Pitt Series in Policy and Institutional Studies

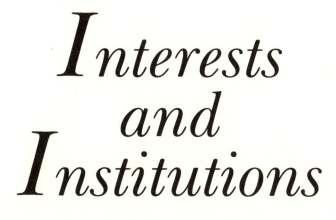

*I*nterests
and
*I*nstitutions

Substance and Structure
in American Politics

Robert H. Salisbury

University of Pittsburgh Press

Pittsburgh and London

Published by the University of Pittsburgh Press, Pittsburgh, Pa. 15260
Copyright © 1992, University of Pittsburgh Press
All rights reserved
Eurospan, London
Manufactured in the United States of America
Printed on acid-free paper

A CIP catalogue record for this book is available from the British Library.

Library of Congress Cataloging-in-Publication Data

Salisbury, Robert Holt, 1930–
    Interests and institutions : substance and structure in American
politics / Robert H. Salisbury.
        p.   cm.—(Pitt series in policy and institutional studies)
    Includes bibliographical references.
    ISBN 0–8229–3724–7
    1. Pressure groups—United States.   I. Title.   II. Series.
JK1118.S33   1992
322.4′3′0973—dc20   92–12242
                                                                CIP

Contents

IV. *Interests and Institutions in the Local Community*

V. *Continuing to Reinterpret*

*I*ntroduction

It requires a good deal of chutzpah to publish a collection of one's essays, written over a thirty-year period on considerable range of topics. One must be persuaded that there is something in them that would be of sufficient intellectual value to an audience to warrant their investment, in money and time, in the price of the book. In this introductory chapter I will attempt to say what that value might be and to identify the audiences that might find these papers useful. Part of what I will say constitutes a kind of intellectual/professional memoir explaining why I undertook particular kinds of research and writing and employed particular methods of inquiry. Scholars should not pretend to have stood apart from the institutional, intellectual, and normative context in which their work has been done and by which it was inevitably affected. We get interested in a topic for many reasons, some of which have little to do with the logic of our professional milieu. Sometimes our theory drives us to the next step of inquiry, sometimes it is the availability of funding, sometimes it is personal idiosyncrasy or happenstance. Apart from their importance to one's biography, the reasons do not matter very much, perhaps, except insofar as describing how they worked for one person may help others, especially graduate students and other fledglings, to think more usefully about developing their own agendas of professional work. There is a difference between the "war stories" of the grizzled veteran and fables that point a moral. My introductory comments attempt to partake of the latter genre, but they may sometimes verge on the former as well. In any case, the value, both substantive and conceptual/theoretical, of the essays in this volume will be enhanced, I believe, by understanding the contexts in which they were done.

In reflecting on my academic experiences I have often criticized myself with the charge that over the years I too easily accepted the invitations of others to pursue one line of research or another. Both my master's thesis and my doctoral dissertation were on topics suggested by my graduate adviser. My work on Missouri politics, state politics and education, policy analysis, congressional staff, and, most recently, inter-est group representation in Washington all originated in the suggestions or invitations of others. I sometimes seem not to have had very many ideas of my own about what to do. When that attitude takes hold I go into a mild funk and accuse myself of dilettantism and other such sins, fundamental failures of character in the serious scholar.

My way out of this slough of despond is to reflect on three related points. When I was a graduate student I read a book by the distin-guished academic whose name I have forgotten. That book sets forth a scenario for a proper academic career in which the scholar proceeds carefully and systematically to move from one topic to the next, picking material in each case that extends out from the previous work and pre-pares the ground for the step to follow. At the end of one's career, there will be a veritable edifice of accomplishment, efficiently constructed to generate an unassailable reputation as *the* person in the chosen field. Philosophy was the field chosen for illustrative purposes, but the strat-egy would be applicable in many disciplines. In any case, I thought as I read it that it certainly might work in political science, and I was ap-palled. Where was there room for surprise? New enthusiasms orthogo-nal to the old? Even then I could not imagine myself working on the same wall for decades. It didn't sound like much fun, but, as I remember, no mention was made of any form of pleasure.

Welcome a change of pace and direction: that was my first rule. Em-brace the unexpected lest, in the course of a forty-year career, you get bored, dried up, or burned out. My second principle of conduct has been that whatever you choose to do should yield intellectual pleasure. It doesn't matter whose idea it was. Work on topics that are intriguing; that challenge and stretch your talent; that enliven both mind and body with the enthusiasm and energy required by the hard slog of scholar-ship. If it isn't any fun, there are probably easier ways to make a living.

The third component of my defense against misplaced self-criticism is that the topic you select for investigation is not the crucial consider-ation. What counts is what you do with it. What kind of analysis can you produce? Are you able to bring generic theoretical perspectives to bear on the material, whatever it is, so as to craft a work of social science? Can you transcend the particular data to develop some more broadly appli-cable insight? These are not questions that are answered by the choice of research methods. Neither abstract formalization nor complex statistical manipulation by itself will lift inquiry above the crowd. Of course, the persuasiveness of these arguments as they apply to me must rest on the reactions of the reader to the papers in this collection. I have told myself often enough through the years, however, that as a political scientist it was possible to bring one's kit bag of concepts and theories into many research milieus and produce work that was not only empirically sound but also, as one moved about from one context to another, might expand and enrich the kit bag's contents as well. To put this another way, the dilettante (generalist is too presumptuous a term) may sometimes have an intellectual advantage over the specialist by virtue of a wider range of intellectual investment. Knowing a little about a lot of things may spark the imagination to find connections that specialists are too deeply embedded to perceive.

The essays in this collection express, I believe, the operation of the three principles in my own professional life. I have worked on a good many different topics over the years. All have been aspects of American politics, to be sure, but they have ranged quite widely in substance and institutional milieu and reached into numerous established subfields of political science. Even though my research has often been stimulated by the suggestions of others, I have taken much pleasure in each piece of the work. What I have done has often involved field work, and I want to emphasize the importance field research—hands-on contact with real political actors—has had for me in provoking my interest and sustaining my enthusiasm for the hard work of analysis and interpretation. The solitude of the study and the blankness of the as-yet-unwritten page are not as hard to face when there have been preparatory encounters with one's data face to face.

Running through the variety of subjects treated in the essays in this volume there is a common thread, a theoretical perspective, or at least an orientation toward the material that I believe gives a degree of coherence and unity that surprised even me when I went back to see what I had done. In all of this work the emphasis is on the interaction of interests—by which I mean the values that groups of people pursue through the various mechanisms of political action available to them—and institutions—the structures of authority by which authoritative political decisions are made. It is and always has been my view that political institutions shape the ways that interest can proceed and, indeed, may create interests by their impact on the things people value. Conversely, the study of institutions is vacuous unless it is conducted with full attention to the substantive interests at stake in the processes of decision and the differential impact on those interests of any particular institutional operation.

Political institutions were the central focus of political science inquiry in the generations just prior to mine, but that focus was generally upon legalistic description of formal rules. It was written in language that too often was bloodless and boring. My graduate school cohort was encouraged to believe that in order to be modern and *au courant* we should reject the emphasis on the formal arrangements of government and look instead at what people really did in politics. The assumption that guided what came to be called the behavioral persuasion was that the rules and structures of government were better understood as masks that political actors wore, and once the formal guises were stripped away we would encounter the real stuff. Institutions were seen as a kind of obfuscation, a mystifying force that distracted attention from the underlying realities of conflicting interests and power relations. A considerable variety of perspectives could make common cause around this principle. Sociologists joined political scientists, Marxists agreed with pluralists, quantifiers allied with soakers and pokers; demystification was the correct route both to effective social science and to a better informed and more active public. This antiformalist animus carried a political message as well. It was primarily the broad political left that was critical of established institutions and sought to expose the manifold methods by which the rules of politics gave further advantage to those who were already well situated in the society. Conservatives, relatively scarce though they were in the academy of the 1950s, defended both the traditional study of institutions and the institutions themselves in operation.

Rejection of institutional formalism carried with it an implicit paradox, however. In order to get behind the mysteries of congressional rules, for instance, it was not enough simply to look at the patterns of roll call votes, as those involved in some early behavioral efforts did. Nor was the published record of committee hearings an adequate data base for the investigation of senators' legislative roles, though an occasional scholar could, as Ralph Huitt (1990) did, make heroic use of just such material. What soon became clear, however, was that in order to gain effective purchase on the "real" behavior of Congress members it was essential to observe them closely and directly. Field work was required, and the Congressional Fellowship Program, begun by the American Political Science Association in 1954, provided the principal funding opportunity to enable young scholars to acquire the necessary field experience.

The discovery that antiformalism and the demystification of institutions required field research did not quickly permeate the consciousness of political scientists. In part, this was due to the fact that survey data on mass opinion and voting behavior did *not* necessitate hands-on encounters with the "real" world, and at exactly this same period, the 1950s, national voter surveys began to expand the available research material at a dizzying rate. Students could and did simply move from one library to another as they enlisted in the mass behavior campaigns of the behavioral revolution. Statistical literacy quickly became a necessary part of graduate education, while explicit training in the methods appropriate to elite interviewing or other aspects of direct observation seldom intruded upon curricula. For the most part still today in political science field research "methods" are rudimentary and self-taught, learned through experience, if at all.

Nevertheless, the point remained valid; if the masks of institutional power were truly to be stripped away, the researcher would be required to spend considerable time watching to see how the institutions worked. And the paradox was that, having watched them in actual operation, one was nearly always persuaded that they mattered; that they were not simply formalized expressions of an already constituted structure of power, but a distinct and autonomous factor constraining behavior and shaping policy outcomes. People behaved differently than they would otherwise have been expected to because of the rules. None of this meant that the institutional arrangements could provide by themselves a satisfactory explanation of political results. The rules took on substantive meaning only in conjunction with the interests, the groups and individual advocates that sought to advance their respective causes through the exercise of governmental authority. Field research taught the lesson, at least to me, that effective political science required the mapping and analysis of the interplay of interests and institutions, and that neither could be adequately understood without close sustained observation.

This realization did not dawn suddenly, and in some ways has not taken full hold even yet. In the comparative politics field the assumption that field research was essential to effective scholarship had long been operative, and the move of American politics students back to institutionally defined research contexts has enabled a degree of methodological rapprochement between the two fields, especially when linked with the acceptance by comparativists of voting and opinion materials generated by survey research methods and of less formalistic but "behavioral" data such as interest group activity. Field work in comparative politics certainly has not always meant a search for the realities of power and interest that lay behind institutional forms. At its best, however, that kind of result rewarded the investigator who had no real choice of research strategies except to settle into the institutional system of some other nation and try to figure out how it worked. The need to "settle in" to the U.S. political context was less obvious since, after all, most American political scientists had spent their lives there. Early life does not always lead to an understanding of the forces at work, however. Without a more self-conscious immersion in a particular institutional setting some sort of secondhand grasp of reality would be the best one could expect.

In my own career the first occasion for a quasi-anthropological foray arose when a close friend and former colleague, Robert Blackburn, took a position as assistant to the mayor of St. Louis. He began telling me stories about what was happening in city hall, and soon had me intrigued. Like a good academic I went off to the university library to read what I could find on St. Louis and on the politics of cities more generally. As Lawrence Herson (1957) had recently pointed out in an *American Political Science Review* article, however, there was not a rich body of "modern," behaviorally oriented literature available on urban politics. In the late 1950s most of that field had not yet experienced the antiformalist onslaught. It was both legalistic and reformist and generally not very helpful regarding the "stuff" of political life. So I turned to old newspaper files covering the previous thirty years or so of St. Louis political and social history. One of the larger delights of this part of the research was the fun of tracing comic strips, pennant races, and other aspects of the American culture back through the years of my childhood and before. All this was useful; indeed, indispensable. But eventually I had to go downtown and get to know city officials, mingle with city hall reporters, visit the political bars where aldermen and ward committeemen did much of their work, attend election rallies, and interview a wide range of knowledgeable informants. It was not a very systematic process at the start and never very sophisticated, but it was immensely instructive at many levels. Throughout I had always to fight off the insecurity of an academic venturing into the real world. But it was often a great deal of fun. In due course, I wrote some articles for the political science community interpreting what I had learned about St. Louis and trying to place it in a broader frame that would bring the experience of other cities into appropriate comparison. I also wrote a long manuscript that I intended to make into a book, but I persuaded myself that the book ought to include more detailed case studies of particular decisions than I was yet able to produce. This was the precise time that Robert Dahl, Edward Banfield, and several other prominent scholars published major books on urban politics. For a rather brief period in the early 1960s this work, building generic interpretations of power and influence on the basis of studying some particular issues in a particular city, enjoyed high status in the profession. Book after book followed this strategy of using case studies to provide the evidentiary basis for their analysis. I thought they were right, methodologically, and so postponed my own book. But I never finished the cases because I had begun another project, this time a collaborative investigation, looking at state politics and public school policy.

Thomas Eliot, then chair of my department and soon to be chancellor of my university, had written a seminal article (1959) reviewing the existing literature on school politics. In a kind of parallel to Herson's earlier plea regarding the urban field, Eliot lamented the absence of serious nonformalistic work on education policy making at the state level. Here was another set of institutional arenas in which to soak and poke, hang around, get their feel, interview, and generally try to understand. Eliot received a grant from the Carnegie Foundation and invited me to join the research project on state politics and school policy. The states we chose for investigation were Michigan, Illinois, and Missouri, and I worked on the latter two. It was necessary, as it had been in St. Louis, to discover what the contending interests were—who wanted what, who opposed whom, what alliances and coalitions were at work, what tactics they used—and how these groups worked within and were affected by the institutional arrangements of the respective state governments. The fact that our study was explicitly comparative was a great advantage because the folkways of the systems differed enormously as did the structures of political power. Rules of the legislative process, similar in appearance, took on very different meanings in the differing political contexts.

The book that resulted from this research and articles that spun off from it captured much of the substance of what we learned. The published work could not report, however, but only at most reflect, the full richness of flavor and insight the field experience conveyed. Though we did not write about it, we learned, for example, that playing poker with lobbyists and legislators and beating them was a very effective way to earn their confidence and gain research access. Apart from these lessons, it was patently clear that the differing institutional settings of the three states we studied had a major impact in shaping both strategy and substance of the interests, specifically the public school groups, and also that school groups and the education committees of the legislature did not operate in exactly the same way that labor unions or farm groups and their respective committees did. Indeed, the K-12 school interests had virtually nothing to do even with higher education groups.

In the years following the completion of the state politics and education project my professional writing shifted away from a field-research base and turned toward theory. Papers on interest group formation and on the policy process built upon the previous decade's experience, enriched by the reading and reflection that must always accompany fruitful field work. Meanwhile, I had entered another institutional milieu in which I learned a great deal about politics, some of its painful but most of it of positive value, at least in the long run. I had become chair of the political science department. These were years of upheaval in academe, provoked in part by the Vietnam War protests but extending to many issues of university governance and curricular direction. I was deeply involved in the politics of my academy, and, though it is not much reflected in the papers included in this volume, the experiences of that period turned my attention much more than before toward some of the normative dimensions of American political life.

At one level the questions I began to ask involved political participation. Who joins and why were central to the understanding of interest groups and therefore well established items on my agenda. Earlier I had investigated such matters with respect to local political party organizations and I was soon to begin a substantial research project involving citizen participation in local school organizations. More broadly, however, I had been impressed by how great the variance was among my academic colleagues in their willingness cheerfully to undertake administrative or even policy-making chores within the university. Some would, others would not. Personal circumstances accounted for part of the difference, and talents differed as well. More than that, however, it seemed to me that some faculty members served on committees when asked because they thought they should; that though it was not stipulated in their contract, it was somehow part of their duty as citizens of the university community. Others, of no less strong commitment to the academic calling, did not really think of the university as an arena of citizenship, in which outcomes depended in some sense upon service, but as a bureaucracy, a hierarchy in which the role of the faculty member was to teach and do research while others raised the money, served the meals, administered the library, and kept the records.

The questions that grew out this recognition were and are at once empirical and normative. They require determination as to what is the case on a far more substantial and systematic basis than my ruminations could provide. Interestingly, as I came to understand the direction of my thinking, this line of concern tied closely to the work of a generation of historians who, since the late 1960s, had reinterpreted the eighteenth-century experience of Americans so as to give central importance to the concept of republican virtue. Virtue, in this context, entails a commitment to serve the public good, to make whatever personal sacrifices may be necessary in order to enable the enterprise—the republic or, by analogy, the university—to function well enough to allow individual interests to be pursued. Wood, Pocock, Bailyn, and other historians have been persuasive in showing how vital a part of the American founding generation's moral philosophy this concept was and how it was operational in the lives of Jefferson, Adams, Washington, and so many others. I stress it here, not so much because I think that notions of republican virtue have become central to my published work (or to my life, for that matter), but because I have quite consciously drawn upon them in much of my personal assessment of contemporary politics, in the academy and in the larger polity, and they may have edged further into my research than I realize. In any case, the "discovery" of republican virtue, a concept that among other things competes quite directly with self-interest as the latter is ordinarily understood, must eventually be incorporated into any effort to provide a full statement of the meaning of interests and interest group politics.

Two other institutional settings have provided me the opportunity to undertake extensive field work and thereby to acquire a foundation of understanding of both the interests that competed and the institutional constraints that shaped the competition. One was the United States Congress. In the late 1970s, in collaboration with Kenneth Shepsle, I undertook to investigate the role of congressional staff. This was a period in which Congress was in great flux. Reforms of various kinds had recently restructured the relationships among its parts, destabilizing patterns that had operated for more than a quarter of a century. New leadership had taken office and, not least, there had been a massive increase in the size and, by all accounts, the importance of the staff. It was a fascinating time to hang around the Hill, and we learned a great deal, some of it about the significance of the staff and some of it more generally about the crucial importance of the rules of congressional procedure in shaping what happens. Apart from our joint efforts Shepsle made more important use of this experience than I, drawing upon his expertise in formal analysis to publish a series of seminal articles elaborating the principles of the "new institutionalism," but this field experience impressed both of us with the immense complexity of the congeries of interests at work in Washington and the webs of connection between interests and officials. For me it was those webs of connection that came to constitute my most recent and most elaborate venture in field research.

As the work on congressional staff was reaching an end, another and, as it turned out, much larger opportunity was presented. My long-time friend and sometime collaborator, John Heinz, was completing a major study of Chicago lawyers. He and his coauthor Edward Laumann approached me to ask whether I would be interested in a study of Washington lawyers that they were considering as a possible next undertaking. They felt that such an investigation should focus on those lawyers who dealt with the federal government as lobbyists, legislators, and consultants, not the real estate or divorce sections of the D.C. Bar. Accordingly, they thought my interest in both Congress and interest groups and my experience in the Washington milieu could be valuable complements to their efforts. The prospect was exciting to all of us, ultimately turning into a project on the representation of private interests, not just on lawyers, and growing to what seem like near-gargantuan proportions. We conducted more than one hundred exploratory interviews in Washington, soaking and poking to a fare-thee-well to learn what we could about how the system worked and how best to frame the instruments for the systematic investigation that we would subsequently undertake. The eventual surveys encompassed 311 organizations in four policy domains. They, in turn, identified the individuals who represented their interests in Washington. We interviewed at considerable length and detail a total of 806 representatives. Further, we asked each respondent to name government officials with whom he or she most often interacted and interviewed 301 of them. The data we amassed from the surveys were immense in quantity and in most respects unique in social science research. We have been able to extend both descriptive comprehension and theoretical formulation in many directions, and when we finally conclude our own efforts to grapple with the bumper harvest of our research we will be exhausted ourselves, no doubt, but our data will still reward the efforts of other investigators.

Part of the importance of the Washington representatives project was in the absolutely essential linkage it displayed between extensive exploratory field work, the soaking and poking phase, and the subsequent design of the systematic data collection. We simply could not have developed an adequate sense of what interests were present and how they went about their business on the strength of the extant literature; that is, by relying on the library. Some of the lessons we learned seemed fairly simple once we had learned them. One of these is the basis of a paper included in this volume on the importance of institutions as claimant interests operating on quite different principles from voluntary associations. Another became the basis for rethinking the nature of the interests that groups pur　·e in the political arena, seeing them more as emergent and contingent rather than as somehow fixed ex ante. As that recognition came ever more clearly from our research it reinforced and more sharply articulated a central point that operates throughout the essays in this collection; namely, that the interests of groups are shaped, not totally but in significant part, by the ways in which those groups interact with each other and with public officials in and through the institutional settings of congressional committees, floor debate, cabinet departments, regulatory agencies, OMB, the White House, the courts, and whatever other units are part of the process. It follows that interest group politics is dynamic and protean over time, and that there are processes of learning and adaptation quite continuously at work among all the active players in the policy-making system. There are many stable components, to be sure. Indeed, we were surprised to discover how much of the lobbying system was staffed by veterans of the policy wars. Still, there is much that changes, not always discernible each week or month, but moving enough to require the scholar to keep coming back to mark the successive modifications.

It is this dynamic conception of the interest-institution interaction that distinguishes the approach represented here from the traditional approach to political institutions, wherein they were conceived as essentially fixed patterns of authority, changing little if at all over long periods of time, and therefore reasonably well captured by documentary declarations regarding powers and procedures. The formal theorists share with the traditional institutionalists a bias toward equilibrium states and a neglect of the dynamics of interest configurations that transform the political meaning of any particular institutional equilibrium. Congressional committee domination of executive agencies means one thing when the committees are controlled by conservative Southern Democrats and something else entirely when consumer advocates are in charge. Decision rules and size principles taken on their meaning in the context of substantive political struggles whose course and ultimate result they help to shape. And if the substantive political impact of some institutional feature changes with time and circumstance—the presidential veto, for instance, was once an instrument mainly advocated by liberals, and has recently been embraced with enthusiasm by social and economic conservatives—a purely formal analysis of the institution will be inadequate.

In the course of this apologia I have not yet said much about my interest in interests, and that is odd, in a way, because it is surely the strongest and most consistent thread connecting the various parts of my research and writing. From my M.A. thesis, in which I tried to characterize the opinions of Chief Justice Fred Vinson in terms of the interests they represented, to my most recent work on pluralism my work has been about the groups that were actively seeking to shape public policy, about why those who took part did so while others did not, and how the decisions made by public officials were linked to the configurations of values—the interests—of various segments of the American population. My enthusiasm for these questions may have antedated my formal training in political science, but that experience was so dominated by the focus on interest analysis that it blots out other possible contributions. My graduate education at the University of Illinois came at a time when the department there included distinguished scholars of several intellectual persuasions, and one's seminar training included substantial work in formal institutions and the history of political thought. But the currents of argument that really mattered involved interest groups and group theory. The Illinois faculty included Charles Hagan, Philip Monypenny, Murray Edelman, Gilbert Steiner, Austin Ranney, and my own adviser, Jack Peltason. All were caught up in the developing behavioral movement, and graduate students soon joined in the impassioned discussions of Bentley, Truman, Easton, et al. Those were heady days, not yet overtaken by survey research and quantitative methodology, and argument over coffee or beer was the dominant mode of intellectual progress.

It is one thing to debate the meaning of Truman's concepts, however, and quite another to learn how to spot substantive interests, to recognize the characteristic plumage and song of each, and to understand their migration patterns and nesting habits. This required extended immersion, not only field work as described above, but in diverse written sources as well. When I first began to teach I offered a senior-graduate course on government and business. I had to work prodigiously to learn enough about the history and present patterning of American business enterprise in order not to have to fall back on formalistic discussions of institutional structures and programs of government regulation. One of my students in that course told me, after it was over, that he had started to keep a file of newspaper clippings that illustrated interests at work and soon discovered that he needed to clip virtually the entire paper. Just so.

In the first few years of teaching I offered a considerable range of courses, some because I wanted to and some because, as the youngest member of the department, I was asked to. In my first year I had quickly to acquaint myself with relevant interest configurations not only in the vast area covered by a course on economic regulation but in American foreign policy as well. In the years that followed I developed a more comprehensive introduction to public policy and also began to teach "Parties and Interest Groups" using V. O. Key's great text.

One way and another I cast a net of curiosity, motivated both by personal interest and by professional relevance, that grew steadily wider and more inclusive as the years passed. I was compelled by my intellectual convictions as well as by my tastes and enthusiasms to study the history of virtually everything. How could one understand present day civil rights politics or the ethno-cultural interests expressed in the religious right without a grasp of the historical processes by which the interests in those areas were shaped? How could one unravel the complexities of price support policies in agriculture without knowing something of both the history and the economics of the diverse commodities and organizations that constitute the substance of farm politics? In actual practice, a consistent and fundamental commitment to interest-based analysis has had a wonderful side effect. It has legitimized as professionally relevant nearly everything I read, the trips I took, and even much of the television I watched. As a student of interests, work and play have never been very well separated for me; not a wholly unmixed blessing, I know, but on balance a blessing nevertheless.

I would be remiss in this introduction to myself if I were to leave out an important feature of my academic experiences during the past several years. I have been extremely fortunate throughout my academic life to have had colleagues who were both personally congenial and intellectually challenging and to work in a university that encouraged us to do the best teaching and research we could. Few restrictions were ever imposed; we taught the courses we wanted to or thought our students needed, and we pursued the lines of scholarly inquiry that interested us. There were no bureaucratic impediments to our initiatives in program development, and few layers of administration to penetrate before reaching the level of authority necessary for approval. At the same time, while we generally could try anything we thought appropriate, we had to make it work ourselves with a faculty of modest size, a smallish graduate program, and not much administrative or infrastructural backup. Autonomy can be a mixed blessing.

One personal product of this rather freewheeling setting has been the opportunity to teach jointly with people from other disciplines and to develop courses of our own design that could, among other things, introduce us to materials and instruct us in ways of thinking quite remote from the routines of our respective fields. In particular, I have taught several courses, both graduate and undergraduate, with Wayne Fields, a writer on many subjects and now chair of Washington University's English Department. Wayne's first love was rhetoric, especially political rhetoric, and his primary area of specialization was nineteenth-century America. Working with Wayne has taught me a great deal; part of it about American writing, about fiction and nonfiction texts in a broad sense of the term; but more importantly about how humanists go about the task of understanding a text and its context. As a social scientist I was accustomed to looking at a book, a speech, a statute, or a building for that matter, from the outside, to see what forces had produced it and acted upon it and to trace its effects, in turn, on subsequent events and conditions. Wayne alerted me to questions about the inside; about what made a speech or novel work; about the symbolic and representational meanings condensed and displayed in the manifold forms that a student of any culture must try to understand.

Indeed, what I came finally to recognize as a result of teaching with Wayne Fields, was that I really was interested not just in American politics but in American culture. If I wrote mostly about governmental institutions and processes, I certainly did not suppose for a minute that they could be extracted from their historical setting or separated from the economic, social, literary, religious, and even geographical contexts that gave so much of the substantive meaning to politics and operated so powerfully as causal factors shaping political outcomes. The corollary of this view, of course, is that political factors affect the other spheres of life as well. For an economist or a literary critic to ignore the political dimensions of the world in which her speciality takes place, or as is more common, to incorporate only a simplistic notion of politics, is a crippling error of intellectual strategy, not always apparent in the short run but productive of work ultimately condemned as narrow, partial, and generally mistaken.

This conviction does not show in most of the essays included here, I'm afraid, partly because there is never enough time or space to include everything that is relevant, and priorities must be set. Nevertheless, I am convinced that fully to grasp and comprehend its politics one should be well acquainted with every facet of the culture of which the politics is so vital a part. This conclusion is self-serving, of course. It provides a *post hoc* justification for being interested in everything, for reading as widely as possible, confident that almost any study or any topic can contribute to one's thinking and often be more narrowly useful to the "work" of writing. I have managed from time to time to publish articles on both baseball and religion, two areas of near-lifelong interest that are certainly vital parts of the American culture. I have taught courses that brought American art museums and symphony orchestras within the purview of a political scientist's concerns. And I have absorbed at least part of the lessons my comparativist colleagues have tried to teach me; that to understand American culture and politics it is necessary to know how it compares with others. That is quite true. It entails a still broader agenda of reading and study, even of the supreme soaking and poking process of foreign travel. That, too, is a self-serving position, perhaps, for it surely can lead one to exotic excitements. But that is exactly what for each of its acolytes the academic enterprise ought to be: a process of continuous growth, not linear so much as in breadth, variety, and complexity; an endless succession of puzzles and mysteries to be solved, with the ever-more-challenging additional feature of discerning that a mystery exists; a life in which the primary tasks, learning and teaching, for which they actually pay us a salary, cannot be exhausted.

There are always new problems, new combinations, new angles of vision, and there are always new students, always the same age, with the same irresistible eagerness. I would not wish to be the kind of scholar who builds a wall of scholarship, perhaps to sit upon, like a guru on a mountaintop, dispensing wisdom and defending the perch against invading successor generations. That sort of embattled, ultimately beleaguered style of life never has had much appeal for me. Indeed, I have always thought that the better metaphor for that approach to an academic career was Humpty-Dumpty, bound eventually to fall from his perch, never again to be taken seriously. I would much rather try to retain some of the innocent naivete of the beginning graduate student, for whom nearly everything is yet to be learned and no restrictions of efficiency or relevance or disciplinary centrality have yet imposed their authoritative weight on curiosity. We never fully match our daily lives to our aspirations, of course. We are always climbing, looking back sometimes but never down. I would like to believe that such a spirit pervades the essays in this collection, and I particularly hope that it will continue to flourish in whatever I do next.

In preparing these essays for publication I was tempted to revise and improve them, sharpening the focus and refining the argument wherever I could. I also considered bringing them up to date in their empirical references, indicating along the way how and in what ways things had changed since the time of writing. I was concerned that the reader might forget when a particular essay had been published and think, for example, that I was referring to Richard Daley *fils* instead of Daley *pére*. In the end, however, I decided to present the material in the original, making only a very few stylistic changes to adapt to contemporary usages. My hope is that, although details of substance have changed, the larger arguments and perspectives continue to have their uses and that it is valuable to see them in their original form so as more accurately to understand the ground on which we build.

REFERENCES

Eliot, Thomas H. 1959. "Toward an Understanding of Public School Politics," *American Political Science Review* 53 (December 1959): 1032–51.

Herson, Lawrence J. R. 1957. "The Lost World of Municipal Government," *American Political Science Review* 51 (June 1957): 330–45.

Huitt, Ralph K. 1990. *Working Within the System*. Berkeley, Calif.: Institute of Governmental Studies.

Part I

✦

*Interest Group
Theory*

Once or twice friends whose central professional interest was in the study of political philosophy have paid me the high compliment of calling me a "closet theorist." Perhaps I am. In any case, in this section are four essays addressing some of the basic theoretical and conceptual issues of interest group analysis. Unlike many of the other essays in this volume, all four were written simply because I wanted to present a particular argument or line of thinking. They sprang only indirectly, if at all, from ongoing empirical research, and they were not produced in response to someone else's invitation.

1

An Exchange Theory of
Interest Groups

In one of those apparently casual passages into which enormous significance may be read David B. Truman remarks that "the origins of interest groups and the circumstances surrounding their orientations toward the institutions of government [are] . . . among the factors most relevant to a description of group politics."[1] He goes on to suggest or imply some fragments of general theory concerning group formation which remain largely undeveloped, either by Truman or by other students of interest groups. Issues of major theoretical relevance are raised in these fragments, however, and we propose to examine them closely to see whether they, and the data concerning interest group formation, may lead to some fuller theoretical understanding of interest group phenomena.

We shall focus much of our attention on the development of American agricultural groups. In part, this focus is the product of convenience and ready accessibility of illustrative data.[2] In part, however, this sector of American group development is especially apt for the testing of extant theories of group formation. In addition to farm groups we shall refer to other types of groups sufficiently often to indicate the range of application of the argument. It should be noted at the outset that the argument presented here has many close links to an intellectual focus now attaining major stature in other social sciences; namely, exchange theory.[3] This paper represents an effort to contribute to that development by applying its terms to, and reinterpreting them in the light of, interest groups in politics.

Reprinted with permission from *Midwest Journal of Political Science* 13 (February 1969):1–32.

Briefly, the argument is that interest group origins, growth, death, and associated lobbying activity may all be better explained if we regard them as exchange relationships between entrepreneurs/organizers, who invest capital in a set of benefits, which they offer to prospective members at a price—membership. We shall compare this approach to others in an attempt to explain the data of group origins and elaborate its terms to explore the implications of the argument for other facets of group activity.

One other prefatory note should be entered. Our concern here is with organized interest groups or, in Truman's term, formal associations. We wish to explain how such associations come into being, the conditions affecting their growth or decline, their internal structures of action, and their role in the political process. We do not wish to develop an interest group theory of politics, a la Arthur F. Bentley. That is quite a different intellectual enterprise and one that is largely unrelated to the present analysis. This is an effort to develop a theory of interest groups, not an interest group theory of politics, and it is hoped that any disputation which might center on the latter issue may be avoided.[4]

Theories of Proliferation and Equilibrium

One fragment of extant group formation theory we may call the proliferation hypothesis.[5] It argues, in effect, that as a consequence of various processes of social differentiation, especially those linked to technological change but including others as well, there is within a given population more and more specialization of function. Increasingly specialized sets of people are observed engaged in a growing range of particular economic activities or specific social roles and from this specialized differentiation of role and function comes greater and greater diversity of interests or values as each newly differentiated set of people desires a somewhat different set of social goals.

For example, it may be argued that American farmers became increasingly specialized in terms of the commodities raised in a particular area or by particular farmers and also in terms of that corollary of specialization—interdependence with other segments of the economy; banks, merchants, railroads, and the like.[6] Ever since the Civil War, it is quite clear farmers have grown more and more differentiated as technological innovations, such as mechanical combines and cotton pickers or refrigerated transport, combined with other factors, such as the increased use of less flexible, arid land, and changing demand patterns in both peace and war, to induce each farmer to concentrate his resources on the commodity he could produce to greatest advantage rather than try to supply himself with a wide range of necessary foods and fibers. In short, the full-scale commercialization of agriculture, beginning largely with the Civil War, led to the differentiation of farmers into specialized groups with specialized interests, each increasingly different from the next. These interests had to do with such questions as prices and market shares for the farmers and also for those with whom the farmers dealt in the marketplace. The interdependence which accompanied the specialization process meant potential conflicts of interests or values both across the bargaining encounter and among the competing farmers themselves as each struggled to secure his own position.

The proliferation hypothesis now simply adds that as a "natural" social response among these conflicting specialized groups formal associations are created, or emerge, to represent the conflicting claims of each differentiated set of interested parties. The association articulates the interest, and by organizing its adherents provides more effective bargaining power vis-à-vis other groups. It may be, as Bentley put it, "mere technique" since the association is seen as a kind of automatic fruit of the process of social differentiation, but it has an independent effect upon the political processes in which the group may be concerned. Thus unorganized groups, i.e., people with differentiated but unarticulated values, are presumed to be weaker than organized groups. The questions of whether truly differentiated interests will actually languish for long in unorganized circumstances is a matter which remains unclear in the theoretical fragments we have to work with.[7] It does seem that, taken over time, such interests are expected to achieve organizational expression even through the specific process by which formal organizations are generated are nowhere examined and seem rather generally to be regarded as inevitable consequences of differentiation itself. In any case, for our purposes, the salient points concerning the proliferation hypothesis are three: (1) associations are products of differentiated sets of values or interests, (2) over time there will appear more and more different, diverse, specialized groups in the political arena as the processes of social fission continue, and (3) it is to the processes by which values are altered that one must look for an explanation of group formation.

A second proto-theory, so to speak, of group formation may be referred to as the homeostatic mechanism hypothesis.[8] This argument places much less emphasis on the processes of social differentiation and the generation of "new interests" thereby. Rather it assumes a certain differentiation and suggests the following sequence as typical of group origins. A putative equilibrium among social groups is disturbed as a consequence of such socially disruptive factors as technological innovation, war, transportation or communications changes, and such macro-social processes as major population movements, business cycle fluctuations, and industrialization. The disequilibrium will evolve a response from the disadvantaged sectors as they seek to restore a viable balance. A principal way of doing so is by organizing a formal association because, as Truman points out, this not only improves bargaining power but it also helps to stabilize and strengthen relationships within the group by increasing the mutually supportive interaction among the members and thereby the range and salience of their shared values. Notice that the organization is seen as a more active agent in this approach than from the proliferation perspective. Its operations contribute directly, if only marginally, to the changing of member values and it is thus much less dependent on underlying social processes to show the interest direction the group should pursue.

Truman observes that "the formation of associations . . . tends to occur in waves"[9] because once a group organizes in order to reassert a satisfactory equilibrium it may inspire counterorganization among rival groups in a kind of dialectical process. Presumably there is an equilibrating tendency underlying this process, however, so that once a set of social group bargaining encounters has been organized on all sides there is an end to the group formation process and a stability to the associational activities. In this respect the homeostatic mechanism hypothesis differs from the proliferation hypothesis since the latter predicts the continuing development of new interest configurations and hence of new associations.

We may well have read distinctions into remarks which were intended for less intensive exegetical use, but the two theoretical sketches outlined above do occasionally appear in the literature. The two approaches differ in emphasis and in certain of their assumptions, but they are not mutually exclusive. The critical question is which hypothesis gives the better empirical return, or, if neither is adequate, is there a superior alternative? Attention to the formation of agricultural groups in the United States leads us to find congenial elements in both hypotheses, but there are disquieting elements as well. Let us examine, albeit briefly, the relevant data.

By either of our hypotheses the growth of politically relevant farmer organizations would be expected in the post–Civil War period. On the one hand, the spectacular rise of the Grange from 1867 until about 1875 is a sufficiently prominent datum that no theory of group formation would be likely to miss it. At the same time, it is clear that agricultural technology changed dramatically in the direction of mechanization during this period. The dislocations of war and the railroad-assisted postbellum westward expansion contributed, as did the growth of corporate industrial power, to the transformation of the farmer's circumstances. In large measure, it appears that the proliferation hypothesis has somewhat the better case for the immediate post-war period in its stress upon the generation of new interest and value configurations as a consequence of social differentiation. Clearly, it was not simply a matter of older groups coming into a new situation, for, outside the South, there had never before been large groups of commercial farmers with such dependence on the market and so vulnerable to its vicissitudes.

But it is also clear that for nearly half a century farm groups did not proliferate into more and more organizations, each with its specialized concerns.[10] At least until after 1900 the overwhelming bulk of farm organizations which were formed were aggregated under the comprehensive embrace of few, though often loose, organizational structures.[11] Thus the Grange was followed by the Farmers Alliance in the 1880's, the Populist Party in the 1890's, and the Agricultural Wheel, the Farmers Union, and finally the Farm Bureau in the first part of the twentieth century. Although each of these organizations was composed of a large number of local and state units, and in the case of the Farmers Alliance there were several distinct regional components which were partly or wholly autonomous, no real evidence can be found of a fission-like process. Rather a rapid series of local organizational successes was followed by official aggregation under a broad banner and then, until this century, by the equally rapid demise of the organization, in its power if not, as usually happened, in its very existence.

This sequence of organizations may seem to disconfirm the proliferation hypothesis, but it does not readily fit the homeostatic mechanism theory either.[12] The rapid rise and fall of actual farm associations in a period, 1867–1900, which was one of consistent market disadvantage for most farm groups could hardly be construed as conducive to the reassertion of a viable equilibrium. It may be argued that whether they were successful or not the groups were certainly organized in order to reassert just such an equilibrium, and of this there can be little doubt. The rhetoric of farm protest groups has consistently stressed the postulate that a primeval state of grace had been violated by this industrial revolution and public policy should work toward the restoration of Eden. But rhetoric which evokes Arcadia may be distinguished from empirical social theory, and neither proliferation nor the homeostasis hypotheses seem adequate to explain the succession of organizational failures among people who, it has generally seemed, were in considerable distress and needed political and organizational help. Both our theories seem to assume that under such conditions organized groups will emerge and in some sense succeed. Yet the empirical landscape is cluttered with abandoned farm group vehicles, and effective theory must deal with the relics as well as the survivors.

Another set of data with which extant theories do not satisfactorily cope relates to organizational membership figures. The proliferation hypothesis implies not only that the number of organized groups will increase over time but also that total membership will probably grow. This might follow for such social psychological reasons as that the more groups there are the more opportunities for a given person to participate actively in one and the more inducement therefore to join. It might also follow from the expectation that the greater the specialization the greater or more wide-reaching the self-consciousness of group involvement and hence the greater the likelihood of formal group membership.

Homeostasis theory, on the other hand, implies a cyclical pattern of membership. If groups are formally organized as a response to bargaining disadvantage, so their membership would be expected to rise in conditions of adversity and, probably, to decline or at least stabilize when adversity was overcome. So long as the organization's existence remained essential to the new equilibrium the membership might not fall off precipitately but it would still follow a kind of cycle over the course of the fluctuating fortunes of the group involved.

Group membership data are generally rather elusive and sometimes a bit suspect too. For some groups, especially those of a professional and technical occupational character, there appears to be a slightly uneven but generally rather steady growth in membership.[13] In some groups there is a rapid surge, often followed by a precipitate decline even to disappearance of the group altogether.[14] In two socio-economic sectors, however, agriculture and labor, the data are reasonably complete and follow similar curves; namely, they show a growth of membership in times of comparative prosperity and a decline during economic recession.[15] For example, in the first decade of the twentieth century, a decade of relatively favorable farm prices and income after thirty-odd years of almost unbroken decline, farm group membership increased five hundred percent! The Grange, by then politically quiescent, more than doubled. The Farmers Union and the American Society of Equity were formed and each quickly attracted one hundred thousand members. Numerous commodity groups were organized at this time, and finally, still under relatively favorable economic conditions which extended until about 1919, the local and state farm bureaus were organized, to be federated in 1919 in the American Farm Bureau Federation.

Once the happy times for farm prices of World War I were over, prolonged farm depression set in and lasted until about 1926. During this period farm group membership generally declined. In the midwestern heartland of the Farm Bureau membership fell by almost one-fourth between 1920 and 1925. The Farmers Union lost forty percent of its strength between 1915 and 1933. Efforts to organize new farm groups out of the disequilibrium conditions of the early 20's uniformly failed. Decline in membership again was noticeable in the early Depression years of the 1930's, but this was followed by a spectacular recovery and growth between 1940 and 1950. In this decade, which was again one of greatly increased prosperity, the three main general farm organizations, the Grange, the Farmers Union, and the Farm Bureau went from a combined total of 866,224 family memberships to 2,108,849. Since 1950 a slow growth has continued despite the continuing decline in farm population.

Broadly, a similar pattern may be observed in the labor movement with substantial union growth during the prosperous periods of high employment, such as both World Wars, and decline in periods of recession. Additional variation is introduced by such factors as the passage of legislation like the Wagner Act, and changes in industrial technology, but the point remains. In these areas, at least, organized group membership varies directly with the relevant portion of the business cycle, going up with good times and down with bad, and this is exactly the opposite of the expectations derived from the homeostasis hypothesis.

Although the proliferation hypothesis is vague with respect to expected patterns of group membership over time, it clearly does not lead to a cyclical pattern linked to the business cycle. This hypothesis fares much better, however, especially in the period of the last thirty-five years, regarding the number and variety of distinct organizations. More or less paralleling the enormous infusion of science into agriculture has been a very striking growth in the number of specialized commodity associations. Cotton and tobacco organizations, like specialization in the production of these crops, are older, dating from around 1900. But wheat, corn, cranberries, turkey broilers, and several dozen other groups have been formed more recently as an undoubted consequence of the proliferation of farming interests.[16]

Yet as we consider the appearance of, say, the National Corn Growers Association in the mid-1950's one cannot seriously regard it as any kind of an organizational manifestation of the differentiated corn growers partly because corn growers had been differentiated for years and partly because they have not joined the group in appreciable numbers. The NCGA seemed much more a kind of letterhead organization which might, if its founder's dreams materialized, someday speak for a sizable portion of the corn growers but it had hardly yet begun to climb toward such eminence. It was still a small, struggling business enterprise, and the example suggests a very important modification required of the proliferation thesis—to establish some analytical distance between the technological and other social forces, on the one hand, and the emergence of organized interest groups, on the other.

Before we pursue this theme, however, let us again consider the implications of the cyclical pattern of group membership. There appears to be a fairly straightforward, one might almost say simple-minded, explanation for this pattern. It is simply that in times of prosperity potential group members are much more likely to have the dues money and be willing to spend it for membership,[17] while in hard times group membership may be one of the first luxuries to be sacrificed. Thus union membership regularly declines in the face of unemployment, and it is clear that for some portion of the members membership itself is a very marginal investment. At the same time, however, group leaders, faced with declining membership in hard times, may step up the tempo of agitation, both to hold on to their organizational membership and to alleviate the underlying group distress. Farm group leaders undoubtedly increased their public militance in the early 1930's,[18] as did unions, while their organized strength was shrinking. But leadership vigor cannot therefore be treated as an unambiguous indicator of group emergence or strengthening. Again, the point is that group strength, insofar as it implies or involves either weight of numbers or the formation of new groups, is generally greater in prosperity than in times of trouble, and thus a significantly revised theory of group origins is required.

Entrepreneurs/Organizers

We find congenial a conceptualization of interest groups which regards them as benefit exchanges. Let us think of them in the following way. Entrepreneurs/organizers invest capital to create a set of benefits which they offer to a market of potential customers at a price. If, and as long as, enough customers buy, i.e., join, to make a viable organization, the group is in business. If the benefits fail, or are inadequate to warrant the cost of membership, or the leaders get inadequate return, the group collapses. *All* interest groups are conceptualized within this frame; it follows therefore that only "organized" groups, in the sense of entrepreneured exchange relationships, whether formally self-identified as organizations or not, are observable. The frame is inclusive and, it is argued, encompasses all cases without altering its basic terms.

It should immediately be noted that the conceptual scheme employed here is closely akin to an analytical frame which presently is of burgeoning interest to sociologists and represented especially in the work of Peter Blau and George Homans. At the same time, there are major identities of thought as well as language with economic theory where, after all, exchange behavior is the heart of an economist's world. Indeed, a partially parallel argument about interest groups has already been presented by economist Mancur Olson, Jr.

Many of the substantive hypotheses to be suggested here are rather direct transfers from simple economic models, and there is every reason to suppose that more elaborate and complex formulations can also be exchanged among disciplines as clarity increases respecting just how much alike our conceptual apparatuses are. The point should hastily be added, of course, that a significant residue of hypotheses in the present work is derived from distinctively political problems of types which other social scientists seldom if ever are compelled to face.

Let us now consider the core meaning of our crucial terms. These are four in number; entrepreneur/organizer, benefits, group member, and exchange. In several ways the notion of entrepreneur/organizer is particularly central to the argument. The entrepreneur in any organizational situation is the initiator of the enterprise. Behaviorally, it is always true that he must make the first move if any exchange activity is to occur. Economics is not simply adopting a useful fiction when it singles out capital formation and investment as critical to economic development and entrepreneurs as the behavioral units involved in putting capital to work. In fact, that is what happens. Entrepreneurs use capital to generate goods or services, which, they hope, will be valued enough to be wanted; people desiring to satisfy wants work and save, and a growth spiral is set in motion. And unless the valued goods and services are offered no latent demand can be observed, only postulated. Capital formation processes must, to be sure, come before the entrepreneur can begin to work, but in terms of any specific organized economic exchange the entrepreneur is the starting point.

If we are to apply this analogy to the phenomena of interest groups, it will be necessary for us to identify specific entrepreneurs whose activities constitute the first visible signs of every particular organized group. It will also be necessary to identify some sort of capital which is invested to launch a group enterprise. If we can meet these tests, we will then also wish to inquire concerning such questions as the sources and processes of recruitment of interest group entrepreneurs.

It would be helpful to have a systematic array of group origins data to work from, but for the moment we must be content with illustrative cases to buttress the assertion that in no instance does an entrepreneurial theory of group formation fail to apply. Again the history of American farm groups demonstrates the point. The first big group to be organized was, of course, the Grange. It was initiated by Oliver Hudson Kelley who, by dint of considerable personal sacrifice and some generous friends, managed to survive until his organizational dream began to take hold.[19] Similarly Newton Gresham, having failed as a newspaper publisher, fed his family on credit and neighbors' largesse for more than a year until his Farmers Union began to attract enough dues-paying members to sustain him.[20] There is evidence of personal investment, though less dramatic, on the part of leading organizers of more recent groups such as the Farmers Holiday Movement, the National Corn Growers Association, and the National Farmers Organization.[21] And clearly a great many contemporary interest groups active in such fields as civil rights or foreign policy are headed by persons who have made heavy personal investments in their respective organizations.

Several of the early, large farm groups were begun by publishers of small newspapers or periodicals serving primarily rural markets.[22] The new organization was partly conceived as a circulation building mechanism and members received an immediate tangible benefit in the form of a subscription. In addition, the publication gave publicity to the group and in various ways capitalized its formation. It should be noted that these publisher-organizers may have had quite diverse *reasons* for establishing their groups. Conceptually, however, the reasons are less significant than the behavioral patterns.

A considerable number of farm groups were subsidized by other, older, groups. In part, of course, the Farm Bureau was organized and long sustained by subsidies, some from federal and state governments and some by local businessmen.[23] The expectation that the Bureau would be a supportive group, economically and perhaps politically, no doubt underlay these subsidies, but similar expectations must usually inform the subsidizing of one group by another. The organizing of sub-units under subsidy from the parent organization may be thought of as a variation on the same theme, though the latter is so "normal" and "legitimate" an aspect of organizational growth that it occasions no comment from observers. Inter-group subsidy, however, is very often regarded with suspicion by observers who somehow expect someone to be corrupted in the process.

In any case, it is clear that both capital costs and specific entrepreneurs have often come from other, older organizations. This seems to be particularly significant as a source of entrepreneurial recruitment, at least in the case of farm groups, but perhaps for others too. Not now as a form of subsidy but rather as a training ground and example of the possibility of establishing viable organizations of farmers, the early Grange provided the first real organizational experience for an enormous number of people. Many organizers of the Farmers Alliance had had experience in the Grange. In turn, Newton Gresham had been a zealot with the Alliance, allegedly organizing some fifteen hundred sub-alliances, before he attempted to establish the Farmers Union. Contemporaneously, other former Alliance and Grange organizers, such as Isaac McCracken of the Brothers of Freedom and Harvie Jordan of the Southern Cotton Growers' Association, were at work organizing their new enterprises. Saloutos is able already to refer to Jordan as a "professional farm organizer and lobbyist."[24]

What seems to have occurred is that once the Grange had set the example of a viable organization of farmers, a large number of people, especially those with direct experience in the prototype group, were attracted by the prospect of establishing farm groups of their own. One might follow as another collapsed. They might be differentiated be region or by crop or both. They might stress somewhat different combinations of material or political or rhetorical objectives. But in a broader sense they were all in the same line of business, and many of these businessmen came to constitute a rather specialized and self-sustaining subset of farm organizers. It seems warranted to suggest that a large portion of labor organizers have come from backgrounds closely associated with the union movement, or that both right and left wing group organizers tend to have long careers in that kind of activity—as *organizers,* not necessarily as heads of any particular group.

One important point which is suggested by the foregoing discussion is as follows. If groups must be organized by organizers investing capital, and if very often these organizers and this capital are derived, either as a subsidy or a legacy, from older organizations, then the emergence of extensive organized group life in a political system will tend (1) to be a gradual process, partially dependent on the spread of the organizational experience to socialize and recruit organizers, and (2) will depend upon the accumulation of social capital sufficient to invest in the formation of durable organizations. To the extent that the capital required is material, group formation requires, and must largely wait upon, industrialization. This is in no sense a novel conclusion, of course, but the argument by which it is reached is quite different from most.

The Nature of Benefits

We turn now to our second key concept. It should be understood at the outset that we do not attempt to assess "real" or "true" benefits. Rather we assume that people do or pursue those experiences and things which they value, for whatever reasons, and *in this sense only* may be regarded as rational. We assume that people mainly do or seek, subject to periodic evaluation and correction, whatever brings them a positive balance of benefits over costs. (It may be simpler to think only of positive and negative benefits since the latter is really what the notion of costs mean.) Notice that this is a conceptual assumption which is useful in thinking about certain kinds of behavior and of no necessary relevance either to normative theories of behavior or to motivational analysis.

How then shall we conceptualize benefits? A useful beginning point is the threefold distinction suggested by Clark and Wilson with reference to organizational incentives.[25] They distinguish among material, solidary, and purposive incentives. By material incentives they mean the tangible rewards of goods or services or the means, such as a job, by which goods and services may be obtained. Material incentives—or, in our terms, benefits—are always extrinsic to the parties involved in the transaction and are typically instrumental toward more fundamental values such as deference or well-being. Solidary benefits, on the other hand, are intrinsic to the parties. They are experienced directly and within the self. Clark and Wilson suggest that solidary values "derive in the main from the acts of associating and include such rewards as socializing, congeniality, the sense of group membership and identification, the status resulting from membership, fun and conviviality, and so on."[26]

Purposive benefits or incentives consist of the realization of suprapersonal goals, goals of the organization or group. Although, of course, the benefits of such achievement may accrue to particular individuals they are not ordinarily divisible into units of value allocated to specific persons or charged against unit costs. Nor can purposive benefits always be confined to the parties seeking them. Thus "good government" or "peace" or "states rights" or "civil liberties" are all desired by individuals and benefit individuals, but the benefits cannot readily be cost analyzed and they accrue to all sorts of people who took no part in the efforts to secure them. Blau employs a related concept when he discusses "expressive" social actions, as distinguished from instrumental actions. Expressive actions are those where the action involved gives expression to the interests or values of a person or group rather than instrumentally pursuing interests or values. Presumably one cannot *express* material values; one must pursue them and achieve them. Similarly, one can only enjoy solidary benefits by having them. But one can often derive benefits from expressing certain kinds of values. Opposition to war on poverty and affirmation of free speech or civil rights are contemporary examples of values many people wish to express and, what is of critical importance for our purposes, they are willing to join groups which provide mechanisms for the public expression of those values. Whether the expression is instrumentally relevant to the achievement of the values in question is, for the moment, not at issue. The point here is that important benefits are derived from the expression itself.

We prefer here to use the notion of expressive benefits rather than Clark and Wilson's term, "purposive." They were dealing only with intra-organizational incentives and consequently were untroubled by whatever complexities might appear regarding transactions between an organization's leaders and other groups. Clearly, however, some interest group leaders lobby for suprapersonal organizational goals—price supports, let us say, or a tax cut—which are purposive in Clark and Wilson's sense but also material in their explicit anticipated consequences. Material, solidary, and expressive benefits would seem to constitute mutually exclusive categories at the conceptual level, though the difficulties of empirical specification and measurement can hardly be exaggerated.

Our argument is that the group entrepreneur invests his capital to create a set of benefits, composed of some combination or mix of the types mentioned, which he offers at a price to a market. The price is group membership, which may cost as little as a supportive signature or as much as the heavy dues attached to some trade association memberships. The market is whatever range of people the entrepreneur chooses to try to attract. This leads us to an examination of the implication of our threefold typology of benefits for the entrepreneurial activities of group organizers. We then shall consider group members and potential members as sets of markets with demand patterns or preference schedules and see what implications this angle of vision may have.

What benefits are in fact offered by the entrepreneur/organizer to potential members of his group? It is clear that in a high proportion of cases the benefits initially offered are largely material. In the case of the early farm groups, for example, beginning with the Farmers Alliance and continuing through the Farmers Union and the Farm Bureau as well as a host of smaller groups, the initial exchange centered around some form of economic cooperation, for buying or selling or both. Co-operatives were sometimes promoted by stressing their ideological virtues, but in every case they were also expected to return direct economic benefits to those who joined. Obviously the same has been true of labor unions and also of most business trade associations.[27]

To observe the initial stress on material economic benefits in so many groups is to call attention to a closely related phenomenon which any theory of group formation and functioning must take into account. This is the phenomenon of organizational failure. No extant theory of interest groups seems to recognize the evident fact that a great many specific organized groups go out of business. Turnover is extremely high. Now if groups are organized through benefit exchange, it follows that they will dissolve whenever the benefits are inadequate to warrant continued support of the group. If the organizer fails to maintain that flow—if, for instance, the cooperative fails—the members will quit. So will they if they can no longer afford the cash dues. And this is precisely what happened to numerous farm groups and sub-groups during the latter nineteenth century. What were essentially small business operations failed; often because of bad management, but in several cases because of the special adversity of recession, as in 1893.

Not every group is organized around material benefits, of course. The early local agricultural societies probably flourished on the basis of the solidary benefits derived from membership, and it has long been standard to attribute much of the success of the Grange to the high solidary benefits resulting from the semi-secret rituals and Grange Hall-centered fraternal activities of the group. From the point of view of an entrepreneur, however, solidary benefits are often difficult to sell unless the market has special characteristics. An organizer can build a clubhouse but he cannot easily guarantee it will be worthwhile to go there. The solidary benefits may develop but the entrepreneur is especially dependent on his customer to help him create his product. Furthermore, it is not clear that for most people sociability is valued highly enough to persuade them to join a new group to get it. They may do so if there are no other alternatives—if the marker is genuine virgin territory regarding group association as the post-bellum farming frontier largely was. Or people may join solidary benefit groups which provide a generous admixture of other types of benefits too. A typical mix is solidary benefits mixed with rather a specialized type of expressive benefits. For example, cell-based organizations, which certainly have structures conducive to providing solidary benefits, tend also to be linked to extremist ideologies, often fraught with conspirational theses. In the small group situation of the cell, "the enemy" can be denounced enthusiastically and thereby maximize both expressive and solidary benefits of membership. Nevertheless, we tend to regard those interest groups which stress solidary benefits as "fringe" groups, unlikely to have much impact on public decisions, perhaps precisely because so much of their membership satisfaction is provided within the group itself.

It is probably the case, however, that we do not concern ourselves with solidary groups, or, for that matter, with material exchange groups either, unless there is also some kind of politically relevant expressive content to the group's internal exchange. Thus we care about the Grange not because of its fraternal rituals but because of the political relevance of the values and interests expressed by its leaders through its various official mechanisms. Still, it is one thing for, say, a material benefits group to acquire an overlay of expressive benefits and quite another to organize a group around the exchange of expressive values to begin with. The latter is a frequent phenomenon but one of special characteristics.

For the entrepreneur it is comparatively easy to essay establishing an expressive group. It requires little capital to articulate a cause and go about promoting the nascent group as guardian of that cause. On the other hand, this type of group presents especially high risks too. The cause may be a popular one without there being any persuasive reason for people who believe in it to join the particular group whose organizer claims to be the *true* defender of the faith. Moreover, it is likely that expressive groups are especially vulnerable to slight changes in circumstances, including many over which the group has no control. For example, America First and the Committee to Defend America by Aiding the Allies were wiped out organizationally by Pearl Harbor.[28] More broadly, for most people the act of joining an expressive group—contributing dues to ACLU or signing a Viet Nam protest petition—is a marginal act. The benefits derived from value expression are seldom of great intrinsic worth. Consequently, even if civil liberties remain equally endangered, a slight change in the member's resources or social pressures may lead to his failure to renew his membership.[29]

Two points of quite general political relevance follow from this line of analysis. On the one hand, expressive groups, being cheap to organize, will abound in a political system to whatever extent there may be entrepreneurs available to organize them, but they will tend to be highly transient. They will be easily established and as easily disappear. They will utilize communications media, especially the mail, more than face-to-face contacts; they may alter their expressed position to meet changing "market conditions." But above all they are unstable organizations. The corollary point is that expressive group organizers may be expected to infuse other types of benefits into the group in order to give it stability. They may attempt to enlarge the solidary benefits, for example, through the use of direct action protests. Whether a group moves from expressive toward solidary or the other way is an empirical question, but our analysis has suggested that a group originally stressing one type will tend to add the other in order to increase its stability as an organization.

We observed earlier that political scientists take notice of groups only if there is some political relevant expressive content to the groups' activities. But, we have argued, strictly expressive groups are unstable and transient. At the same time, stable groups such as those based on viable economic benefit exchanges may not have any politically relevant values. Must our concern with groups be only sporadic, incorporating them only when they enter the political arena and ignoring them otherwise? It would appear that, in fact, this is what we have done and it has led us to assume a durability and politicization of interest groups far in excess of reality. The theoretical posture adopted here, which deals with organized groups as generic phenomena, not simply in their politically relevant aspect, leads to the conclusion that most group activity has little to do with efforts to affect public policy decisions but is concerned rather with the internal exchange of benefits by which the group is organized and sustained. But surely, one may argue, some significant fraction of the universe of groups is established *in order to affect* and with the consequence of affecting policy outcomes. To consider this question properly we just also consider the work of Mancur Olson, whose argument is in many ways parallel to this one.[30]

Olson is concerned with the question of why people maintain membership in interest groups. He demonstrates that in most familiar group situations it is not rational for any member to be part of an interest group in order to support a lobby, even though he genuinely desires the goals toward which the lobbying is directed. The argument hinges primarily on the distinction between what Olson calls *collective benefits*—those which accrue to people in a particular situation or category regardless of their organizational affiliations—and *selective benefits*—those which accrue only to members of the association. Thus the Farmers Union may lobby for price supports, i.e., collective benefits, but its members will receive the benefits of price supports whether they stay in the Union or not. Olson shows that therefore its members would not stay if they rationally balance the cost of membership against its benefits insofar as these benefits are collective. But cooperatives and cheap insurance may be available only to members. They are selective and may be entirely sufficient to induce continued membership.

Thus far Olson's argument differs little from the present one except that it is less clearly couched in exchange terms and thus does not explicitly examine the entrepreneur/organizer as a functionally distinct role from that of group member. Olson does not contend that all group members are rational, but only that to the extent that they are they will not normally join organizations in order to seek collective benefits. Two main exceptions are noted: where the members are philanthropic and seek through group membership to obtain benefits for others; and where membership is coerced, as in a union operating under a closed shop agreement. Yet the broadened conception of benefits we have employed, including the notion that costs, e.g., of coercion, are the same as negative benefits, allows us to subsume these exceptions under the same headings as in the central argument. Moreover, as we noted earlier, we can assume that rationality in the sense of purposiveness or goal-orientation is characteristic of such a preponderance of behavior that any observed exceptions will not affect the main contentions.

There are two typical critical points in Olson's argument, both of
them points of omission, with which we must take issue. Olson does not
examine how groups are first organized but assumes a going system. As
a consequence he does not adequately deal with group development
through time.[31] If one looks at group formation, however, one finds
that some organizations such as the Farmers Alliance were indeed organized around the exchange of selective benefits but that others, such
as the Grange, were organized initially, at least in significant part, in order to alter public policy; i.e., to secure collective benefits. Granted that
many of the groups in the latter category may later have introduced selective benefits in order to hold the members, we must still account for
the initial appearance. And Olson's argument does not hold for this
situation. Is it relevant for farmers to join together in order to bring
about policy change? Does organization improve their bargaining
power? Political lore and science agree on the affirmative. How many
farmers must join before this power is sufficient to secure any collective
benefits through policy change? The answer is, within very broad limits,
indeterminate. Accordingly, it may be entirely rational for any potential
member to join until the benefit is achieved as long as his costs in joining
are exceeded by his anticipated benefit from the collective good. Once
the latter is a reality, however, the indeterminacy disappears and Olson's
analysis comes into play; the member ought rationally to withdraw unless selective benefits are introduced. Thus a sizable array of organized
groups *may* appear on the political scene to lobby for collective good but,
lacking selective benefits, their mortality rate is likely to be high.

Olson's second omission is any explanation of the phenomenon of
lobbying. We shall deal with this whole subject in greater detail below,
but it should here be noted that Olson's argument accounts for the maintenance of groups without regard to their impact on public policy but
does not explain why groups lobby or how lobbying is related, if it is, to
the dynamics of intra-group relationships. Nevertheless, Olson has performed an important service in destroying the comfortable myth of an
interest group behaving in a simple representational way, seeking public
policy goals because these goals are desired by the group's members.[32]

Group Membership

We must now consider a very tricky but important component of our
conceptual structure, the matter of consumer, or member, preferences.

It seems fair to say that at bottom extant interest group theory assumes that group members have public policy-related interests, values, or preferences which (1) antedate the existence of the organized association, (2) are the rational basis for joining and remaining as members of the association, (3) are articulated and heightened by virtue of the associational interactions, and (4) are represented through the association to the policy-making arenas by virtue of lobbying activities. As we have seen, Olson undermines the logical plausibility of points 2 and 4 and, in a sense, renders point 3 beside the point for explaining interest group phenomena. But there are additional difficulties even in the first item. How do we know that a particular array of interests exists? Conventionally we have approached the issue in two very different ways. We may impute interests to categories of people—workers, farmers, etc.—on the basis of some theory about how individual values are derived and ordered, say Marxism or its variants. Thus we conclude that factory workers desire policies which raise wages, or give authority to unions, or the like. Alternatively, we may infer preferences from observed behavior. Thus some types of workers join unions more readily than others and are presumed therefore to place a different valuation on union membership. Most behaviorally derived preference schedules look far more diverse than do those imputed on the basis of more abstract theories about how values are formed. One might therefore suppose that empirical inquiry into preference schedules ought to be urged to test competing analytic strategies. But here one runs into the problem that intersubjective comparisons of utility schedules are, in virtually all cases, impossible.[33] Without examining the large body of literature on this point, we may apply this conclusion to our situation in the following manner. Preferences and their orderings may be established for any set of people only on the basis of their behavior. Although he may make a reasonable estimate in advance, say on the basis of some kind of market research, the only way a producer really determines what consumer preference schedules are is by offering a good at a price, or at varying prices, and observing the differential demand schedules. Similarly, the only way empirically to determine the existence of an interest is to articulate a position (expressive benefits) or offer material or solidary incentives at one or more price levels and to observe the incidence and distribution of support—membership, votes, money, or whatever else is valued political currency. Price, a behaviorally derived result of exchange activity, resolves the dilemma posed by the noncomparability of inter-subjective preferences. And this means that interests of a group or class of people may be observed *only* by examining exchanges between political entrepreneurs and consumer/member/voters.

The analytic problem is thus, *a fortiori*, resolved by conceptualizing interests and interest groups in terms of exchanges of benefits between entrepreneurs/leaders and consumer/followers. This point does not, however, affect the relevance of individual preferences or of questions concerning how those preferences are formed or changed. Thus one may still argue that technological changes affecting the structure of economic activity may alter the preference schedules of many persons. These new schedules may constitute a promising potential market for political entrepreneurs, or, indeed, they may adversely affect a particular entrepreneur's market. Variables affecting market potential are relevant to an understanding of group formation and development. But, as we have stressed, they are never a sufficient explanation of interest activity and their aggregate structure cannot be more than guessed at in the absence of group organizing activities.[34]

The Exchange

It follows from what we have said that the "potential group" or market is a matter of great uncertainty from the point of view of the group organizer. The latter, having invested his capital in an array of benefits, offers these benefits at a price—membership in the group—which he hopes will attract members and also maintain a viable organization. Entrepreneurs/organizers generally appear to select their markets on the basis of their own experiences and contacts or by emulating other, similar, organizational efforts, as when they purchase or borrow mailing lists of similarly inclined groups or publications. Farm organizers are closely affiliated with farmers, labor organizers with workers, rightists with rightists, and so on, and seldom do group entrepreneurs seem to cross over from one field to another. Thus, they have some expectation concerning the probable demand curves of the market they seek to reach, but they must be unsure whether the response will be sufficient to sustain the organization. And in order to sustain a group organization, it is necessary to maintain an adequate flow of benefits both to members *and* to the organizers themselves. In short, there must be a mutually satisfactory *exchange*.

Now what kinds of benefits are derived from these group organization exchanges by the entrepreneurs? The economists have no difficulty with this question, which they assert is answered by the notion of profits. If, in addition to profits, an entrepreneur derives other types of job satisfactions, profits remain the key requirement for continuation of the enterprise, and in abstract economic models of entrepreneurial activity the profit must approach some optimal return on the capital investment or the investment will be transferred to some other, more promising, enterprise.

It may be that many kinds of group organizing capital are not as easily transferred as straight money capital; a prosperous labor union probably will not subsidize other enterprises randomly nor will a farm organizer equally well defer his spending in order to organize in the urban ghetto. The *tendencies* would surely be for investment to go toward expressively supportive organizations, cognate markets, and relatively familiar territories, geographical and functional. Yet we can cite numerous examples to show that even this capital is transferred from one enterprise to another within quite broad limits. Let us, therefore, consider what is implied by the notion of profit in respect to political entrepreneurs.

As a minimum we may assume that, so long as the entrepreneur desires to maintain the organization as a going enterprise, he must get a sufficient return in the form of membership support to enable him to continue to provide the benefits which attract members. Over some initial period of time the benefits may be more costly than membership will pay for, but, unless the enterprise is permanently subsidized, the returns must ultimately match the cost of providing the benefits. Where the benefits to members are material, of course, the membership must also provide material rewards in exchange. But even in solidary and expressive groups the entrepreneur must derive enough material return to pay the overhead costs *and* keep him sufficiently satisfied so as not to shift his energies to some other enterprise. Conceptually, the entrepreneur's reward may be viewed as profit. Thus: Entrepreneurs provide benefits to members whose membership must entail a return sufficient to pay the costs of the benefits received plus some profit to the entrepreneur.

What form does group organizer profit take empirically? A common form is that of the salaried executive. In some groups the organizer may be chosen president of the group he develops and paid a salary. In other cases he may occupy the position of executive secretary or its equivalent. In either situation he must maintain an adequate flow of benefits to members or lose his position, either because the enterprise goes bankrupt or because he is dismissed somewhere short of organizational catastrophe. If the organizer does not desire or cannot obtain a paid position from his entrepreneurial activities, he may nevertheless persist in them if they have sufficient expressive value for him, and many expressive groups probably are developed in this fashion as avocational or philanthropic concerns substitute for entrepreneurial "profit motives." Even here, however, organizing is costly, and there must be subsidies drawn from other extra-group sources to sustain the activity or the group will shortly be bankrupt. The great difficulty experienced by many civil rights groups in keeping their leadership afloat illustrates the point.

I do not wish to argue that group organizers are classic "economic men" whose conscious motives are to secure the largest possible financial return. Indeed, although there surely are examples of such motivation among extant interest group entrepreneurs, taken as a whole their conscious intentions are undoubtedly very diverse. The point is rather that "profit" to the leadership is a necessary part of the exchange with the members and without it the leaders cannot continue.

One implication of the foregoing discussion is that any *election* of leaders by members, or of representatives by constituents, may be regarded in terms familiar to economic analysis of the firm.[35] Thus the minimum return required on investment is reelection to office, and office must provide sufficient resources to motivate and to maintain the flow of benefits to members/constituents. Dissatisfied members of a voluntary group may quit or switch to a rival group; dissatisfied constituents may be expected to switch to a rival candidate. But the logical and conceptual relationship is the same. It is an exchange which must satisfy both parties.

Now, let us go an additional step. It may be observed that large numbers of organized interest groups do go bankrupt in some sense. They fail as enterprises. Their organizers/leaders must find some other line. But large numbers of groups survive over long periods of time. Moreover, it is characteristic of many relatively stable groups, especially those involving primarily material benefits exchanges, to exhibit great stability in their paid leadership personnel. Further, it may be suggested that the "profits" accruing to this leadership from providing members with selective benefits, available only to group members, very often exceed by a comfortable margin the minimum requirements of sustaining the enterprise. How may we think about this "surplus"?

From the standpoint of the entrepreneurs, whose decision it is to dispose of his "surplus profits," there may be a number of options. He may, for example, enlarge the benefits available to members in order to restore the balance between his costs and his profits. Or he may spend his profits in various private, but personal, activities—higher salary, extra-group activities, or whatever. Perhaps he builds a fancy new building as an organizational headquarters. But, if his enterprise is internally prosperous, he may spend some of his "profits" in public activity. He may, for example, lobby for legislation which *he* thinks desirable and do so quite independent of any views his members have on the questions.[36] When he does so, he cannot expect his members to agree with him, but, as long as his organization survives and he with it, it does not really matter. He takes his policy positions and invests what he has in the way of profit in promoting them not because his membership demands that he do so but only because his membership makes it possible for him to pursue his private desires by providing him a profitable exchange. Now it may be that his desires are not incongruent with those of his members. It may also be that he seeks legitimation and support for his desires by asserting that they conform to those of his members. But it may also be that those whom he attempts to persuade to his views are unimpressed by his claims of membership support, and his success must then be achieved by other bargaining tactics. Applying this same conception to a legislator we often say that he has a considerable number of "free votes" on which constitutency demands are absent or conflicting or vague and which he casts according to bargaining criteria which he derives independent of constiuency pressure. Yet unless he satisfies the minimum constituency expectations of benefits he will not survive in office long enough to spend his profits in his "free votes."

It is not argued that "profit consumption" is the sole explanation of lobbying or influencing activity or that all such activity is equally well explained this way. It is contended, however, that a significant portion of what we observe to be lobbying activity by group leaders may result not from a mandate derived from membership demands but from the personal choices and values of the group leaders. This conception would fit and make sense of a broad spectrum of data which show group spokesmen taking public policy positions at variance with the apparent views of their members and still suffering no reprisals. Indeed, as Milbrath among others has pointed out, a major focus of lobbying is not the policy makers at all but the group members themselves.[37] If lobbyists were simply reflecting membership demands, they would not spend so much time "farming the membership."

Moreover, we may in this way more easily make sense of the reported disregard of lobbyists, or at least extremely uneven response to them, by

policy makers.[38] And, finally, we may thus square the lack of logical necessity for lobbying by group spokesmen, which Olson shows, with the
obvious fact of extensive lobbying in the observable world.

There remains a significant portion of lobbying activity which may be
regarded as instrumental to the benefit flow and exchange of the group
and it would be wrong to ignore this portion. As we noted in criticizing
Olson's argument, the problematic but presumably positive relationship
between group strength and activity and the achievement of public decisions providing collective good makes it rational, within broad limits,
for individuals who value the good to join a group which proposes to
lobby for it. Moreover, many collective goods are provided in discontinuous or, at least, recurrently renegotiable form so that simply because
an act is passed providing a given level of farm subsidies for three years
does not guarantee it will be renewed or, if renewed, maintained at the
same level. Group lobbying may often, therefore, be instrumental in securing or maintaining the flow of collective benefits, and, while not all
those affected by the benefits will join the group, or join for that reason,
some may do so and press the entrepreneurs to act accordingly.

In addition, for some groups potential policy decisions constitute a
significant source of the selective benefits by which the group's internal
exchange is sustained. This would be true, for example, of a significant
portion of the licensing regulations applicable to professional groups
who secure the legal authority to control entry to the profession, and,
having such authority, make it attractive thereby for prospective prac-
titioners to join the association. Or for a labor union, policy decisions
involving picketing, antitrust applications to union activities, yellow-
dog contracts, and the like directly affect the ability of the union leadership to provide selective benefits to its members through favorable
contracts. Whenever this is the case, it is obvious that lobbying by the
entrepreneur leaders requires no additional conceptual trappings for
satisfactory explanation.

Continuity of Group Leadership

In the analysis we have presented the focus has been mainly on the initial organizer/entrepreneurs of the group. There are good reasons for
this emphasis. It reminds us that existing organizations such as unions
or major farm groups, which sometimes seem to be permanent features
of the political landscape, have quite specific origins and originators.

Moreover, it has been useful to examine those origins and the individuals who played the key entrepreneurial roles in establishing the groups. But one need not rely on state of nature assumptions in the analysis of contemporary groups. A large proportion of the extant roster of politically relevant groups are durable enterprises with origins which may or may not shed light on their present affairs. Implicit in our argument, however, is the view that all groups may be approached in the same terms. If the entrepreneur/organizer is easier to identify through examining group origins, his role is conceptually identical with that of the leader of a going group concern. It is, therefore, group leadership generally that we are discussing in a framework of benefit exchange. The entrepreneurial role is generically identical with that of leader; the leader is perforce an entrepreneur.

We will not repeat what has already been said of the entrepreneur in order to make clear its application to leadership generally. Nor is it possible here to do more than assert that the argument may be transferred *in toto* to the consideration of leadership generally, not simply group leadership. Suffice to say that although we begin with an attempt to develop an empirically valid and logically secure theory of interest groups we find ourselves with a formulation of truly general proportions.

Let us here add only one additional point of substance derived from our general argument. We have already noted that among material benefit groups leadership tenure has generally been very secure. There are, of course, some notable exceptions, but most union or farm or business group leaders have had long careers, seldom challenged. On the other hand, what we have referred to as expressive groups are frequently characterized by bitter schisms. Does our formulation contribute to an explanation of this phenomenon? We indicated earlier that expressive groups are cheap to organize but fragile. If they are cheap to organize, they are also cheap to factionalize. A rival to the leadership needs only a membership list and a better line to support a factional fight. The fruits of victory may be great or small, depending on what the faction leaders value and how prosperous or prestigious the group is. What are the potential costs of attempting a factional fight? The ultimate cost is expulsion. But seldom is an expressive group the sole guardian of expression of a value. If one is kicked out of CORE or the John Birch Society one is not thereby denied the opportunity to express one's position but probably only of whatever solidary values the group conferred on its members.

On the other hand, consider a comparable situation in a union or a farm organization. In order to mount a serious effort to unhorse the leadership, factional leaders must, in effect, assemble enough capital, perhaps from anticipated profits, to promise enough increased benefits to attract support for themselves and away from their rivals. This is typically very difficult to do partly because the capital to organize a factional drive is hard to assemble, partly because the existing leadership faced with factional opposition may often reinvest more of their profit into membership benefits, and sometimes may simply coopt potential factional leaders into the existing leadership cadre. Moreover, uncompromising factional rivals may be met with exclusion from the group which in turn may mean exclusion from a substantial array of material benefits available only to group members. For all these reasons then factional efforts in established material benefits groups are comparatively rare and often come to grief.[39] And this is true even though the profits available to material benefit group leaders are often substantial and hence might be expected to attract rival entrepreneurs. But the capital requirements to capture control of the UAW or set up a rival union in the same employment markets would surely not be much less difficult to manage than capturing control of, or establishing a rival to, General Motors. Finally, material benefit interest groups have been successful as have business firms in coopting potential factional leadership into an orderly hierarchy with sufficient profits derived from the group's exchange structure to sustain the full cadre.

Conclusion

In concluding a paper of this kind one is tempted simply to restate the core of the argument, recognizing that for the most part the usefulness of the kind of conceptual orientation presented here depends upon its plausibility and suggestiveness as a heuristic model. In the main it is neither true nor false but to be tested by its intellectual utility. Nevertheless, the utility of such a scheme must ultimately rest on whether one can imagine ways by which to derive reasonable empirical applications which are amenable to testing against data. One such application has been illustrated here in the discussion of farm group origins, and our conclusion was that an entrepreneurial exchange hypothesis both fits and explains the data better than alternative hypotheses. It has also been suggested that this formulation accounts for the high incidence of schism among ideological or expressive groups and the low incidence of severe factionalism among material benefit groups. One must recognize, however, that in the latter explanation the data are largely impressionistic since they assume more knowledge than we have of the kind of benefits exchanged in the two categories of groups. In principle, however, such data could be obtained by inquiring of group members, and of people solicited to join who decline, what benefits they derive from membership and determining the points at which, under various conditions, marginal costs equate with marginal benefits or utility.

Another empirical test might be undertaken by examining closely and systematically the behavior of group leaders over time. It was argued that much lobbying activity by group leaders may be understood as a form of personal consumption of profit derived from their intragroup exchanges. If this is correct, it would follow that when their membership declines or is threatened with decline such profit is reduced and the lobbying for policies that are non-instrumental to the group's exchange structure would also decline. If, that is, UAW membership declines, Walter Reuther should spend more time on contract bargaining and union-related instrumental lobbying and less time on policy issues of a more personally expressive character. Without gainsaying the difficulties of making such observations, one may suppose that they are possible and would constitute an empirical test of the theory.

Finally, and whatever the empirical outcomes of the specific inquiries proposed or of others which might be imagined, we must assert the crucial importance of developing systematic empirical theory, of interest groups as of other politically relevant phenomena, to bring greater order and clarity to the extant array of literary theory. Nearly two decades ago David Truman demonstrated extraordinary imagination in assembling a vast array of fragments into a richly suggestive fabric of commentary and insight. Ironically, his accomplishment was so complete that remarkably few political scientists have worked ahead with the tools he sought to fashion. By employing a more generic conceptual orientation to examine interest group phenomena, perhaps we may at least hope to revive the substantive investigation into their characteristic properties and more systematically relate them to other facets of the political system.

NOTES

1. THE GOVERNMENTAL PROCESS, New York: Knopf, 1951, p. 66.

2. Professor John P. Heinz and I are engaged in an extended study of U.S. farm policy formation and that inquiry stimulated much of the present analysis as well as providing much illustrative material for it.

3. The principal works thus far which attempt to develop reasonably general statements of exchange theory include Peter Blau, *Exchange and Power in Social Life*, New York: Wiley, 1964; George Homans, *Social Behavior: Its Elementary Forms*, New York: Harcourt, Brace and World, 1961; James A. Coleman, "Foundations for a Theory of Collective Decisions," *American Journal of Sociology*, Vol. LXX, May 1966, pp. 615–628; Mancur Olson, Jr., *The Logic of Collective Action*, Cambridge: Harvard University Press, 1965.

4. It may be noted that, Truman aside, there is remarkably little recent literature which deals, empirically or theoretically, with interest groups as primary units for analysis, as dependent variables, rather than independent variables related to policy outcomes or processes. Among the exceptions may be cited Lester Milbrath, *The Washington Lobbyists*, Chicago: Rand McNally, 1963; Norman Luttbeg and Harmon Zeigler, "Attitude Consensus and Conflict in an Interest Group: An Assessment of Cohesion," *American Political Science Review*, Vol. LX, September, 1966, pp. 655–667; Frank Nall, "National Associations," in W. Lloyd Warner, ed., *The Emergent American Society, Large-Scale Organizations*, New Haven: Yale University Press, 1967, pp. 276–314.

5. For elements of this argument, see Truman, *op. cit.*, especially pp. 52–62. See also, Robert MacIver, *The Web of Government*, New York: The MacMillan Company, 1947, pp. 52 ff. The formulation is familiar in the standard sociology and anthropology writings also, and Truman cites representative authorities.

6. The growth of specialized commercial agriculture is traced by a number of agricultural historians. See, for example, Everett E. Edwards, "American Agriculture—the First 300 Years," in *Farmers in a Changing World, The Yearbook of Agriculture, 1940*, U.S. Department of Agriculture, 76th Congress, 3rd Session, House Document No. 695, Washington, D.C., 1940, pp. 171–277; Fred A. Shannon, *The Farmer's Last Frontier*, New York: Farrar and Rinehart, 1945.

7. The theoretical uncertainty in which Truman left his concept of the "potential group" is examined in Roy C. Macridis, "Interest Groups in Comparative Analysis," *Journal of Politics*, Vol. XXII, February, 1961, pp. 25–45; and in Mancur Olson, Jr., *op. cit.*, pp. 128–130.

8. Again, cf., Truman, *op. cit.*, pp. 52 ff.

9. *Ibid.*, p. 59.

10. One must distinguish between the politically relevant groups of this period and the older, localized, agricultural improvement societies organized mainly for self-help and the promotion of fairs. See Carl C. Taylor, "Farmers Organizations," in *Encyclopedia of the Social Sciences*, New York, 1931–7, Vol. 6, pp. 129–131.

11. A particularly valuable discussion of farm group organizations in this period is Theodore Saloutos, *Farmer Movements in the South, 1865–1933*, Berkeley: University of California Press, 1960. For the early twentieth century see Theodore Saloutos and John D. Hicks, *Agricultural Discontent in the Middle West, 1900–1939*, Madison: University of Wisconsin Press, 1951.

12. See also Olson's observation that Truman "assumes *organized* (italics his) groups arise because there is dislocation or 'need' for them, and this is neither factually nor theoretically substantiated." *Op. cit.*, p. 123, n. 50.

13. In the ABA and AMA membership shows rather a rapid early growth, averaging more than ten percent per year until up to one-fourth of the potential members were enrolled. Thereafter growth has averaged approximately three percent per year. There are very few periods of absolute decline, however, with 1933–34 being much the worst. Membership in the NEA, an organization of more ambiguous professional status and with a less well-defined market, has fluctuated much more widely.

14. The Farmers Alliance is estimated to have gone from one million members in 1890 to near extinction in 1893. See Robert L. Tontz, "Membership of General Farmers' Organization, United States, 1874–1960," *Agricultural History*, Vol. 38, July, 1964, pp. 143–157.

15. See Tontz, *passim*, and sources cited therein. Tontz himself argues that membership does go up when farm conditions go down but with a three to five year lag. The data fit as well, however, to a direct and positive relationship between prices and membership.

16. In 1957 and 1958 some thirty-seven regional and national farm commodity organizations joined the National Conference of Commodity Organizations, an organization attempting to build a program agreement among the disparate interests of commodity groups. NCOO had brief success in 1958 but shortly foundered.

17. Saloutos notes that, "The farmers joined the Farmers Union for various reasons. The quest for higher cotton prices naturally was an important factor, but the fact that producers were benefiting from a rising market was equally significant. It was much easier for farmers to pay dues in 1903 when cotton commanded 13 cents a pound than in 1898 when it brought only 6 cents." *Op. cit.*, p. 187.

18. See, for example, John L. Shover, "Populism in the Nineteen-Thirties: The Battle for the AAA," *Agricultural History*, Vol. 39, No. 1, January, 1965, pp. 17–24.

19. See Saloutos, *op. cit.*, p. 32. Generally, on the Grange, see Solon J. Buck, *The Granger Movement*, Cambridge: Harvard University Press, 1913.

20. Saloutos, *op. cit.*, pp. 184–186.

21. The origins of the National Farmers Organization are described by Charles Walters in "History of the National Farmers Organizations," *Farm Tempo USA*, Vol. 3, November, 1966, pp. 16–20.

22. Milton George, editor of the *Western Rural,* founded the National Farmers Alliance and the paper advanced the early money and absorbed headquarters costs. Saloutos, *op. cit.,* pp. 77–78. William Hirth did much the same later on in organizing the Missouri Farmers Association. See Ray Derr, *The Missouri Farmer in Action,* Columbia, Missouri: Missouri Farmer Press, 1953.

23. On the formation of the Farm Bureau see O. M. Kile, *The Farm Bureau Through Three Decades,* Baltimore: The Waverly Press, 1949; and Grant McConnell, *The Decline of Agrarian Democracy,* Berkeley: The University of California Press, 1953. See also the convenient summary in Olson, *op. cit.,* pp. 148–153. The efforts of John L. Lewis and his associates in subsidizing union formation, especially through the Steel Workers Organizing Committee, in the mid-1930's, provide other well-known examples.

24. *Op. cit.,* p. 156.

25. See Peter B. Clark and James Q. Wilson, "Incentive Systems: A Theory of Organizations," in *Administrative Science Quarterly,* Vol. 6 (September, 1961), pp. 129–166. Clark and Wilson are concerned more generally with organizations than with interest groups *per se,* but their analysis is generally relevant even when only implicitly so. Some of their hypothesis are similar to those suggested here, some are not. For example, they suggest that organizations will stress purposive incentives in the formative stages. We argue the contrary for farm groups and many others. See especially p. 151. See also the similar typology developed by Amatai Etzioni for discussion of ways of inducing compliance of members of organization with leaders. His typology include utilitarian, coercive, and normative incentives. *Comparative Analysis of Complex Organizations,* New York: The Free Press of Glencoe, 1961.

26. *Op. cit.,* pp. 134–135.

27. A recent careful history of the development of cotton textile trade associations describes the early importance of exchanging technical information about a rapidly changing technology as a motivating factor inducing cooperation. See Louis Galambos, *Competition and Cooperation: The Emergence of a National Trade Association,* Baltimore: The Johns Hopkins Press, 1966, pp. 11, ff. The list of additional examples among trade associations alone could be enlarged to almost any desired length, limited only by gaps in our information about the specific entrepreneur/organizer.

28. See Wayne S. Cole, *America First,* Madison: University of Wisconsin Press, 1953.

29. Unfortunately, there are large gaps in our knowledge about membership in most types of voluntary organizations. Most studies have concentrated on characteristics of members compared to non-members or in the grosser aspects of organizational involvement generally in the society. Important reviews of pertinent literature include J. M. Scott, "Membership and Participation in Voluntary Associations," *American Sociological Review,* Vol. 22, 1957, pp. 315–326; Charles R. Wright and Herbert Hyman, "Voluntary Association Memberships of American Adults," *American Sociological Review,* Vol. 23, 1958, pp. 284–294.

Lacking a viable typology of groups, few have inquired into differential propensities to join or withdraw from different types of groups. For illuminating case studies, however, see Joseph Gusfield, *Symbolic Crusade,* Urbana: University of Illinois Press, 1963; Raymond E. Wolfinger, Barbara Kaye Wolfinger, Kenneth Prewitt, and Sheilah Rosenhack, "America's Radical Right: Politics and Ideology," in David Apter, ed., *Ideology and Discontent,* New York: The Free Press of Glencoe, 1964, pp. 262–293.

30. *Op. Cit.*

31. Indeed one might argue that in most interest group studies the two elements most often missing have been individual behavior associated with differentiated roles and changes over time. Concern with origins forces us to consider interest groups longitudinally and we are led to useful insights in the process.

32. I do not wish to imply that in stressing any differences with him I have adequately represented everything Olson says in his remarkably suggestive book. Many of the points he stresses are very much like the arguments here, and I am delighted to acknowledge my debt to him.

33. See, for example, R. Duncan Luce and Howard Raiffa, *Games and Decisions,* New York: John Wiley and Sons, 1957, pp. 33–34, and Chapter 14; Kenneth J. Arrow, *Social Choice and Individual Values,* 2nd ed., New York: John Wiley and Sons, 1963, especially pp. 109 ff.

34. The discussion here of potential markets, a familiar enough notion in economic analysis, would seem to incorporate the principal meaning of Truman's oft maligned concept of potential group. Truman imputed a political impact to potential groups, however, which is quite absent from any understanding one might have of potential markets. Again, the latter are truly fallow until cultivated by entrepreneurs.

35. I do not wish here to offer more than the mere suggestion that the conceptual orientation employed here has extremely general application to politically relevant phenomena and that, if pursued, it may yield enormous returns in terms which subsume many types of representative relationships under the headings of exchange theory.

36. Olson also notes that group leaders may employ "profits" to lobby for objectives rather than those desired by the members. He suggests that these "profits" are often a consequence of some degree of monopoly power vis-a-vis the potential membership market and would be absent if there were perfect competition among groups. As we have said earlier, however, Olson does not clearly differentiate the role of the entrepreneur and so does not emphasize the personal choice he may exercise in lobbying as we have done. *Op. cit.*, pp. 133–134, n. 2.

37. *The Washington Lobbyists,* p. 205.

38. Cf., for example, Raymond A. Bauer, Ithiel de Sola Pool, and Lewis A. Dexter, *American Business and Public Policy,* New York: Atherton Press, 1963.

39. It may be observed that the argument here and throughout this paper has major implications for discussion more commonly framed in terms of

oligarchy or, in Truman's terms, the active minority. What we are saying, in effect, is not that such formulations are wrong, but that by employing an exchange schema we can account for a much wider variety and range of data, including oligarchy data, within the same theoretical framework.

2

Interest Representation: The Dominance of Institutions

*I*t *is common* for academics to divide the American political world into two parts, governmental and nongovernmental. In turn, the actors occupying nongovernmental roles of significance sufficient to require textbook chapters treating them are individual citizens (also aggregated into "public opinion"), political parties, and interest groups. The latter two were once often closely tied together, in texts and in courses, with parties clearly the dominant concern (e.g., Key, 1964). In recent years interest groups have come to constitute a largely autonomous subject matter, but almost always they are placed into a conceptual framework that links them closely to parties. Functional arguments assign groups and parties to the articulation-aggregation portions of the functional space, and process formulations place both on the input side of policy making. By treating parties and interest groups as two types of political organization, Wilson (1973) has perhaps best reflected the implicit conceptual assumption governing descriptive work and shaping the definitions of theoretical problems.

The American political universe, in fact, contains a considerably more diverse array of actors than these conventional headings suggest. In particular, notable omissions from textbook treatments and most research literature include individual corporations, state and local governments, universities, think tanks, and most other *institutions* of the private sector.[1] Likewise unnoticed are the multitudes of Washington representatives, freestanding and for hire, including lawyers, public relations firms, and diverse other counsellors. Ad hoc coalitions, issue networks,

Reprinted with permission from *American Political Science Review* 78 (March 1984): 64–70.

and other "loosely coupled" cooperative structures of activity are occasionally acknowledged, but are rarely described or given a place in academic characterizations of the essential features of the American system. Yet, attentive readers of what might be called the "inside press" of American politics, such as *Congressional Quarterly* and *National Journal*, are regularly informed about these kinds of activity and given to understand that they are often of critical importance to policy outcomes.

In this article I propose to argue that institutions have come to dominate the processes of interest representation in American national politics. Institutions present somewhat different theoretical problems from those we are accustomed to encountering in regard to membership-based interest groups. Moreover there are important empirical differences between a system driven by membership groups and one in which institutions occupy center stage. As the characterization of Washington representation undergoes reconstruction, two important strands of empirical theory come under scrutiny, interest group theory and theories of representation. It is thus an enormously ambitious undertaking, even presumptuous, that is attempted here. It is intended really as a beginning, however, or perhaps a midstream rechanneling, so as better to accommodate the observables of Washington politics.[2]

There are four essential concepts involved in the proposed reconstruction: interest, organized interest group, institution, and representative. I will seek where appropriate to incorporate the results of recent discussions of these ideas, and in the latter part of the article I will present some fragmentary data illustrating and amplifying the arguments. In general, I will not be concerned as much with defining the key terms with unchallengeable clarity as with conveying rather more ostensively the meanings and uses I believe important. In any case, the words bear such heavy accumulations from centuries of everyday employment that it would be of little help or effect to legislate. And, of course, there remains Arthur Bentley's rather insouciant sentiment, "Who likes may snip verbal definitions in his old age, when his world has gone crackly and dry" (1908, p. 199).

The Concept of Interest

Toward what end is political activity directed? At one level we might speak of justice, equity, or the redress of grievances. In a more neutral vein, a number of terms are employed, often more or less interchangeably; e.g., values, objectives, and interests. But it is interest that is most often incorporated into our skeins of theory and thus merits special attention. Interest refers to attitudes, of course (Truman, 1951; cf. MacIver, 1932). It involves values and preferences. But it is the perceived or anticipated effects of policy—government action or inaction including all its symbolic forms as well as more intangible allocations—upon values that create politically relevant interests. Similarly, interested behavior expresses policy-related purpose, sometimes very broadly defined and sometimes highly specific and detailed. To be sure, preferences may be inert, quiescent, held *in pectore,* or otherwise unattached to any visible action. Yet it is often risky for an outside observer to impute interests, asserting that a given policy *ought* to be seen as having such-and-such an effect on certain values, thus producing interests and, perhaps, eventual political action. Finally, interests are certainly perceived by individuals, one at at time and sometimes uniquely, but it is also possible for other reasonably "unitary" actors to perceive and act politically upon interests. Here we come to the institutional actor, and in examining institutions and their interests we must consider how, if at all, they differ from more conventional notions of organized interest groups.

How Interests Are Organized into Groups

Until the publication of Mancur Olson's *The Logic of Collective Action* (1965), comparatively little serious attention had been given to the question of how and whether interests would become organized into associations capable of politically interesting action. Some commentators (e.g., Hagan, 1958), following Bentley's lead, refused to make a distinction between interest and group, treating them as identical phenomena, two words for the same observable activity. In this tradition the main intellectual task was one of mapping, locating the actors involved in the political situation and specifying the policy direction they took. Once all the interests were thus plotted, one would have a complete picture (Bentley, 1908, p. 269), and such a picture, it seems, was expected to yield satisfactory understanding. In any case, Bentley was so anxious not to step outside a strict empirical frame of analysis that little attention was given to the question of how interests developed, or failed to, and why some were more readily mobilized than others.

David Truman, building on and sometimes departing from Bentley, did ask specifically how groups emerged. He specified an initial condition, the sharing of attitudes or interests among potential members, and suggested that these shared values would most often be brought into being by some exogenous disruption of a social equilibrium, such as war or technological change. Formal association for Truman, as for Bentley, was a matter of "mere technique," and not given special theoretical status, but as a practical matter the discussion of group emergence focused mainly on organized groups. Truman went on to suggest that group formation was often a "wave-like" process with organization begetting counter-organization until some new equilibrium was reached within the broad social sector in which the interests were located. In addition to this "homeostatic hypothesis," Truman presented a broader argument to the effect that groups proliferate as a consequence of the processes of social fission that result from the growing complexity of modern society (1951, p. 57).

Homeostatic and proliferation models both operate on a macrosocial level, and neither has anything directly to say about the specific formation of particular organizations. Truman assigned a functional meaning to group organizing—the stabilization of tangent relations—but he did not seem to regard the actual organizational process as problematic. He may well have shared the view that seems to have been the pervasive wisdom before 1965, namely, that like minded people join together to enhance their political power in order to achieve public policies that serve their common interests. It was this conventional view, of course, that Mancur Olson sought to redress.

Olson challenged the assumption that individuals would join an organization in order to press for public policies, the benefits of which they would enjoy whether they had joined or not. Philanthropy, coercion, or downright irrationality might lead some people to join some groups, but those considerations could not be expected to hold for the discernible profusion of extant organizations. It was Olson's central insight that interest groups, at least those concerned with economic interests, are not in the first instance organized for public policy-related reasons at all. Rather, they are constructed around the provision to members of selective incentives, material benefits unavailable outside the organization. Lobbying on public policy, if it occurs, is a by-product, an activity made possible by the internal exchange of selective benefits, but not necessarily given purposive direction by the values of the group's members. For example, a UAW member may or may not support the leadership's stand on a nuclear freeze or extension of the Voting Rights Act so long as his or her group membership is assured by a job and a union contract, and a doctor may read the *Journal of the American Medical Association* without sharing AMA politics.

Walker (1983) has shown that in many cases some kind of subsidy, either from other groups or from the government, underwrites some part of the cost of creating and sustaining the organization. Nevertheless, one must still account for the ability of a group to attract members to that group and not some other, and for this problem Olson's argument still holds.

In subsequent revisions of Olson's original thesis, I (Salisbury, 1969, 1975) and others (Berry, 1977; Moe, 1980) contended that, although Olson excluded them, his argument applied fully as well to all the many groups that were organized around public policy goals. These, too, were vulnerable, highly vulnerable indeed, to the free rider problem. Why should any particular environmentalist join the Sierra Club or the Wilderness Society? Each organization must provide selective incentives, different from the competition and compelling enough to attract the potential free rider, or go out of business. These incentives might include a distinctive formulation of policy purposes—a better "line"—as well as some combination of material and solidary attractions. In more intimate settings interpersonal pressures may supplement the advantages of membership. Moreover, as Olson argued, relatively small groups may be created out of the self-interest of a few large powerful members willing to bear the costs of organization in order to gain the political advantages of group expression.

In all of these cases, however, the political strength of the organization is derived from the support of its members, whatever the means by which that support may have been secured; that is, we grant an organization legitimacy and pay attention to its policy requests because we assume that in some sense the spokesmen for the group represent the interests of the members. To be sure, this assumption is often challenged; we may charge the group with oligarchical tendencies, or in other ways suspect that the leadership is not representative of rank-and-file opinion. Many groups go to elaborate constitutional and procedural lengths to obviate such doubts and establish their *bona fides* as to the reflection of membership sentiment in the group's policy stands (see, for example, McFarland, 1976). The widespread use of mechanisms providing a "democratic mold" (Truman, 1951, pp. 129–139) clearly indicates that groups which are believed to represent organized membership constituencies have both a legitimacy in the policy-making arenas and potential clout, especially through votes and campaign funds, which "unrepresentative" organizations lack. Further, it is assumed that the policy interests expressed reflect either explicit or tacit concerns of the members, for otherwise they would leave the organization.

In fact, there are several modes of "interested activity" in which the assumption that group policy actions are driven by member preferences might be unwarranted. Under some circumstances, one example would be Olson's by-product situation. Conceivably the internal exchange of selective benefits might be so secure that no public policy inanity the leadership commits will alienate the faithful. Quite often group leaders espouse policy positions with only tenuous support from their members, although *severe* discrepancies between leader actions and member wishes are probably rare and generally short-lived. A second type of deviant case is the organization that is nothing more than a letterhead, lacking membership altogether. Interest groups to which no one belongs and which do not even provide for the possibility of membership are quite common among public interest groups, as Berry (1977) has shown. Similarly, Sorauf (1976, p. 19) has noted that in the field of church-state politics a good many "groups" are little more than institutionalized personalities. Leaders without organized followings may claim to have the sympathy of millions, of course, or at least to represent their "true interests," but such claims are likely to be received at a heavy discount.

At the other end of the spectrum there is the political movement, a congeries of organizations and individuals, participating in various ways in an effort to achieve a common set of policy goals (Asch, 1972; Gamson, 1975; Gusfield, 1963; McCarthy & Zald, 1973). It is characteristic of movements that many of the formal organizations within them have brief and highly volatile lives, and a large share of the sympathetically inclined individuals takes part only sporadically, if at all. Consequently, even though a movement may be very large in sympathy, it is typically uncertain in its mobilizable strength. Political movements are often characterized by great uncertainty also concerning who authentically speaks for those who identify themselves with the cause, with or without some formal membership, and typically there is considerable competition among several would-be spokespersons. Despite disputes over the correct line to take on a particular policy question, however, there is little doubt that the interests a movement represents are those of the "members," however that constituency is defined. Hence, all the norms and apparatus of representative democracy are applicable, and, in a society in which those norms are widely admired, that in turn places constraints on the tactical options available to movement leaders.

The several kinds of groups we have been discussing—political movements, voluntary organizations of members recruited through the use of selective incentives, and institutionalized personalities—all face the problem of establishing the legitimacy of their representational claims. The policy interests or values addressed are said to consist of the values of the group members, supporters, and identifiers. Mechanisms to allow consultation and display responsiveness are adopted. Moreover, since representational claims are so central to group legitimacy, the designation of group spokesman or representative is also a matter of critical importance. Many lobbying tasks can be performed by any competent hired hands, to be sure, but public articulation of group positions, if they are to be taken seriously, are inevitably caught up in the legitimation process and therefore cannot lightly be delegated or farmed out. The central point to be made is that in crucial respects the representation of membership-based interest groups differs significantly from the representation of institutional interests. Let us turn to the other side of this pairing to examine the difference further.

How Institutions Differ from Groups

In an earlier phase of the political science discipline a great deal of attention was paid to the theoretical meaning and position of institutions. Nearly all of this discussion, however, was focused on governmental institutions; the state and its parts and subdivisions. Very little mention was made of nongovernmental institutions except occasionally when it was noted that private groups also have governing structures and may exercise power over their members as well as influencing the larger society. Even this observation makes no distinction between voluntary associations of members and hierarchical structures which exercise authority over people within their jurisdiction. A corporation, a local government, most churches, and even universities are different, not totally but in crucial ways, from our conventional notion of interest groups, and the traditional literature on the nature of institutions does not tell us about the difference.

First of all there is the question of interests. We presume that people who join interest groups respond to selective incentives that appeal to their particular values and that whenever the incentives lose their appeal or their personal resources fail, they will drop out—voluntarily. Exit is obviously possible as well from any particular institutional setting (cf. Hirschman, 1970). One may quit one's job (or be laid off), move to another town, be graduated from school, or otherwise depart. Yet in most cases these acts send no message to the institution's leaders, nor are they intended to. To be sure, if half the population leaves, the city fathers may search for a new service formula; if a large number of students transfer, the college will be in trouble. Institutions of this kind must satisfy the needs and serve the interests of those who "belong." But when a corporation seeks to affect public policy—regarding pollution standards, for example—it does not justify its effort by alleging that it is reflecting the values of its employees. Nor does a university seek increased student loan funds on the grounds that its student body has expressed its desire for the money. It is not member interests as such that are crucial, but the judgments of organizational leaders about the needs of the institution as a continuing organization.

A central distinction between an institution and an interest group is that institutions have interests that are politically and analytically independent of the interests of particular institutional members. In part this derives from the continuing nature of a corporate institution. For example, it is presumed in both law and fact that a university has an existence transcending any agglomeration of individuals who happen presently to occupy its diverse roles. Inasmuch as students surely, and faculty often, are "mere birds of passage," trustees are admonished to be careful not to mortgage the future or rashly to spend the endowment. Similarly, the directors of a corporation can be held liable if they distribute to the stockholders everything not nailed down, with no thought of the long run. A voluntary association does not have the same expectation of eternal life. It must recruit members every year to stay alive.

Unless liquidation or merger destroys its identity, a corporate institution not only has a continuing existence, but it also possesses significant assets which belong to the corporate entity, not to the individual members thereof. It is from this foundation that institutional interests in public policy arise. Institutional leaders are charged with protecting, strengthening, and otherwise enhancing the assets of their institutions, both in the short run and to assure reasonable financial safety and stability for the institution in the future. Much of what they do has no direct political significance, of course. But in the latter twentieth century public policy is of such immense scope that issues continually arise which affect the assets of particular institutions, thus generating politically relevant interests (Salisbury, 1980). Environmental regulation, safety and health regulation, rules regarding employment practices, the host of grants and entitlement programs, tax policies—the list is long. Even an institution of the most modest size and aspiration will encounter both threats and opportunities in this policy array, and insofar as its resources permit may seek to increase its understanding of these possibilities and to influence them.

An institution can monitor public affairs and lobby to affect them only to the extent that it can afford to, of course. It must have resources available for such purposes. What we are calling institutions are generally complex organizations, highly differentiated and often with multiple functions. Such organizations typically command substantial and diverse resources and within limits a meaningful fraction may be allocated to policy-relevant tasks if and when these are perceived as useful to the maintenance and enhancement of the enterprise. Moreover, in most cases such allocations may be made without extensive consultations with members, employers, stockholders, or other constituent groups. They are, in effect, management decisions. And here lies a key distinction between institutions, as we use the term, and interest groups. Institutions are managed organizations. They are primarily hierarchical in their internal structures of authority, at least with regard to when and how far to become involved in the policy-making process. Membership groups must look far more carefully to the desires of their members, both to assure political legitimacy and to keep their supporters happy.

In distinguishing membership groups from institutions we do not mean to suggest that they are completely unlike. Most interest groups hope to survive into the indefinite future and thus take on institutional characteristics. Many possess substantial assets which they manage with a view to their long-term organizational health, and whenever public policy affects their institutional concerns, appropriate political action may be taken. Similarly, corporations and other hierarchies are not completely unconstrained by the views and needs of various groups both inside and outside the organizational boundaries (see, for example, Vogel, 1978). Demands for "socially responsible" behavior and for adoption of mechanisms to ensure democratic control are part of the political environment of all organizations in the United States, not just of membership groups. Nevertheless, there are important differences. Institutions have greater latitude—more discretionary resources and more autonomous leadership authority—to enter the political arena. Institutions have less need to justify their political efforts by reference to membership approval or demand. Institutions may also have a wider range of specific policy concerns. The instances in which policy impinges upon institutional interests will be numerous indeed for large complex organizations.

One result of these differences ought to be that institutions, not conventionally defined interest groups, will have come to dominate the roster of nongovernmental actors in Washington. This should follow inexorably upon the growth of government and of the scope and impact of policy. Before we turn to some examination of the empirical situation, however, let us consider briefly and in general terms the modes and motives of entering the political arena.

Entry Into the Political Arena

Until the publication of Olson's *Logic,* the question of how and why groups undertake political activity was scarcely acknowledged to be problematic. Interest groups were essentially defined by their political presence, and although perceptive students clearly understood how much ebb and flow there was in the vigor and direction of political action, they gave it little theoretical attention. Olson showed that the mere existence of politically relevant shared values or interests could not account for the effective mobilization of those interests into politically relevant action; i.e., action aimed at effecting policy decisions that would supply collective policy benefits. Olson, as we have seen, did provide for the possibility that small homogeneous groups might so act, especially when one or a few members of the group had a particularly large stake in the collective good outcome. Otherwise, however, while persuading us that much lobbying had to be seen as a by-product of the internal organizational exchange of selective benefits. Olson did not explain why groups should bother to engage in political action. Why should the "by-product" of successful group formation be "spent" on political purposes rather than, say, on increased perquisites for the leadership?

One possibility is that securely entrenched group leaders act out of personal whim or conviction, unconstrained by member preferences, institutional needs, or factional threats. Some of the late George Meany's positions on foreign policy come to mind in this connection (cf. Radosh, 1969), but it is probably very rare for leadership autonomy to be complete. More often, one suspects, group leaders lobby because they perceive potential effects of some government action on their members or members' values which the members might urge trying to influence if they were fully informed. A second and far more significant explanation is that group leaders are active on policy questions because that is why their members or followers support them in the first place. Here we speak of purposive or expressive groups. Despite Olson's reluctance to include such consumption values among the incentives that organization offer their adherents, it is clear from subsequent empirical work, as well perhaps as being intuitively pleasing and logically persuasive, that members do often support organized efforts to secure collective public benefits, whether it is truly rational to do so or not. In any case, such purposive group activity presents no mystery regarding why political action is undertaken; it is of the very essence.

A third motive for action is institutional; that is, institutional leaders estimate that investment in political representation would be beneficial to the interests of the organization. One might treat this kind of decision as a rational calculus problem essentially like that faced by individuals in determining whether or not to participate politically, in groups or otherwise. Three considerations make it inadvisable to do so. One is that institutions are *far* more likely to be part of relatively small, similarly situated groups—Olson's privileged groups—and thus be able to organize more readily and to anticipate being more effective politically than most individual citizens can expect. Second, although a given individual may hold a large number of distinct values or interests and even embrace a considerable set of political causes, available resources for participation are quickly exhausted, and multiple modes of individual participation are comparatively uncommon. Institutions possess more resources which, combined with a greater sense of efficacy in political action, lead to a considerably increased probability of participation at any given level of intensity of interest or concern.

Finally, the very size and complexity of an institution renders it vulnerable to a much broader array of specific policy impacts, positive and negative, present and prospective. Indeed, insofar as individual citizens are themselves embedded for work and play in large institutional settings, as so many are, they experience many of the effects of policy only indirectly, through their respective institutions, rather than immediately and in person. This would largely be true for much of the "new regulation" of environment and job safety, for example, as well as for national programs affecting state and local government budgets and services. A given corporation is quite likely to find itself in several encounters at once, on different policy issues, being worked on in different institutional settings, and requiring different modes of political action. Perhaps individual level interests also possess such complexity in principle, but in actual practice they do not generate comparable diversity of interest representation.

The forms of political action undertaken by institutions are indeed diverse, although none is exclusively utilized by institutions rather than membership groups or even, in some cases, individuals. One common form is to join organizations of similarly situated institutions. Some of these are trade associations organized along specific industry lines. Others may be closer to "peak associations," attempting to encompass an entire sector of economic activity. A large research university might belong to several organizations or universities—AAU, NASULGC (if public) or NAICU (if private), AAMC (if they have a medical school) and other professional school groups, ACE (as the peak association for higher education), and perhaps some others (King, 1975). A manufacturing corporation may belong to several trade associations, depending on how complex its product line is, as well as the NAM, the U.S. Chamber of Commerce, and the Business Roundtable. Part of these memberships may be expressive (the NAM would seem often to have been a forum for venting spleen regarding public policy rather than seeking realistically to affect it), and part may be more conventionally political, lobbying by small groups for beneficial collective policy goods.[3]

A mode of political involvement that has recently taken on Brobdingnagian proportions is the Political Action Committee (Conway, 1983; Malbin, 1980). Not all PACs have been created by institutions, but most of them have, and the prominence of PACs in campaign finance further illustrates how important institutional actors have become in our political life. Again, it must be stressed that although some PACs have raised significant sums from individual enthusiasts of liberal and, especially, conservative causes, business corporations, trade associations and, to a much lesser extent, labor unions dominate this form of activity, constituting nearly 78% of 3,371 members active at the beginning of 1983 (*National Journal*, 1983).

Finally, institutions enter the political arena directly. Several thousand corporations maintain permanent Washington offices to monitor the political scene and to help represent organizational interests.[4] Corporate divisions of public or governmental affairs are standard organizational components, not only of business enterprises but on a smaller scale of universities and many other institutions of contemporary American society. Further, many of these institutions retain outside firms, primarily lawyers and public relations counsel, to represent them in

Washington in particular aspects of their wide-ranging institutional encounters with the federal government. The key word here is "represent," for it carries some current meanings that have not adequately been incorporated into the formulations of political science discourse in representation. Let us turn next to that issue.

Washington Representatives and the Nature of Representation

It is rather startling to pick up a large volume entitled *Washington Representatives, 1982* (Close, 1982) and find that among the thousands of individuals listed, not one is a member of Congress. Yet, although these representatives are not accorded that status by customary formulations of social scientists and philosophers (Eulau, 1952, 1967; Pitkin, 1967; Wahlke et al., 1962), they clearly are so designated by the world. There are some differences in functions and activities, of course, between nongovernmental representatives and those who hold authoritative office. Let us consider of what these differences consist.

First, an official representative is said to have a constituency to which he is (or is not) responsive. An elected representative has a legally defined constituency, but he also has an effective one, those who supported him and those whose preferences he actually seeks to advance in policy-related actions. In this second sense, every official may be said to represent a constituency, i.e., to reflect some values rather than others in decisions. A "Washington Rep," on the other hand, typically represents a client, an organization, group, or individual (and occasionally only himself) who retains the representative and defines the scope of interests to be represented. The concept of client ordinarily implies a narrower range of policy concerns and a more limited set of representational activities than are contained in the idea of constituency representation. A corporation may retain a lawyer to represent it before the Federal Communications Commission on a specific licensing case, or alternatively to monitor the Federal Energy Regulatory Commission decisions on a continuing basis. Client representation may take many forms, but generally it is more specialized in subject matter, more limited in both scope and time, than constituency representation. At the margin the differences grow indistinct. The AFL-CIO is represented in Washington by a substantial crew of people and is actively interested in a range of questions that very nearly matches the full congressional agenda. Nevertheless, labor lobbyists have broad discretion to choose whether or not to get actively involved, whereas congressmen can hardly pick and choose so as to avoid all the issues about which their constituents disagree or are indifferent.

Client representation is relatively specialized and often quite discontinuous. Any specific representative may work on behalf of a particular client for a purpose that has a short life of relevance. Often, moreover, the representation is directed toward a specific agency, committee, or other unit of government, and once the policy issue moves away from that institutional setting to another, a different representative more familiar with the new arena may be brought in. Thus, specialized client representation often results in a given client retaining several representatives to perform highly focused representative services. The corollary of this is that a given representative often specializes in working with a particular piece of the governmental policy machinery and may represent numerous clients with problems involving that agency or committee.

Implicit in the foregoing discussion is the notion that representation involves three essential components rather than two, as conventional discussions of the topic assert. In addition to the representative and the represented, there is also the agency of government to which the representation is directed. Actually there are several prepositions employed to describe this side of the relationship. A lawyer may speak for a client *to* a congressional staffer; he may testify *in* court, *before* a judge; he may negotiate *with* an agency over a compliance schedule; indeed, he may only monitor what government does and counsel the client, in which case no prepositional connection with government is made. Even this last is seen as a form of representation, however, and requires the third party's presence to be meaningful.

It is not clear whether a third party is necessarily implied in traditional conceptions of representation. It is rarely if ever mentioned explicitly, but apart from descriptive representation, which can occur simply by possessing the appropriate personal characteristics, representation of constituency interests cannot logically occur unless there is some sort of "other." A legislator does not achieve his or her constituents' interests or even express them meaningfully without official status in an institutional arena where negotiations may be undertaken to accomplish his or her representational purposes. Nevertheless, ordinary speech vocabulary does not force us to recognize the institutional arena as a separate element in constituency representation as it does in considering client representation.

A full analysis of Washington representation requires us then to identify individual clients as well as broader constituencies, to examine who the representatives are and the diverse terms and conditions governing their service, and to understand the specific governmental institutions that serve as the focus of any particular representation activity. As we have said, much of that activity, although by no means all, is highly specific as to client, representative, and agency. It is often short-lived in duration and limited, even imperceptible, in its impact on any part of public policy or the world. Representational activity is very often ineffectual, redundant, or otherwise useless. Moreover, like the dog that Sherlock Holmes realized had not barked in the night, effective representation may entail doing nothing. In any case, however, this conception of representation is broader and more highly differentiated than either of two traditions in mainstream political science to which it is related, legislative representation and interest group lobbying.

Nevertheless, there remains a profound difference between the governmental official who, in either a Bentleyan or a Burkean sense, represents some interest in a specific authoritative choice among policy alternatives and the nongovernmental representative who can never do more than advocate that interest. Each may represent a client or constituency, but there remains a significant gulf between their respective capacities to act. Thus, even though only one key word is used, there are two quite different component processes involving two quite distinct sets of people, a nongovernmental set engaged in policy advocacy and a governmental set engaged in policy determination. If ordinary parlance calls both groups representatives, can we mitigate the confusion somewhat by using sharply distinct terms for the two processes? The answer is probably yes, but not if the advocacy process is called lobbying. That much-abused word is so fraught with ordinary language meaning, most of it unsavory, as to defy rehabilitation anyway, but it is also true that none of its historic uses comfortably fits what many Washington representatives do. The word lobbying does not well convey the meaning of a presentation by a drug company representative seeking approval of a new drug from the Food and Drug Administration. Nor does it capture the character of discussions between a committee on technical standards of the Aerospace Industries Association and Pentagon procurement officials. Amicus curiae briefs presented to the Supreme Court have sometimes been called "lobbying" instruments (Barker, 1967; Krislov, 1963), but they are different in much more than tactical form from the efforts of the National Rifle Association to prevent gun control legislation or of

Chrysler to secure financial help. The latter are surely examples of lobbying; amicus briefs and FDA appearances involve a much more restricted kind of policy advocacy, by representatives acting in behalf of clients.

Interest representation is an encompassing term that embraces lobbying in its ordinary use as well as narrower, more rule-bound forms of policy advocacy. Interest representation incorporates the client-representative relationships of a corporation and its lawyer, the membership group and its president, and the congressman and his constituents. Within that conceptual frame we distinguish governmental officials from those outside, policy formulation and enactment from advocacy. Within both those distinctions we may wish also to distinguish among specific institutional settings in which representational activity occurs. The forms of policy advocacy in courts are different from those in legislatures and so are the forms and norms of policy making. One reason that the term lobbying is so awkward is that it was developed initially to characterize policy advocacy in and around legislative settings where its connotations made sense and only later applied to other contexts. In any case, we should try to establish a vocabulary that is compatible with observable political life and is as consistent and straightforward as possible.

If we turn from a focus on process to a focus on role, we find, to begin with, the same confusion between lobbyist and representative as between the equivalent verb forms. The two words have vastly different connotations in the American lexicon but frequently refer to the same phenomena. Again, lobbyist more often is used with reference to policy advocacy in an around legislative bodies (Milbrath, 1963; Zeigler & Baer, 1969). A less clearcut but not uncommon distinction uses *lobbyist* to refer to an organizational employee, subordinate to those who make policy for the organization, whereas *representative* connotes a free-standing agent, retained on a fee-for-service basis and often on the assumption that the agent possesses particular skills or credentials of relevance to the advocacy role that are not readily available within the interested organization, whether institution or membership group. Even when we do not distinguish between the two *words* in that manner, however, the two *roles* are distinguishable and of both theoretical and descriptive interest.

As a first approximation of our descriptive needs it will be helpful to know what proportion of the very large community of Washington representatives are employees of the organizations whose interests they represent. Milbrath (1963, p. 150) found that as of 1956, 74.6% of the 114 registered lobbyists he interviewed were employed by the organizations represented. Of the remainder, 21% were outside lawyers, hired on a fee basis, and 4.4% were non-lawyer consultants. Table 1 reports comparable data compiled from the listings in *Washington Representatives, 1981* in four broad policy areas, selected to reflect reasonable diversity in subject matter and styles of representation. Not only are the 1981 proportions remarkably similar to those Milbrath found 25 years before, they are essentially constant across the four policy domains.

This consistency is all the more impressive when we remember that it has survived an explosive growth in the numbers of groups and institutions seeking Washington representation as well as in the numbers of individuals providing it. Estimates of raw numbers for earlier years are neither plentiful nor, probably, very reliable. Schlesinger (1949, p. 46) claimed that in 1942 some 628 organizations maintained offices in Washington, whereas Albig (cited in Blasidell, 1957, p. 59) counted 1,180 organizations located there in 1947–1948. By 1981 there were approximately 1,600 trade and professional associations, about 100 labor unions, over 200 individual states, cities, counties, and other units of government, numerous foreign governments, more than 4,000 corporations, and membership interest groups numbering well over 1,000, all located in the Washington area. Temporary and ad hoc issue coalitions and other short-lived organizational efforts make it difficult to establish exact magnitudes, but it seems reasonable to suppose that the contemporary Washington community of interest representation includes more than 7,000 organizations in more or less permanent residence.

When we turn to individual representatives, the numbers are even more startling. In 1981 the total capital area employment of trade and professional associations headquartered there was estimated to be more than 40,000 (Helyar, 1981).[5] In addition, as is well known, the number

TABLE 1
Organizational Forms of Washington Representation

	Agriculture	Labor	Health	Energy
Law firms	17.9%	18.1%	16.8%	15.9%
Consulting and public relations firms	6.6	4.9	6.4	5.7
Corporations, trade associations and other institutions	75.5	77.0	76.8	78.4
N	832	304	722	1574

Source: Washington Representatives, 1981.

of lawyers in Washington has grown enormously. Membership in the District of Columbia Bar Association became mandatory in 1973, and between then and September, 1981, it went from 10,925 to 34,087. This number is somewhat misleading. Significant numbers of lawyers belong to the D.C. Bar who live elsewhere in the country. At the same time, however, a considerable number of people with law degrees who work in Washington do not actually practice law; many work for the federal government. Hence, the total number of lawyers residing in the capital may well exceed 40,000.

We may easily be overwhelmed by these numbers, and they are truly impressive, but we should remember that by no means all trade association employees or all lawyers in Washington are really representing politically meaningful interests. A sizable percentage of the lawyers are engaged in the private practice of private law. The so-called "Fifth Street Bar," for instance, centers around the local District of Columbia courts, and its members never have occasion to lobby on Capitol Hill. Similarly, many association employees are engaged in internal administration and support and are not really relevant to our concerns here. On the other hand, an unknown but substantial number of representatives come to Washington from elsewhere, some often and some only occasionally, advocating policy positions but never becoming part of any register or roster of representatives. If we look only at the Washington-based individuals actually performing policy representation roles, again drawing on our examination of the listing in *Washington Representatives,* we can observe that in our four broad policy areas, 4,227 individuals were listed, of whom 35.6% were lawyers. This proportion is remarkably close to that reported by Milbrath and also to the proportion of lawyers among public interest group lobbyists of the early 1970s examined by Berry (1977, p. 88). In the 1981 listings the labor area had a significantly smaller percentage of lawyers (17.1%), but in the other three policy domains the lawyer presence ranged from 31% to 39%.

We pay particular attention to the prominence of lawyers, in part because of the considerable publicity that has been given to them in recent years, but in greater part because the concept of the lawyer as representative carries some interesting connotations. Lawyers traditionally and predominantly operate as free-standing professionals retained by clients for relatively specific defined services and compensated by fee. Although many lawyers actually work in large organizational settings on a salaried basis, we would still expect that lawyers will, more often than non-lawyers, be found outside the organizations retaining them. Table 2

TABLE 2
Lawyers and Non-Lawyers, In-House and External Representatives

	Lawyers		Non-Lawyers	
	In-house	External	In-house	External
	%	%	%	%
Agriculture	12.4	79.4	87.6	20.6
Labor	8.3	71.4	91.7	28.6
Health	15.2	84.1	84.6	15.9
Energy	18.9	73.7	81.1	26.3

Sources: Washington Representatives, 1981; Martindale-Hubbell law directory, 1981.

indicates that this is indeed true and that the proportions of lawyers who are in-house employees remain quite similar across the policy domains.

One consequence of the large number of lawyers around Washington may well be increased specialization in the representation process, possibly because lawyers are typically hired as outside counsel. Their services are sought when, and only when, the client firm requires those services, and their billing is ordinarily based on hourly charges. In-house counsel might work on anything the organization requires, but external representatives typically have a more limited assignment in both the time to be given and the official governmental segments to which the representation is made. A law firm might attempt to provide full representational services to a given client, advocating policy positions before all the legislative, executive, and judicial agencies that affect the client's interests, but no individual representative can hope to do so. The ever-increasing scope and variety of government and policy impact make this strategy a difficult one for even a large firm to employ successfully, however, and the more common response is the use of multiple representation by a given client. Ford, General Electric, IBM, GM, Exxon, and other giants may hire eight or ten separate outside representatives in addition to working through trade associations and their own substantial governmental relations staffs. The government of Japan in 1982 retained nine different representatives for its embassy and four for other parts of its government, while several dozen others work for specific Japanese firms and associations (Madison, 1982).

The heavy reliance on representatives, typically lawyers, chosen to speak to government officials on behalf of a limited set of client interests is more characteristic of institutional representation than of membership groups, especially when the membership is composed of individuals. Such groups séldom can afford the investment in hourly legal fees that such specialized representation calls for, and they are much more likely to adopt a jack-of-all-trades style. The sheer financial scale of institutional representation vastly exceeds the magnitude of purposive group activity, and the respective personnel pools reflect this differential investment level. Only about 1,200 of the nearly 8,000 individuals listed in the 1982 *Washington Representatives* worked for purposive groups, and as numerous case studies attest, the salary and support levels enjoyed by this disparate group of advocates are hardly commensurate with the resources available to most institutional representatives.

We can round out this part of our discussion by reporting one other set of data demonstrating the importance of institutional representatives, especially of business corporations. For a single policy area, agriculture, Table 3 compares, first, the representational presence in Washington of different kinds of organizations declaring significant concerns with agricultural policy; private business corporations, rural cooperatives, governmental institutions, nonprofit private institutions, foreign interests, agri-business trade associations, general farm organizations and commodity groups, and other groups with purposive inter-

TABLE 3
Agricultural Interest Representatives in Washington

	Washington Representatives, 1981	Congressional Committee Testimony, 1977, 1979, 1981	New York Times References, 1977–1982
Business corporations	33.5%	10.3%	16.8%
Rural cooperatives	4.3	10.7	6.3
Governmental institutions	1.5	12.8	5.2
Non-profit private institutions	.4	6.4	4.7
Foreign interests	12.2	.6	1.6
Business trade associations	29.8	16.0	14.1
Farm organizations	9.9	30.7	22.5
Citizens groups, including labor	6.3	9.5	27.8
Not classified	2.1	3.1	1.0
TOTAL	100.0%	100.1%	100.0%
N	466	2579	191

Sources: Washington Representatives, 1981; Congressional Index Service; *New York Times* Index Service.[6]

ests in agricultural policy. Only the last three categories are in any sense membership groups, and only in the last two sets are individuals enrolled. Thus, individual membership groups constitute only one-sixth of the community of agriculture interests more or less continuously represented in Washington. It should not be assumed that all individuals listed are equal in political importance or policy input. On the other hand, the representational presence reflected in column 1 permits a wide array of interest-serving activities to be undertaken. Informal lobbying, monitoring and grass-roots mobilization, and representation before administrative agencies are all greatly enhanced by an organizational presence on the scene. Rather than organizations of farmers, it is institutions, especially those of business, which clearly dominate that presence.

In more public and visible arenas, however, the picture changes. In testimony before congressional committees on matters of farm policy (column 2), farm organizations play the most prominent role. Newspaper mentions of organizations in connection with farm issues (column 3) are even more fully dominated by membership groups. Business corporations and trade associations recede. The lesson to be drawn is partly one concerning legitimation. The public process of policy making gains more legitimacy through hearing and appearing responsive to self-interested individuals and groups than by deferring to organized institutions and institutional interests. In addition, however, it is probably the case that much of the substantive policy concerns motivating institutional advocacy consists of quite small items of no interest to most groups of farmers or the general public. This is especially likely when, because of the multiple representation phenomenon we have described, a corporation or trade association retains a representative for a single, highly specialized task. This kind of thing counts in column 1 but is not otherwise noted. When all the small specific policy items are added together the list can be formidable indeed, of course, but few of them may have attracted the attention of the *New York Times* or congressional committee hearings. Nevertheless, we can surely say that for much of what happens in Washington to influence the authoritative allocation of scarce resources in agricultural policy, the general farm organizations, such as AFBF, NFU, Grange, and NFO, once thought to be so powerful, are less prominent than conventional textbook treatments suggest.

The importance of institutional representation has some significant implications for the likely course of public policy as well as for our theories of how and why things work. The use of multiple representatives, each concentrating on a specialized set of policy concerns, surely must intensify the fragmenting, disaggregating tendencies in public policy so often alluded to in recent literature. Secondly, institutional representation may be expected to be far more durable and persistent in policy-making circles than most purposive groups or even membership groups based on material incentives. Institutional resources are not infinite, of course, but neither are they as often subject to membership demands for review or as vulnerable to shifts in political tides and entrepreneurial fortunes. Institutional representation may be more durable, but it is also typically more prosaic, more pragmatic, than purposive group advocacy. Institutional interests more often concern export licenses than anti-Communism, city budgetary assistance more than a war on poverty. (Corporate PACs continue to give significant financial support to their supposed ideological enemies, liberal Democrats. Surely this is a prime example of the pragmatism of institutions (Handler & Mulkern, 1982, esp. pp. 20–27).) In a very important sense, the conservative bias that Schattschneider (1960), McConnell (1966), and other critics of pluralist America have long attributed to interest groups is rooted far more in the power of institutional representation than in conventional membership groups. Indeed, it is the comparative weakness and fragility of membership interest groups of every point of view and persuasion, not their strength, that may be argued to be responsible for whatever malaise the American polity has lately suffered from interest-based politics.

This effort to clarify the conceptual map of American policy-making processes has yielded three main conclusions. First, I distinguish between institutions, institutional interests, and their representation, on the one hand, and what we have rather awkwardly called membership interest groups on the other, and I argue that important theoretical differences exist between the two. Second, I note that both these organizational forms of nongovernmental interests are represented in Washington by large numbers of people whose roles have many conceptual similarities to those in formal policy-making positions and who, like their official counterparts, are called representatives in everyday usage. Nevertheless, there remains a critical difference in status and function between policy advocates and policy-makers which the fuzziness of language should not be allowed to obscure. Washington terminology is not more precise than that used by political scientists to describe and analyze what happens there, but it is somewhat different and in recent years has grown more so with regard to interest representation and policy advocacy. Finally, we urge that the power and scope of institutional representation is such that our teaching, our research, and our normative evaluations will all go awry unless we make the appropriate corrections in analytic focus.

NOTES

This article owes much to the stimulus of a collaborative research effort, sponsored by the American Bar Foundation, on the role of Washington representatives, in which John P. Heinz, Edward O. Laumann, Robert L. Nelson, and I are currently engaged. Michael Powell was associated with an earlier stage of this work and contributed to my thinking. My colleagues at Washington University—Robert Blackburn, John Kautsky, Michael MacKuen, and Kenneth Shepsle—read earlier drafts and as usual provided trenchant and constructive criticisms, as did the anonymous referees of the *Review*.

1. Business corporations are sometimes considered, sensibly enough, among business interests, but the profound differences in organizational structure and motivation between, for example, General Motors and the Chamber of Commerce have not been remarked, nor has the implication these differences have for interest group theory.

2. I make no effort in this article to compare American patterns of interest representatives with those of other advanced industrial democracies. Membership associations with high rates of sectoral participation are considerably more common in European systems, and individual institutions may therefore have less room for assertive advocacy. Some aspects of "American exceptionalism" are treated in Salisbury (1979) and in Wilson (1981). See also Berger (1981).

3. Trade associations present some special complexities for our argument. They themselves are membership organizations, but their members are corporate institutions. The members must be kept satisfied with association policy, selective benefits of other kinds, or both, but being institutions, their calculus regarding membership benefits may contain considerable slack. Moreover, corporate institutions may seldom confine their policy-related activity to association membership. That trade associations do operate under member-induced constraints has recently been illustrated by the cutbacks in association staff and programs brought about as a consequence of the economic recession (Teeley, 1983). Trade associations, like other groups, are often fragile organizations financially, begun with very shadowy support out of an enterprising lawyer's office, or on some otherwise flimsy basis. One result of this is the appearance of association management companies, interest group wholesalers, which manage the affairs of several small organizations. For example, Smith and Bucklin, a Chicago firm, operates more than 70 trade associations, and the National Center for Municipal Development assists dozens of local governments in their quest for federal support.

4. Governmental affairs offices have existed for a considerable time, of course. The Public Affairs Council, an organization composed mainly of corporate government affairs officers, was formed in 1954, and the Brookings Institution sponsored a roundtable discussion among 19 of them in 1958 (Cherington & Gillen, 1962). Little notice has been taken by political scientists, however; the Cherington and Gillen volume was never reviewed in the *American Political Science Review.*

Dexter (1969) discusses Washington representatives in some detail, but unlike his earlier work (Bauer, Pool, & Dexter, 1962), this book does not seek to tie his discussion into more general theories of interest group performances.

5. Twenty-nine percent of all such organizations are located in the Washington area, up from 19% in 1971 (Close, 1981).

6. References in congressional committee testimony and *New York Times* references were calculated by reference to keywords "agriculture" and "farm," combined with "policy" and "legislation." *New York Times* references covered the period from January 1, 1977, to June 30, 1982.

REFERENCES

Asch, R. *Social movements in America.* Chicago: Markham, 1972.

Barker, L. J. Third parties in litigation. *Journal of Politics,* 1967, *29,* 41–69.

Bauer, R., Pool, I. de S., & Dexter, L. A. *American business and public policy.* New York: Atherton, 1963.

Bentley, A. *The process of government.* Chicago: University of Chicago Press, 1908.

Berger, S. *Organizing interests in western Europe: pluralism, corporatism and the transformation of politics.* Cambridge: Cambridge University Press, 1981.

Berry, J. M. *Lobbying for the people.* Princeton, N.J.: Princeton University Press, 1977.

Blaisdell, D. C. *American democracy under pressure.* New York: Ronald, 1957.

Cherington, P. W., & Gillen, R. L. *The business representative in Washington.* Washington, D.C.: Brookings Institution, 1962.

Close, A. C. (Ed.). *Washington representatives, 1981* (5th ed.). Washington, D.C.: Columbia Books, 1981.

Close, A. C. (Ed.). *Washington representatives, 1982* (6th ed.). Washington, D.C.: Columbia Books, 1982.

Conway, M. M. PACs, the new politics, and congressional campaign. In A. J. Cigler & B. A. Loomis (Eds.). *Interest group politics.* Washington, D.C.: Congressional Quarterly Press, 1983.

Dexter, L. A. *How organizations are represented in Washington.* Indianapolis: Bobbs-Merrill, 1969.

Eulau, H. The role of the representative: some empirical observations on the theory of Edmund Burke. *American Political Science Review,* 1959, *53,* 742–756.

Eulau, H. Changing views of representation. In I. de Sola Pool (Ed.). *Contemporary political science: toward empirical theory.* New York: McGraw-Hill, 1967.

Gamson, W. A. *The strategy of social protest.* Homewood, Ill.: Dorsey, 1975.

Gusfield, J. R. *Symbolic crusade: status politics and the American temperance movement.* Urbana, Ill.: University of Illinois Press, 1963.

Hagan, C. B. The group in a political science. In R. Young (Ed.). *Approach to the study of politics.* Evanston, Ill.: Northwestern University Press, 1958.

Handler, E., & Mulkern, J. R. *Business in politics: campaign strategies of corporate political action committees.* Lexington, Mass.: Lexington Books, 1982.

Helyar, J. Capital's service sector gives area economy a safety net. *Wall Street Journal,* April 28, 1981.

Hirschman, A. O. *Exit, voice and loyalty.* Cambridge, Mass.: Harvard University Press, 1970.

Key, V. O. Jr. *Politics, parties and pressure groups* (5th ed.). New York: Crowell, 1964.

King, L. R. *The Washington lobbyists for higher education.* Lexington, Mass.: Lexington, 1975.

Krislov, S. The *Amicus Curiae* brief: from friendship to advocacy. *Yale Law Journal,* 1963, 72, 694–721.

MacIver, R. M. Interests. In E. R. A. Seligman (Ed.). *Encyclopedia of the social sciences.* New York: Macmillan, 1932.

Madison, C. Is Japan trying to buy Washington or just do business capital style? Washington: *National Journal,* October 9, 1982.

Malbin, M. J. (Ed.). *Parties, interest groups, and campaign finance laws.* Washington, D.C.: American Enterprise Institute, 1980.

McCarthy, J. D., & Zald, M. N. *The trend of social movements.* In *America: professionalization and resource mobilization.* Morristown, N.J.: General Learning Press, 1973.

McConnell, G. *Private power and American democracy.* New York: Knopf, 1966.

McFarland, A. S. *Public interest lobbies: decision making on energy.* Washington, D.C.: American Enterprise Institute, 1976.

Martindale-Hubbell law directory. Summit, N.J.: Martindale-Hubbell, 1981.

Milbrath, L. W. *The Washington lobbyists.* Chicago: Rand McNally, 1963.

Moe, T. M. *The organization of interests.* Chicago: University of Chicago Press, 1980.

Olson, M. J. *The logic of collective action.* Cambridge, Mass.: Harvard University Press, 1965.

Pitkin, H. F. *The concept of representation.* Berkeley: University of California Press, 1967.

Proliferating political action committees. *National Journal,* January 29, 1983.

Radosh, R. *American labor and U.S. foreign policy.* New York: Random House, 1969.

Salisbury, R. H. An exchange theory of interest groups. *Midwest Journal of Political Science,* 1969, *13,* 1–32.

Salisbury, R. H. Interest groups. In N. Polsby & F. Greenstein (Eds.). *Handbook of political science*. Reading, Mass.: Addison-Wesley, 1975.

Salisbury, R. H. Why no corporatism in America? In P. C. Schmitter & G. Lehmbruch (Eds.). *trends toward corporatist intermediation*. Beverly Hills, Calif.: Sage, 1979.

Salisbury, R. H. Are interest groups morbific forces? Paper presented to the Conference Group on Political Economy of Advanced Industrial Societies. Washington, D.C., 1980.

Schattschneider, E. E. *The semi-sovereign people*. New York: Holt, Rinehart and Winston, 1960.

Schlesinger, A. M. *Paths to the present*. New York: Macmillan, 1949.

Sorauf, F. J. *The wall of separation*. Princeton, N.J.: Princeton University Press, 1976.

Teeley, S. E. Trade associations are shrinking with economy. *Washington Post*, January 31, 1983. p. B1.

Truman, D. B. *The governmental process*. New York: Knopf, 1951.

Vogel, D. *Lobbying the corporation*. New York: Basic Books, 1978.

Wahlke, J. C., Eulau, H., Buchanan, W., & Ferguson, L. C. *The legislative system: explorations in legislative behavior*. New York: Wiley, 1962.

Walker, J. The origins and maintenance of interest groups in America. *American Political Science Review*, 1983, 77, 390–406.

Wilson, G. K. *Interest groups in the United States*. New York: Oxford University Press, 1981.

Wilson, J. Q. *Political organizations*. New York: Basic Books, 1973.

Zeigler, H., & Baer, M. A. *Lobbying: interaction and influence in American state legislatures*. Belmont, Calif.: Wadsworth, 1969.

3

Political Movements in American Politics: An Essay on Concept and Analysis

A merican politics, past and present, is rich in political movements. The civil rights movement, the environmental movement, the student movement, and the labor movement are but a few of the phenomena to which the term is attached as a defining concept. And lest we suppose that movements come only from the left, the neoconservative movement of recent years or the Prohibition movement of an earlier time give witness to the contrary. The Progressive movement gave the dominant tone to an entire political era in the United States, and democracies elsewhere in the world have also experienced substantial impact from forces that both participants and observers designated as movements.

Among sociologists, social movements have long been of central concern, providing a standard subfield in the discipline and generating a considerable body of literature (Zald and McCarthy, 1987). The neighboring social sciences have less often incorporated the sociologists' work into their own analysis, however. Political scientists have quite generally failed to give explicit attention to movements, tending instead to divide their attention to movement phenomena between mass behavior (mainly electoral behavior), on the one hand, and interest groups, on the other. The one studies mobilization; the other looks at organization, but few political scientists examine the interaction—how organizations mobilize public support and thus build a movement. Recent scholarship has begun to incorporate social movement theory and research into political science, but there still is little or no attention to whatever might be

Reprinted with permission from Lucius J. Barker, ed., *New Perspectives in American Politics. The National Political Science Review* 1 (1989):213–31.

distinctive about movements within the context of the political arena (cf. Morris and Herring, 1987).

In this essay, I propose to explore the conceptual elements involved in the study of political movements, drawing in part on the social movement literature to do so but focusing specifically on those movements that seek to enter the political arena and the impact that arena has on the dynamics of movement activity. I will argue that neither organizational nor individual behavior alone provides an adequate focus if we are to encompass the full range of what is politically important.

The Concept of a Political Movement

Let us consider the essential elements involved in the observables we call movements. The most common definitions of social movement begin by stressing the importance of a particular configuration of opinion that aims at "changing some elements of the social structure and/or reward distributions of a society" (McCarthy and Zald, 1977:1217). Immediately, however, we must restrict this definition. To include every desire to alter the reward distribution of a society would make *movement* virtually synonymous with *human striving*. What we call movements seek relatively major changes, and it seems preferable therefore to confine the term to those who advocate changes in the *structure* of the socioeconomic-sociopolitical order. Thus the civil rights movement encompasses all those who have worked to reconstruct the status relationship among racial groups, whereas the Urban League, a "mere" interest group, has generally confined its attention to enlarging job opportunities for blacks. An interest group as such typically seeks to achieve an optimum payoff from the existing structure. It hopes to win within the system, not to alter the system's structure. Particular groups may, of course, become integral parts of movements in which their goals are linked to larger purposes. Thus the distinction between interest groups and movements can be shadowy, and often quite dynamic as groups shift their focus from narrow to broad "change" objectives and back again. Moreover, some discrete interest groups may couch their purposes in the encompassing rhetoric of systemic change without ever becoming part of a movement. Figure 1 expresses the movement—group distinction schematically.

Because they seek structural change, many movements are thought to be radical, critical of "the system" from the "outside," so to speak, rather than accepting the system as it operates and working to maxi-

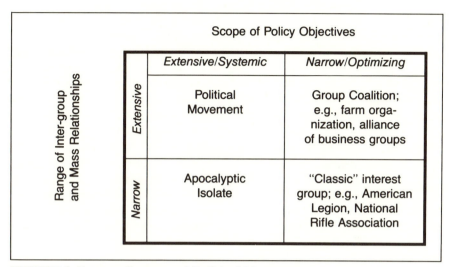

FIGURE 1 Interest Groups and Political Movements

mize advantage within it. Whether a structural change is regarded as truly radical depends a good deal on one's analytical perspective, of course, and also on the scope and magnitude of consequences likely to result from the movement's recommendations. Many a reform movement in American urban experience, for example, has discovered that the consequences of institutional change were much less significant than they had expected. Nevertheless, we commonly call these campaigns movements, as did the participants themselves, and we should therefore define the term to include them. The key is thus the movement's definition of goals in terms of structural change rather than simply redistribution of valued outcomes. To be sure, at the margin that distinction becomes blurred. Many movements draw support from people who mainly want more of what there is, but their mobilization is predicated on the assumption that, in order to achieve meaningful redistribution of values, some structural/institutional change is required. In some cases, the rhetoric of protest so confounds structural change with redistribution that it becomes impossible to differentiate between them. Still, there is a difference between the quest for "more" and the effort to restructure social relations.

Movements themselves have structural characteristics; they are not mere aggregations of opinion. A movement includes one or more formal organizations (SMOs in the parlance of sociological usage) that act as the "carriers" and mobilizers of the movement. These organizational components often operate in ways that are very similar to other interest groups and are commonly included in most treatments of interest groups. Yet to define the civil rights movement solely in terms of the NAACP and other active organizations, even to equate the labor movement with the AFL-CIO, would lead us to misunderstand the special characteristics of movements. The latter embrace followers as well, identifiers who endorse the movement's goals and may take part in some or all of a considerable repertoire of supportive activities without formally joining any organized association. It was appropriate to refer to an American labor movement so long as the cause of enhanced working-class power and associated income redistribution evoked broadly sympathetic support from intellectuals, opinion leaders, and diverse other segments of the population. Once that support waned, the "movement" became a mere constellation of interest groups.

The extent to which people have come to identify with a movement is usually difficult to measure precisely, but that very uncertainty may serve to enhance the bargaining position of movement leaders who can claim a strong following that opponents cannot confidently disregard. A movement, then, has organizational components—and is thus different from a crowd—and an uncertain number of identifier-followers ready to act in concert with the organizations that lead the way.

Very often we employ the word *mass* in conjunction with movement, and although that word is no model of measurement precision, its central implication—that the scope of the movement's support is, actually or potentially, large—is one we embrace. It makes little sense to designate a neighborhood clean-up campaign a movement. Its potential support is too small for such promotional hype. Higher prices for soybeans likewise is a poor prospect for movement status. Indeed, most of the activities described by Lowi (1969) under the heading of interest group liberalism are clearly *not* movement material. Nevertheless, political/social entrepreneurs quite often will call their efforts *movements* in order to imply the existence of a mass support base, at least in potential. In part, this claim may stimulate a bandwagon effect among the previously uncommitted, but there is another implication as well. A movement, seeking structural change that will putatively benefit a large number of people, far in excess of the participants so far associated with the cause, can usually enjoy a more favorable moral position among intellectuals and publicists than the self-interested pursuit of benefits by interest groups and institutions. The prospect of a mass base confers a degree of democratic legitimacy on movements—what Useem and Zald (1982) call the legitimacy of numbers—that interest groups often lack.

There are other reasons for adopting the movement label as well. It implies dynamic growth and an optimism about the possibilities of collective action that are nontrivial assets in mobilizing support. The well-known arguments of Mancur Olson (1965) and others regarding the difficulty of recruiting members to an organization in order to strengthen a campaign for supraorganizational collective benefits is, as Moe (1980) and others have shown, considerably modified when the "rational individual" is unclear regarding what it would take to secure the collective purpose. One may well join a movement whose momentum promises to sweep away all obstacles, especially if refusing to join threatens to leave one isolated from one's peers. If everyone seems to be flocking to the movement's banner, the appeal is more persuasive. Calling a group of farmers the American Agriculture Movement (Cigler, 1986) conveys a good deal more of this dynamism than naming the same group with the same purposes the American Farmers Association.

A movement is thus characterized by the rhetoric and, when it prospers, the reality of dynamic growth. Closely related is the strong preference among movement tacticians for direct expressive action rather than, or at least prior to, bargaining and negotiation. Associations have conventions and speeches, but movements have songs and marches, sit-ins and picket lines. Associations are prosaic; movements are dramatic. Associations seek to secure and maintain access to decisionmakers, and the maintenance of friendly communication channels is of the highest priority. Movements accept a degree of risk, sometimes though not always great, that extant elites will be offended and authorities alienated by direct action tactics that may reach all the way to martyrdom.

From one perspective, the expressive emphasis of movement tactics reflects the heavy dose of moral self-righteousness that so often accompanies movement rhetoric. One ought not to compromise or bargain over what is morally right; rather, one should declare it forthrightly from the housetops and put the burden of compliance with rectitude on those in authority. From the more mundane perspective of detached analysis, however, dramatic expressive action has other advantages. It confers upon participants the "selective" benefit of personal excitement, the delights of enthusiasm for a noble cause, and the very real sense of solidarity with those of like persuasion. Moreover, dramatic expressive acts have a better chance than many more conventional tactics of gaining

the attention of potential sympathizers, sometimes raising their consciousness that they are in fact sympathetic and sometimes persuading
identifiers that this expressive core of "the movement" is actually "doing
something" directly and not just sitting around the mimeograph machine. The combination of mobilization effects with the intrinsic pleasures to participants of being noticed go far toward explaining the
tactical emphasis by modern political movements on media events with
all the concomitant uncertainty about what is real and what is manufactured in this kind of tactical exercise.

A final element of definition can be disposed of quickly. It involves
the distinction between political movements and social movements. The
latter is clearly the broader term, for it encompasses all movements,
whether or not they involve activity within the political arena. Movements are political whenever and insofar as they undertake actions intended to affect governmental officials, by persuading them to act in a
particular way or indeed by determining who will hold office. Any
movement whose goals require some governmental response is political.
Many movements are almost entirely so; the Progressive movement, for
example. The American labor movement, on the other hand, despite its
extensive political agenda, finds its primary raisons d'être in the economic bargaining relationship with employers. In modern times, a very
large share of the phenomena we call movements in the United States
plainly have involved at least some action in the political arena and so
may properly be included in the set of political movements. Sometimes
an aggregation of groups and followers may largely abandon the political arena but maintain enough dynamism and sharpness of purpose to
qualify as social movements. One might regard the feminist movement
in the late 1980s in this light. Since the demise of the ERA, feminism has
been an important social movement, but without very much immediate
political presence. Again, the point is that a distinction between social
and political movements, although often blurred in real life, is of analytic and descriptive utility.

Movements and Their Enemies

Movement rhetoric in American (and other democratic) politics is often
filled with apocalyptic metaphors, emphasizing that the desired structural change can come about only through the destruction of hostile

forces and stressing verbs of action, adjectives conveying great intensity, and adverbs of moral virtue. Interest groups, despite Truman's conception of them as adverse to others, often find themselves without visible opposition (Salisbury et al., 1987; Walker, 1983) and to a large extent appeal to members in Olsonesque fashion by offering selective benefits unavailable except through the association. Movement organizations, those associations that are a movement's active agents, must likewise offer specific membership benefits. But the recognition of an enemy and a commitment to oppose are not selective organizational benefits, restricted to those who join. They are matters of attitude and conviction that anyone may come to share. Once the beliefs are in place, selective benefits to participants, especially of a solidary character, will more readily follow, but first there must be the shared belief in social structural change. Is conflict a necessary condition of such belief? Is it possible to be emotionally committed to changing the system without also being committed to the view that there are social forces or groups or elites or somebody on the other side, preventing the change, acting out of self-interest and perhaps corruption also to block the desired reform? Logically, it does not appear to be a requirement. Social systems and political institutions may be thought of in essentially impersonal terms in which no individual or group wills the undesired outcomes, but neither can anyone overcome the institutional barriers; hence the movement, born out of frustration. Such arguments are surely possible and sometimes employed, but it is clear that movement rhetoric is seldom content with such detached analysis. Instead, appeals for support are predicated upon opposition—to "the bosses," including those in charge of political machines, capitalist employers and hierarchical superiors both inside and outside of government, or to such other putative oppressors, exploiters, and despoilers as have been defined by the movement's rhetorical foundations and proposed reforms.

The sense of embattlement carries a message of urgency; the stakes are great, and time is short. Armageddon is at hand; the battle is on, and failure looms unless potential members promptly and generously make a commitment of support. If we were to postulate a continuum of political rhetoric along which appeals for support may range from the most intensely apocalyptic to the mildest nonconflictual expression of a group's policy desires, it is clear that those political formations we call movements would be bunched together toward the high-conflict end of the spectrum.

Movements and Movement Organizations

Discussions of political and social movements commonly separate out from the "mass of activity" those formal associations that have been constructed in support of the movement's goals. In some movements, there is a single core group. Often there are several. Sometimes organizations vie for movement leadership; sometimes they work out a kind of functional division of labor. Some movements are characterized as "reticulated," networks of organizations and more inchoate followings bound together by contacts among leaders who move back and forth across the landscape of both geography and political society (Freeman, 1983).

Movement organizations, as we have noted, must maintain themselves as viable enterprises against all the challenges of apathy, disappointment, and rival associations. In so doing, they face the free-rider problems that Olson outlined. Insofar as a movement organization seeks to attract and hold members primarily with selective benefits composed of expressive rhetoric—espousing the purest doctrine or the correct line—the association risks swift collapse. Expressive groups are easy to start but hard to maintain. And this is especially true if the costs of membership are at all burdensome, as, for example, they were when what Wilson (1973) refers to as redemptionist organizations in the civil rights movement required such sacrifices as going to jail or suffering physical beating.

The history of political movements in America is replete with examples of organizational failures, to be sure, but in a sense what is more surprising is how many movement organizations survive, at least for considerable periods of time. How is it that groups whose symbolic emphasis is on achieving structural changes in society and that typically couch their appeals in relatively conflict-centered language filled with moral outrage can last so long? A part of the answer lies in the findings of Walker and others (cf. Berry, 1977; Freeman, 1983; Salisbury, 1969) regarding subsidies granted to one group by another. Walker attributes a significant share of the success in organizing various kinds of public interest movement organizations during the 1960s and early 1970s to the infusion of financial aid from sympathetic groups already established and from foundations and government agencies. A similar story may be told of much union organizing and farm group development, among others.

It would not provide very dependable support for movement organizations if the subsidizers were themselves highly vulnerable to the vicissitudes of movement momentum, factional strife, or rapid decline in resources among potential members. In fact, however, a large share of the subsidizing agents are quite securely institutionalized. Foundations, churches, universities, and government agencies may decide to stop funding change agents or, if they do not, risk losing some of their own support, but they generally remain in existence, and movement organizations may be able to come back again and again for help. From the perspective of the movement entrepreneur, sympathetic institutions typically constitute a more dependable base of support than individual members or identifiers, however important the latter may be as indicators of the movement's broad appeal. In American experience, churches have played a particularly important role as institutional bases for such diverse movements as abolition, temperance, civil rights, peace and disarmament, and the "right-to-life." We will return to and elaborate on this theme later in this essay.

A second basis of movement survival, at least of its core, is to be found in the dedicated commitment of relatively small numbers of faithful adherents who do not accept defeat or bow to what others see as inevitable demise but continue on in the hope that success will yet crown their efforts. Minor political parties and many interest groups operate on essentially the same kind of slender foundation, of course. When such a fragmentary enterprise calls itself a movement, however, observers should not accept the designation at face value. It may again become one; the civil rights movement might well regain the momentum and broad support it had in the early 1960s. Until that happens, however, to give the interest groups seeking civil rights policy objectives the label of *movement* would misrepresent their character and misread their short-term prospects.

Disruption and Organization: Can Movements Survive?

Piven and Cloward (1977) present in most explicit form the argument that political movements are inevitably robbed of their vital essence as change agents when they become institutionalized and the active movement entrepreneurs turn their energies away from leading direct action and concentrate on maintaining formal organizations. They contend that significant structural changes can sometimes be forced by means of disruptive protest, which so raises the cost to society of maintaining the status quo that dominant elites are forced to accept new arrangements.

Once the protestants are organized and begin to negotiate, however, the momentum is lost, and "the system," either as it was or as modified, once more begins to function with the usual results of excluding the unorganized from its benefits.

This interpretation—that organization only means power *within* a given system and is thus antithetical to systemic change—is an interesting, if extreme, variation on the more familiar argument of Michels to the effect that bureaucratization and oligarchical dominance tend to affect all organizations, even those imbued with democratic dogma and revolutionary objectives. The needs of organizational maintenance supersede movement elan and momentum, and, as this happens, the possibility of dynamic growth itself fades very quickly. Thus it takes a feat either of memory or retrospective empathy to speak in the 1980s of the labor *movement* or the student *movement*. In 1984, Jesse Jackson's presidential campaign mobilized many previously inactive black citizens, but it did not reinvigorate the civil rights *movement*. It may well be, of course, that movements accomplish less policy change than more narrowly focused interest group pressure. The NAACP Legal Defense Fund litigation strategy was surely an important adjunct and perhaps even a necessary precondition to the marches of Martin Luther King. In the context of the legalistic culture of American politics, it is often helpful to have tested the possibilities and explored the limits of legal action before appealing to people to take to the streets. But test cases and *amicus* briefs are not the same as the direct-action tactics of a movement. They do not hold the potential for altering the consciousness of large numbers of people or of mobilizing them to action. And the political logic that underlies movements is that only large-scale action and demands can get beyond incrementalism to achieve fundamental changes in the structure of social relations, political power, or economic reward.

On the Origins of Movements

Samuel Huntington (1981) has argued that a cyclical pattern can be discerned in American political experience in which periods of "creedal passion," manifested in a burgeoning of movements and righteous causes, alternate with periods of relative quiescence. Albert Hirschman (1982) has advanced a somewhat similar argument, in which the cycles of movement and retreat result from the frustrations and disappointments of each phase as accomplishments fall short of promises. Related to these hypotheses is that considerable body of literature on part realignment that, in some versions at least, sees the rise of various political movements and third parties as the major signal of structural strain and upheaval that eventually force the major parties into departures from past coalition appeals and thereby bring about significant realignment and reinvigoration of voter loyalties. It is not entirely clear whether a new party alignment is expected to "solve" the structural crisis sufficiently to quiet the movement impulse. Clearly, the "System of 1896" did not; thereafter the congeries of Progressive, socialist, and Prohibition reform movements picked up speed. Nor was the 1928–1932 realignment followed by notable quiescence—labor organizers, the Townsend Plan, and others provided the "politics of upheaval" (cf. Schlesinger, 1960). Conversely, the movements of the 1960s—civil rights ,antiwar, environmentalist, and so on--quieted down without any lasting party realignment taking place. The connections between party development and political movements are obviously important but would seem to present more complexity than either cyclical or realignment theories can well accommodate.

A useful clue to the conditions likely to generate movements as compared to those leading to the formation of conventional interest group associations may be found in David Truman (1951), who does not even mention movements as one of the "stages of technique" in organized group action. Truman locates the source of group foundation in the disturbance of an equilibrium of interactions. Although he is not very explicit about the distinction, he speaks of some disturbances in terms that involve quite large numbers of people and involve interactions that are best described in the language of social structure—labor versus capitalist management, for example, or wheat farmers against the banks and railroads. Other "disturbances," however, such as many of those resulting from technological changes, are discussed in terms of relatively small differentiations of detailed interests, such as those leading to the formation of trade and professional associations.

Neither large structural shifts nor lesser differentiations of interests generate politically relevant activity with complete spontaneity. Leadership and mobilization are necessary ingredients for anything beyond the fragments of anomic outbursts. But whereas entrepreneur—organizers are necessary, they are never sufficient. Their efforts must find responsive audiences, and responsiveness is conditioned in part by the more or less objective positions people occupy in the complex of social relations we call political society. When these "market conditions" are experiencing major shifts in status relations among social groupings, for example, movement entrepreneurs may find rich opportunities. And, inasmuch as American society has long been characterized by extraordinary dynamism and growth, with correlative status uncertainties, movement politics, for all its high risk, has generally been an enticing opportunity. Meanwhile, however, and often in almost unnoticed parallel through time, the processes of social fission and marginal differentiation of interests go on apace, creating new opportunities, without much melodrama or fireworks, for interest associations to be formed and for them, along with institutional representatives, to go about the business of pursuing their comparatively modest policy objectives in the corridors of power.

The Movement Market and Its Customers

If our social imagination permits us to envision potential movement entrepreneurs "raising capital" from sympathetic institutions and investing their own commitment as dedicated believers in the cause, where may we expect them to find their most likely adherents? What sectors of the population will most readily respond to a movement's appeal? Part of the answer depends of course on the existing distribution of beliefs, values, and preferences. One finds supporters among those who share the movement's values and believe in its goals. But that is not a very satisfactory answer for at least two reasons. One is that commitment is not simply a given. People can be converted; from unbelief to acceptance, from acquiescence to enthusiasm, from applauding spectator to dedicated, even fanatic, activist. A movement depends upon and, indeed, is defined by those whom it *moves*—those who are mobilized to act in ways they would not were it not for the movement's impact upon them. And this mobilization is problematic. It may be great, swiftly achieving momentum sufficient to effectuate major social change. Or it may fall short, lapsing into the petty wrangling that, for example, characterized left wing movements of the 1920s and after; perhaps settling into comfortable bureaucratization with meetings in Las Vegas and Key Biscayne, a la the present day labor movement; or, like the student movement of the 1960s, disappearing almost totally with only a faded bit of poster or graffiti to show it was ever alive.

Many movement markets are quite volatile. One might suppose that an effort to restructure some basic social relationship would draw a relatively stable level of latent public support, but, at least at the overt level, many movement causes have experienced quite wide and rapid swings in saliency and popularity. McAdam (1982) shows, for instance, that the issues of civil rights fluctuated greatly in their perceived importance in the period from 1963 to 1966 when they were, in effect, displaced by concern over Viet Nam.

There is another side to this same phenomenon. Movements tend to come in sets (Freeman, 1983), often only loosely connected but sharing a degree of sympathy, drawing on the same organizations and social strata, articulating values and espousing causes that occupy adjacent locations in the issue space of the day. Thus, in the three decades prior to the Civil War, abolition was political kin to feminism, prison reform, concern for the mentally ill, and public education (Tyler, 1944; Rothman, 1971). The New Right of today embraces a congeries of movements, some of them uneasy about their allies but caught up in a context, a "market" of potentially responsive opinion, that has been identified as offering the most promising route to rapid growth and effectiveness. Right-to-life demonstrators do not necessarily share the views of the economic conservatives or nuclear power advocates, and the elites of each movement component may be very different. Nevertheless, they function to some degree in common political harness because their most likely prospects of broad mass support, needed to enact or sustain their basic policy or structural change objectives, are found in the same social sectors.

Thus the "market" for movement organizers is often fluid and problematic, but there may be rather clear limits constraining conversion and mobilization. Predispositions can be identified. Sympathies are not randomly distributed. The logic of modern mass mailing technique rests on the increased likelihood of a positive response to a second appeal tapping the same or a related social value. Movement entrepreneurs therefore tend to work primarily within particular value sectors of society (Salisbury, 1969, 1975), some of which have been revealed by past behavior and some even better illuminated by present affiliations.

Having said this, however, it remains true that movement leaders must take a further step to identify the most likely sources of people who, apart from their sympathy with the values espoused, will be willing to undertake the activity that specifically distinguishes a movement from "mere" interest group support, namely direct action (Judkins, 1983). Who are the people most likely to respond to exhortations to march, to sing, to sit down, or sit in? Surely they will tend to be people not otherwise engaged, with few existing commitments of time or dependent interests that might be placed at risk by disruptive direct action.

Thus the young, the restless, the unemployed, and those who, like writers and entertainers, have some autonomous control over their working schedules are more promising movement material than those with families to support or with employers who might look askance at demonstrators. Farmers are more readily mobilized in winter than when crops require tending. Senior citizens seeking policy relief may not always be able to travel long distances or endure physical hardship, but, within limits, their very freedom from obligations makes them an attractive market for movement recruits.

At the same time, however, the very condition that enables these people to undertake direct political action—the absence of competing obligations—greatly reduces their inclination to care very much about the cause to which the movement is devoted. Even when the movement's purpose is quite directly linked to the differentiated needs of the putative market—draft resistance for students, jobs for the unemployed, or better pensions for the aged—free riderism combines with inertia and, often, an absence of reinforcing social context to keep most potential participants far removed from the movement in question. And when the movement does not seek differentiated group benefits, as with the anti-nuclear-energy campaign, for example, it is especially difficult to exploit these markets of comparatively unattached, otherwise uncommitted people.

Just as the mobilization of "loose" voters—first-time voters and those previously not participating—is a key element of party and candidate strategy in elections, the mobilization of people with scanty networks of affiliation is of surpassing importance to movement development. We have stressed the short time frame within which movement mobilization must build if it is to have significant impact, and this has two interesting connections with what we have said about the attractiveness of the underaffiliated segments of society as the prime market for movement recruitment. The first is that these segments are composed of people for whom the appeal of movement participation is likely to have an especially short life. In part, this is because people with little to lose from risky direct action are also likely to be highly oriented toward the present, taking a short-term view of both gratification and adversity, and are less willing to remain committed to any group promising only long-run rewards. In part, however, it should be noted that, for many of the less densely affiliated, that condition itself is of rather short duration. The young get older and acquire more compelling responsibilities. Students eventually leave the carefree protected sanctuary of academe.

(Faculty members, by contrast, remain in this institutional setting, permitted by tenure rules and academic norms to indulge their expressive fancies in all sorts of movements without much risk.) Some of the unemployed obtain jobs. And, even though new cohorts of individuals replace them, the problem of movement mobilization is nearly continuous. Movement causes typically are difficult to accomplish and hence frustrating to their supporters, and they draw support disproportionately from social sectors that themselves undergo rather rapid turnover of individual members.

A consequence of this is seen in the studies of student protest and civil rights movements of the 1960s in which "generational" change and intergenerational conflict developed in a remarkably brief period of time (Ross, 1983). In those movements, a generation lasted approximately five years, after which new recruits came in with different expectations and values, and the older generation gradually withdrew. The new cohort itself, however, was gone in another five years. This tendency to suffer frequent generational turnover and conflict reflects what might be called the "sunshine patriotism" of much movement support—it will be remembered that George Washington Plunkitt (Riordan, 1948) called reformers "morning glories"—and contributes to it as well. The result is that movements very often have brilliant but brief prominence, and fade very quickly, losing all but a hard core of deeply committed activists for whom the cause remains important or appealing enough to keep them at work.

We come back then to the organizers, leaders, and core activists, upon whom must rest a very large share of any effort to understand movement growth and decay as well as the residual survivals of what might be called movement shells, once-prominent centers of political action now moribund save for the dedicated true believers who keep the faith against all the evidence around them of public indifference or even contempt. The WCTU and the American Council on Alcohol Problems are virtually all that remain of the Prohibition movement that, having achieved such success under the guidance of Purley Baker and Wayne Wheeler, fell quickly into disrepute and caricature when Bishop Cannon took over (Gusfield, 1969; Odegard, 1928). Antiwar movements, influential in the 1930s, quiescent from Pearl Harbor until the late 1950s, flowered again in the Viet Nam years, led by some of the same figures, such as David Dellinger and A. J. Muste (Hentoff, 1963), who had kept the flickering light of pacifism alive throughout the period (Wittner, 1984). These two examples remind us not only that movement leaders can, by their wrangling and internecine struggles, quickly bring a movement down, but that continued dedication to the cause may sometimes bring the reward of revived support and social impact. It is the latter lesson, of course, that sustains the optimism of those who remain committed to a movement that has ceased to move, losing its momentum, and finding its best rhetorical flourishes greeted with stony indifference. That same confidence, however, often encourages the very intramural conflict that speeds decline, as rival leaders, *knowing* that they are *right* and that the future will confirm it, refuse to yield or compromise.

Movements are concerned with causes, with matters of principle, defined in terms of moral, even theological, right and wrong. To adopt the wrong doctrinal position is not merely mistaken, therefore: It is sinful. Error must be combatted by every available means, especially within the family of movement sympathizers, for if they do not get things right, how can the larger world ever be expected to understand the truth? It would rarely be quite correct to say that a movement has been wracked by heresy, for that term implies the existence of an agreed-upon standard of truth and, usually, some degree of hierarchical authority to establish and enforce that standard. Politically interesting movements in America have not often or for long had such clearly established central leadership. Yet, if they have avoided heresy trials, they have been rife with schism. Abortionists, feminists, prohibitionists, socialists, right-to-lifers, participatory democrats, and on and on, virtually without exception, have shown a wonderful ability to find grounds for doctrinal dispute of sufficient seriousness to lead one faction to exit and found a new organization, still within the larger movement perhaps, but presenting a different interpretation of its moral purpose, its enemies, or the strategies of action that should be followed. In this respect, clearly, political movements in the United States closely resemble, just as they often have drawn vital organizational support from, American Protestantism.

The Institutional Foundations of Political Movements: The Case of the Churches

Social scientists have recently begun to discover that their assumption that religious beliefs and institutions would wither away in the face of postindustrial modernity was false, at least in the United States. Rather than fading away, religiosity has fully maintained its strength at the level of individual belief and practice, and churches, in the aggregate, are not only flourishing but displaying unwonted vigor with respect to political affairs. The specific importance of institutional religion to the study of political movements is enormous because, in both past and present, church organizations have provided major sources of support for political movements of many kinds.

The civil rights movement is a well-known example in which Southern churches came to constitute key elements in the organized infrastructure of the movement, providing leadership, workers, communication centers, funds, and even physical asylum for those active in the campaigns (Zald and McCarthy, 1987). A similar dependence on local congregations was exhibited by the classic campaign for Prohibition; the right-to-life movement has found wide support in Catholic parishes. New Right campaigns of various kinds have drawn resources from fundamentalist churches, especially some of the large Southern Baptist congregations, conservative Presbyterian churches, and Pentacostals. At the other end of the spectrum, various manifestations of peace movements throughout the twentieth century have rested on support from sympathetic church groups, such as the Methodist Church Washington office, or what Morris (1984) calls "halfway houses," groups such as the American Friends Service Committee or the Fellowship of Reconciliation, which themselves depend largely on churches for support, and which, in turn, provide organizational cadres for such campaigns as the nuclear freeze movement (Dwyer, 1983).

The importance of churches as institutional foundations of so American political movements is twofold. First, they are relatively secure organizations with indefinite longevity. Unlike the volatile movements, the churches will continue to function for years to come, and even though one movement fades, another may soon rise up from the same resource base to pick up the campaign threads and try again. The peace movement, as we have noted, is a prime example wherein key leaders resurface again and again as new wars and threats of war raise once more the old questions. To the extent that political movements can build upon such stable institutional foundations, they can become permanent fixtures on the political scene. Despite the considerable ebb and flow of their strength, they never entirely disappear because their organizational core remains in operation. Thus we find the irony: Specific political movements tend to rise and fall within relatively brief spans of time, but many of what might be called movement streams, including

peace, civil rights, and the moral reforms espoused by religious funda-
mentalists, are quite enduring parts of the political system.

A second consequence of the fact that church organizations constitute the core of so many political movements in the United States is rhetorical. Movements, by definition, must appeal to a far broader audience
than can be made content with solidary or material selective benefits.
The structural reform goals a movement pursues must be articulated in
ways that first capture the attention and then the commitment of large
numbers of people who have not previously been motivated to care. A
movement must therefore fashion powerful rhetorical tools.

It may be a truism that any time rhetoric can draw upon widely
shared symbols and patterns of belief its prospects of persuasion are enhanced. Certainly, it is true that the continued breadth of acceptance of
Christian symbols and beliefs among Americans offers an attractive opportunity to many types of entrepreneurs, political and otherwise, and
would-be movement leaders partake of this opportunity. Beyond this,
however, the fact that churches themselves are so often the institutional
core of movement action guarantees that goals and aspirations will be
cast rhetorically in religious terms. Not content to argue in behalf of one
social class against another or to urge the prudential advantages of a
particular course of reform, all sorts of movement leaders in the United
States state their cases in the language of moral principle, pitting sin
against salvation, and either they draw upon Holy Writ for inspired justification or they endow more worldly documents such as the Constitution with quasi-divine qualities. We need not argue that this is the only
reason for the importance of political rhetoric grounded in religious
themes to recognize the role of American churches as institutional in-
frastructures serving political movements.

Conclusions

It may be inappropriate to label the final observations of this chapter as
conclusions because their purpose is really to open some issues for discussion and enlarge the scope of both our theoretical and conceptual
understanding and our descriptive accomplishments. By explicitly
bringing the concept of movement into harness with interest group, association, institution, and so on, we can perhaps establish a sufficiently
broad frame within which to discern more clearly the different organizational modes employed by people seeking political purposes, track

more accurately the progress (and decay) from one mode to another, and map the interrelationships among these several forms of activities. Thus, we have suggested that movements typically encompass one or more movement organizations, which we would ordinarily call interest groups, and often depend upon the long-term support of institutions such as churches and other subsidizing agents for the survival of the movement shell or core.

One of the most important differences between a political movement and a "mere" interest group is in the language employed. Movement activists use a language of action. They stress the imminence of the crisis and the great magnitude of the stakes. Their characteristic rhetoric reflects the fact that they tend to have so little time in which to succeed. The language of interest group advocates, by contrast, tends to be circumspect in emotional tone and constrained by the particular norms of the institutional setting—congressional committee, regulatory agency, appellate court, and so on—in which their policy advocacy is expressed. Most of them will be back year after year to pursue their concerns, goals that are largely incremental and distributive rather than matters of basic structural change.

The term *movement* itself is often a political weapon, used in order to convey a sense of dynamic growth and prospective impact, as well as an analytic concept. Accordingly, we must be careful in according the analytic status of movement to activity simply on the basis of self-referencing rhetoric. It is important to pay close heed to political rhetoric, however, precisely because of this conflation of political with analytic usage. Any ambitious optimist may call a cause a movement; social scientists should always be clear enough about the meaning of their concepts to know the difference.

REFERENCES

Berry, Jeffrey. 1977. *Lobbying for the People*. Princeton: Princeton University Press.
Cigler, Allan. 1986. "From Protest Group to Interest Group: The Making of American Agriculture Movement, Inc." In Allan Cigler and Burdett Loomis, eds., *Interest Group Politics* 2nd ed. Washington, D.C.: Congressional Quarterly Press.
Dwyer, Lynn E. 1983. "Structure and Strategy in the Antinuclear Movement." In J. Freeman, ed. *Social Movements of the Sixties and Seventies*, New York: Longman, pp. 148–161.

Freeman, J. 1983. "On the Origins of Social Movements." In J. Freeman, ed., *Social Movements*, pp. 8–30.

Gusfield, Joseph. 1969. *Symbolic Crusade*. Urbana: University of Illinois Press.

Hentoff, Nat. 1963. *Peace Agitator: The Story of A. J. Muste*. New York: Macmillan.

Hirschman, Albert O. 1982. *Shifting Involvements: Private Interests and Public Actions*. Princeton: Princeton University Press.

Huntington, Samuel. 1981. *American Politics: The Promise of Disharmony*. Cambridge: Harvard University Press.

Judkins, Bennett M. 1983. "Mobilization of Membership: The Black and Brown Lung Movements." In J. Freeman, ed., *Social Movements*, pp. 35–51.

Lowi, Theodore. 1969. *The End of Liberalism*. New York: W. W. Norton.

McAdam, Doug. 1982. *Political Process and the Development of Black Insurgency*. Chicago: University of Chicago Press.

McCarthy, John D., and Mayer N. Zald. 1977. "Resource Mobilization and Social Movements: A Partial Theory." *American Journal of Sociology* 82:1212–41.

Moe, Terry. 1980. *The Organization of Interests*. Chicago: University of Chicago Press.

Morris, Aldon, and Cedric Herring, 1987. "Theory and Research in Social Movements: A Critical Review." In Samuel Long, ed., *Annual Review of Political Science*, Vol. 2. Norwood, N.J.: Ablex Publishing Corp., pp. 137–98.

Morris, O. D. 1984. *The Origins of the Civil Rights Movement*. New York: Free Press.

Odegard, Peter. 1928. *Pressure Politics: The Study of the Anti-Saloon League*. New York: Columbia University Press.

Olson, Mancur. 1965. *The Logic of Collective Action*. Cambridge: Harvard University Press.

Piven, Frances Fox, and Richard Cloward. 1977. *Poor People's Movements: How They Succeed, How They Fail*. New York: Vintage.

Riordan, William. 1948. *Plunkitt of Tammany Hall*. New York: Knopf.

Ross, Robert J. 1983. "Generational Change and Primary Groups in a Social Movement. In J. Freeman, ed., *Social Movements*, pp. 177–89.

Rothman, David J. 1971. *The Discovery of the Asylum: Social Order and Disorder in the New Republic*. Boston: Little, Brown.

Salisbury, Robert H. 1969. "An Exchange Theory of Interest Groups." *Midwest Journal of Political Science* 13:1–32.

———. 1975. "Interest Groups." In Fred Greenstein and Nelson Polsby, eds., *Handbook of Political Science* (IV, pp. 171–228). Reading, Mass.: Addison-Wesley.

———, John P. Heinz, Edward O. Laumann, and Robert L. Nelson. 1987. "Who Works with Whom: Patterns of Interest Group Alliance and Opposition." *American Political Science Review* 81:127–34.

Schlesinger, Arthur M., Jr. 1960. *The Political of Upheaval*. Boston: Houghton, Mifflin.

Truman, David B. 1951. *The Governmental Process*. New York: Knopf.

Tyler, Alice Felt. 1944. *Freedom's Ferment: Phases of American Social History from the Colonial Period to the Outbreak of the Civil War.* Minneapolis: University of Minnesota Press.

Useem, Bert, and Mayer N. Zald. 1982. "From Pressure Group to Social Movement: Efforts to Promote Use of Nuclear Power." *Social Problems* 30:144–56.

Walker, Jack. 1983. "The Origins and Maintenance of Interest Groups in America." *American Political Science Review* 77:390–406.

Wilson, James Q. 1973. *Political Organizations.* New York: Basic Books.

Wittner, Lawrence S. 1984. *Rebels Against War: The American Peace Movement.* Philadelphia: Temple University Press.

Zald, Mayer, and John D. McCarthy, eds. 1987. *Social Movements in an Organizational Society: Collected Essays.* New Brunswick, N.J.: Transaction Books.

4

Interest Advocacy and Interest Representation

T*his paper is* much too ambitious. It attempts to stake out positions in three broad conceptual issues and then to explore how most fruitfully to link the ideas that have been articulated. Most of the discussion will rest upon examples and circumstances specific to the United States, though much of what I have to say may have more generic relevance. In the course of the paper, I shall have occasion to tread upon many toes, contending that in one way or another other commentators have misunderstood either the conceptual apparatus, primarily that which is implicated in thinking about pluralism, or the American historical experience—or both! Thus ambition is joined with presumption, a dangerous combination in any hands.

One focus of attention will be two concepts that have been fundamental to much modern political analysis. These are the concepts of "interest" and "representation." It should be apparent immediately that I will not be able to give much more than a cursory review of the many decades of deliberation scholars have devoted to these concepts, but I will try nevertheless to sort out some of the core meanings of the notion of "interest," and at the end of the paper connect it more explicitly to a concept of representation. My second "project" is to examine the several foundations of political interests, largely in the U.S. context, so as to be able to consider American pluralism with appropriate reference to substantive interests and their interplay with institutional arrangements.

Paper presented at a conference on Pluralism and Democracy, sponsored by the Feltrinelli Foundation, Cortona, Italy, May 1990.

The third part of this paper will seek to articulate some models of the policy-making process which are in reasonably widespread heuristic use. These models have both normative and empirical dimensions that are often difficult to disentangle. I will argue, however, that to a considerable extent the normative disputes that have arisen over the years regarding how best to understand the American political experience derive from differences in the level at which we think about policy alternatives. To put it much too simply, if interests are conceptualized in macrosocial terms, certain models of how policy decisions are or ought to be reached make sense. If, on the other hand, interests and their political representation are considered in microterms, a very different "spin" is imparted to the analytic pitch. I shall not offer a resolution to the intellectual dilemma that results from this line of reasoning—viz., that disputes about the existence of the public interest or the moral status of interest group liberalism cannot be resolved without opting for one level of analysis over another. I do hope, however, to reduce what seems to be a large amount of confusion.

The Concept of Interest

When it is said that the Northern Widgetinkers Association (NOWA) or the Peoples United for Future Favors (PUFF) are interest groups, two distinct meanings of "interest" immediately come to mind. One is that members of the group hold certain values they wish to see incorporated into public policy. NOWA may want tariff protection for widgets, for example, while PUFF might strive to nationalize the airlines, but, in turn, those policy goals are intended to serve more fundamental values, higher incomes for widget makers and for PUFF members more equitable distribution of airline profits and service. The policy is a means toward the goal, often only one of the relevant methods of advancing its realization. But we employ the term interest to refer to both means and end and thus we introduce one kind of confusion.

Another source of confounded meanings is the frequent interchange of objective and subjective concepts of interest. We use two slightly different adjectives to identify objective interests. Sometimes we speak about the "real" interests of a political actor. When we do so, we generally mean that lurking behind the arguments and assertions being advanced are unstated but actually dominant criteria or judgment and action. What is being said is a mask for what is "really" desired. Thus during the 1940s it might be and often was said that to argue in behalf of states' rights or unlimited debate in the Senate was essentially a "front" for the defenders of racial segregation. Similarly, an organization urging aid to "anti-Communist" forces in Central America might "really" reflect property interests there threatened by "reformist" regimes.

The other word we employ to modify interest is "true." Marxists historically have placed great emphasis on what they believe to be the "true" or objective interests of the workers and have sought to combat the alleged false consciousness that misdirects their political understanding. Thus it is said that the failure of workers to realize that their "true" interests will best be served by collective class action leads to working class Toryism and weakness in the labor movement. To be sure, it can be argued that allegations of "real" or "true" interests, which by definition are different from those observably articulated in the political arena, are rhetorical devices by which contending parties strive to persuade others that their cause is deserving and ought to be supported. In any case, however, these apparently minor linguistic modifications of the central concept of interest can introduce further confusion.

Interests, like policies, may be material, symbolic, or both. Reductionists may wish to argue that one type of interest (usually symbolic) "really" consists deep down, of the other, but such disputes may best be regarded as part of the process of interest conflict rather than essential conceptual matters. There seems to be no reason a priori to insist that some values people hold constitute interests or the basis of interests while others do not. The question is empirical; what, in fact, do people value sufficiently to engage in political activity (such as participating in voluntary associations or lobbying their congressmen) to get it. The full range and variety of human motivation is potentially involved, which is one of the reasons that the study of interest groups is so rewarding.

There is a distinction of real importance to be made, however, between self-interested motivations and those that are non-self-interested. Actually, that rather misstates the matter since all motivation must be regarded as self-interested. People want, in some sense, to do everything they do, and they serve their personal values (though not always their "true" or "best" interests) with their every act. In the world of political interest groups, however, there is a difference between the group whose actions are directed toward improving the lot of its own members—the widget makers, in our earlier example—and one devoted to improving the condition of others. A classic example of the latter would be the National Coalition Against the Death Penalty devoted to the elimination of capital punishment, a fate that none of the likely members of such a group could ever realistically anticipate for themselves. Of course, they derive some satisfactions from the effort; otherwise, they would stay home. But there is a difference nevertheless, not only in motivational basis between what are often called "public interest" groups and "private" or "special" interests, but also over their place in the "moral economy" of the political order. Public interest groups, not being "selfish," are regularly applauded by editorialists and academics while many public officials, noting the absence among such interests of any direct personal stake in the outcome of political conflict, may deride them as "morning glories," or at least give them less credence then they accord to those more directly affected by the issue at hand.

There is a significant political difference, then, between "selfish" interests and the "others." Is there a fundamental conceptual distinction also? I think not. In actual practice a great many self-interested groups assert and believe that what they are after will be good not only for them but for the nation, even the world. To identify one's own interests with those of a larger public was not simply a maladroit expression by the former General Motors president Charles Wilson (back in 1953, during his confirmation hearings to become secretary of defense, he said, "What's good for General Motors is good for the country and vice versa"), but a very standard self-justification shared by people of many different persuasions. The observable combinations of selfish and generous motivations are surely enormous in number and range.

What is the core of the concept of interest, I believe, is the particular motivation as it is related to governmental action, past or prospective. For the student of interest groups what engages attention is never simply the values or "goods" sought by a group but how those values are expressed in or affected by some action of government, by public decision. The interest may be negative; that is, the prevention of action. Indeed, the underlying value itself may be negative; e.g., opposition to social change. The differences in signs are not important. *It is the conjunction of private wants and public action that constitutes the interest of an interest group.*

It follows that a particular organization is very likely to move into and out of the status of interest group depending on whether or not its values are entangled with public policy. No firm or permanent line of demarcation differentiates "political" interest groups from those that are not political. Interests change, emerge, or are discovered; the actualization of interests is a dynamic process. I will elaborate the implications of this point below. First, two other points can be made. One is that, given this definition of interest, the larger the scope of public policy, the more interests there will be. Note that I say nothing about why policy expands; that may or may not be a consequence of group pressure, of "interest group liberalism." I am only forecasting that as government expands its activities more and more people will discover they have been or might be affected. Thus interests are generated as government grows.

The second point, however, involves the question of whether and to what extent the perception of interests, as I have defined them, will be followed by the formation of an organized group or by political action undertaken by an existing group. Here, we encounter the heart of Mancur Olson's classic argument (1965), that rational individuals will not pay their share of the costs of organizing or acting to achieve a collective (i.e., public policy) benefit, the pleasures of which, if enacted, cannot be denied them whether or not they contribute to the effort. Various scholars have shown that uncertainty concerning the possibly critical impact of one's participation can help partially to overcome "free riderism" (e.g., Moe, 1980). So can the spirit of philanthropy. So, as Olson himself acknowledged, can face-to-face pressures in small group situations. Still, there surely remains a substantial residuum of potential groups for which Olson's argument holds and which, therefore, are likely to be far smaller than they would be if all those sharing the same value positions and similarly affected by government action (i.e., having the same interests) got together. Selective benefits, as Olson showed, may overcome part of the problem, but substantial "free-riderism" undoubtedly remains.

Now, however, let us reconsider "the Olson problem" from the perspective provided by the conception of interests I have used here. How, for example, are we to think about "free riders" when the interest in question emerges *after* the fact of government action being taken? Olson said it would not be rational to organize, let us say, to secure old age pensions. Most senior citizens could be expected to await the policy outcome without saying much or doing anything. But after legislation is passed and a social security system is in place, two things change. One is that "rational ignorance" now helps to *sustain* the program, not prevent enactment. "Free riderism" now works in favor of the unorganized, since most people will not bother to make an effort to repeal an unfavorable law any more than they would work for one to their benefit.

The second change results from the vastly increased awareness on the part of the pensioners that they are in fact affected by the policy and vitally so. Each month's social security check reminds them. By no means all the recipients of Medicare have joined AARP to help maintain the benefit flow, of course, but that organization's growth to some 30 million members surely reflects in part the discovery of policy interests by people who previously had been largely unaware of their possibilities. The usual way of thinking about interests treats them as "givens," as priors that have been defined by a group before entering the political thicket to advance them. Environmentalists know they oppose acid rain and favor wilderness protection. This is where they start; indeed, it is what defines them as environmentalists. Those interests are appropriately treated as givens. But consider the position of an oil industry association executive who reads in the *Federal Register* of proposed regulations requiring more detailed flight plans to be filed by noncommercial planes (Laumann and Knoke, 1987, p. 3). He realizes that with the Freedom of Information Act oil companies might have to divulge to competitors the flight plans of their aerial explorations looking for oil under the sea. An interest has emerged requiring his best lobbying efforts. Or take the case of a university whose tax-free borrowing for construction would be cut off because the Tax Reform Act of 1986 set an upper limit on how much could be borrowed in this way. Again, a policy interest has emerged that had not been there before the tax reform proposals took shape. To be sure, the core values of both the oil companies and the university predate the policy development and are far more stable. But those core values do not in fact tell us much about the particular policy issues in which the interaction of private values and public action generates interests among various groups. And it is on those issues that "interested" political activity occurs and interests, in the sense used here, are continuously being discovered and redefined; they are *emergent*.

There are several further implications of the point. Insofar as interests emerge from the interactions of the political process, it is necessary for the protagonists themselves to observe that process with care so that they can spot emerging concerns in a timely way. Private interest representatives must spend much of their time monitoring what goes on in government so that they can identify relevant policy developments, alert their respective groups, and develop constructive strategies of reaction. Again, we are accustomed to thinking of interest groups as aggressive protagonists, urging policies upon lawmakers or bureaucrats, and pushing hard to get things done. To this we must add that much of what group representatives do is react to the initiatives of others, including the officials themselves, and try either to turn those initiatives to their own advantage, neutralize their effects, or perhaps only adapt their organization's actions to fit new conditions.

The Foundations of Interests

In this section I want to present what must be only the merest sketch of a review of the principal bases from which the policy-focused interests discussed in the previous section emerge. As I argued there, these diverse sources of value are not themselves what I have defined as political interests, though some are surely very close to that station; rather they are the factors that generate values which in turn may, through encounters with present or prospective governmental action, become interests and lead on to processes of advocacy and representation. My presentation may seem very like an outline of a much fuller treatment of the subject, and indeed that is how I regard it myself, but there are contained within it, and I hope with clarity, some points with important effect on the later discussion of interest representation.

Pervasive Value Orientations

Ever since the American political experiment began commentators have sought to characterize and explain its uniqueness, and many of these analyses have contended that some fundamental factor deeply embedded in the structure of American society provided an explanation of politically decisive value orientations. Louis Hartz's well-known *Liberal Tradition* (1955) exemplifies this genre, while F. J. Turner (1984) and David Potter (1954) represent variations on the theme. What these three agreed on—and what the great Tocqueville had already articulated—was that for various reasons the American society lacked the deep social cleavages that characterized most of the modern world and that therefore U.S. politics were composed largely of shallow and shifting disputes over small stakes with little ideological gloss or rhetorical passion.

More recent developments in scholarship have led to the rediscovery of republicanism as a pervasive and rather more conflict-centered perspective very widely shared in the early days of the Republic and continuing in the present day to provide a basic orientation, primarily in a deep suspicion of any form of power, a fear of the corrupting effects of office upon civic virtue, and a generalized doubt about the legitimacy of political parties, factions, and "special interests" of any kind. Republicanism clearly sprang from a particular social and political configuration in which, among other things, a rough equality of condition among white males really did exist, but its subsequent impact has been felt in very different circumstances, not least in the way it underlies the "public interest group" movements of the last thirty years.

Ethno-Cultural Origins

The pervasive value orientations described above were rooted in the equally pervasive Anglo-Protestant origins of the American people, and the growing cultural diversity of the nineteenth-century immigration was bound to lead to politically relevant value orientations that differed, sometimes almost diametrically, from those of the earlier settlers. As David Hackett Fischer (1989) has recently shown, however, there were significant cultural differences even among the various groups of Britons who came during the seventeenth and eighteenth century and having settled in different parts of the continent, laid the foundations for distinctive political cultures that Elazar (1966), Kleppner (1979), and others would map in their later manifestations.

Ethno-cultural factors include race and religion, and we know how profoundly those sources of value leading to political interest have been and continue to be. In this brief review I would make only two points regarding the impact of this category of items on interest development. First, the immigration and settlement patterns of distinct ethno-cultural groups have always tended as they still do to be sharply differentiated in geographical location. In the early days of low density this often led to what Robert Wiebe (1975) has called "island communities," loosely linked together in a "segmented society." Later, in more urbanized settings the islands were often ghettoes or wards. In more aggregated form they might be regions or sections; Southern sectionalism certainly had some basic ethno-cultural foundations that only incidentally were related to cotton production.

The second feature to note concerning the effect of ethno-cultural factors is the extent to which these groups, especially as they reflected differential religious commitment, built institutions. Not only churches, both physical edifices and denominational structures, but schools, hospitals, colleges, settlement houses, recreational centers, and social clubs all sprang in abundance from the differentiated and often competitive ethno-cultural streams of Americans. The impact of these institutions on U.S. politics has been an enormously important "second stage" effect of the fact that the United States is a nation of immigrants.

Industrialization

It is obvious that not much of importance can be said in such a brief compass about the effects of industrialization and its siblings, commercialization and urbanization, on the foundations of interests. I will confine myself therefore to a very few assertions. First, with these massive macrosocial processes a class structure emerged in the United States that, compared to the period before about 1840, was far more sharply differentiated in income and life style, in values and aspirations, and very often in religion and even language. Further, the emergent structure not only contained a working class largely urban and heavily infused with recent immigrants, but a middle class as well, also largely urban but mostly Anglo and Protestant, genteel in manners and involved in the rapidly growing commercial and professional enterprises of the nation. Although he anticipated both parts of this development, as well as the rise of a third class fragment, the quasi-aristocracy of wealth, those are all really post-Tocquevillian features that become intertwined with but do not efface the older sources of value orientations we have discussed.

Second, one of the most palpable consequences of the macrosocial processes in question was the creation of large organizations including local governments, industrial corporations, trade and professional associations, financial structures, universities, and eventually the various bureaucracies of the federal government. This burgeoning of institutional actors transformed the political world, among others, not just by accentuating the demands and conflicts growing out of industrial capitalism but by generating a large array of new players in the game. I have written elsewhere (1984) about the distinctive character of institutional interests and will not repeat that discussion here. Having made the point about institutions, however, let me proceed to my third observation regarding the effects of the macro forces of industrialization, et al., which is that it was these forces also that led to the flowering of what we now think of as interest groups. This is a matter that is often misunderstood. Tocqueville, after all, had stressed the American tendency to form voluntary associations in order to solve collective problems and before him Madison had talked of the ubiquity of factions. Neither of these acute observers was really taking about the kinds of groups that devoted substantial and sustained effort to the task of persuading government to act, or avoid acting, in ways that would be helpful to the group or to its conception of the public interest. Lobbying organizations, both self-interested and otherwise, begin to appear in significant numbers in the late nineteenth century, and of course they eventually transformed the process of interest advocacy and representation.

The Growth of Office

No account of the development of politically relevant interests in the United States would be adequate without giving due attention to the proliferation of governmental offices and of the potential "opportunities," as G.W. Plunkitt called them (Riordan, 1948), that went with control of office. In the early days of the Republic the opportunities for tangible advantage were comparatively modest, but as the scope of government grew, and especially with the vast undertaking of providing the physical infrastructure for American cities in the latter nineteenth century, the stakes of successful political action were greatly increased and so were "the interests," the groups that hoped to profit from the play.

Even before rapid urban growth provided such a cornucopia of possibilities to successful political entrepreneurs, generations of town founders and promoters had sought to enhance land values in their respective communities by such means as locating the county seat and courthouse, building a college, inducing a railroad to come through town, or attracting such public facilities as prisons and asylums for the jobs they would provide local residents. Along with other forms of "public improvements" these actions typically involved the use of governmental authority as an integral part of the enhancement of economic growth and speculation-bound prosperity.

The important thing to recognize about this sometimes shabby and often reckless history is that nearly all of the "interested" impact of governmental action was experienced in specific locales. It was of little concern to the active parties whether land values appreciated in general; it was the particular community effects that mattered, that gave rise to and sustained politically relevant electioneering, lobbying, and so on. It is also true, of course, that the vast bulk of officialdom is chosen at the local level, so that the combination of thousands of positions to fill and massive opportunities for specific localized economic advantage accruing to those who prevailed in local elections meant that, as Tip O'Neill belatedly observed, "all politics is [or was] local."

Obviously, in the late twentieth century the level of concern has shifted somewhat. Real estate continues to be a powerful source of interested political action, but values may sometimes be more affected by generic features of the federal tax code than by what the local zoning commission does. Nevertheless, no assessment of politically relevant interests in American politics can afford to neglect those of public officials and of those groups that are in some way dependent on those officials for favorable treatment. On many occasions American reformers have failed to reach their noble objectives because they forgot that officials have interests which often resonate sympathetically in the community and which constitute relevant components of the political process as much as do groups more fully external to the state apparatus.

The Dynamics of Interest Development

Once again I must ask indulgence; it is plainly impossible to provide a full account of the ways that the structure of interests grows and changes over time. I do want, however, to distinguish two quite distinct dynamic processes of interest development and to suggest that when both are simultaneously in operation the result is a particularly complex pluralism. I recognize fully the importance of growing population density and of the negative externalities that have accompanied that growth, of the increased affluence and leisure which permit new styles of politics to flourish, and of the myriad of other changes that have been at work. I skip over them here only to stress some less often noticed components of social change.

One dynamic involves the differential growth of the demographic structure of the population. Improved health leads to more senior citizens. Differential birth rates yield faster growth among the poor than among the rich. Social mobility is more rapid for Asians than for Hispanics. And so on. The point is that various political interests emerge from these demographic developments; Asian-Americans come to dominate public institutions of higher education, seniors protect the tax exemption of their social security pensions. Intergenerational tensions and ultimate public policy conflicts are implicit in such demographics.

A second dynamic involves the physical mobility of productive resources, especially capital, as it seeks the greatest advantage. One plant is closed while another, nonunion, is opened with a smaller work force and lower wage structure. Not only production and other elements of business are potentially mobile. Writers, composers, and many other types of professional can quite easily pick up their baggage, move to a new site, and be back at work in an hour or two. When Lindblom (1977) talked about the privileged character of business in a democratic polity, what he meant, I believe, was that business has a particularly advantageous position from which to shift its investment from one location to another. This gives a firm a good deal of leverage over civil authority; it can move elsewhere and the mayor, the governor, the senator, and so on cannot. Nor can the local bureaucracy, the local utility firm, or the local real estate speculator. Indeed, the ethno-cultural islands are also locally circumscribed, largely dependent on a particular configuration of spatial boundaries for attaining political impact. What I want to emphasize is that there are many interests in the United States which are essentially fixed in geographical location and these, in turn, are often closely tied to a structure of political representation that is also organized in terms of geography. Those interests that are mobile, especially those residing in the comforting toils of capital, may whipsaw government by threatening to leave but still be less than ideally served by particularistic localism as a pattern of representation.

Some Models of Politics

In this section I want to sketch four models of the political process, each of which is quite commonly employed for both descriptive and critical purposes, and each of which contains quite distinct implications for the way that interests, whose foundations I outlined in the previous discussion, are represented.

Since this paper is largely about interest groups it seems appropriate to begin with Lowi's well-known formulation (1969), *interest group liberalism*. In this model organized groups, speaking with an "upper class accent," make policy demands on officials who, to get and hold group support and thereby public office, yield to those demands. For the most part these demands are relatively disaggregated and thus permit coalitions of the whole to form through logrolling, but some groups may be more encompassing—e.g., labor or corporate business—and significant policy conflict is certainly possible. But the unorganized are poorly served by this system, and the dominating criterion for making policy decisions is interest group strength.

A second model of the process can be called the *party responsibility* model. In this kind of system political parties offer competing packages of policy to voters in order to gain their support, especially for presidential candidates. The successful candidate, drawing support from partisan colleagues in Congress, pushes through his or her program. Interest groups in this model are subordinated to party leaders, who tend to frame their policy options in macrosocial terms such as inflation, unemployment, growth, or national defense rather than in more group-specific language. There are group winners and losers, of course; indeed the party responsibility model, by emphasizing a two-party choice between programs, often emphasizes the conflicts among groups and makes explicit which groups do well and which do badly.

A third version we will call, with a bow to Tip O'Neill (1987), the *all politics is local* model. In this system the elected representatives of geographically distinct areas seek policies and programs that will provide benefits to their particular constituencies. They frame these programs either by logrolling, often under universalistic criteria allowing every member to get something for his or her district, or by seeking out representatives of similarly situated districts—cotton growers, urban slums, etc.—and building coalitions in behalf of beneficial programs.

Notice that in all three of these models it is assumed that the electoral process is the critical determinant of what policies get enacted. Under interest group liberalism, to be sure, the elected officials are granted no real function other than to receive and transmit group demands. Nevertheless, elections may generate varying combinations of group-responding decision makers, and when they enact policies they are presumed to be motivated by their desire to be reelected. The party responsibility model may come closer to reality at times of significant realignment in party strength, but in its normative form it is presumably operative in every election.

Our fourth model for the policy process does not necessarily depend upon the mechanism of elections to achieve the representation of particular interests. We may label this the *synoptic rationalism* model. Problems are defined (within some paradigm, to be sure) and solutions developed to solve them. Typically the solutions are "enacted" by invoking authority and/or by reference to reasoned argument. Judicial decisions exemplify this form, but so do the many technical/rational policy determinations made by the Pentagon, NASA, the State Department, and elsewhere in the bureaucracy. I am not suggesting that bureaucrats or judges are never caught up in interest group pressure or local politics; quite the contrary! Nor do I want to suggest that in the most technically rigorous analysis and solution of a problem some interests will not do much better than others. I do want to argue, however, that our expectations regarding how interest advocacy will occur and what patterns of representation will follow depend upon the policy process model we employ.

Now let us consider the very important matter of policy advocacy in the light of these four models. Who articulates the alternatives under interest group liberalism? The organized groups. Under party responsibility? The party leaders, conventions, and presidential candidates. Under localism? Local interests and their elected representatives. Under synoptic rationalism? Experts and authorities, sometimes through adverserial proceedings, sometimes through hierarchy, but often in less structured formats. Now any clear-eyed observer of the policy process in the United States will reach the conclusion that in actual practice all of these sources of policy advocacy are likely to become involved in any large issue and many small ones. There is certainly no organized group monopoly of policy argumentation virtually ever to be found. Even on the narrowest, most obscure slice of any legislative action elected officials must have some say and *may*, though they certainly do not always, put forward the cause of any interests they choose. That is, and this point is vital to a proper understanding of pluralism in American, people in official positions are quite capable of advocating the interests of whomever they regard as worthy, whether or not the latter are well-organized, provided either that the latter, though not organized, may still be responsive to legislative initiatives favorable to them and vote accordingly, or that the elected official, relatively indifferent to the electoral payoff of his actions, chooses to pursue what he or she deems desirable public policy.

Policy advocacy can and does come from all sorts of sources and, while there is no assurance that in the aggregate the political system will produce an evenly "balanced" flow of policy arguments, or one proportionate to the numerical strength of all interests involved, neither is there much reason to assume that the array of organized interest groups will succeed in dominating this flow. Party leaders and candidates do put forward proposals that are not simply restatements of organized group demands. Bureaucrats often urge policy initiatives of one sort or another precisely because they believe there are valued interests in the society not adequately represented by the organized group spokesmen (cf. Long, 1952). Denzau and Munger (1986) have argued formally that elected representatives may often find it advantageous to represent the interests of unorganized constituents.

In the end, of course, the question of which interests in a society find their policy concerns effectively represented does not depend entirely on the patterns of interest advocacy. Before turning to some further consideration of interest representation, however, let me briefly develop one other point. How do the principal institutions of American politics shape and constrain the advocacy of the various types of interests discussed earlier in this paper?

The Interaction of Interests and Institutions

Broadly speaking, we can divide the many interests extant and articulate in American politics into two groupings. One group would include all those whose concerns are essentially ideological, rooted in some basic value orientation or commitment from which a broad spectrum of policy positions is deduced. Liberals and conservatives, republicans (in the eighteenth-century sense) and populists, socialists, and libertarians would all be in this group, as would most of those whose conceptions of politics pits the "public interest" against the "special interests." Allied with what we might call these *macropolitical interests* would be many others, mainly from the realm of corporate business, that are more narrowly specific in their substantive concerns but also are relatively independent of any particular geographical location. Their capital resources are often quite mobile and can move where it is advantageous. Hence they do not depend so much upon particular geographic representation.

It will be obvious that I mean to suggest that this broad array of interests tends to favor the American presidency as the institution most likely to express their policy needs. Not all of them can expect to have satisfactory access at any one time, of course. Conservatives did well from 1921–33, badly for the next two decades, but after 1980 discovered once again how superior the presidency was to Congress or the courts. Liberals, for their part, praised the executive in Franklin Roosevelt's day, worried some with Truman and Eisenhower, renewed their faith with JFK, but have fallen away since then. Yet they never have truly embraced Congress as a sympathetic alternative, nor have the public interest groups. The latter, in their Progressive era manifestation, tended to urge the use of independent regulatory commissions, but those mechanisms have had less appeal in recent times.

For the geographically rooted, functionally specific and disaggregated interests, including many of the ethno-cultural groups in their "islands," the localists of various kinds, and many of the institutional interests, Congress has been the institution of choice. Its representational structure makes it responsive to disaggregated group demands. Not all such interests will be successful in constructing coalitions large enough to enact or even block legislation, but Capitol Hill is the place to try. Its policy products tend to have a distinct *micropolitical* form, filled with ear-marked provisions and special clauses, and much decried by those whose policy focus is more broadly defined. Yet micropolitical actions, such as the unreformed tax code, have massive macropolitical implications, and the reverse is equally true. A campaign against inflation, for example, differentially affects the building trades, older manufacturing core cities, and Wall Street brokerage houses among many others.

The position of the judiciary in relation to the major interest configurations seems to me quite ambiguous. On the one hand, there is the view that the courts have offered an institutional refuge to a variety of interests that are not able to compete effectively in the other institutional arenas. In the twentieth century racial and religious minorities have often found this to be true. On the other hand, there is the Dahl-Dooley-Funston (Dahl, 1957) hypothesis to the effect that the courts tend to follow along, though sometimes with a lag of a few years, with whatever coalitions are dominant in national politics. Still a third view, which I think comes close to the mark, is that the courts are in fact quite marginal to the process of interest representation. Two large empirical studies of interest group activity in the 1980s (Schlozman and Tierney, 1985; Nelson et al., 1987) found that litigation was the least often used technique of advocacy, and most interest groups rarely use the courts except for ad hoc tactical moves.

The principal interest group activity that focuses on the courts does not involve a matter of strategic choice where there is a preference for one institution over another because of its rules or representational tendencies. Rather, it stems from the substantive jurisdiction that belongs almost exclusively to the judiciary. On such matters as criminal prosecution, liability, bankruptcy, and numerous others the courts are the primary arenas of decision. Statutes may frame the rules and processes of deliberation, and executive branch officials are involved, of course, in prosecution, but the judges are key actors across a considerable jurisdiction of substantive concerns. My point, however, is that this jurisdiction is a rather minor fraction of the total policy agenda of the organized interest groups in American politics (and undoubtedly an even smaller fraction in other democratic systems).

Although most interest groups will tend to prefer one institutional branch to another, most of them will try to attain and utilize access across the whole system. At the level of the individual lobbyist there is less specialization than one might expect. One cultivates members and staff in both houses of Congress and within the executive in proportion to one's substantive needs (Where is the issue located along the path of decision? Who has the needed information?) and the permeability of the institution (the White House is more difficult to penetrate than a Cabinet official's office, for example). Pragmatic adaptation to political circumstances continually modifies the institutional preferences noted earlier. Corporate business learns to work with Congress, and sometimes even the most parochial localists establish sympathetic ties with the executive (the Defense Department comes to mind).

Pragmatism prevails in part because both ends of Pennsylvania Avenue are involved in the development of most programs and no relevant component of the decision process can safely be ignored. But there is another factor of rather paradoxical character which works to modify the emphasis a group might otherwise place on one institution to the near exclusion of the other. This factor is the joint product of party and ideology. Most lobbyists are partisans, Republicans or Democrats, and many have had quite substantial involvement in party organizations and election campaigns. Moreover, most lobbyists work for client organizations with partisan and/or ideological inclinations. By that I mean that a large proportion of the organized interest groups active in Washington find one party more responsive to their policy desires than the other. It follows that they prefer an institutional arena if their favorite party controls it but otherwise are less enthusiastic. I would emphasize that what I have called the macropolitical interests do not cheerfully run over to Congress every time the presidency falls into the wrong hands. Ideological liberals and public interest groups wrung their hands during the Reagan years, but they remained highly ambivalent about Tip O'Neill and Jim Wright. Similarly, localists such as many commodity groups might find a Republican Senate less hospitable than a Democratic House but still prefer to keep the locus of decision on price supports firmly in Congress rather than delegate it to the executive.

Interest Representation: A Dynamic Process

In this last section I will try to connect the lines of argument developed earlier to the ultimate focus of concern; namely, what interests are represented in the policy-making processes of American politics. Although I recognize that there are other usages for the term, I shall employ what I regard as the Bentleyan meaning of representation; that is, those interests are represented which are benefited by the activities of public officials. Not all represented interests will prevail. Many members of Congress or justices of the Supreme Court are on the losing side of issues, but whatever authoritative actors do represent some interests. I would stress that the whole range of activities, formal and informal, involves interest representation, not simply such ultimate acts as votes. Speeches, backstairs negotiations, legislative proposals, amicus curiae briefs, committee hearing exchanges, and, of course, floor votes, ve-toes, and judicial opinions are all among the total array of representa-tional acts.

Two important points follow from this. One is that when interest rep-resentation is considered in this light it can be seen as involving far more than the pressures and demands of organized groups. Some of what of-ficials do undoubtedly reflects such pressures. It would be foolish indeed to dismiss as ineffectual all the lobbying, all the PAC contributions, and all the amicus briefs. But it would be equally foolish to suppose that ev-erything public officials do is in response to such pressures. Amicus briefs do not so dominate judicial opinion writing as to screen out other sources of ideas and arguments. Nor do organized group protestations monopolize the argumentation processes in Congress or the administra-tion. Those processes are, in a sense, intellectual as well as political, cre-ative as well as responsive.

That being so, it follows that the whole question of bias in the inter-est group system—the notion that, because there are so many business groups present in Washington with such extensive resources, competing interest groups, such as consumers or labor, are at a severe disadvan-tage—becomes much more problematic. It may still be true, of course, that business interests are more effectually represented than labor, but that may be as much because of the persuasiveness of current economic theory as it is because of organized group pressure. (Indeed, organized labor might do better politically by investing more in "academic" re-search and intellectual innovation and less in Washington lobbying.) In any case, the full pattern of interest representation is, or may be, signif-icantly separate from, even largely independent of, the structure and shape of the organized group presence.

The second point I want to make in this context has to do with those organized groups. Just as interest representation in the political system is only partly a function of group pressures, so the activities of organized groups are only partly directed toward influencing public policy. A great deal of what so-called lobbying groups do in Washington is to monitor what is going on; keeping an eye on the policy processes, checking up on the activities and plans of other groups, and generally trying to keep on top of the complex of developments that might affect the groups' interests. Or, to put it more accurately (and bring back into our discus-sion the concept of emergent interests introduced early in the paper), lobbyists spend much of their time trying to discover what their respec-tive interests are as policy impinges or threatens to impinge upon group concerns. Often, once those emergent interests are recognized, the lobbyists may go to work to affect the ultimate policy result. In other circumstances, however, the information gleaned from the monitoring activity may be used to enable the interest group or organization to adapt its own activities to adjust to the new policy conditions. Note that *access* is nearly as vital for purposes of securing timely information about the policy process as it is in order to influence that process.

These two assertions may serve as conclusions. Not all the policy-relevant actions of public officials are to be explained by reference to interest group pressures and demands. Not all the activities of organized groups are designed to influence policy outcomes. Both are essentially empirical questions calling for separate and distinct investigations. Recent research has begun more carefully than before to explore some of these issues, primarily those involving the activities of organized groups. But the relationship between group activities and interest representation in the policy process itself remains highly problematic.

REFERENCES

Dahl, Robert A. 1957. "Decision Making in a Democracy: The Supreme Court as a National Policy-Maker," *Journal of Public Law* 6 (Fall): 279–95.

Denzau, Arthur T., and Michael C. Munger. 1986. "Legislators and Interest Groups: How Unorganized Groups Get Represented." *American Political Science Review* 80 (March): 89–107.

Elazar, Daniel. 1966. *American Federalism: A View from the States*. New York: Crowell.

Fischer, David Hackett. 1989. *Albion's Seed*. New York: Oxford University Press.

Hartz, Louis. 1955. *The Liberal Tradition in America*. New York: Harcourt, Brace and Co.

Kleppner, Paul. 1979. *The Third Electoral System, 1853–1892*. Chapel Hill: University of North Carolina Press.

Laumann, Edward O., and David Knoke. 1987. *The Organizational State: Social Choices and National Policy Domains*. Madison: University of Wisconsin Press.

Lindblom, Charles E. 1977. *Politics and Markets*. New York: Basic Books.

Long, Norton. 1952. "Bureaucracy and Constitutionalism." *American Political Science Review* 46 (September 1952): 808–18.

Lowi, Theodore. 1969. *The End of Liberalism*. New York: W. W. Norton.

Moe, Terry. 1980. *The Organization of Interests*. Chicago: University of Chicago Press.

Nelson, Robert L., John P. Heinz, Edward O. Laumann, and Robert H. Salisbury. 1987. "Private Representation in Washington: Surveying the Structure of Influence." *American Bar Foundation Research Journal* 1987 (Winter): 141–200.

Olson, Mancur. 1965. *The Logic of Collective Action.* Cambridge: Harvard University Press.

O'Neill, Thomas P., and William Novak. 1987. *Man of the House.* New York: Random House.

Potter, David. 1954. *People of Plenty: Economic Abundance and the American Character.* Chicago: University of Chicago Press.

Riordan, William L. 1948. *Plunkett of Tammany Hall.* New York: Knopf.

Salisbury, Robert H. 1984. "Interest Representation: The Dominance of Institutions." *American Political Science Review* 78 (March): 64–76.

Scholzman, Kay, and John Tierney. 1985. *Organized Interests and American Democracy.* New York: Harper and Row.

Turner, Frederick Jackson. 1984. "The Significance of the Frontier in American History." *American Historical Association Annual Report, 1893.* Washington.

Wiebe, Robert. 1975. *The Segmented Society.* New York: Oxford University Press.

Part II

◆

Macropolitical Analyses

The papers in this section all seek to characterize particular elements of the U.S. political system, to describe how things work and explain why. They address directly the interplay of interests and institutions and, in particular, how American political rules and institutions shape and channel interests in the quest for political advantage.

The "Theory of Policy Analysis" paper was developed as a revision of an earlier attempt of mine to develop a theory of policy making that would appropriately take into account both interests and institutional milieu. The first attempt seemed to me static and ultimately formalistic, and so this second effort, in which my friend and fellow worker John Heinz joined me, was recast along quite different lines. Ironically, although it was, we thought, a great improvement over the earlier version, it received much less attention from the profession.

The essays on corporatism and centrifugal tendencies reflect forays into the company of comparative politics scholars. My effort in these papers was to show how a significant part of "American Exceptionalism" was rooted in the interaction of interest groups and political institutions.

The "Allies and Adversaries" paper is one of several which, along with a lengthy book, resulted from a long-term collaborative research project investigating Washington lobbyists. The last paper in this section also stemmed from collaborative research in Washington.

5

A Theory of Policy Analysis and Some Preliminary Applications

*T*his *essay continues* a line of inquiry which for the last several years has considered the questions: How can we think about public policy decisions in ways that are (1) relevant to the development of empirical theory in the discipline, and (2) grounded in the data and techniques of systematic empirical investigation? This literature includes such work as that of Lowi and Froman regarding the theory development side, and the by now formidable array of Dawson and Robinson, Dye, Hofferbert, Sharkansky, and a number of others who have assessed the data.[1] Most if not all of these studies are set in a general frame which is at least quasi-Eastonian. Policy decisions are of central theoretical concern, viewed as the outputs of a political system which is responding to the inputs of resources, demands, and supports. (This general orientation may be contrasted with the functional process orientation associated with Gabriel Almond and his colleagues wherein policy decisions receive comparatively scant attention in either the theoretical or empirical treatment.)

The thrust of a substantial number of the empirical studies of policy is that variations in the political system do not explain much of the variance in outputs. Rather than such classic political variables as party competition, apportionment patterns, or gubernatorial strength, the critical independent variables appear to be such items as income, urbanization, sectional or regional value orientations, and habit patterns regarding

John P. Heinz coauthored this essay. It is reprinted with permission from Ira Sharkansky, ed., *Policy Analysis in Political Science* (Chicago: Markham, 1970), pp. 39–60.

policy. Whatever relevance political system characteristics may have in other contexts, they do not greatly affect the *amount* of public expenditure in any of the numerous categories investigated once system resource variables are controlled.

It should be noted that (1) these findings deal mainly with expenditures and are concerned, at various levels of refinement of observation, to explain variations on a "more or less" dimension; (2) these findings are not asserted on theoretical grounds to have general validity—indeed there is contrary evidence for some earlier periods—but only to describe the situation, and the "normal" situation not the innovative one, as it has existed in recent American times; and (3) these findings accept and work within the policy categories "given" by the real political world and have therefore a low level of abstraction. Consequently, apart from the need for continuing refinement of this line of analysis, a number of major issues of policy analysis remains unsettled. One, which is perhaps the most completely unsettled, is the function of the political system in translating or processing demands into outputs. Hitherto the assumption underlying most discussion of this part of the process seems to have been that the political system accomplished its processing tasks by, in some sense, *representing* the demands and therefore securing outputs which would satisfy the demands. John Wahlke has argued persuasively that we have overstressed demand representation and underestimated the significance of supports.[2] Even this view, however, leaves the dynamics of the decisional system unclear since if decision-makers do not act by virtue of pressure on them, why, then, do they act? We shall not settle this issue here but only observe that it is opened, elevated to major theoretical importance, and left up in the air by the recent research on public policy.

A second issue which will be a major preoccupation of the rest of this paper is, in effect, what about all the policies which are not cast in the form of expenditures? How shall one analyze decisions which make or revise rules, establish or disestablish structures and programs, or administer justice in a court? A basic thesis of this paper is that there is a fundamental distinction to be made between decisions which allocate tangible benefits directly to persons or groups, as expenditures generally do, and decisions which establish rules or structures of authority to guide future allocations. Further, we shall argue, political system variables of the kind alleged to have little impact on the *amount* of expenditure may still have significant effect on the *kind* or the *distribution* of the amount.

I

There are by now several extant efforts at establishing a typology of public policy which would not simply accept the conventional categories of education, highways, welfare, etc. We shall not again review these, but we will indicate briefly the intellectual lineage of the typology proposed here. In a genuinely seminal essay Lowi argued that there are three fundamental types of policy: distributive, redistributive, and regulatory; that these types are distinguishable mainly according to the degrees of disaggregation of the treatment the policy in question provides to those groups it affects; and that there is some sort of developmental sequence that occurs in a technologically sophisticated system, roughly from distributive to regulatory policy.

Salisbury revised and extended Lowi's approach by suggesting that different policy types—distributive, redistributive, regulative, or self-regulative—could be expected to emerge as outputs of various types of interaction between two key variables, the pattern of demand and the structure of the decisional system.[3] The two variables were placed on axes depicting the degree of fragmentation-integration in each. A highly fragmented demand pattern, *e.g.,* where each county seeks a subsidy for its roads, might interact with a fragmented decisional system, *eg.,* most legislatures, and the result would be a distributive policy of the classic pork barrel variety. An integrated decisional system, a strong executive, for example, facing a relatively integrated demand of two conflicting groups, might be forced into choosing sides in what was interpreted as a zero-sum game.

Self-regulatory policy might be anticipated when an integrated group made demands of a fragmented decisional system with the policy decision being to delegate authority, say in the form of self-administered licensing authority, to the demand group. The fourth type, regulatory policy, was interpreted as resulting from the interaction of fragmented demand and integrated decisional system and was characterized by continuing governmental agency control over the demand groups. Characteristic of both regulatory and self-regulatory policies is ambiguity regarding winners and losers. The benefits are unclear because they are expressed in the abstract terms of rules and structures, and the tangible benefits themselves are deferred in a regulatory decision.

It was argued in that paper that political scientists have for generations been preoccupied with regulatory policy and particularly with constitutional policy, or policy decisions which establish or revise authority structures. It was argued further that in the American case the interactions of demand and decisional systems have tended historically to be concentrated in the distributive portion of the matrix, although modern times may have brought about somewhat greater aggregation of demand and integration of decisional systems, notably manifested in increased strength of the executive.

As we see it the major difficulty in the argument advanced previously lay in the conception of regulatory policy. More than the other three types identified, the meaning of regulation as distinguished from distribution was fuzzy to say the least. Perhaps this was a natural consequence of a conception which stressed ambiguity regarding beneficiaries as the criterion of classification, but we remained unsatisfied nevertheless. It will be recalled that regulatory policy was asserted to result from the interaction of fragmented demand and integrated decisional system. Regulatory policies, such as constitutional revisions, would thus be postulated to follow from diverse group interests pressing claims upon a decisional body which was integrated enough to defer specific benefit decisions in favor of more general rules. But the concept of integration in the decisional system is troublesome. Is a constitutional convention, or for that matter a Supreme Court, more integrated a system than a legislature? Any measures of decision system integration one might devise might have great trouble discovering less unity on public works appropriations, undoubtedly a distributive policy, than on constitutional changes. The terms integration and fragmentation are often used to identify significant features of decisional systems but their empirical meaning is not clear.

On reflection, it appears to us that *any* decisional systems must achieve some degree of integration in order to make *any* decision. The minimum required is provided in the formal decisional rules; fifty percent plus one, two-thirds, a constitutional majority, or what not. Informal norms may add to or alter this minimum. But some measure of agreement is essential. The agreement in a decisional system comes, however, at the conclusion of the decisional process. And sometimes this process may be arduous, sometimes easy. The question then is not the amount of integration achieved but rather how difficult or costly is it to achieve the requisite coalition. From this perspective if we say that a legislature is likely to be more fragmented than an executive agency, we mean that it is generally more difficult or costly to organize the majority required for action in the former than in the latter. And this alters our original argument considerably. We now regard the decisional system under scrutiny not as fixed along an integration-fragmentation axis but as a variable whose functioning is problematic. The more costly it is to organize decisional coalitions, the more fragmented we may regard the decisional unit. But these costs will vary depending on the type of policy under consideration. A legislative majority can be organized more readily for some things than for others. So, indeed, in any decisional systems. Can this observation be generalized and linked to our earlier typology?

Let us do so in the following way. Let us conceptualize the linkages between demand, and support as well, and a decisional system in terms of cost-benefit ratios to decision-makers. That is, decision-makers will behave, *ceteris paribus,* so as to optimize their cost-benefit ratios operating in regard to a particular set of activities. The calculus involved will include the value, positive and negative, to the decision-maker of acting so as to confer benefits upon some relevant constituency; the costs of informing himself about the substantive issue sufficiently to develop a position; and the cost of investing time, energy, and resources in negotiating a favorable winning coalition. These costs will vary from issue to issue and individual to individual within a decisional system but we may generalize about their relative magnitudes and modes among institutions as well.

Now our initial formulation of this cost-benefit argument involves a fundamental distinction between two types of policy, allocative and structural. By allocative policies we mean decisions which confer direct benefits, material or symbolic, upon individuals and groups. Structural policies we take to mean policies which establish authority structures or rules to guide future allocations. The latter policies are more abstractly formulated and more ambiguous in their effect than the former. Allocative policies may vary along a distributive-redistributive axis; structural policies may vary as between regulatory and self-regulatory outcomes. We shall explore this further at a later point. For now let us assert our most *fundamental* hypothesis linking the cost-benefit calculus we described above to this distinction in policy outcomes: The more costly it is to organize the requisite coalition on an issue, the more likely it is that the policy outcome will be structural rather than allocative.

II

Let us consider a brief example. One state legislature receives the budgetary requests for the several state colleges and universities and makes the decisions about how much money each will receive. A neighboring

state legislature makes a *de facto* delegation of authority to a state board
of higher education to receive and adjust the budget requests for the
state schools and ratifies the board's recommendations. In the former
case the legislature makes an allocation decision, typically a highly distributive one in which each institution gets an incremental increase over
its last appropriation. In the latter state, however, the legislature has, in
effect, opted out of the allocation and instead chosen to make a structural, or regulatory, decision by establishing the state board. Why the
different *types* of decision? Our explanation rests on the relative costs, as
perceived by the decision-makers, of the one kind of decision as against
the other. In the state where the Board makes the allocative decision the
key legislators no longer perceive much constituency-linked advantage
to the old system. Where once the groups with the greatest active interest in higher education were concentrated in the districts containing the
institutions, now the demand for expanded public higher education
comes from everywhere and, indeed, there are state institutions of one
kind or another almost everywhere. To logroll in this context would be
exceedingly complex and individual legislators might find it very difficult to show their constituents where they had gained any advantage.
For constituents as well as legislators it is vastly easier and more relevant
to contemplate higher education in terms of a statewide system. Moreover, demand for higher education is not simply for places to accommodate Johnny. It is directed also toward developing the training and
research facilities which are universally perceived as vital components of
the state's economic growth. The demand is thus strong and steady but
little tied to constituencies and hence to electoral benefits of interest to
legislators. To make an allocative decision will be of small benefit to
them. We may say that the constituency exchange values are low. At the
same time, the growing magnitude and complexity of the state higher
education system markedly increases information costs to the legislators.
It becomes ever more difficult for them to learn enough about the problem to reach a policy preference of any substantive detail. And the diffusion of constituency interest helps to render the task of negotiating a
winning coalition in the legislature uncertain and therefore potentially
expensive. It has become more costly (and less beneficial) for legislators
to allocate college and university monies, and so they opt out by creating
a structural unit to do it for them.

Now why does the other state legislature continue to make its own
allocations decisions? Reflecting perhaps a lower rate of economic
growth and a less sophisticated urban and industrial base, the demand

for higher education expansion is less vigorous. It continues to be fragmented regionally and expressed in ways that sustain viable legislator-constituent exchanges in the principally affected districts. Moreover, the slower pace of change makes it seem less difficult for key legislators to remain abreast of the issues. It is thus not so costly and more profitable to negotiate directly among themselves and the legislators do.

It is characteristic of many decisional systems to meet rising information and negotiation costs and/or declining exchange values by adopting *de facto* structural rules which call for the actual allocations to be worked out elsewhere. The deference paid legislative committees is a well-known example. Delegation to administrative agencies is another. The "agree bill" phenomenon described by Steiner and Gove,[4] wherein the principal demand groups work out their differences in advance, illustrates a type of self-regulative structural decision. Codification of the criminal code offers still another illustration.

An early president of the American Political Science Association, Paul S. Reinsch, observed many years ago that American legislatures had never been particularly interested in code revision and tended to accept the recommendations of expert commission.[5] He noted that this behavior could be observed as far back as the first thorough-going code revision in this country, which took place in New York in the 1820's under the sponsorship of Governor DeWitt Clinton. The same tendency has been observed somewhat more recently by Heinz in connection with the 1961 Illinois Criminal Code.

The Bar Association Committee responsible for the new Illinois Criminal Code was rather explicitly instructed by leaders of the state legislature that, wherever possible, controversies were to be resolved before the draft code was presented to the legislature. It was understood that compromises or agreements were to be reached with all important groups having serious objections to the draft, so that the legislature could give the matter minimum time and attention and avoid becoming embroiled. And that is what happened. The drafting committee consisted entirely of Chicago lawyers, with the exception of its secretary, Professor Charles Bowman of the University of Illinois School of Law. The result was quite a liberal and progressive code, by any standard, which rather closely followed in many respects the American Law Institute's Model Penal Code. In spite of its liberality, especially in the area of sentencing, the Code sailed through the legislature with a minimum of trouble—and, not coincidentally, a minimum of notice. On the one part of the draft code which gave rise to really serious conflict—the sex crime provisions—the drafting committee worked out a compromise which eliminated the problem before it got to the legislature. The drafters had substantially adopted the view of the Model Penal Code on both homosexuality and abortion—briefly, permitting private, consensual homosexual acts and therapeutic abortion. (These were, of course, very significant changes in the existing law.) The Catholic Church took strong exception to both of these proposals, but especially to the abortion provision. Before the controversy got very far, Professor Bowman sat down with the Church's lobbyist, one Mr. Claire Driscoll, and reached the rather simple agreement that the committee would instead recommend no change in the State's strict laws against abortion, in return for which the Church would cease its opposition to the homosexuality provisions. Both sides kept their agreement, and there was no trouble in the legislature.

Any legislature would have had great difficulty with these delicate issues had they attempted to work out the reallocations of legal status themselves. The structural decision to delegate and ratify was a great deal less costly to achieve and apparently did not cost much in exchange values.

The situation we have just described involved *de facto* delegations of authority by the legislature. In addition, of course, there are many examples of formally more complete and *de jure* delegation, as when a legislature (or a legislature plus the executive) decides to delegate a part of its Constitutional decision-making power to an independent regulatory commission. This kind of policy also appears to reflect the inability of the decisional system to meet the rising costs of making its own allocative policies. Often the demand may have become so intense and diffuse, as it was both for and against railroad regulation in the 1880's,[6] that the legislature throws up its hands in despair. The same kind of thing happens when a patronage-dispensing system, having tired of creating "nine enemies and one ingrate" with every appointment, decides to set up a civil service commission. By taking such action, the decisional system either delays the time when it must choose whom to indulge and whom to deprive, or avoids the choice entirely.

Federal regulatory commissions make both structural or regulatory and allocative policy. Indeed, administrative law recognizes the distinction between the two types of decisions, terming the former "rule making" and the latter "adjudication." The reason why we class rule making as regulatory is obvious—in fact, the legal term is quite descriptive of our definition of the concept "regulatory." Most "adjudication" decisions, on the other hand, are allocative (distributive or redistributive) precisely because they allocate a television channel or an air route or whatever to one applicant rather than another. It is interesting that the Administrative Procedure Act in a sense recognizes and reinforces this pattern by requiring a more cumbersome decision process for rule making than for adjudication. The Act requires more steps in a rule making proceeding, and requires that more people become involved. In short, it invites a fragmentation of demand and makes the decisional process more costly to the interested parties. Thus, the characteristics which we would expect to find in a system producing regulatory policy have in this case been institutionalized by the Act as legal requirements of the system.

It will be apparent that the interpretation pursued here, though formulated independently, is closely akin to that recently presented by Adrian and Press.[7] Their more extended formulation of a cost typology stresses what we here have aggregated under two headings, negotiation costs and information costs. For our purposes, and without disputing the validity of their more detailed formulation, we shall treat most of their other costs as sub-types of our negotiation costs. Adrian and Press use the term information costs but appear to mean something else by it. Our use of information costs stresses information about the *policy* issue rather than, as with them, information about value orderings of other decision-makers. In effect, it is the cost of developing a value or preference ordering for oneself. Information of special relevance to our scheme is that dealing with the predicted impact of alternative allocations upon the objects of the policy: farmers, taxpayers, constituents, persons accused of crime, or whatever. Information costs include the cost to the decision-maker of finding out what, if anything, his constituents want—the cost of determining the exchange value. Adrian and Press do not include exchange values as part of their argument. We think that the value accruing to the legislator from his constituency of making or participating in making a policy choice is clearly a significant and variable part of his implicit calculations.

III

Let us move another step in the argument. From the basic hypothesis—if costs to decision-makers exceed some level, structural decisions will be preferred to allocation decisions—and from the above discussion what corollaries can be deduced? Let us briefly suggest several more to illustrate how the three cost-benefit components are worked into the general argument.

> If demand is strong, relatively stable, and district-specific—*e.g.*, for rivers and harbors improvements—information costs will be low, exchange values high (and costs therefore low), and allocative decisions will be preferred.
>
> The more diffuse the demand, the greater the information costs (and under some conditions exchange values will also be low), and structural decisions, *e.g.*, delegation of authority, will be preferred.
>
> If demand is strong and *ad hoc, i.e.*, confined to one issue and one segment of time rather than continuous and incremental information costs will be high and structural decisions, *e.g.*, granting permissive authority to the *ad hoc* demand group, will be preferred.
>
> The more integrated (cohesive, unified, hierarchical) the decisional system, the lower the negotiation costs, and the more likely allocative decisions will be preferred.
>
> The greater the procedural distance the decision-maker is from the site of the evidentiary record, the greater his information costs, and the more likely a structural or rule decision will be preferred.

Now let us proceed still another step, and, in doing so, forge another link to our original analytic schema. Once the choice is made between an allocative policy and a structural policy what additional *types* of choices are open to decision-makers? Here we would preserve the distinctions offered earlier. Allocative policies may range along a distributive-redistributive continuum. That is, they may distribute the resources in question equally among all the putative objects of policy, or they may distribute in any of a nearly infinite number of unequal ways, or they may redistribute resources so that some policy objects (districts, groups, firms, individuals, nations) are more or less explicitly deprived and others advantaged.

We are prepared to adhere to the earlier hypotheses also regarding the conditions governing the extent of redistribution. That is, redistributive policy is likely to result from relatively high integrated demand operating on a relatively integrated (*i.e.*, where costs of reaching a decision are relatively low in proportion to the exchange values involved) decisional system. Demand integration refers to the unity of the groups demanding a policy decision. It does not refer to mere parallelism of interests, as when many districts desire defense contracts, but requires more explicit and usually organized unity of action pressing for the decision. We would also reassert our earlier contention that in the United

States demand is seldom sufficiently integrated and/or decision costs are seldom low enough to eventuate in much seriously redistributive policy—at least not without side-payments to assuage elements of the demand structure. At the same time, however, much policy has moderately redistributive elements, and a large portion of the policy *proposals* advanced by various contending parties may be highly redistributive.

If the costs of decision are high, and a structural or regulatory decision is chosen, there remains open the question of whether it may be one granting self-regulation to the group whose demands precipitated the decision. Here we would argue, as before, that when the policy objects are heterogeneous, or uncertain, or simply numerous and unorganized, regulatory policy results. Where, however, the object group generates the policy demand, is clearly identified, and highly integrated the likely policy result is to grant the authority to engage in self-regulation. Again the classic case occurs in the area of professional and quasi-professional group licensing. The disputed issues of self-regulation policy are those where a group demands such a delegation of authority to itself, claiming a high degree of integration, only to have the policy-makers perceive additional interests which would be affected and which, while perhaps silent at present, might be provoked into action by such a policy.

Let us represent in diagrammatic form the two fundamental arguments made, the one in Salisbury's earlier paper and the present one. Figure 1 shows both axes representing the degree of fragmentation-integration, one of the demand pattern and one of the decisional system. Figure 2 preserves the vertical axis from Figure 1 but presents the

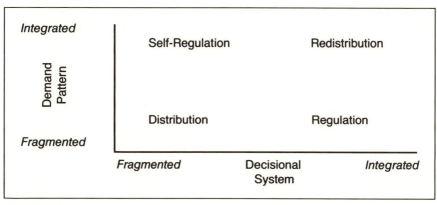

FIGURE 1

variable of decision costs along the horizontal axis. It will be noted that this alters the relationships among policy types along the lines and for the reasons indicated in the previous discussion. Let us turn to some further examples of policy decisions to see how the argument may be useful in organizing data.

IV

A theory of policy formation must, if it is to be comprehensive, account for policies made by all kinds of governmental agencies. Thus far we have concentrated attention on legislative decisions with a brief note on regulatory agencies. Let us now consider the courts with particular reference to criminal law policy.

All courts are relatively highly integrated decisional systems, as compared to legislatures, for example, and thus one might expect all courts to produce allocative policy decisions. But appellate courts, being more remote from the facts in question, ordinarily have higher information costs than do trial courts, and we argue that appellate courts are, consequently, more likely to produce regulatory or structural policy decisions than are trial courts. This is not to say that appellate courts *always* produce regulatory decisions. On the contrary, they produce a good many allocative decisions—as we shall shortly note—and this is consistent with the degree of integration of their decision-making structures.

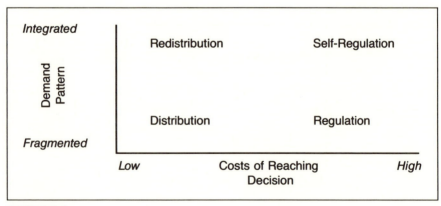

FIGURE 2

But the point is that appellate courts may produce policies of *either* of the two major categories, depending on the level of the information cost to them in a particular case. (Though the same is, of course, true of trial courts, it is less costly for them to produce allocative decisions because they are closer to the facts.)

Perhaps the classic case to illustrate an appellate court's information costs is the United States Supreme Court's decision in *McNabb* v. *United States,* 318 U.S. 332 (1943). A very important step in the development of the law of confessions, that case held that a confession obtained after an unreasonable delay in arraignment could not be used at trial. In his decision for the Court, Justice Frankfurter made the flat statement that the McNabb brothers "were not brought before a United States Commissioner or a judge" during the two days they were held prior to their confessions. He was simply wrong. Though the record was silent on the point, the McNabbs *had,* in fact, been arraigned promptly. Thus, an important Supreme Court decision rested its rationale squarely upon a mistake of fact. (And given the legendary meticulousness and ego of Justice Frankfurter, one can imagine what his reaction must have been— especially since it came relatively early in his years on the Court.) No decision-making body can afford to have very many such incidents come to light, and especially not one where the expectation is so strong that the decisions will reflect a maximum of reason and informed deliberation.

Thus, the U.S. Supreme Court—like all appellate courts—will refuse to decide a case if it feels that the state of the formal record before it does not permit sufficient certainty about the crucial facts. For example, on the final decision day of its October 1967 term (which was June 17, 1968), the Supreme Court announced its dismissal of the writ of certiorari it had previously granted in the case of *Wainwright* v. *New Orleans,* 88 S. Ct. 2243 (1968). That is, after granting certiorari, receiving briefs, and hearing argument, the Court decided that it was not going to decide the case. The reason was succinctly stated by Justice Harlan: "I find this record too opaque to permit any satisfactory adjudication." And Justice Fortas, with whom Justice Marshall joined, said:

> Upon oral argument and further study after the writ was granted it became apparent that the facts necessary for evaluation of the dispositive constitutional issues in this case are not adequately presented by the record before us. It is also entirely clear that they cannot now be developed on remand with any verisimilitude. . . . Our jurisprudence teaches that we should decide issues on the basis of facts of record. (88 S. Ct. at 2244–45)

We would classify the action of the Supreme Court in the *Wainwright* case as a regulatory decision. The policy of "judicial restraint," along with doctrines of "ripeness," "mootness," "comity," "Waiver," and "exhaustion of remedies," are all structural rules the future benefits of which are uncertain.

On the other hand, many of the Supreme Court's most famous and controversial decisions, such as those which have changed the law of criminal procedure (*e.g., Mapp* v. *Ohio, Gideon* v. *Wainwright, Escobedo* v. *Illinois,* and *Miranda* v. *Arizona*), might well be classed as allocative decisions. In those cases, the allocation of many of the benefits and costs was relatively immediate. When what is at stake is whether defendants in all felony cases will receive advice of counsel, a decision requiring that it be provided to them constitutes, in a very real sense, a present allocation of a benefit to defendants (and perhaps the perceived deprivation of some law enforcement groups), even though subsequent action would be necessary before counsel was actually furnished to any particular defendant.

Not all of the great "landmark" cases produce allocative decisions. If the information costs to the court are too great, regulatory decisions will result. And, in fact, it seems likely to us that the information costs in important test cases are generally higher than in the cases that are of more limited significance. Almost by definition, a "test" or "landmark" case is one which is expected to lay down rules *for the future.* And because those cases are perceived to be important and of continuing significance, a premium is placed on knowledge of the probable impact of each of the various decisional options open to the court. In other words, information costs increase.

The matter of exchange values derived by a court is more difficult to ascertain. Without taking part in the discussion the literature offers regarding judicial "constituency" or interest representation, we can observe that judicial role orientations commonly lead to the conclusion that a particular allocation of benefits cannot or should not be avoided. If it were, values of importance to the judges would be lost.

Thus we would argue that in those major cases in which appellate courts render allocative decisions, they (1) feel that they have secured the necessary information (perhaps at high cost), and or (2) feel that the benefits to be derived from an allocative decision outweigh the information costs. The "Brandeis brief" sometimes used in major cases (and *only* in major cases), and the numerous *amicus curiae* briefs offered and received in such cases, may be regarded as an attempt to meet high information costs. Moreover, the U.S. Supreme Court's opinions in cases like *Miranda* v. *Arizona* or *Brown* v. *Board of Education* are typically at pains to demonstrate that the Court is informed of all the facts of the social context relevant to its decision—in other words, that it has met the information costs. Conversely, where the information is inaccessible and the court does not feel that the benefits are sufficiently high, a court will not render an allocative decision, but will instead usually avoid deciding the issue—"judicial restraint," again, being a regulatory decision. For example, the U.S. Supreme Court's opinion in *Witherspoon* v. *Illinois*, 88 S. Ct. 1770, 1774–75 (1968), refused to decide the more sweeping of the two issues presented to it:

> The data adduced by the petitioner . . . are too tentative and fragmentary to establish that jurors not opposed to the death penalty tend to favor the prosecution in the determination of guilt. We simply cannot conclude, either on the basis of the record now before us or as a matter of judicial notice, that the exclusion of jurors opposed to capital punishment results in an unrepresentative jury on the issue of guilt or substantially increases the risk of conviction. In light of the presently available information we are not prepared to announce a *per se* constitutional rule requiring the reversal of every conviction returned by a jury selected as this one was. [*Justice Stewart writing for the Court.*]

Trial courts, of course, also make regulatory or structural decisions— when they decline to take jurisdiction of an action, for example. As with appellate courts, we would argue that they do so when their costs, including information costs, are higher than the benefits they would anticipate from an allocative decision. Many judges have been dubious about the value to them and their self-images of entering certain controversial "political thickets." This may have been the situation when the United States District Court in Chicago dismissed a civil suit brought by Dr. Jeremiah Stamler against the House Un-American Activities Committee. In that case, Dr. Stamler had been cited for contempt by HUAC, and he was asking for a declaratory judgment enjoining further proceedings by the Committee. The District Court rested its dismissal of the action on an extension of the Constitutional provision (Art. I, § 6) that Members of Congress cannot be held answerable in court for "any speech or debate in either House." The issue which had been raised, of course, was whether HUAC's proceedings constituted *legitimate* official action.

The more typical, run-of-the-mill trial court action, on the other hand, seems to us more likely to result in an allocative decision—either

distributive or redistributive. Let us take as an example the lowly traffic
court (assuming *arguendo* that the decisions which result can be called
"policy"). The traffic court is a quite highly integrated decisional system.
The decisions are made by a single magistrate who has a very large degree of discretion—usually, no transcript is made of the proceedings, so
the magistrate does not even have to worry about the potentiality of an
appellate court looking over his shoulder. The rules of procedure are
notoriously loose. The defendant is usually not represented by counsel;
somewhat more often an Assistant State's Attorney is present. Thus, in
the typical case, the only persons present in court are the magistrate, a
clerk, the defendant, other defendants in other cases, the complaining
police officers, and perhaps a State's Attorney. The traffic court decisional system is thus highly integrated—and the demand pattern is too,
at least when the defendant is not represented by counsel. When the defendant does not have counsel, little attention or weight is typically given
to whatever he may have to say. Thus, all of the effective demand is from
the State, for his conviction. And the result in the vast majority of cases
is a redistributive decision, depriving the defendant of money and
awarding it to the state. But if we introduce a defense counsel into the
system, the result often changes dramatically. The demand pattern is
more fragmented, and the decisions tend to be more distributive—*e.g.*,
the defendant may still be found guilty but given a suspended sentence,
or, instead of receiving a stiff fine or a license suspension, the defendant
may be sentenced to go to traffic school.

The same is true of more serious criminal cases—misdemeanors and
felonies. Very few criminal cases result in structural decisions which have
any future effect. It is almost always a matter of deciding how to apply
well-settled rules (regulatory policies) to the facts of a particular case.
Something over seventy-five percent of all criminal defendants are convicted. And only a very small percentage of the total convictions are appealed. Thus, relatively few criminal cases ever reach the stage where
the decisions are "reported" or have precedential value. Most criminal
case decisions, then, lack future effect, and we would class them as allocative. These decisions may be either distributive or redistributive.

It does not often happen that a criminal trial court decides a case in
a way that is redistributive in favor of the defendant—*i.e.*, a trial court
does not often release a defendant who is regarded by the prosecution as
"obviously guilty" of a serious crime. In our view, it is no accident that
the decisions which raise the outcry that criminals are being turned
loose typically come from appellate courts (and the outcry then may be

raised even though the decision is not redistributive in favor of the defendant, but instead "regulates" the police, or is distributive when the State felt entitled to a redistributive result in its favor). Thus, when a trial court reaches a redistributive result in a criminal case, it is usually redistributive in favor of the prosecution. The defendant may certainly be deprived, and the prosecution may even be benefited in a very real sense—*e.g.*, the State's Attorney gets a good conviction record.

In explaining why trial court decisions in criminal cases may often be redistributive in favor of the State, but seldom in favor of the defendant, we would point again to the variable of the presence or absence of defense counsel. (The demands of the State may also vary in criminal cases, of course, and if the State reaches an agreement with the defendant, as in a negotiated plea situation, a distributive result may be expected.) *Gideon* v. *Wainwright*, 372 U.S. 335 (1963), may be viewed as a recognition of the fact that defendants tend to get lighter sentences when they are represented by counsel. And the research recently completed by Vaughan Stapleton and others on the effect of counsel in juvenile delinquency proceedings—comparing the treatment of juveniles represented by counsel with that of an unrepresented control group—confirms that observation even in a court which is in theory the "friend" of the defendants before it. Again, in our terms, the presence of defense counsel tends to fragment demand and to produce a more distributive policy result.

V

Let us finally attempt to illustrate our scheme applying it to a larger policy array—the major pieces of agricultural legislation proposed or passed, of the past twenty years. The initial task before us is to specify the major criteria by which to differentiate our several policy types. This we do in the following way, noting, of course, that many ambiguities and uncertainties remain:

Redistributive Policy

Establishment of price support program

Reduction or increase in mandatory price support levels

Significant changes in groups covered when changes are controversial among the groups affected

Limitations in level of support payment ceilings

Distributive Policy

Addition of groups covered or benefited by program without inter-group conflict

Addition of program components of broadly applicable expected benefit, *e.g.*, soil bank and diversion payments, certain research programs, credit facilities expansion, etc.

Extension of existing programs for short terms, one to three years, so as to maintain the status quo, usually in the face of impending redistribution of resources previously authorized but not yet implemented

Limitation of time covered by authorization to not more than three years in order to leave open the option to renegotiate in Congress the existing benefit distribution

Regulative Policy

Policies which vest discretionary authority in the Secretary of Agriculture to raise or lower price supports, to adjust acreage, or to sell surplus commodities without specific criteria to guide his decisions in these areas, so long as the discretion can in fact be used in either direction, up or down.

Policies which establish study groups to make recommendations on future policy.

Self-Regulative Policy

Policies which vest discretionary authority in farmers generally, or in commodity or geographical groups, to establish quotas, eligibilities, acreage allotments, benefit levels, or other benefit components.

The initial establishment of a farm price support program in 1933 was a substantially redistributive policy, taking resourcs from some groups in the population and allocating them to various classes of farmers. This result is in accord with our theoretical expectations since for a brief period farm group demand was highly integrated while the First Hundred Days presented an unusually integrated (low cost) decisional setting. Subsequent policy decisions have generally been distributive, however, as the diverse farm groups jockeyed for position. Controversy has centered on the level, range, and commodity coverage of supports; the extent and severity of growing and marketing controls; and on the range and impact of additional benefit programs to farmers. These conflicts have involved party, administration, and congressional leaders, farm organizations, and commodity groups. During the 1950's the heart of the policy issue was high rigid v. flexible support policy, but many additional dimensions have entered the debate and we will try only to hint at some of these, showing how our theoretical argument leads us to view this tangled political struggle. From 1933 at least until 1961 the Administrations quite consistently proposed redistributive agricultural policies, varying in the extent of redistribution envisioned, in the particular groups to be benefited by the proposed reallocation of resources, in the strategies and alliances employed and the willingness to accommodate divergent groups, and in success. Beginning in 1961, and off and on since then, administration proposals have tended to include substantial regulatory and, perhaps, self-regulatory elements in an effort to escape the impasse over conflicting redistributive proposals[8] and, at the same time the growing money cost of farm programs and the threat of drastic redistribution implied by that cost.

Throughout most of this period we find that most of the key components of the Congressional system, especially in the House, and especially, of course, in the Agriculture Committee of the House, were strongly oriented toward distributive policy outcomes. For much of the period the Senate was more receptive to the introduction of flexible, *i.e.,* lower, support levels, but there, too, the price was often temporary deferment of lower supports or special treatment for one or more key commodities. Key legislators consistently defended the particular commodity interests of their constituents, and they were reasonably clear about the relationships between those interests and the policy issues under consideration. Their information costs were not high, therefore, and the benefit they perceived to accrue to them from effective constituency representative was substantial.

Had all or most farm groups generally shared the same policy interests there might have been relatively little difficulty in assembling the necessary votes to pass broadly distributive or even pro-farmer redistributive bills in Congress, regardless of what the USDA and the President desired. But in fact, from the 1940's on these interests conflicted rather than united. The Farm Bureau and Farmers Union split; the Farm Bureau itself lost internal cohesion; commodity interests competed; regions with different commodity patterns developed conflicting interests. The proliferation of specialized policy interests accordingly made it increasingly difficult to organize a majority coalition for any program or package of programs in Congress. The growing fragmentation of demand, given the close and continuing linkage of commodity groups and representatives, thus increased the negotiation costs within the decisional system.

Yet this development, important though it is, should not be regarded as operating in isolation. Had it done so we would expect to observe a slow but steady growth of difficulty in assembling majorities to pass distributive polices, perhaps with the resultant policy vacuum filled by Administration efforts at securing regulatory authority to control farm policy administratively. To some extent the Eisenhower Administration consciously followed such a strategy, exacerbating commodity conflicts in order to secure greater discretion in dealing with surpluses. But the commodityization of farm policy demand has been greatly complicated by the concomitant partisanization of demand. Increasingly during the 1950's and still strongly in the 60's party unity has been striking in congressional voting on major farm legislation. Particularly has this been true of Republicans who on several occasions have demonstrated complete unanimity. Republican unity, usually in behalf of redistributive farm policy in the form of reduced controls and supports has been countered by substantial Democratic cohesion on the other side of the high rigid v. low flexible support issue that dominated farm policy debate for most of the Eisenhower years. But Democratic unity was, and is, less complete and much less committed to any particular redistributive policy line. Rather, the several key commodity groups, many led by influential Southerners, tended to negotiate distributive policy compromises, including on occasion benefits for urban Democrats to such as food stamps and promises on minimum wage bills. Democratic unity was problematic nearly every year depending on what agreement could be worked out and on how much leverage Republican opposition or a Republican administration might have. But in one way or another the Democratic majority was able to conclude agreements leading to policies that were mainly distributive. Democratic efforts at redistribution were vetoed by the President; Republican proposals were stymied in Congress; distributive compromises were passed. The only change in the 1960's was that Administration and Congressional majority were on the same side. The former sought to interject regulatory policy elements but generally settled for more distributive results. The greatest regulatory achievement was perhaps the four-year time period covered by the 1965 Food and Agriculture Act, longer than any previous authorization and thus giving more time for the Administration to seek administrative solutions to farm problems.

The persistence of distributive policies in agriculture has often been attributed to the strength of "the farm bloc," a mythical body of congressmen representing farm interests and organizations who allegedly get together on a bipartisan basis to secure subsidies and related goodies from an apathetic majority. In fact, farm policy disputes, since the Brannan Plan was proposed in 1949, have been highly partisan, major farm organizations have disagreed violently and consistently about most questions, and commodity interests have had a hard time to negotiate compromises among their divergent and often conflicting positions. Farm policy has remained so largely distributive because (1) non-farm Congressmen have generally opted out of the issue; exchange values derived from farm issues for them are low and information costs are high so they adopt a rule policy of party unity in support of whatever position their leadership, Administration or legislative, develops; (2) Democratic legislators from farm regions tend to dominate the relevant committees; they derive high exchange value from farm issues and have correlative low information costs; this balance is so strong that they are fully prepared to pay the very high costs of negotiating with one another to reach that agreement necessary for decision. Party unity or Administration support rules adopted by neutral congressmen greatly reduce the negotiating costs but the inter- and intra-commodity conflicts still make these high for Congress as a whole. Nevertheless, the exchange values are so great that the price is acceptable. That this continues to be true is partly the result of the fact that agricultural production is so fully bounded by geographical space. More than almost any other industry the specialized interests of, say, durum wheat or long-staple cotton producers have specific geographical referents and these are closely linked to the boundaries of legislative constituencies. Moreover, the demand for assistance to farmers through governmental programs has been strong and nearly continuous for decades, not always for the same programs but for policies adapted to the changing technology and economic structures of agriculture. The continuity of demands keeps information costs relatively low and the dynamic character of the industry maintains the exchange value to the congressmen of regular efforts at making new policy. And the geography of farming, specialized to locale, accentuates the exchange values as it reduces information costs. If agricultural production were to grow more sophisticated and flexible, as it has done to some extent, it might lose some of this geographical specialization and render the exchange values of legislators more uncertain. If a farm congressman found himself unable to determine what kind of program his constituents wanted, or if he was unable to discover any policy alternative he thought would do them any good, he might accept administrative regulation more readily.

Our model predicts that regulatory policy will result when demand is fragmented or diffuse and the costs of making allocative policy decisions are too high. Acceptance of party unity, Administration support or agriculture Committee leadership are all types of *de facto* decision rules that illustrate the point for some legislators within Congress, and the modest step toward granting the Secretary of Agriculture the authority to affect market prices by selling surpluses on the grain market is a example in substantive policy. But rule or structure decisions may also be self-regulatory if operative demand has sufficient unity and there are illustrations of this available too in recent farm politics. One was the Administration proposal in 1961 that commodity groups be organized to create their own programs which when certified by the Secretary of Agriculture would become operative unless vetoed by Congress within sixty days. The proposal foundered, partly because congressmen were still unwilling to delegate their authority and lose the exchange values and partly because commodity groups were neither so clear cut nor so unified as to be able readily to regulate themselves. Indeed, critics of the proposal alleged that because of the lack of definition among commodity groups it would be the USDA which would really make the policies, *i.e.*, it would be regulatory not self-regulatory. Another recent current of activity which aims at self-regulation is the NFO with its drive for collective bargaining between farmers and processors. NFO is explicitly opposed to government farm programs for purposes other than those necessary to permit the bargaining process to function, but they too depend on unity among farmers, *i.e.*, integrated demand, in order to make self-regulation of this type work to their advantage.

VI

Efforts at conceptualization often and properly may be faulted for their lack of specific indicators by which to test whether the formulation is merely an engaging metaphor or a genuine step toward empirical theory. We acknowledge our vulnerability on this score. We have been concerned to explicate and illustrate our schema in the hope that it will seem both plausible and useful as a device to order a wide variety of policy data. In so doing we have incorporated a number of rather familiar propositions from the lore of political science—regarding delegation of authority, for example—and clothed them in language that places them into more contemporary modes of analysis. But this is not the same thing as utilizing unambiguous measures to test the hypotheses advanced. We must be content by pointing, if a bit lamely, to two elements of research strategy which our formulation indicates to be critical. One is that empirical research pursuant to our argument must concentrate much attention on the specification of decision costs. Here we are at one with an important current of the discipline, most recently exemplified by Adrian and Press. Secondly, our analysis points to an approach to the analysis of constituency—decision-maker interaction in terms that may be both feasible and fruitful; namely, in terms of exchange values derived from particular policy issues. Patterns of demand which are district-specific on the one hand, or diffuse on the other, continuous or *ad hoc,* and so on, represent potentially measurable ways of getting at this issue which has so often proved intractable to political scientists. We would simply conclude by voicing our agreement with the position that unless and until empirical specification is possible our schema remains in that overpopulated category of inelegant literature, the exploratory essay.

NOTES

1. Most of this literature is well known to students of public policy analysis. Theodore Lowi, "American Business, Public Policy, Case-Studies and Political Science," *World Politics* (July, 1964), 677–715; Lewis A. Froman, Jr., "An Analysis of Public Policies in Cities," *Journal of Politics* (February, 1967); Richard E. Dawson and James Robinson, "Inter-Party Competition, Economic Variables, and Welfare Policies in the American States," *Journal of Politics,* 25 (May, 1963), 265–89; Richard I. Hofferbert, "Ecological Development and Policy Change in the American States," *Midwest Journal of Political Science* (November, 1966), 464–86; Hofferbert, "The Relation Between Public Policy and Some Structural and Environmental Variables," *APSR,* 60 (March, 1966), 73–82; Thomas R. Dye, *Politics, Economics, and the Public: Policy Outcomes in the American States* (Chicago: Rand McNally, 1966); Ira Sharkansky, "Economic Development, Regionalism and State Political Systems," *Midwest Journal of Political Science* (February, 1968), 41–62.

2. John C. Wahlke, "Public Policy and Representative Government: The Role of the Represented" (paper presented to the Seventh World Congress of the International Political Science Association, Brussels, September, 1967).

3. "The Analysis of Public Policy: A Search for Theories and Rules," *Political Science and Public Policy,* ed. Austin Ranney (Chicago: Markham, 1968).

4. Gilbert Y. Steiner and Samuel K. Gove, *Legislative Politics in Illinois* (Urbana: University of Illinois Press, 1960).

5. *American Legislatures and Legislative Methods* (New York: Century, 1907), pp. 316–17 and 322–23.

6. J. J. Hillman, *Competition and Railroad Price Discrimination—Legal Precedent and Economic Policy* (1968), describes the deliberate ambiguity of the Interstate Commerce Act as a device adopted to unload a conflict Congress could not resolve.

7. Charles Adrian and Charles Press, "Decision Costs in Coalition Formation," *APSR* (June, 1968), 556–64.

8. Robert Eyestone examined farm policies of the past thirty-odd years and attempted to classify House Committee Reports according to criteria somewhat similar to ours. He, too, finds a significant increase in regulatory and self-regulative proposals over time though he interprets this finding in terms that are quite different from ours. "The Life Cycle of American Public Policies: Agriculture and Labor Policy Since 1929" (paper presented to the Midwest Political Science Association, May, 1968).

6

Why No Corporatism in America?

In the early 1970s, after President Nixon had created tripartite machinery to bring labor, business, and government together to try to halt inflation, several scholars proclaimed that the corporate state had arrived in America (Fusfeld, 1972: 1–20; Peterson, 1974: 483–506). For the most part it was the strength of corporate business in the circles of decision that most impressed these observers, but the new institutional arrangements were taken to be confirming evidence of corporatist tendencies stretching back through World War II, the National Recovery Administration, all the way to Theodore Roosevelt. But the evidence quickly disintegrated. Official labor-management collaboration in an incomes policy was ended and the machinery abandoned. Part of the reason could be found in the curious weakness of those peak associations that would be expected, in a corporatist system, to play crucial roles. Despite the temptations to seek unity major sectoral groups remained divided.

In January 1977, a small newspaper item announced that the national Association of Manufacturers and the US Chamber of Commerce had suspended talks about the possible merger of their two organizations. Later in the Spring, accompanying the accession of Douglas Fraser to the presidency of the United Auto Workers were speculations about whether the union would now reenter the AFL-CIO. These two stories were among the recent examples of a phenomenon that has long been known but not much examined; peak interest group associations in

Reprinted with permission from Philippe Schmitter and Gerhard Lehmbruch, eds., *Trends Toward Corporatist Intermediation* (Beverly Hills, Calif.: Sage Publications, 1979), pp. 213–31.

the United States have great difficulty achieving enough comprehensiveness of membership to be able effectively to represent their respective sectors in the political process. The analysis of this condition provides the basis for this paper.

To begin, let us say what we mean by the notion of peak association. Comparativists may not think there is much difficulty here. In Britain such groups as the National Farmers Union, the Confederation of British Industries, or the Trades Union Congress include some 80–90 percent of their respective potential members. In West Germany the *Spitzenverbände* must be consulted in drafting legislative proposals. And elsewhere in Western Europe the phenomenon is not only familiar, it is a critical organizational ingredient in the emergence of what Schmitter calls societal corporatism. But in the United States it is not quite so clear which organizations are the "peaks," and so we must seek definition for our term.

It turns out that the interest group literature does not provide much help. The term "peak association" is used, often in passing, by such scholars as Key (1964) and Eldersveld (1958). It is employed as an important part of his analysis by Wooten (1970). But none of these writers defines the words very clearly, and Eldersveld seems to imply that he thinks the notion is unclear. My own previous comments concerning "peak associations" are brief but nearly all of what there is. I suggested that the term referred to "sector-wide organizations which embrace a comprehensive array of constituent sector organizations" (Salisbury, 1975: 187). This is a reasonable beginning but uncertainties remain. First, it is not clear what is meant by saying that a peak association is composed of other organizations. Indeed, the entire notion of group membership itself is far more ambiguous than is commonly realized. For instance, in the National League of Cities the unit of membership can be either the individual city or the state leagues of municipalities. The American Trucking Associations include both individual firms and specialized associations. And the National Association of Manufacturers has several different kinds of membership. Moreover, there is a considerable difference between a group like the American Farm Bureau Federation, a federation of state farm bureaus, and the Consumer Federation of America, an amalgam of over two hundred very diverse kinds of organizations. Yet both are "organizations of organizations."

A second uncertainty arises over the definition of sector. The term is most commonly employed to refer to the major sections of economic self-interest in modern industrial society; labor, business, and agriculture. What is unclear is how many such sectional or producer groups should be designated as sectors without destroying the meaning of the term. What of the professions? A good case can be made for including medicine, law, and education as sectors. Each is reasonably well-bounded. Each has an "interest," a stake in society and in public policy. In recent years the "PIGs," the Public Interest Groups which include public official organizations of mayors, governors, counties, and the like, have certainly emerged as a self-interest set with clear stakes in public policy [Stanfield, 1976]. The Nader groups and Common Cause are probably outside the definition. So perhaps are the environmentalists. Consumers are a borderline case. We need not come to a definitive position on the matter; only indicate the fuzziness of the boundary.

Let us attempt a definition. *A peak association is an organization which purports, and is taken, to speak for a particular sector of society.* The term leaves out those groups who defend the public interest, for they deny a "selfish" sectoral concern. The term sector is intended to apply to larger rather than smaller slices of society. Neither the petroleum industry nor Texas constitutes a sector in this sense. The definitions involves a reciprocal relationship. A group cannot simply declare itself to be the spokesman of a sector. It must be acknowledged to be so by those to whom it speaks; decision makers, elites more generally, or the broad public. Once the notion of audience response is taken into account, it makes the concept probabilistic rather than definitional. An organization may be acknowledged as the legitimate representative of a sector by some elites but not others. It may be supposed that there are threshold points beyond which a group achieves the status of peak association, and these points are located at the intersection of the organization's actual hegemony in its sector—density of membership, absence of intra-sector rivals, forceful assumption of sector leadership—and the recognition of that hegemony by the relevant "others." Presumably, the greater the hegemony, the fuller the recognition. But the opposite is also true. By conferring recognition on a group as the rightful spokesman of a sector, policy makers may greatly enhance its actual dominance. Indeed, it appears that many of the peak associations in Western Europe reached their hegemonic status with major contributions from the more or less official recognition by key government agencies, especially in the bureaucracy.

In the United States, however, it has been unusual for official recognition to be granted any organized interest group, and it has been even more rare for such recognition to be given to groups purporting to speak for an entire sector. There are some examples, however, and let us note them. One of the best known is the support given through the Extension Service to the formation and continuing strength of the American Farm Bureau Federation (Block, 1960). It took decades for this connection to be severed, and during at least part of the time from the Bureau's establishment in 1919 until the late 1940s there were many, inside of government and out, who asserted or acknowledged the Bureau's suzerainty (McConnell, 1953). Yet all the while the Grange and the Farmer's Union existed as general farm organizations open to all kinds of farmers, and when there was a major consultation with USDA or Congress about farm policy they too were included (Campbell, 1962). From the time of the Brannan Plan in 1949 until 1977 the dominant motif of American farm politics was partisan division with each party joined together in close working relationship with a general farm organization, Democrats with the Farmers Union and Republicans with the AFBF (Key, 1964: 159; Heinz, 1962: 952–78). Even though the latter was much the largest, it could hardly be regarded as a peak organization when its access depended so heavily on having Republicans in power. And periodic efforts to transcend the partisan division by establishing ad hoc coalitions of farm organizations have all quickly failed as the coalitions find themselves unable to contain the centrifugal forces generated by diverse and conflicting farm interests.

Another substantive area has witnessed several efforts of federal government officials to encourage the formation of interest groups (Zeigler, 1964: 94–109; Fainsod et al., 1959: 467). First during World War I, again under Secretary of Commerce Hoover in the 20s, during the NRA period of 1933–35, and in World War II trade associations were organized with the active support of government, primarily in order to assist in the administration of federal regulatory programs. At other times federal policy has sought to restrict trade association activities, too, of course, but even during the periods of encouragement there was no sustained move to support or consult with groups that purported to speak for all of industry. Organizational recognition was confined to the level of the specific industry. When Washington officials wanted to acknowledge the importance of business (or labor) as a whole, to confer symbolic recognition, and to consult with private interests about public policy they worked with individuals, like William Knudsen and Sidney Hillman, whom they, the officials, not the sector organizations, chose (Blum, 1976).

A case for full peak status might be made for the AFL-CIO. Certainly since the 1955 merger there has been no rival organization in a position to speak on behalf of all of organized labor. Nevertheless, when compared, say, to the TUC, several points of difference appear. For one, in the 1970s the AFL-CIO included only about 75 percent of unionized workers who consist, in turn, of less than one-fourth of the total work force. Moreover, any labor group that does not include the auto workers, the teamsters, or the mine workers must stand in stark contrast to the TUC in which the three equivalent unions are among the most significant. AFL-CIO hegemony is further reduced by its declining rate of success in winning representation elections. This is not meant to dismiss them as unimportant. George Meany certainly had a significant voice in national policy discussions, and Andrew Biemiller led what was widely regarded as among the most skilled lobbying crews in Washington (Singer, 1976). But neither lobbying strength nor electioneering clout was sufficient to assure the AFL-CIO of a decisive, officially acknowledged, voice on labor questions. It is the President who selects the Secretary of Labor and other labor representatives on official bodies, not the AFL-CIO, even when a Democrat is in the White House.

A final example of the difficulties of sustaining peak association status in the United States can be drawn from medicine. When Oliver Garceau's splendid study was published in 1941 there was little doubt of the AMA's dominance over the "medical profession in politics" (Garceau, 1941). This remained largely true through the 1950s. But it is not true any longer. Rival organizations of doctors have been formed, and other groups with different interests, such as the hospital administrators, have emerged to contest with the AMA for position and power in health policy making.

Thus peak associations in the United States are either weak and incomplete or ineffectual. None can claim quasi-monopolistic hegemony over a significant sector of socio-economic self-interest. Consequently, the United States lacks an essential ingredient of a corporatist polity, "a limited number of singular, compulsory, noncompetitive, hierarchically ordered and functionally differentiated categories" (Schmitter, 1974: 93–4). Now there is a long tradition among American intellectuals that asks, "Why no Socialism in America?" (Laslett and Lipset, eds., 1974). To that query, or perhaps instead of it, we now would ask, "Why no corporatism in America?" I propose to approach this question from three quite different perspectives: one, macro-social; two, in terms of the patterns of public policy; and three, as a problem in organizational analysis.

Social Diversity and Institutional Fragmentation

Perhaps the most immediate and common response to the question of "Why no corporatism?" would be the one that harks back to the *Federalist Papers* and identifies two interrelated factors, social diversity and institutional fragmentation, as primarily responsible. The relative extent of social diversity and its effects in American life can be argued. Beer and Sapolsky, for instance, both point out that British agriculture is also diverse in commodity interest, yet successfully brought under a single organizational tent (Beer, 1958: 130–140; Sapolsky, 1968: 355–76). How much diversity is too much to contain? To the element of heterogeneity one may add that of sheer size. Compared to the nations of Western Europe the physical scope and diversity of the United States is immense. This is undoubtedly true, yet corporate concentrations of power have emerged, despite the anti-trust laws, in sufficient proportion to suggest that American heterogeneity can be overcome by skillful entrepreneurs.

A variant on the diversity factor, and one of considerable interest, is presented by those who contend that the pace and timing of socio-economic growth significantly affects the prospects for corporatist organization. At one end of the spectrum we find Sweden with its rapid and nationwide advance into mature industrialism. The United States is surely close to the other end (Sharkansky, 1975). Industrialization struck New England a century and a half before it reached many parts of the South or West; today, while Utah, Wyoming, and Montana emerge as fuel-rich industrial sites, the Northeast attempts to shore up its sagging employment prospects. The unevenness of growth is not confined to a single period of history. The late-starting sections do not eventually catch up and smooth out the differences. The Old South may become part of the Sun Belt, but Phoenix remains different from Savannah in the values and interests of those who live there.

Within any given sector, therefore, the tensions among competing groups will be greater and more difficult to reconcile to the extent that historical socio-economic growth and development has been distributed geographically in uneven pattern. If the historical pattern has been uneven, it will continue to be. Moreover, this tendency will be greatly accentuated if political institutions are designed to accommodate this spatially distributed diversity. And this is what American institutions are preeminently designed to do. The structural elements are familiar; federalism, separation of powers, legislators nominated and elected from single-member districts. The elements interact to perpetuate the pattern where groups have multiple access points and governmental officials find it extremely difficult to assemble enough authority to act on a comprehensive scale, whether it involves enacting policy or negotiating with a socio-economic sector. At the same time, the continued existence of dispersed centers of authority provides opportunities for influence to interest groups which are similarly organized in a fragmented, geographically dispersed manner (Truman, 1951; McConnell, 1966). Simply to illustrate the familiar point: if lawyers are able to affect the selection of judges and the development of procedural rules at the state level for state courts, the need to act on a national basis is much reduced and the ability of the ABA to mobilize the legal profession is likewise reduced.

If federalism makes it difficult, or unnecessary, for a sector to be mobilized on a nationwide basis, so all the devices for fragmenting governmental authority make it difficult, or impossible, to assemble the capacity to act in a focused and forceful fashion. The other side of the corporatism equation is "the state," an entity capable of recognizing, licensing, or creating a peak association and then bargaining with it in a substantively meaningful way. But in the United States no such monistic state exists in any real behavioral sense. The Department of Agriculture cannot meaningfully engage in an annual price review, even if there were an agreed spokesman for agriculture (Self and Storing, 1962), because neither that bureaucracy nor the administration of which it is a part can commit "the state" to a specific course of action except within a very narrow range. Congress has not allowed it even in its most extreme moments of delegation of authority. HHS cannot exercise even its delegated authority over universities or the medical profession without multiple end runs immediately going to Congress to mitigate the effects of the order. Corporatism is a form of collective bargaining. In the United States there is no party, on any side, with enough authority to bargain effectively and commit a sectorwide following to accept the result.

It is instructive to note that the partial exceptions to this statement have mainly occurred during emergencies. The extensive (and, as the Supreme Court ruled in the Schecter case, excessive) corporatist delegation contained in the NIRA was a response to the Depression. Trade association formation and cooperative bargaining flourished also during the wars, especially in conjunction with administering wage and price control. But even national emergencies have not suppressed for long the centrifugal tendencies built into America's governing institutions. And yet, governmental arrangements are, after all, subject to change. Public policy might have overcome the tendency toward fission. The mere existence of fragmented institutional structures does not guarantee their persistence, though it helps. Corporatist institutional possibilities might have been established by law, as they were in a good many countries after World War II. In the United States the functional need for a "stable, bourgeois-dominant regime" was surely as compelling as in other industrialized democracies (Schmitter, 1974). But policy has not moved that direction. Why not?

Interest Group Legitimacy

The factors adduced already surely help to account for the predominant thrust of public policy. The central point to be added here is this. An important reason the American public policy has not enhanced corporatist tendencies is that monopolistic interest groups are regarded with deep suspicion in the American political culture.[1] It may seem absurd, at first blush, to suggest that in the United States, where interest group analysis was, in a sense, invented and given its most enthusiastic hearing, where associational membership has been the very hallmark of national character, the legitimacy of interest group activity is less than it is in other democratic systems. Nevertheless, it is the case.

First, we offer as evidence the point made earlier; namely, there is virtually no official incorporation of formal associations as participants in policy discussions. They are not invited to designate sector representatives on governmental advisory bodies, or to name key policy makers who are to deal with their sector. There have, of course, been occasional advisory relationships, such as the ABA's role in "clearing" judicial appointments (Grossman, 1965). And we are in no way suggesting that groups have less *informal* influence in the United States than elsewhere. We shall comment on this aspect later. Here our point is only that their formal position is negligible.

A corollary to this is that bureaucrats in America deal directly with constituent units, not with associations. HHS negotiates with individual hospitals or universities, not with the organizations of hospitals or universities. The Defense Department does not contract with the Aerospace Industries Association but with individual firms. It is specific unions which must conform to pension fund regulations, and the AFL-CIO does not formally intervene.

A second piece of evidence bearing on the legitimacy issue is the amount of official regulation of group activity. We do not have a comprehensive survey on the matter, but it seems clear that no democratic nation even remotely approximates the seriousness of the American effort to regulate the details of group-government interactions. For a long time scholars seemed to believe that this was because there was so little group activity in other systems, but once interest groups were discovered abroad some two decades ago that illusion was swept away.

Lobbying regulation in America plainly rests on a deep suspicion of organized groups and of the probable consequences for the polity of their activities. This same suspicion permeates significant fragments of the academic community. In political science the heirs to the progressive tradition characteristically regarded interst groups as the enemy of the public interest.[2] Schattschneider, Lowi, and a rather disparate array of latter-day anti-pluralists have kept this perspective very much alive (Schattschneider, 1960; Lowi, 1969). The point is that an anti-group orientation is widely diffused through the American polity, and it permeates both textbook literature and newspaper editorials. The organizational success of Common Cause, itself an interest group to be sure, cannot be understood apart from this profound conviction that organized interest groups are not fully legitimate participants in the processes of government.

Why, then, is this so? The matter can be approached from at least two directions. One is that fount of so much interpretation of American politics; John Locke, Louis Hartz and the Liberal Tradition (Hartz, 1955). The argument is that American political culture is so rooted in individualist assumptions that groups have no integral place. Our theorists and publicists have sustained a mythic structure that was created in order to undermine an older corporatism of post-feudal Europe.

> [I]t is clear enough why the democratic image these men gave us should be hostile to half of the machinery that was later invented to make democracy work. . . . Seeking to emancipate men from the rigid pluralism of church, guild, and province, those thinkers were bound to be "individualists." How could they say, even if they understood the fact, that democracy itself would function through a new pluralism of associations, parties, and groups (Hartz, 1960: 13–14).

Presthus is one of the very few who has recognized how hostile American political culture is toward organizing groups as policymaking participants [1974]. He regards Canada as possessing substantially more

of a corporatist value orientation, though the empirical data he develops
are not entirely compatible with this interpretation.[3] But we need not
rest the argument entirely on the elusive variable of political culture.[4]

Tentatively, I would suggest that group legitimacy and group hegemony are mutually interdependent. What makes an organization the legitimate spokesman for a socio-economic sector? Confidence that the
organization is representative of the values, opinions, and interests
(which terms may all mean the same thing) of the members of that sector. How can we be confident of this? From evidence that the organization encompasses a substantial portion of the sector in either actual or
virtual membership; from evidence that the organization's leaders are
not embroiled in internal conflicts over policy (Truman, 1951: 84; Masters et al., 1964); from the existence of procedures, such as elections or
referenda, that give some reason to suppose the leadership to be reasonably representative of the membership. There are examples of this
kind of unity/legitimacy which, in turn, results in a very impressive accumulation of group influence, albeit informal, over policy (Masters et
al., 1964; Bailey et al., 1963). But in the United States these cases are
rare and generally rather fragile. The overwhelming tendency is for
membership to be fractional, cohesion to be threatened, and representatives to be very doubtful. Hence, no legitimacy. Hence, no corporatist
role.

The importance of the legitimacy dimension is that it makes it highly
unlikely that American public policy will move in a corporatist direction,
granting privileged access to particular organizations so that they gain
enough organizing advantages to achieve quasi-monopolistic status vis-
à-vis their respective sectors.[5] This being so, the only way for a corporatist system to develop would be for would-be peak associations to
achieve hegemonic status through their own organizational processes.

Peak Association and Organizational Exchange

If it is up to organized groups to make themselves into legitimate peak
associations, what would they need to do? To consider this question we
employ the analytical framework that Mancur Olson and others have
used to think about interest groups generally (Olson, 1965; Salisbury,
1969). The would-be peak must offer prospective members selective
benefits, unavailable outside the peak organizations, which are sufficiently appealing to induce a large proportion of the sector involved to

join. (We pass over Olson's other possibilities, coercion or one member bearing the whole cost.) What kinds of benefits could hold such appeal?

Since we are dealing with peak associations we can assume that, despite the ambiguities we noted earlier regarding the nature of membership units, the prospective members of the peak are themselves organizations, such as labor unions, business firms, or universities. It would be rare that material benefits in their usual forms—cheap insurance, charter flights, or strike funds—could be utilized to build a peak organization. The main reason for this is that the constituent units themselves are organized around the exchange of material benefits. Moreover, each of the constituent units typically has a substantial staff. This staff is unlikely cheerfully to surrender this autonomy nor the membership to subordinate a prospering benefit exchange to a peak association, and, conversely, the peak group cannot prevail merely by offering staff support or selective material benefits. American constituent groups tend to be far stronger in staff and material resources than their counterparts elsewhere, and hence less susceptible to this kind of appeal from peak organizations.

Let us consider four types of benefits that are sometimes utilized, or at least proposed, as having the potential to attract and hold the requisite membership. These are information, the regulation of jurisdictional disputes, recognition of the sector organization as legitimate and/or expert, and increased sector weight in policy making. All are of material concern, but their value is not as direct as such things as insurance, and indeed their worth to prospective members is highly problematic.

Sapolsky suggests that a major benefit accruing to peak association members in Britain is access to information about ministry intentions regarding sector policy (1968: 368). There is no doubt that information is a very valuable commodity. But in the United States two factors conspire to make it extremely difficult for peak associations to monopolize such information so as to make it a selective benefit available only to its members. One is that given the institutional fragmentation of American government there are multiple sources of information about what is happening in Washington. It is very difficult to imagine who could sign an exclusive dealing agreement on behalf of the government, effectively limiting the flow of information to a single peak group, and make it stick. The second reason is that there is a highly developed and enormously competitive information business already developed, and any organization already has many options available to find out what it needs to know.[6]

Differential access to information gives advantages to specific organizations vis-à-vis competitors in their own sector. At some point, of course, such access may become too costly to maintain and a common information pool, as would be provided by a peak association, would then be attractive. Essentially, this is the calculus followed by a newspaper that uses a wire service rather than maintaining its own Washington correspondent. But it has not yet become operative in labor, business, or the other major interest sections. Aspiring peak associations in most sectors seem not to have been as efficient in providing information to members as more specialized groups, and the prospects for peak group hegemony over this function are not at all encouraging.

The regulation of jurisdictional disputes is a different kind of matter. The possibilities can best be seen in the case of labor unions. One of the chief advantages of union participation in the AFL-CIO is protection against raiding by rival unions and support from rival unions in organizing activities. A good recent example can be seen in the AFL-CIO support for the United Farm Workers against the Teamsters in their efforts to organize in California. Surely this kind of help can be of significant benefit to all but the very strongest organizational units in a sector. The Teamsters, of course, are very strongly situated and hence quite content to remain outside the AFL-CIO fold.

For other unions and in other sectors, however, there is an additional factor that limits the ability of organizations in the United States to establish sector hegemony by regulating jurisdictional disputes. There is an extensive array of extant public policy that already deals precisely with this problem in both positive and negative ways. On the negative side the antitrust laws preclude business organizations from allocating markets among competitors, and there is a considerable number of cases in which trade associations have been convicted on exactly those grounds. The NRA period was an exception, of course, and enforcement of competition has always been uneven, to say the least. But in large sectors of the economy peak associations would be legally forbidden to provide the "benefit" of settling jurisdictional arguments for the members.[7]

Consider also such policies as commodity marketing orders, which do indeed have the effect of regulating conflicts among potential competitors and which have been written into positive law as a result of the specialized pressures of particular commodity groups. In this situation there is no regulatory function left for a peak organization to perform. When an organization is put together, as the National Conference of

Commodity Organization was in the late 1950s, it is left with the much weaker function of coordinating a log-rolling alliance based on the mutual support of each commodity group for every other group's needs. Hence the peak group does not long survive. There is a broad array of legislation regulating group operations, including representation elections and pension fund disclosures in the labor field, securities issues in business and degree program certification in higher education, to mention only a few which might have been subject to private control of strong peak associations. Conversely, it seems generally to be the case that in the more fully corporatist systems of Western Europe, with vigorous associations of comprehensive sector-wide scope, there is considerably less legislation regulating the internal affairs of that sector.

We have already discussed the question of peak association legitimacy at some length. In the present context the point is that legitimacy requires substantial sector unity and this can perhaps best be achieved by means of an effective peak organization. Let us consider further, however, what else is associated with sector unity, what kinds of groups especially need it, and what trade-offs there are against it. Professional groups provide good illustrations of the arguments. When doctors or lawyers or educators are cohesive and speak with one organizational voice, their associations are often regarded as legitimate spokesmen for their sectors. More broadly, the whole profession is conceded a degree of expertise that entitles its members to deference on sector-related public policy, and to substantial self-regulation. One aspect of this is the right to charge a fee for services which, if they are incompetent, will not be discovered until it is too late to do much about it, except, of course, to sue for malpractice. Such a reputation for expertise is thus highly valued and placed at risk whenever significant policy conflicts develop within the sector organization.

Once there is substantial internal disagreement about what is best for the sector, there is no choice but to have non-experts make the decision, in coalition with some portion of the sector and against some other part, and to do so according to standard political considerations. From the perspective of the sector, the thing to do is first to suppress the conflict or mask its expression. If the decisive forces cannot be contained, however, the indicated strategy is to cultivate political clout. Mobilized electoral strength can affect political decisions when deference is no longer afforded to expertise. In both education and medicine the decline in professional unity has been met by a rise in political militance.[8] The point is that within virtually every professional sector policy conflicts have erupted with increasing frequency and severity, reducing thereby the chances of sector hegemony.

The fourth possible basis for peak association formation is to increase the weight or influence of the sector in bargaining over policy. Surely there is appeal to potential members in enhanced influence, but this really is a problem in organizing for collective benefits, and Olson's arguments apply. He does provide for the possibility of small groups organizing for collective purposes and some sectors might already be organized into oligopolistic form with a sufficiently modest number of discrete units to qualify as a small group with the accompanying face-to-face pressures that help overcome free rider tendencies. Elsewhere I have argued that within some limits, that might be fairly broad, it would be in the interest of each potential member of large groups to join so long as it is uncertain whether that membership increment may be decisive to the establishment of requisite sector influence (Salisbury, 1975). But above those limits free riderism must reappear in the absence of selective benefits, and, as we have seen, these are difficult to manage effectively in peak organizations. We cannot say, on these grounds, that strong peak associations are impossible in the United States but at a comprehensive sectoral level the odds are against them.

There is another factor in the American context that makes sector influences itself of problematic value. The assumption that influence is desirable for a sector is tied to another assumption; namely, that policy decisions will affect the entire sector in substantially the same way. For that to be so the policies themselves must be framed in comprehensive terms, and the members of the sector must be in sufficiently similar circumstances as to have a common interst in the outcome. In fact, however, heterogeneity of interest or situation characterizes most sectors of American life. Pension fund regulation will not affect the Teamsters the same way it does the Steelworkers, for example. Nor are Harvard and Slipper Rock similarly situated regarding NSF policy. More than that, much American public policy tends to be highly disaggregated so that the differential effects within a sector are further heightened. The general point is that whenever a given policy has differential impacts, it adds to the centrifugal tendencies of the system, and in the United States the continued reinforcement of those tendencies constitutes a formidable obstacle for would-be peak associations to overcome. Again, medicine serves as an example of a sector where the expansion of explicit public policy has resulted in the steady proliferation of interests, each somewhat differently affected by existing programs and taking a distinct and separate posture toward new proposals.[9]

Another Possibility

In one sense the point of this essay is a small one, and perhaps some might consider it even trivial. We are not suggesting that organized interests are without influence over American public policy. That influence is informal and often suspect, but it is not necessarily less consequential because it is unofficial. Some observers indeed have interpreted American politics as very largely a public, legitimate, process that masks the exercise of private and unaccountable power of the business elite.[10] From this perspective the absence of corporatist mechanism might be regarded as irrelevant or even a matter of deliberate choice to hide the realities of economic power over political decision and to exclude potential rivals from the bargaining table.

If there were genuine corporatism in the United States, labor would have to be a full participant in the negotiations over economic policy. They would have a full voice in determining which social sectors were to get what share of the national product. Government, in turn, would hold not only the swing vote between business and labor but an important potential for affecting the demands and interactions of both sides. Moreover, corporatist mechanisms presumably operate regardless of election outcomes, whereas informal· access may be much affected by them.

Thus corporatist arrangements might well make a difference and a perceptive business elite might therefore wish to prevent a political evolution in that direction. Such an hypothesis cannot be refuted, of course, and the possibility, even as only a part of the total explanation, should not be dismissed. My own judgment is that insofar as a self-conscious business elite exists in the United States it has not devoted much attention to what economic planning mechanisms would or would not best suit its needs. Most of its energies have gone into the more general defense of the free market, on one hand, and the quest for specific subsidies and other direct benefits for particular industries, on the other. Still, the political strength of business in America and the concomitant weakness of labor may well help us understand why it has only been in times of severe crisis that both sides have been willing to sit together.

Conclusion

It is possible that there is a somewhat simpler answer, or partial answer, to our original query. The argument put forward by Schmitter is that corporatism is a response, perhaps the modal response, to the need for stability in an advanced capitalist system. Shonfield (1965: 231) stresses the need for stability but sees corporatism as one of three possible styles of national economic planning by which such stability may be sought. In addition to corporatist planning there is state intervention, utilizing the levers of public power, and indicative planning whereby the planners persuade rational economic men to accept dispassionate analyses and act accordingly. In the United States there is some of each of these kinds of planning but not much use of corporatist devices. On that policy area most representative perhaps of corporatist tendencies, wage-price or incomes policy, the American approach has been mainly to utilize jawboning, occasionally to exercise the levers of federal power, and to play off one sector against the other. But there has been almost no serious effort to cultivate consensus or to facilitate the development of labor-management agreements which would hold down inflation (Goodwin, ed., 1975: 368–9). Panitch has argued that in Europe corporatism has not really worked as well as Schmitter and others believe, that the stability it brings is brief and the problems soon return (Panitch, 1976, also Wilensky, 1976 and Wheeler, 1975). In the United States there has generally been enough slack within each sector that a relatively free market process could operate at least some of the time, to bring downward pressure on prices. But even in the face of stubborn stagflation there is not much corporatism in America.[11] Corporatism, in turn, is an aspect of comprehensive national economic planning and we may conclude this review by observing that there is not much planning in America either.[12]

NOTES

An earlier version of this paper was presented at the annual meeting of the American Political Science Association, Washington, DC, September, 1977.

1. For a parallel argument; *viz.*, that it is values that differentiate American from European practice, see Anthony King, "Ideas, Institutions and the Policies of Governments: Part III," *British Journal of Political Science*, Vol. 3 (Oct., 1973), pp. 409–423.

2. In a wonderfully revealing statement Jewel Cass Phillips once distinguished between "good" pressure groups and "bad" pressure groups. He then asked, "Are good pressure groups desirable?" After careful deliberation he concluded that they were not! *State and Local Government in America*, New York: American Book Co., 1954, p. 122.

3. Another example is provided by Joseph La Palombara's characterization of the British style of operation: "When in doubt, clear it some more before taking action." *Politics Within Nations*, Englewood Cliffs: Prentice-Hall, 1974, p. 354.

4. Roy C. Macridis is the author of another well-known argument embedding patterns of interest group behavior in the context of political culture. "Interest Groups in Comparative Analysis," *Journal of Politics*, Vol. 23 (Feb., 1961), pp. 24–45.

5. One might add that insofar as there is increasing insulation of elected officials from electoral insecurity, there will be still less reason to negotiate with organized associations. Rather, officials may feel more and more able to dominate the discussion. It would seem that such a development characterizes the contemporary politics of medical care more than would have been thought possible in the 1950s. On the increasing safety of electoral margins, see Morris P. Fiorina, *Congress, Keystone of the Washington Establishment*, New Haven: Yale University Press, 1977.

6. As a single example of a large and mostly uncharted area, see the large volume published by Congressional Quarterly entitled *Washington Information Directory*, 1977–78.

7. A notable exception to the general ban on peak organizations resolving disputes among their members is provided in the exemption from anti-trust prosecution granted to organized baseball.

8. On the rising militance in the National Education Association, see "NEA's Growing Political Power," *National Journal*, August 30, 1975. An instructive recent evaluation of the politics of medicine is John K. Iglehart's "No More Doctor Nice Guy," *National Journal*, March 6, 1976.

9. A part of this proliferation process is treated by John K. Iglehart, "Health Report/Economy Taking Steam from National Insurance Drive," *National Journal*, January 18, 1975.

10. I am grateful to G. William Domhof and Robert Alford for their perceptive and probing comments on an earlier version of this paper. Both of them, in somewhat different ways, made suggestions that persuaded me I could not ignore the relevance of de facto corporate influence in a discussion of corporatism in America.

11. N. H. Keehn has written a rather interesting essay in part predicting and in part urging the coming of corporatism to the United States. I think he is wrong, but the analysis deserves attention. See "A World of Becoming: From Pluralism to Corporatism," *Polity*, Vol. 9 (Fall, 1976), pp. 19–39.

12. I have tried to address this side of the problem in another paper, "On Centrifugal Tendencies in Interest Systems: The Case of the United States," pre-

pared for the World Congress of Sociology, Uppsala, Sweden, August, 1978, and presented in this volume, *infra*.

ADDITIONAL REFERENCES

Bailey, S. K., et al. 1963. *Schoolmen in Politics.* Syracuse: Syracuse University Press.

Beer, Samuel. 1969. *Modern British Politics.* London: Faber and Faber.

Block, W. J. 1960. *The Separation of the Farm Bureau and the Extension Service.* Urbana: University of Illinois Press.

Blum, John M. 1976. *V Was for Victory.* New York: Harcourt, Brace, Jovanovich.

Campbell, C. M. 1962. *The Farm Bureau and the New Deal.* Urbana: University of Illinois Press.

Eldersveld, S. J. 1958. "American Interest Groups." In Henry Ehrmann, ed., *Interest Groups on Four Continents.* Pittsburgh: University of Pittsburgh Press.

Fainsod, Merle, et al. 1959. *Government and the American Economy.* 3d ed. New York: W. W. Norton.

Fusfeld, D. R. 1972. "The Rise of the Corporate State in America." *Journal of Economic Issues* 6 (March): 1–20.

Garceau, Oliver. 1941. *The Political Life of the American Medical Association.* Cambridge: Harvard University Press.

Goodwin, C. D. 1975. *Exhortation and Controls: The Search for a Wage-Price Policy, 1945–1971.* Washington, D.C.: Brookings Institution.

Grossman, Joel B. 1965. *Lawyers and Judges: The ABA and the Politics of Judicial Selection.* New York: John Wiley.

Hartz, Louis. 1960. "Democracy: Image and Reality." In W. N. Chambers and R. H. Salisbury, eds., *Democracy in the Mid-Twentieth Century.* St. Louis: Washington University Press.

———. 1955. *The Liberal Tradition in America.* New York: Harcourt, Brace.

Heinz, John P. 1962. "The Political Impasse in Farm Support Legislation." *Yale Law Journal* 71 (April): 952–78.

Key, V. O., Jr. 1964. *Politics, Parties and Pressure Groups.* 5th ed. New York: Crowell.

Laslett, J. M., and S. M. Lipset. 1974. *Failure of a Dream? Essays in the History of American Socialism.* Garden City, N.Y.: Anchor/Doubleday.

Lowi, Theodore. 1969. *The End of Liberalism.* New York: W. W. Norton

Masters, Nicholas A., Robert H. Salisbury, and Thomas H. Eliot. 1964. *State Politics and the Public Schools.* New York: Knopf.

McConnell, Grant. 1966. *Private Power and American Democracy.* New York: Knopf.

———. 1953. *The Decline of Agrarian Democracy.* Berkeley: University of California Press.

Olson, Mancur. 1965. *The Logic of Collective Action.* Cambridge: Harvard University Press.

Panitch, Leo. 1976. "The Development of Corporatism in Liberal Democracies." Paper presented to the American Political Science Association. September. Chicago, Ill.

Peterson, W. C. 1974. "The Corporate State Economic Performance and Social Policy." *Journal of Economic Issues* 8 (June): 483–506.

Presthus, Robert. 1974. *Elites in the Policy Process.* London: Cambridge University Press.

Salsibury, Robert H. 1969. "An Exchange Theory of Interest Groups." *Midwest Journal of Political Science* 13 (February): 1–32.

———. 1975. "Interest Groups." In Fred Greenstein and Nelson Polsby, eds., *Handbook of Political Science* 4: 171–228. Reading, Mass.: Addison-Wesley.

Sapolsky, Harvey. 1968. "Organizational Competition and Monopoly." *Public Policy* 17: 55–76.

Schattschneider, E. E. 1960. *The Semi-Sovereign People.* New York: Holt, Rinehart and Winston.

Schmitter, Philippe. 1974. "Still the Century of Corporatism?" *Review of Politics* 36 (January): 85–131.

Self, P., and H. J. Storing. 1962. *The State and the Farmer.* London: Allen and Unwin.

Sharkansky, Ira. 1975. *The United States: A Study of a Developing Country.* New York: David McKay.

Shonfield, A. 1965. *Modern Capitalism.* London: Oxford University Press.

Singer, J. W. 1976. "Buttonholing and Buttering Up for Labor—and 'the People'. " *National Journal* (April 24).

Stanfield, R. 1976. "The PIGs: Out of the Sty into Lobbying with Style." *National Journal* (August 14).

Truman, David B. 1951. *The Governmental Process.* New York: Knopf.

Wheeler, C. 1975. *White Collar Power.* Urbana: University of Illinois Press.

Wilensky, Harold. 1976. *The New Corporatism: Centralization and the Welfare State.* Beverly Hills, Calif.: Sage.

Wooten, Graham. 1970. *Interest Groups.* Englewood Cliffs, N.J.: Prentice-Hall.

Zeigler, Harmon. 1964. *Interest Groups in American Society.* Englewood Cliffs, N.J.: Prentice-Hall.

7

On Centrifugal Tendencies in Interest Systems: The Case of the United States

In the preceding essay attempting to account for the absence of societal corporatist development in the United States I focused my attention on the weakness of so-called peak associations which, being unable to speak authoritatively for their respective economic sectors, could not bargain effectively to achieve the stable equilibrium among themselves and with the state that corporatism entails.[1] As I ponder the matter further, it seems to me that there are a good many other elements involved as well, many of them quite fundamental to the workings of the American politico-economic system. The deeper one goes, indeed, the more one is led to a kind of rediscovery of some of the most elementary truths, clichés virtually, that are too often passed over in a search for sophisticated models and macrocosmic theories.

In my earlier paper I suggested that in answering the question, "Why no corporatism in America?" one also encountered the question, "Why no national economic planning in America?" In the discussion that followed Robert Alford suggested that perhaps a part of the answer was to be found in the same place as that to the more familiar question, "Why no socialism in America?" And the search for explanations to these puzzles leads quickly also to such factors as the institutional configuration; ideological commitments and/or cultural norms regarding individualism, centralization, and economic growth; the party system as it interacts with the class structure, on the one side, and governing institutions, on the other; the "Liberal Tradition," and especially the ab-

Paper prepared for the meeting of the International Sociological Association, Uppsala, Sweden, August 1978.

sence of statist practices and ideas; the patterns of public policy and the American brand of distributive "interest group liberalism"; and, ultimately, to the structure and shape, functional and spatial, of American society. I cannot hope to pursue all of these routes (perhaps the better metaphor would be to see them as facets of a brilliant stone, brittle enough that excessive or careless cutting risks shattering the object and destroying the chance of understanding). I will concentrate mainly on the latter two items, the shape of American society and the pattern of public policy, and attempt to articulate what seem to me to be the vitally important connections between them.

The most important concept in the American political system is *constituency*. It dominates the behavior of virtually every political actor and institution. Its corollary concept is representation, and unless one understands how constituencies are defined and how they command the processes of representation, one's theories are likely to go astray. I am not here saying only that every political actor or institution must have some sort of "support" in the society, which is doubtless true but not very interesting. Nor am I repeating the Bentleyan lesson that every political act "represents" some larger interest. My point is more restricted and more specifically American. It is that in this system political actors more or less consciously "look to" particular segments of the society as their primary reference points, as having by right first call over them, and see themselves as dependent on constituency approval, in this segmented sense rather than in the more general terms of "the people" or "the public interest," for their political survival.[2]

Most of the societal segments that function as constituencies in American politics are defined primarily in geographical terms. There are, of course, states, cities, and legislative districts that contain such concentrations of particular economic or social interests that we refer to them as labor, farm, Italian, or black districts, etc. Further, the constituencies of administrative agencies are typically characterized by functional groupings—labor, agriculture, the handicapped, the aerospace industry. Even so, the effective "clout" such functional constituencies bring to bear on their administrative "representatives" is largely exercised through the geographical units of legislative and executive branch electoral politics. One gets one's congressman to harass the HUD regional office or Pentagon procurement or whatever, threatening to investigate agency ineptitude, or without appropriations, or in some other way bring pressure on administrative policy. Conversely, agencies build support to be exercised through similar instrumentalities, by doing useful things in this district and that state as well, as by working with functional groups which themselves have grass-roots constituencies organized within specific geographical districts. In the discussion to follow I will concentrate mainly on legislative constituencies, but the latter-day incorporation of administrative agencies into a constituency-centered system is also of great importance, and I will consider it further toward the end of the essay.

The essential dynamic that enforces constituency primacy on American politicians is, of course, election. But many political systems elect legislators from districts without cultivating in them such a sharply differentiated sense of the needs and demands of the specific district. Explanations of American constituency centeredness involve not only the institutional arrangements of election but those of candidacy as well; in short, the party system. For at one level, at least, the power of local constituencies is simply the obverse of the weakness of political parties in America. That this is such an old question, not very much in fashion since the rise of survey research on voting behavior,[3] does not necessarily render it irrelevant to our needs. A part of the question of "Why no Corporatism?" involves "Why such weak parties?"

By "weak" we mean, at one level, the inability of party leaders to enforce policy agreement on recalcitrant members, especially within legislative bodies. At a deeper level, however, a "weak" party is one that lacks the capacity to develop a coherent policy program to which its principal official members will adhere. The weak party cannot aggregate interests and values sufficiently well to achieve a clear party position. Greatly strengthened disciplinary machinery would probably slice away major segments of the loose voting coalition that identifies with the party and/ or its candidates. The "strong" party in terms of its internal institutions would thus become a very "weak" party electorally.[4]

In a "weak" party system the elected official cannot look to party leaders for much electoral help in his district since the leaders themselves are weak in authority and resources and likely to be diverse in policy views. He cannot simply depend on a sufficient core of dependable party identifiers to reelect him so long as he has behaved as a faithful party follower—though there may be districts where this can still be done. There are too seldom such dependable cores available, and even when they do exist they often differ, among themselves and with other partisans elsewhere, as to what constitutes proper adherence to the "true" party tradition. So in a weak party system candidates for election devote much of their efforts to building their own personal bases of support within the district through constituency service and personal favor as well as with their own policy action. They hope in the process to insulate themselves from rival candidates and also from national tides of partisan fortune. And they do so by shaping their policy-making activities, great and small, in such a way as to strengthen their constituency links rather than in broader, more highly aggregated forms that tighter party associations, for example, might entail.

In a sense this is quite a familiar litany, of course, going far back in time and only needing to have the modern development of casework and the disaggregated distributive policy making of interest group liberalism to make a consistent analytic package embracing Schattschneider, Bryce, and most traditional textbook discussions of the American party system. But to note that constituency-centered political behavior is associated with a weak party system does not tell us why either or both came to be, and for this we must undertake a brief historical excursion.

First of all, it is apparent that the *initial* basis of political action in American was the geographical constituency. Whether colony or state, Tidewater or Piedmont, Old East or New West, manufacturing North or agricultural South, all politics up to 1865 was surely and obviously dominated by questions and conflicts that were seen to be cast in specific geographical terms. Moreover, the politician was expected in his actions to represent his geographically defined constituency and, after the rise of political parties, to bend the shape of party philosophy to fit the needs of the locale. The reverse relationship seems hardly ever to have occurred to anyone.

This does not mean, of course, that there were no principles larger than the promotion of this canal or that railroad or turnpike to undergird political action. Free soil, "The Bank," and the tariff, to name a few, were great issues, indeed. But all three, and most others in the period, evoked conflicts that largely followed regional or sectional lines, so that effective representation of one "philosophical" point of view or another was quite compatible with, and generally required politically by, election from a particular state or district.

Now, according to Beer,[5] this is not so very different from the parliamentary politics of Great Britain in the nineteenth century. There, although geographical units of representation were not so compelling, they were not irrelevant, and the dominance on the agenda of essentially parochial interests, expressed largely though private bills, was striking. And it was accompanied by a lack of clear party policy or discipline. But in Britain at the end of the nineteenth century this system gave way to "responsible" parties representing broad socioeconomic sectoral interests, and in the United States that did not happen. Why not?

One factor surely was size. A population eventually to become four times larger was situated in a land some thirty-six times greater in area. What began as greater heterogeneity of cultural backgrounds and value of orientations in the United States of, say, 1850, was greatly reinforced by barriers to the type of easy communication that made Britain a national community during the Victorian age, and also by the more tangible differences of interest growing out of differences in climate, resources, and opportunities in such an immense subcontinent. That American politics would continue to be geographically defined was, in a sense, symbolized by the fact that while most European polities were "expanding" their membership by extending the suffrage, the United States was expanding chiefly by enlarging its territory. In both situations, no doubt, each new addition brought its own set of interests to add to the nation's agenda. But the interests of the British working class added by the Second and Third Reform Bills of the 1860s were spread simultaneously throughout the nation and affected every district and every electoral situation. The addition of Montana or Oklahoma or Hawaii did not, as such, alter the politics of Ohio, while the struggle for statehood carried over inevitably to shape the character of subsequent policy efforts by the newly enfranchised politicians.

Let me make the point this way. A political system operates partly in response to the imperatives of its economic arrangements, to be sure, and accordingly advanced industrial societies all display certain common tendencies. But a system also operates as a resultant of the accumulated historical experiences that shape the habits and practices of interaction and desire. Now it is a commonplace to suggest that America is and has ever been diverse, heterogeneous, and generally composed of many "different sentiments and views." My point is that this diversity is heavily geographical, and it has worked through, and been perpetuated by, political constituencies. The heterogeneity of geographical constituencies was sufficiently great and politically compelling that when industrialization led to the potential emergence of class-based values, these were very largely absorbed and often muted and even transformed by the continued dominance of localist concerns.

There are innumerable consequences. One, of course, is the South with its long confinement to practices which, seen from the perspectives of industrial growth and development, were anachronistic but which remained protected by the encapsulating cocoon of localist constituency politics. For decades liberal reformers urged the virtue of party responsibility precisely because it would help bring the South into the mainstream of national development. And Southern politicians declined, emphasizing the virtues of states' rights and local autonomy. Another example, so decried by Schattschneider as the other half of the "system of 1896,"[6] was the acceptance by labor in the Northeast of the Republican Party in return for tariff protection rather than embracing their "natural" class allies in other parts of the nation.

The possible examples are nearly infinite, but the essential point is this. Geographically defined constituencies absorbed and redefined a large portion of the impulse toward class-based politics in the United States, especially insofar as class politics needed strong centralized political parties as the mechanisms of program formulation, effective electoral mobilization, and coherent policy enactment and administration.

We speak throughout this discussion of tendencies and degrees rather than absolutes, of course. And in this spirit we may focus on another nationalizing impetus that emerged in America as it did in Europe during the late nineteenth and early twentieth century but was in time largely subordinated to the fragmenting influence of constituency policies. Beer calls this element in British politics the Radical theory. It postulated the existence of a public interest, more or less coincident with the views of the popular majority, and labeled opponents "special" or "sinister" interests. In its American incarnation this orientation has at least two variants, one Populist and the other Progressive.[7] Both condemn special interests. Both assert that the public interest is a fact. Populists have been more likely than Progressives to accept electoral majorities as valid expressions of that public interest, but both have insisted that the will of the people taken in general and as a whole, not merely as the sum of particularistic fragments, ought to govern the policy-making process.

At the national level there were surely elements of this universalistic standard in the administrations of Theodore Roosevelt, but their peak may well have been reached during the first two years of Woodrow Wilson's presidency, 1913–15. Wilson himself certainly embodied the universalistic, often moralistic, political style, appealing less to section or group than to national and even world standards of virtue. He was working with a Congress that had just emerged from the dominance of authoritarian leadership and had not yet developed the system of control by committee chairmen that was to characterize the next five decades of Congressional politics. Wilson's opportunity to create a program and carry it through to enactment was thus unusual and impressively successful. A substantial array of economic reform bills became law. Many of them had quite broad national support and, like the Federal Reserve System, many were intended to operate on a fully national basis, rather than on a geographically segmented basis as did the Interstate Commerce Commission or even the Sherman Antitrust Act, the two main earlier econmic reforms of the period. But it is not too much to say that by 1915 the Populist-Progressive impulse toward comprehensive legislative action had faded, absorbed back into the system of constituency politics. From then until 1933 "Progressive sentiment" fared badly at the polls. Its legislative proposals either reflected the special needs of particular, sectionally defined groups such as farmers, or as with the Versailles Treaty, they fell victim to coalitions of constituency-oriented "special interest" representatives. Moreover, one of the main tenets of the Progressive faith in America was its commitment to the reform and rejuvenation of state and local government. Such a platform, insofar as it succeeded, could hardly avoid strengthening the centrifugal tendencies of American policy making. Indeed, many articulate Progressives, while urging the triumph of "the people," spoke glowingly of the advantages of federalism and local home rule. "The people" would best realize the public interest within each state and local community, it seemed, and such a perspective could not serve for long to restructure politics along lines of nationwide cleavage, liberal versus conservative or progressive versus reactionary.

When American politics next came to a crucial juncture at which the possibility of the nationalization of conflict would again be at hand and much debated, this same ambivalence in Progressive thought was to help abort the shift. The time, of course, was 1933, and the much heralded prospect was the emergence of a liberal-labor coalition to give at least quasi-ideological coherence to national policy.

It was customary to regard the New Deal as the climacteric of partisan realignment whereby a genuinely national coalition was forged in support of policy initiatives soon to be opposed by an equally firm and increasingly uncompromising coalition of big business, small towns, and the racist South.[8] In some respects the caricature has verisimilitude, of course, and in our effort to accentuate the continuing force of centrifugal factors I do not wish to be understood as disregarding utterly the impact of nationalizing, aggregating tendencies. The United States was an industrializing society throughout the past hundred years, and it has not fully escaped the consequences of that fact. Even the New Deal, however, incorporated a tendency toward decentralization, a confirmation of geographical dispersion, that rendered it far less revolutionary than either its fondest supporters or severest critics ever confessed.

We know, of course, that some steps in the direction of national economic planning failed, either because of their own internal contradictions or because of external factors such as the Supreme Court. The National Recovery Administration, indeed, suffered grievously from both. What is less familiar is the fate of the New Deal planning efforts, involving those agencies explicitly charged with developing and coordinating plans for future policy developments, some against contingencies that might never occur, and some against realities that, in the Depression decade, were inescapable. The key member of Roosevelt's National Resources Planning Board (the agency had several titles during the 1933–1943 period of its life) was Charles Merriam, professor of Political Science and old-line Progressive.[9] Merriam was actually a Republican who had worked with Herbert Hoover as well as Harold Ickes, and he had run for mayor of Chicago in earlier times. But when it came to "the idea of planning" he was much more influential, or perhaps simply representative, than the more expansive, proplanning liberal Democrat Rexford Tugwell. Merriam thought not at all of developing the capacity for comprehensive national economic planning. Indeed it does not appear that his concept of planning went very far beyond a vague commitment to the desirability of collecting economic data and support for advance project planning so as to have things "on the shelf" and ready to go. What was uppermost in Merriam's mind was the importance of creating and stengthening the capacity of state and local governments to plan, in pretty much the same vague sense of the term. And he used his position to bring about grant-in-aid stimuli for the creation and strengthening of state and local planning bodies.

Merriam was ever a product of the Progressive impulse, and his primary contribution to the New Deal was to push it into the decentralized grooves of Progressive institutional development. But Merriam did not work in a vacuum. His efforts coincided with the 1933 creation of the U.S. Conference of Mayors, for example, whereby big cities constituted themselves as lobbyists in behalf of distributing federal money to the urban centers of the country.[10] The expansion of federal program activity that marked the New Deal and after has been, throughout, paralleled by an equally swift growth in the sophistication of potential grant recipients. Nearly all of them are located in particular geographical places, represented by specific members of Congress, and urging that programs be designed to bring an optimum share of the benefits to their particular locale.

Many observers of the New Deal, then and later, have felt that an historic opportunity to create a vigorous sense of national economic purpose and the plans and machinery to implement it had been allowed to slip away.[11] A number of factors have been offered in explanation. Some lie in the realm of belief systems and some in the structure of interests in the socioeconomic sphere. In the remainder of this paper we shall consider each of these and, in the end, how they continue to interact in the formation of public policy.

Economic planning requires that future actions be programmed and resources allocated according to a conscious strategy for achieving an explicit set of goals. One clear necessity for the articulation of goals, the devising of strategy, and the control of decisions is the existence of centralized institutional authority. In the United States construction of such machinery has not been possible and, indeed, the whole idea of centralized authority is regarded with the deepest suspicion. We need not review the whole history of American political ideas to be reminded that hostility toward the idea of a strong national government was not limited to Southern slaveholders. Institutional arrangements such as federalism expressed the attitude, but they also reinforced it by creating a large set of autonomous state and local officeholders with an interest in perpetuating decentralized decision making. To be sure, in the 1930s there were those who hoped for a fundamental shift in power toward Washington, but apart from the short-lived NRA it is instructive to see how little of that shift involved central planning, and how vital (as with Merriam) the decentralized units remained.

During and after World War II, likewise, there was much resistance to the creation of authoritative central machinery either for war mobilization or postwar reconversion. Indeed, in the immediate postwar period the most that could be salvaged for "the planning idea" was the emasculated Employment Act of 1946.[12] We are edging over into American attitudes toward planning now, and we will pursue that topic directly below. First, this point should be underscored: a part of the resistance to national economic planning is rooted in the resistance, both ideological and political, to centralized governmental power.

The concept of economic planning enjoyed its first important American flowering in the early part of the twentieth century, and it was among businessmen. Impressed with what seemed to be the arrival of a consolidation phase and the end of "frontierlike" economic growth, business leaders such as Gerard Swope began to talk of business self-government whereby businesses would administer their respective industries in a stable fashion, equitable among firms, protecting against "chiselers" and other predatory competitors. Assisting in this process would be the newly developing techniques of scientific management, and even organized labor would be invited to sit at the table in return for accepting the status quo of mature capitalism. These arrangements were not to be administered by government, of course, but through trade associations operating under the constraints of quasi-professional codes of ethics. Government's role was to be benign and facilitative, helping to prevent "unfair" competitive practices and sometimes hosting the summit banquets at which the stately sentiments of business self-government could be uttered.[13]

This orientation underlay Herbert Hoover's support for the trade association movement in the 1920s. It was an important source of inspiration for the NRA in 1933.[14] It contributed to such legislation as the 1936 Robinson-Patman Act and the 1937 Miller-Tydings Act, and was still a significant part of "responsible" business thinking during the whole of World War II. The fundamental assumption was that of essential stability in the size and shape of economic opportunity. Given that stability, planning was reasonable, perhaps essential. As labor gained greater organized strength these same "responsible" business thinkers could accept unionization and long-term labor contracts because they added to the stability of expectations and made rational planning more feasible.[15]

American experience from the end of World War II to the beginning of the 1970s cut a large part of the intellectual ground from under this whole proplanning orientation. The era was anything but stable. There was rapid expansion in the aggregate, but this often obscured greatly uneven rates among industries, firms, and sections of the country. Few groups could be sure that their present positions were the best they could hope for. Even if it had been technically feasible, neither businessmen nor constituency-conscious politicians were willing to accept some point in time as the basis for planning future shares of the national product.[16] Helping to rationalize this dynamic system were two important theoretical arguments, one affirming the viability of modified competition and the other doubting the feasibility of centralized planning.

During the New Deal period itself the position that the cure for economic misery was enhanced competition had important support and was generally dominant, though never exclusively so, during the Thurman Arnold-TNEC period of roughly 1935–1940. The theoretical ground on which this line of policy rested was thin. It stressed the concept of "bottlenecks," structural impediments to market determination of resource allocation which could be cleared away by vigorous policy and the power of the invisible hand thereby restored.[17] But General Motors, Alcoa, and Du Pont could hardly be understood as mere bottlenecks, technical and correctible flaws in an otherwise smooth and impersonal system. Nor, for that matter, could the UAW or the United Mine Workers be regarded as lacking in market power. Consequently, it was very helpful all around when John Kenneth Galbraith published his modernized version of Adam Smith cum James Madison.[18] Galbraith was understood to be saying that large corporate interests were, in effect, balanced by big labor with government playing the role of creative broker, shoring up weak trading partners to make sure no one "countervailed" his rival out of existence.

The importance of the argument in postwar America is that it provided a justification of oligopolistic competition that seemed to make it unnecessary to undertake conscious, centralized planning in order to achieve the public interest. The contention that countervailing power could have the same beneficent effects as old-fashioned entrepreneurial competition rehabilitated the marketplace as a respectable alternative to planning, and Galbraith's own shift away from this view did not destroy its continuing credibility.[19]

Meanwhile, another perspective was taking increasingly persuasive shape. Some of it may have stemmed from the ideological conservatism of such economists/philosophers as Hayek and von Mises who pretty much equated planning with tyranny. Mainly, however, this line of argument was quite pragmatic. It is most familiar in the writings of C. E. Lindblom,[20] and its essence is that comprehensive "synoptic planning" does not work because human circumstances are too diverse and too complicated to admit of effective incorporation within the planning scope that the mind of man can devise. "Muddling through," mutual partisan adjustment, and incremental change are all terms that Lindblom and many others have found preferable both as descriptions of how policies are made and prescriptions of how they ought to be.

The effect of these arguments was to justify the view that centralized economic planning was neither necessary nor desirable. Superior economic performance, and thus rewards to contending sectoral groups, would result from letting those groups have at it, while government played the marginal role of umpire and periodic adjuster of the balance of forces. The resulting system was thought to be benign and to contain a fundamental self-correcting device, the pluralists' favorite, the potential formation by aggrieved interests of countervailing groups of their own, sometimes with some help from the federal government, often achieved by mobilizing political strength to make up for economic inadequacy.

The last decade or so has, of course, greatly altered the standing of these interpretations and for obvious reasons.[21] Both the interpretive "bias of pluralism" and the realities of stagflation are too well known to require repeating here. It will suffice for our purposes to observe that while confidence in the efficacy of markets and uncoordinated resource allocation has been severely eroded, it has not followed that in the United States the desirability of central economic planning has been rehabilitated. Instead what has happened is a retreat from comprehensive interpretation and prescription toward a combination of value exhortative rhetoric and piecemeal fragments of public policy steps; an incrementalism not as the result of intellectual conviction or preference but of political necessity. We turn now to examine that necessity.

Resources, cultural traditions, economic development, and all the other sources of politically relevant values are distributed in uneven geographical patterns in the United States. Copper is found only in the mountain states. Nonferrous metals policy issues affect Montana far more than Iowa. Those who represent the areas primarily affected will, quite understandably, seek and very often secure a dominant role in the process of making public policy on that particular problem. Oil state representatives historically have dominated oil policy. Farm state spokesmen have wrangled over agricultural policy. Foreign trade conflicts involved representatives from constituencies with different interests in international commerce. Even so-called collective goods, such as national defense, are collective only to consumers. They involve the geographically specific interests of those who produce them, such as defense contractors or areas with military bases.[22]

In a society with heterogeneous spatial distributions of interests virtually every policy action will have geographically differentiated impacts; greater here than there, favorable in one area and negative in another. That being so, each geographical area will seek to utilize its political representation to optimize its share of the benefits of public policy. It does this by insisting that representatives look primarily to the differentiated constituency for political reward. In turn, constituency-oriented representatives will shape policies, as far as possible, so as to yield rewards that the district or state can recognize and be grateful for. As we noted earlier, the power of this dynamic has quite generally absorbed and redefined tendencies toward strong national parties, strong class identification, and strong sectoral interest groups.

The last point bears further examination. If we watch U.S. labor unions in politics we sometimes see the AFL-CIO, operating in close harmony with the UAW and other unions outside its control, presenting a cohesive "labor front" on an issue of public policy. But very often we may observe two other tendencies: one, specific unions taking stands on issues pertinent to them but not to others, or in opposition to other equally self-interested unions; and two, the AFL-CIO leadership hedging its statements, even growing silent, because of an inability to resolve conflicts of view and interest among different unions. Now a given representative is seldom likely to represent labor-in-general. Rather, his or her district will contain a heavy dose of steelworkers or miners or public employees. He or she will respond to their pressure out of electoral necessity but to "labor" only insofar as the AFL-CIO head is in tune with locally powerful unions. Exactly the same can be said regarding business interests, farmers, or even environmentalists. The political strength of the sector depends ultimately on the ability to mobilize votes (and other electoral resources such as money) within constituencies one at a time.

The resulting impact on policy is to bring about disaggregation, implicit or explicit, in the political evaluation and accounting systems. Thus an urban policy means very little in the abstract. Its significance to any particular judge/citizen is calculated in terms of how much money it funnels into Cleveland or Buffalo or Phoenix. Defense procurement devolves from strategic debate into the question of which companies in which areas receive contracts. Farm policy has always been a loose package of specific crop programs. The crops and commodities are produced in quite specific ares of the country and are appropriately represented in the policy process. Energy policy is little more than a label pasted on a grab bag of more specific bits and pieces designed somehow to appease a sufficient array of constituencies to enable the necessary majority to be assembled.

The problem is not as Lowi argued[23] that American politicians have no standard by which to judge the legitimacy of interest group claims and therefore incorporate them all into policy. The standard is quite clear. It is constituency strength, geographically disaggregated power to influence specific election outcomes. The systemic constraint, and it often is quite powerful, is the need to build a legislative majority to enact the district's desires. Logrolling is one majority-building process. Partisan collaboration and sectoral interest strength that is spread through many districts are others, though both remain subordinated to the claims of individual constituency values. The clear result is that fiscal policy is transmuted into tax incentives for local industry or relief for visible groups of home owners; the issue of mass transit becomes whether Baltimore or St. Louis will receive federal funds for light-rail development; and wilderness protection runs up against a campaign for Alaskan development by and for Alaskans.

Every public policy decision affects different constituencies in the United States differently. From the recognition of this fact spring the political processes by which those policy decisions are made. In addition, however, each decision tends to create vested local interests with a stake in at least maintaining if not expanding whatever resource commitment the decision first entailed. The other half of "interest group liberalism" is the tendency, growing stronger with each year of accumulated policy investments in specific interest formations, to generate interests, with effective self-consciousness and political clout, that were not previously a part of the scene. It has frequently been observed that the War on Poverty stimulated and even subsidized the formation of organized groups which, in their turn, pressed for expansion of that war. So it has been also with "the handicapped," who have been repeatedly brought together with federal funds and helped to interact until they were able to exercise their own autonomous pressure on the policy process. Reaching back in time we find the American Farm Bureau Federation subsidized by Agriculture Department activities. And the military-industrial complex is unimaginable without government procurement of weapons.

Virtually every new policy action of the federal government cuts unevenly into the existing array of socioeconomic and politico-governmental interests in the country. In so doing it creates new groupings of advantaged and disadvantaged, each of which seeks to defend or redress its position through constituency-based political action. In this context comprehensive policy planning, with or without corporatist components, is literally unthinkable. Distributive politics continues to characterize the system, whether it solves objective problems or not. For the first and always the overriding criterion of American policy making is whether the decision makers can be reelected. And that takes place in each member's district, always one at a time.

NOTES

1. See the previous essay, "Why No Corporatism in America."

2. I will not seek to review the very substantial literature dealing with representation in American politics. A recent and helpful work on relevant Congressional behavior is John Kingdon, *Congressmen's Voting Decisions* (New York: Harper and Row, 1973). I would make the point that remarkably little attention has been given to the question of what effectively constitutes the constituencies of American policy makers. Much of what has been written concentrates on the rather peripheral issue of numerical equality in population size.

3. A recent and incisive review of the party responsibility issue is E. M. Kirkpatrick, "Toward a More Responsible Two-Party System: Political Science, Policy Science or Pseudo Science," *American Political Science Review,* vol. 65 (December 1971). See also Austin Ranney, *Curing the Mischiefs of Faction* (Berkeley and Los Angeles: University of California Press, 1975).

4. This, of course, is the position taken by Pendleton Herring among others. See his *The Politics of Democracy* (New York: W. W. Norton, 1940).

5. Samuel H. Beer, *British Politics in a Collectivist Age* (New York: Knopf, 1965).

6. See, especially, *The Semi-Sovereign People* (New York: Holt, Rinehart and Winston, 1960).

7. Richard Hofstadter's *Age of Reform* (New York: Vintage Books, 1955), remains a superb commentary on the political ideas of both these elements, though there has been much additional work since he wrote.

8. Actually, this characterization most accurately applies to earlier journalistic and beginning textbook discussions. The complexities of party realignment have been acknowledged to be enormous and terribly hard to sort out. Compare, for example, Samuel Lubell's *Future of American Politics* (New York: Doubleday, 1952), with Walter Dean Burnham, *Critical Elections and the Mainsprings of American Politics* (New York: Norton, 1970), or James Sundquist, *Dynamics of the Party System* (Washington, D.C.: Brookings, 1973).

9. I am indebted to Barry D. Karl's careful study, *Charles E. Merriam and American Politics* (Chicago: University of Chicago Press, 1975).

10. Suzanne Farkas, *Urban Lobbying* (New York: New York University Press, 1975).

11. See, for example, Tugwell's reminiscence of the New Deal and its loss, *Off Course* (New York: Praeger, 1971).

12. The story of the Employment Act is given its classic telling in Stephen K. Bailey's *Congress Makes a Law* (New York: Columbia University Press, 1950). The history of post-1933 attitudes toward planning are treated in Otis Graham, *Toward a Planned Society* (New York: Oxford University Press, 1976).

13. See James Weinstein, *The Corporate Ideal in the Liberal State* (Boston: Beacon Press, 1968).

14. See Ellis Hawley's excellent review of this period, *The New Deal and the Problem of Monopoly* (Princeton, N.J.: Princeton University Press, 1966).

15. The Committee for Economic Development was organized in 1942 to express exactly these kinds of views in behalf of many of the same business interests that were at the same time supporting the antilabor NAM. See Karl Schriftgeisser, *Business Comes of Age* (New York: Harper and Row, 1960).

16. It is instructive to note that when in 1938 American farmers and legislators sought an appropriate period in which to base price supports their choice was the best five years of post–Civil War history, 1909–14.

17. One of Arnold's books is titled *The Bottlenecks of Business* (New York: Reynal and Hitchcock, 1940).

18. *American Capitalism: The Theory of Countervailing Power* (Boston: Houghton, Mifflin, 1953).

19. Galbraith's later position, of course, was that in a predominantly private economy public goods would be provided in very suboptimal amounts. See *The Affluent Society* (Boston: Houghton, Mifflin, 1958). He eventually embraced a sort of socialist view in *The New Industrial State* (Boston: Houghton, Mifflin, 1967). I have chosen to ignore the socialist perspective throughout this paper, by the way, because although it has come into more favor among American intellectuals in recent years it has never had much strength in the political arena.

20. The best known statement is in *The Intelligence of Democracy* (New York: The Free Press, 1965).

21. Criticisms of the alleged pluralist model are widespread in the writings of Kariel, Bachrach, Connelly, Lowi, and others. The pluralist position itself is presumably to be found in the work of Dahl, Truman, and Latham, though it is seldom easy to find the sterotypical pluralist phrases without doing violence to their context.

22. See the analogous argument by Peter Aronson and Peter Ordeshook, "Incrementalism, the Fiscal Illusion, and the Growth of Government in Representative Democracies," unpublished manuscript, 1977.

23. In *The End of Liberalism* (New York: W. W. Norton, 1969).

8

Who Works with Whom?
Interest Group Alliances and Opposition

S*ome fields of* intellectual endeavor enjoy the luxury of exploring well-defined problems whose difficulties, however intractable, are themselves part of a self-conscious culture of inquiry. Other fields of academic effort may well have substantial common ground, but its contours and possibilities have not yet been fully recognized by those committed to its exploration. One such field is interest-group politics. For two decades now we have gradually been coming to appreciate that the questions and concepts we had thought were central to this area of investigation were substantially misspecified and that quite another tack was needed if we were to make sense, theoretical or descriptive, of the burgeoning mass of activity to which we attach the label of *interest groups.*

Since Mancur Olson (1965) turned us in a different direction, we have been the beneficiaries of important work on the origins and maintenance of voluntary associations (inter alia, Berry 1977; Moe 1980; Salisbury 1969; Walker 1983). Concepts have been reformulated in order to encompass institutions within the interest-group frame of reference (Salisbury 1984). We know much more than we did before about lobbying tactics and strategy (Berry 1977; Schlozman and Tierney 1985). We have accumulated sophisticated treatments of both individual group and sector-level development and change over time (Browne and Salisbury 1972; Hanson 1985; Laumann and Knoke 1987; Starr 1982; Walker 1983). And we have useful cross-national comparisons of the

John P. Heinz, Edward O. Laumann, and **Robert L. Nelson** coauthored this article. It is reprinted with permission from *American Political Science Review* 81 (December 1987):1217–34.

structural ties among business, labor, and the state (Schmitter and Lehmbruch 1979; Wilson 1985). Here we propose to extend the range of our attention to a topic central to many fields of political science but not yet addressed by students of interest groups—the structure of conflict.

Whenever a more or less well-defined system of interactions can be observed or inferred—in legislatures, electoral politics, or international relations, to take three good examples—we move quickly to characterize that system in terms of the conflicts over scarce resources that have so long been held to be the defining feature of politics. We may focus on particular episodes—the struggle over a bill in Congress, a specific presidential contest, or the Falklands War. We may select out some feature of the overall structure for attention—the committee system, third-party challenges, or coalition patterns in the United Nations. We have developed quite a few fragments of theory regarding both generic conflict patterns and behavior conditioned thereby and the operation of specific institutional systems. It may be that the linkages between the more abstract and the more particular are sometimes weakly forged, but it seems plain that substantial progress has been registered by growth in cumulative understanding, theoretical and empirical.

We propose to argue that interest-group politics in the United States constitutes a system, or set of systems, defined by interaction among organized groups and between those groups and public officials. The structure of this system, and of subsystems within it, may usefully be characterized in terms of the extent and shape of conflict among participants. This structure is not evident in every instance of policy dispute, nor is it necessarily revealed by any particular case example of interest-group activity. But, as with voting studies or congressional roll calls, the interest-group system or systems can be discerned at more aggregated levels of observation.

The Research Design

It is ironic that it should have taken so long to get at the structure of interest-group conflict. Since the conceptualizations of Arthur Bentley (1908) began to work their yeasty way into political science, it has been commonplace to put group conflict at the very core of our thinking. Having done so, however, we have been so far unable to go beyond examples to reach more comprehensive formulations of how group interactions are structured. Is there much conflict or little? Are the main group players aggregated into two opposing camps or fragmented among several "parties"? Does the structure vary from one policy area to another? We cannot speak to these questions from existing literature. Recent work has greatly improved our understanding of how groups are formed and what they do, but it has not addressed the structure of conflict (for a partial exception, see Schlozman and Tierney 1985, 283–88). Part of the reason may be the absence of any readily observed defining behavior. Party systems can be examined by looking at the distribution of votes. So can legislatures. So can the Supreme Court. The executive branch is more difficult because criterion actions that could be the basis for characterizing their relationships are not visibly undertaken by all participants. Interest groups presented the same difficulty. No set of observations of group activity with enough scope of coverage or iterations of behavior has been made to allow reasonable inferences to be drawn regarding the existence and shape of systemic structure. Our data overcome these difficulties.

The design of our research began with the construction of lists of organizational participants in each of four policy areas—agriculture, energy, health, and labor. It was our firm belief that unless we linked our analysis of interest representation to the substantive policy concerns of the groups involved we would have a bloodless set of responses, interest-group activity without interests. In order to secure enough respondents in a given policy area to enable our analysis effectively to incorporate these substantive considerations, it was necessary to limit ourselves to a few policy domains. Our selection was bound to be somewhat arbitrary, but we have sought to tap some of the important dimensions of interest representation and to capture a reasonable portion of the range and diversity of representational activities.

The policy domains we examine exhibit very different patterns of institutional and policy change over recent decades. In agriculture and labor there has been a relatively stable set of executive agencies and congressional committees and subcommittees; and the programs in these fields, while not without controversy, have displayed substantial continuity in general design. Health and (especially) energy, by contrast, have undergone much greater changes. The past decade has seen each come under the jurisdiction of a new or redesigned cabinet-level department. Congress has developed new mechanisms to deal with energy issues, and the issue agendas of these two fields have been in great flux.

Both level and form of conflict were expected to vary. Labor policy typically pits two broad constellations of interests—business and labor—

against each other, and the struggles are sometimes of epic proportions. Health matters, by contrast, were once the focus of great struggle, but, although health-care-cost containment continues to inspire sharp disagreement, most health issues in recent years have attracted quite muted political voices. Apart from the labor field, we expect to find a general tendency toward interest proliferation and fragmentation as the interests of various types of specialized producers—doctors, insurance companies, medical schools, and so on in health; oil and gas, coal, nuclear, and other fuel interests in energy; various crop and commodity interests in agriculture—grow increasingly differentiated. To be sure, there are peak associations in some domians—agriculture and health, as well as labor—but no organization can claim even this status in energy, and in the other fields the hegemony of the American Medical Association or the American Farm Bureau Federation has been badly eroded in recent years.

We expect our domains to display diversity, therefore, in the patterns of interaction among organizational actors, and we will be able to investigate to what extent this diversity reflects differences in the substantive policy and organizational composition of the domains. Alternatively, we can estimate how much of what individual-interest representatives *do* reflects their personal backgrounds and present job circumstances and how much is, in effect, imposed by the contemporary context of political and institutional forces within which interest representation must operate.

Our selection of policy domains is skewed toward domestic policy. Issues of foreign trade and other international concerns do arise, but they are not of central concern in any of the domains in our study. Interest representation on domestic matters may be larger in volume and differently structured than on matters of national defense, foreign aid, and other issues involving international considerations. Even those differences are hardly total, however, and we would hope that our findings sufficiently reflect the bulk of the policy process to be of some relevance to the understanding of private-interest representation well beyond the four domains of policy examined.

The procedures employed to identify organizations active in a particular policy domain required substantial documentary investigation and preliminary interviewing. No existing list adequately defines the population of interested participants. Each policy area includes several subsystems that attract somewhat different types of participants, and any single method of locating participating organizations has a systematic bias toward identifying certain kinds of groups and neglecting others (Salisbury 1984). We used four different listings of organizations for each policy domain, and the resulting rosters are broadly inclusive not only of the highly active groups but also of the marginal and intermittent participants. The sampling methods are more fully described in the Appendix.

Having defined the universe of group participation (and welcoming the natural weighting that resulted from multiple nominations), we drew a sample of 311 organizations, equally distributed across the four domains. By telephone we interviewed an appropriate official from each, asking, among other things, who represented their interests in Washington. Each group could name up to four individuals within the organization and up to four people from outside. These nominations (totaling 1,716 individuals) then became the basis for sampling respondents. A total of 774 were interviewed in person, a response rate of 77%. Interviews averaged about 75 minutes in duration. These data form the heart of our research. We asked each respondent to name three government officials with whom he or she regularly interacted and then interviewed 301 of those officials. Finally, we added 32 persons who had been among 72 nominated by informants as notable participants in the four policy domains but who, unlike the other 40, had not appeared in our sample.

Some of the analysis that follows treats respondents as individuals constrained by operating within a policy domain and other factors as well but giving their personal reactions and estimates. In some of the analysis, however, we let the individuals stand for the organizations that employ them and treat the organizations as the actors. This is appropriate for purposes of examining the patterns of organizational conflict, but it generates one unanticipated and unfortunate side effect. Approximately 20% of our respondents are external lawyers and consultants. Each was nominated by an organization, but in a fair number of instances they work also for other clients. We found that when asked about allies and adversaries or about actions and attitudes relating to specific events, these respondents gave replies that could not dependably be assigned to the nominating organization. Too often we could not tell what interests were reflected. Consequently, we determined to treat external lawyers and consultants as employees of their respective firms and not try to include them in the ally-adversary structures.

Quite a few of the larger organizations are represented by more than one respondent in our sample; indeed, there are as many as four from the AFL-CIO, the chamber of commerce, and a few others of comparable significance. There are also some state and local chapters or branches of national organizations, which we treat as part of the same category as the parent group.

We turn now to our empirical findings regarding the structure of group conflict in the four policy domains. We have three distinct sets of data bearing on the general question. First, for both Washington representatives and government officials, we report perceptions of conflict in each domain. We compare domains to see what differences appear in these perceptions and also examine some likely indicators of individual variation in perception. Second, we look at the patterning of alliance and opposition as revealed by responses to questions asking interest representatives to nominate other groups they worked with or considered as adversaries. A third set of data, to which only brief references will be made in this paper, is drawn from responses to questions regarding actual participation in each of some 20 very specific events that occurred during the five years prior to our interviews in 1983–84. If a group had been active and taken a particular position, it could then be located, through smallest-space analysis, in relation to all the other groups active in that domain. From these quite different data sets we derive reasonably consistent pictures of the extent and shape of group conflict in each domain. In turn, we can compare those structures and draw inferences regarding both policy-domain characteristics and, more generally, the character of interest-group conflict in the United States.

The Perception of Issues

As we attempt to assess the nature of interest conflict in our four policy domains, it will be helpful to have some idea of how the interest representatives themselves characterize the issues they deal with. In this section we examine three dimensions: *stability, scope of participation,* and *intensity of conflict.* Our data are drawn from responses to pairs of opposing statements. Respondents placed themselves on a five-point scale, but in the presentation that follows, rather than treat them as interval data, we simply subtract the percentage of *disagree* responses from the percentage of *agree* choices. In no instance was there any discernible bimodality of responses; thus we are satisfied we have not lost or obscured anything substantial in opting for this simple procedure. The data are presented in Table 1.

TABLE 1
Perceptions of Issue Characteristics
(in percentages)

Domain Issue Characteristics	Agriculture Representatives	Agriculture Government Officials	Energy Representatives	Energy Government Officials	Health Representatives	Health Government Officials	Labor Representatives	Labor Government Officials	Total Representatives	Total Government Officials
Issue stability										
Issues are long-lived	68	52	78	88	71	59	68	56	72	64
Coalitions are stable	26	5	21	17	28	28	35	19	27	22
Scope of domain participation										
High public visibility	38	47	78	65	43	65	54	63	53	60
Large number of actors	17	35	52	53	33	61	34	47	34	49
Level of domain conflict										
High intensity of conflict	49	6	70	88	44	45	70	69	48	67
Strong partisanship	-18	-11	11	31	-7	3	37	46	4	15
Number of respondents	189	74	181	80	214	73	190	74	774	301

Note: Figures are the percentage of positive responses minus the percentage of negative responses.

We present two measures of issue stability, one on the long-livedness of issues in the domain and one on the stability of group coalitions. A large majority in each policy area sees the issues as long lasting, and both government officials and interest representatives share this view. Indeed, the agreement is sufficiently great that it might be accepted as settled that most of the business of policy-making entails working and reworking issues with a long history. Not many "new" items get on the agenda, and few matters are ever truly disposed of with dispatch.

There is far less agreement regarding the stability of issue coalitions, though in each domain a modest majority perceives stability rather than flux. The size of that majority is reasonably consistent across policy domains, though higher in labor than elsewhere. Except in the health field, government officials perceive substantially less stability than do interest representatives. We will explore the possible meaning of these differences after we have reviewed the other two sets of issue characteristics.

To assess the scope of interest-group activity in each domain, we asked respondents to estimate the amount of attention given by the general public to domain issues and the relative number of groups actively interested in them. Two points can be made. First, the energy field is seen as considerably broader in participation and attention than the others. Second, agriculture is seen as the narrowest. Doubtless this reflects the excitement surrounding energy issues in the period of our inquiry, but it may also be true that there is a particularly wide array of substantive concerns in this domain. It is interesting that energy representatives offer such high scope estimates. In the health field the representatives give much lower figures than the government officials. This suggests that the health representatives are more substantively specialized than the officials, and hence encounter a smaller slice of the domain's business. In energy, it appears, this distinction is not present. Energy politics have been in such turmoil that it is not surprising that both officials and representatives have been exposed to a broad scope of activity.

A third dimension of domain-issue characteristics involves the degree of group conflict. We asked about the intensity of conflict in general and also about the extent to which domain issues were contested in partisan terms. The two questions draw sharply different responses—conflict is generally said to be high and partisanship to be low. Government officials rather consistently perceive somewhat greater conflict than do private-interest representatives. As one moves from one domain to the next, however, responses on the two questions move more or less together and display rather startling domain differences. Agriculture and health are less conflict-dominated and much less partisan than energy and labor. The labor domain appears to be intensely partisan in comparison with the other domains, and this characteristic ought to appear in the data on allies and adversaries as well. Partisan conflict should be expressed as essentially bipolar opposition whereas the ubiquitous but less partisan disputes of the energy realm might be expected to take a more dispersed, pluralistic form. When we examine the ally-adversary data, we can see whether this expectation is confirmed.

In an effort to probe more deeply into the sources of variation in the issue perceptions of individual representatives, we undertook an extensive probit analysis, employing a considerable number of independent variables. The results were not sufficiently robust to warrant their full presentation here, but they did generally support one important conclusion. We employed several different indicators of individual characteristics, including organizational position, prior government experience, present degree of policy representation effort, and personal values. A contrasting set of considerations consisted of the policy domain involved and the substantive type of organization represented, including labor unions, farm groups, and so on. In virtually every case the latter considerations had much more substantial effects. Agriculture is quiet and nonpartisan; labor is noisy, conflictual, and partisan. Energy and health are highly visible with many participants, while agriculture is perceived to be otherwise. Peak-association representatives see themselves more embroiled in controversies of broader scope and attention (apart from the actual range of their issue involvement) than do those who serve more specialized interests. These differences make reasonable sense and give support to our hope of capturing some diversity by our choices of policy domains.

Allies and Adversaries: Who Works with (and Against) Whom?

In this section we examine responses to two questions. First, we asked whether the organization employing the respondent regularly encountered other organizations, as either allies or adversaries, in the particular policy domain. If they answered affirmatively, we asked the respondent to name up to three of each. The responses allow us to chart in considerable detail the patterning of interorganizational relationships. We will distinguish between organizations that are deeply embroiled in group conflict and those that remain on relatively friendly terms with others in the domain. We will also examine how domains differ in their conflict structures and the extent to which those differences are embedded in the substantive differences among interests in different domains.

Overwhelming majorities in each domain are able to identify both allies (89.9%) and adversaries (74.8%). Labor is most completely defined in ally-adversary terms, health and agriculture somewhat less so. Responses do not differ much by organizational position, though government-affairs specialists are a bit more likely than others to name adversaries.

Probit analysis of the same kind referred to in the previous section indicates that indeed the labor domain is especially likely to generate adversaries. Moreover, labor groups, in whatever domain they participate, are significantly more likely to identify adversaries than are business peaks, business corporations, citizen or externality groups, and energy producers. Time spent by the representative in the domain also makes it likely that adversaries will be named. The full equation produces an estimated r-square of .27 and correctly predicts 77.5% of the cases. That seems a reasonably robust result and one in which most of the predictive power is found in the categories of organizations rather than in individual-level variables or in the domain. As we examine the interconnections among these organizational types, we will thus have good reason to regard them as meaningful, apart from other considerations.

When we turn to the actual nominations, we find a very sizable array of organizations named. Table 2 presents the total numbers for each domain. We really cannot say whether the domain differences in Table 2 are large or small because we lack any comparative standard, but it is clear from the ratio of nominators to nominee organizations that in the energy domain the players agree somewhat more fully about both friends and enemies. In the labor area, the adversary list is relatively concentrated, while in both agriculture and health allies and adversaries are more diffuse.

In order to comprehend the specific alliances and antagonisms in each domain, we have sorted both the nominating organizations and their nominees into groups of similar organizational types. We wished to make the process as parsimonious as possible, but we also felt it necessary to adjust our categories somewhat to take account of elements specific to each policy domain. Many organizations defy easy cat-

TABLE 2
Nominations of Interest-Group Allies and Adversaries

Domain	Allies	Adversaries
Agriculture		
Total nominations	422	287
Organizations named	186	116
Nominators	161	133
Energy		
Total nominations	449	321
Organizations named	143	95
Nominators	165	142
Health		
Total nominations	497	244
Organizations named	215	96
Nominators	185	125
Labor		
Total nominations	446	349
Organizations named	184	99
Nominators	167	151

egorization. Energy firms are often involved in the production or sale of more than one kind of fuel, for example, and a classification of organizations based on fuel type, of critical importance in energy politics (Chubb 1983), encounters difficulties. In agriculture some commodity groups are composed entirely of farmer-producers while others include processors, shippers, commodity brokers, and so on (see Guither 1980). We do not claim to have escaped error, but we believe that most of the more than 1,000 organizations named were sensibly classified, and that the findings, accordingly, are credible.

The agriculture domain presents the simplest array of categories, though not the plainest structure (cf. Bonnen 1980; Browne 1986; Hanson 1985). The four categories in Table 3 are *farm peak organizations,* the general organizations of farmers and their subsidiaries; *commodity groups,* producers or producer-dominated organizations specializing in a single crop or farm commodity; *trade associations,* organizations of corporations not directly involved in agricultural production; and, borrow-

TABLE 3
Allies and Adversaries in Agriculture

Nominee Organization	Nominating Organizations			
	Farm Peaks	Commodity Groups	Trade Associations	Externality Groups
Ally				
Farm peaks	30	26	9	6
Commodity groups	27	60	13	5
Trade associations	8	10	41	4
Externality groups	5	0	6	38
Number of respondents	26	35	27	24
Adversary				
Farm peaks	20	18	3	9
Commodity groups	12	3	2	5
Trade associations	2	6	1	15
Externality groups	6	25	41	9
Number of respondents	22	28	19	20

ing Hadwiger's (1982) term, *externality groups,* including environmental, welfare, labor, and consumer groups concerned about the externalities of farm policies.

Table 3 presents the number of nominations received by organizations in each category (omitting the considerable number scattered across other kinds of groups). It shows several things of importance. First, the groups in each category tend very strongly to find their allies within their own organizational category. As we will see, this is true also in every other domain. Secondly, farm-peak organizations are internally divided. Both friends and enemies are found there, by the peak organizations and by each of the other sectors. To a lesser extent this is true also of the externality set. Neither commodity groups nor trade associations, on the other hand, often find adversaries internally or in the other. Despite the great diversity within each category and the real potential for conflict between, say, feed producers and livestock interests, the reported organizational alignments do not suggest such conflict. The primary object of adversarial concern among these two sets of specialized interests, commodity groups and trade associations, is the externality category. Apart from the externality groups themselves, few organizations choose them as allies, and they loom very large as opponents. As we will see, a comparable tendency can be observed in other policy domains as well.

The energy field reflects a pattern much like that of agriculture, with one principal exception. In energy politics the role of peak associations—those that transcend particular industries, like the chamber of commerce or the National Association of Manufacturers (NAM)—is quite modest. Here again, however, we see specialized-producer interests working closely with one another and with relatively few adversaries within the industry. Trade associations are less differentiated from producers in energy than they are from those in agriculture, though in both domains they seem to avoid making enemies among producer groups. Hostility from the producer interests and peak business organizations is visited on the environmentalists. Three-fourths of the adversaries named by the energy groups included in Table 4 were environmental groups. Rarely were they said to be allies. Thus they occupy the same functional position in energy as externality groups in agriculture, a category that in that domain also includes environmentalists.

TABLE 4
Allies and Adversaries in Energy

Nominee Organization	Nominating Organizations				
	Business Peaks	Oil and Gas	Nuclear and Electric	Trade Associations	Environmental Groups
Ally					
Business peaks	3	10	1	15	3
Oil and gas	11	57	4	23	0
Nuclear and electric	4	3	38	11	0
Trade associations	6	7	5	24	0
Environmental groups	0	1	8	1	18
Number of respondents	9	32	27	31	8
Adversary					
Business peaks	0	0	0	0	0
Oil and gas	1	14	0	5	4
Nuclear and electric	0	1	5	1	5
Trade associations	0	2	3	1	4
Environmental groups	14	37	51	46	3
Number of respondents	8	27	26	29	8

The health-policy domain presents some features resembling energy and agriculture. Here, too, we find that interests select their allies primarily from within their own organizational categories. The externality groups—citizens organizations of various sorts including the Nader-related groups, and labor unions—are often the targets of adversarial relations. More often than in other domains we have examined, however, these groups are also chosen as allies. We take this to mean that the health domain is somewhat less rancorous than others. We noted earlier that a smaller proportion of health respondents had indicated that they regularly encountered opposing groups. Moreover, health representatives perceived their issues to be less conflict ridden and less partisan than did participants in other domains. The diversity of relationships with the *citizen and labor* category is further evidence on the same point.

In the health domain there are no genuine peak associations. The American Medical Association might be so regarded, but only for doctors, and it is obvious that doctors are only one among several sets of interest-group participants, albeit a highly significant set. No health group successfully transcends the several major categories of interested parties and lays a persuasive claim to speak for the health-policy community. It may well be that this very fact helps account for the somewhat lower level of acrimony characterizing health politics. Indeed, in an earlier era, when the AMA did largely dominate the full agenda of health issues, the domain seems to have been considerably more conflict ridden (Starr 1982). Analogies to superpowers in international politics may be farfetched, but it is not implausible to argue that the existence of superpowers tends to polarize conflict and that polarization tends to lead to intensification.

Other points of interest in Table 5 include the fact that academic and hospital groups are especially reluctant to name any adversaries. Veterans, a group category not included in the table, carry this strategy to perfection; they claim to have no organized group opponents at all. The congressional politics of health issues is often strenuously contentious, of course, but what these data indicate is that the conflict is not so much among competing interests represented by adversary organizations as with the more amorphous forces of budget constraints and administration priorities. Group politics is an important, sometimes even decisive, part of the overall policy-making process; but it is seldom, if ever, all one needs to know to explain policy outcomes.

We turn now to the labor-policy domain. Here it is plain that we encounter a bipolar conflict structure. The peak associations of labor

TABLE 5
Allies and Adversaries in Health

Nominee Organization	Nominating Organizations					
	Medical Associations	Academic Groups	Hospitals	Disease Groups and Nonfederal Officials	Trade Associations	Citizens and Labor
Ally						
Medical associations	41	10	6	3	0	6
Academic groups	15	39	8	0	0	0
Hospitals	14	10	42	3	2	4
Disease groups and nonfederal officials	6	1	0	29	0	10
Trade associations	1	0	0	0	46	1
Citizens and labor	5	5	6	8	6	50
Number of respondents	31	25	23	19	20	25
Adversary						
Medical associations	19	1	0	0	0	7
Academic groups	1	0	0	0	0	0
Hospitals	3	2	1	5	0	11
Disease groups and nonfederal officials	0	0	0	3	2	0
Trade associations	2	1	2	4	3	8
Citizens and labor	17	9	11	6	21	16
Number of respondents	21	13	14	10	16	19

and business dominate the poles, and there is almost no trafficking with the other side. Individual unions and trade associations are slightly less implacable foes. The latter, especially, have worked out some alliances with the unions. Citizens groups in this domain are a diverse lot, primarily aligned with labor but including a significant number of antilabor groups, producing substantial intracategory conflict. One revealing feature of Table 6 is that in the conflict-charged climate of labor policy, unlike the other three domains, nearly every respondent was willing to name adversaries as well as allies.

These findings confirm our data regarding the characteristics of issues, where the labor domain evidenced the highest levels of conflict and partisanship. The ally-adversary structure mapped in Table 6 is congruent with the perceptions of labor issues. It is also confirmed by the patterns of event-specific activity reported by our respondents. Groups' relationships to one another in respect to what positions, if any, they had taken on particular policy issues revealed a clear bipolar structure on labor issues. In the other domains, the event-triggered patterns were segmented along lines essentially similar to the organizational

TABLE 6
Allies and Adversaries in Labor

Nominee Organization	Nominating Organizations				
	Labor Peaks	Unions	Citizens Groups	Trade Associations	Business Peaks
Ally					
Labor peaks	2	32	8	2	0
Unions	9	37	11	11	2
Citizens groups	15	17	30	3	4
Trade associations	0	1	5	54	15
Business peaks	0	0	5	30	42
Number of respondents	10	35	26	43	23
Adversary					
Labor peaks	0	0	6	20	22
Unions	1	3	3	20	12
Citizens groups	4	24	24	2	4
Trade associations	1	11	5	7	0
Business peaks	15	41	17	4	2
Number of respondents	10	33	24	33	21

groupings identified in Tables 3–6. (For further discussion of these events-based data see Laumann et al. 1986.)

Conclusions

We began by suggesting that the interest-group universe could be regarded as a system of structured conflict (and cooperation). Our data suggest that this is certainly valid at the subsystem, or policy-domain, level (though we are really not able as yet to portray or characterize in any detail the complete "pressure system," to employ Schattschneider's [1960] convenient, if misleading, term). Domain subsystems have been seen to have relatively stable patterns of interaction, quite sharply ideological and bipolar in the labor-policy domain but fragmented, primarily among sets of specialized producer organizations, in the other areas.

Specialized producers, with relatively narrow policy agendas, tend to avoid becoming embroiled in adversarial encounters. As becomes the protagonists in a system of distributive politics, they try instead to confine their efforts to building whatever support they can for their primary policy goals. These live-and-let-live efforts are complicated in some domains by the presence of peak associations, organizations that seek to transcend the limited membership potential of specialized groups like trade associations and to formulate broader policy agendas as they try to speak persuasively on behalf of an entire economic sector. Peak associations tend to express their policy goals in the more encompassing language of doctrine and ideology, using abstraction to rise above the tangible differences of interest among more specialized producers.

The more prominent and unified the peak associations in a policy domain, the more polarized its group structure and policy struggles become. The limiting case in our data is labor, where the peak associations of business and labor do battle and pull the more specialized groups into one orbit or the other. In agriculture, by contrast, the peak associations, once the basis of cohesive bloc politics, are themselves divided. Farm policy-making tends now to be dominated by narrower and often shifting coalitions and to be articulated with less partisan or doctrinal fervor than was the case, say, in the 1950s.

In each of these policy domains, the role of externality groups—environmentalists, consumers, and other "citizens" aggregations—is a kind of mirror image of the peak associations. Where, as in labor, the latter are powerful, the externality groups are diverse, divided, and often serve as satellites to the "superpowers." Where peak associations are divided or nonexistent, the externality interests provide the principal focus of opposition, perceived as getting in the way of the realization of specialized producer interests (see also Scholzman and Tierney 1985, 285–86). Externality groups often like to think of themselves as the guardians of the "public interest" against the diverse claims of multifarious "special interests." With or without that normative language, we find that this structure does indeed characterize three of our four policy domains.

Our interpretation of the role of peak associations in structuring interest-group conflict moves in a very different direction from the principal lines of argument regarding societal corporatism and from the widely discussed contention of Mancur Olson (1982) regarding the significance of encompassing groups. In the corporatist model, effective peak associations of labor and business are necessary elements along with the state in a tripartite structure of cooperative negotiation (Schmitter and Lehmbruch 1979). The singularity of the United States in failing to develop along these lines has been examined elsewhere (Salisbury 1979; Wilson 1982). Our data suggest that even when we do find reasonably effective peak associations, group relations are more rancorous, not more cooperative.

Olson's argument also would lead one to expect that the more encompassing the group (i.e., the more effective the peak associations), the more efficient (i.e., less dominated by narrowly focused producer interests) the policy decisions. The finding that intense conflict develops when the group politics moves from a fragmented, "special" interest-dominated pattern to one in which more broadly encompassing groups are the main players, does not seem compatible with most notions of efficiency. There may, of course, be a stage beyond bipolar group politics in which a single encompassing "group" is able to accomplish fully Pareto-optimal results, but at that point it would appear that we had passed beyond the sphere of democratic politics.

We believe that our findings are relevant to the ongoing debate concerning the validity of pluralist models of U.S. politics. It is obvious that our design has been premised on the assumption that a multiplicity of groups compete in meaningful ways for the rewards at stake in public decisions. But the patterns of group action we have reported go well beyond that. In his classic study of New Haven, Robert Dahl (1961) rests much of his pluralist interpretation on the discovery that business interests (and other interests also) pursued agendas that stopped far short of the full range of public issues and policy decisions. Consequently, their resources, though imposing, were often not brought into play. In his more recent statements, characterized by a considerable degree of recantation, Dahl (1985) and his colleague Lindblom (1977, 1983) place less emphasis on the theme of selective participation as the crucial factor limiting power and protecting pluralism. They stress instead the structural distinctiveness of business interests and the inherent political advantage derived therefrom.

Our data probably cannot illuminate the debate regarding the more abstract properties of business power in a capitalist order. They do show, however, that there is great variety in the forms of politically active business interests (as well as of labor, farmers, professional groups, and others), and that the variety of form is systematically related to the agendas and strategies of action. Trade associations and specialized producers are not simply smaller, narrower segments of a larger class or sector. They often have different goals and operate in different ways, not as anomalies or deviations from some class-defined normalcy but through rational strategy calculated to advance genuine interests.

If, as we have found, the substantive policy domain is a dominant factor in determining the way interest representatives perceive the political context in which they operate and if, further, the structures of domain conflict and cooperation are built from the particular configurations of interest organizations that participate in domain politics, it follows that an adequate understanding not only of interest-group politics but of the full policy process requires us to keep a careful descriptive watch on the group composition of a domain. Unless we know who the organizational players are, how they relate to one another, and what dynamics of organizational development and change are at work, we are unlikely to secure an adequate analytical grasp of the situation. Neither research monographs nor beginning texts should continue to talk about "the farm bloc," the dominant role of the American Medical Association, or the unity of "business" interests when events have long since rendered those empirically invalid. Our effort to describe the structures of conflict and cooperation among organized groups may thus be taken as a contribution to an ongoing obligation to attend systematically to the *substance* of interest-group politics.

In the end, of course, we must be concerned not only with the structures of interest-group relations but with their policy outcomes as well. What is the reflection in substantive decisions of the fragmented politics of agriculture or the bipolar conflicts over labor issues? Does a "play-it-safe" trade association accomplish more of its objectives than a contentious citizens group? In the next phases of our research, we hope to be able to speak to these questions. Meanwhile, however, showing that interest-group interactions display patterns interpretable in their own terms and comparable in structure to those in other realms of political analysis provides an avenue of potential linkage to the broader bodies of theory on which a coherent discipline of political science must rest.

Appendix: Methods of Sampling Client Organizations

We arrived at our sample of client organizations by drawing on four sources of nomination that could measure levels of policy-making activity (Shapiro 1984). Our first method for locating interested actors in a policy domain was especially attentive to issues attracting mass-media attention because of their controversiality and broad popular interest. Such issues are especially likely to appear in the congressional arena. Organizations taking partisan public stands on popular issues are especially likely to be identified by this technique. We conducted a computerized search of stories in national and regional newspapers and magazines dealing with federal policy-making in each domain from January 1977 to June 1982, noting the number of stories mentioning each organization. The data regarding newspaper coverage of organizational participation were compiled from the Information Bank, a data base of the New York Times Information Service (NYTIS). To compensate for regional effects, the data base included the *Chicago Tribune, Houston Chronicle, Los Angeles Times, New York Times, San Francisco Chronicle, Seattle Times, Washington Post,* and *Time* magazine. The product of the computer search was an extensive set of newstory abstracts from the source newspapers. These abstracts were then searched and tagged for the names of organizations, and lists of organizations in each domain were compiled. The number of mentions for each organization was recorded, a mention being defined as an appearance in one newspaper abstract. Duplicate abstracts of stories reported in two or more news sources were eliminated.[1]

Second, we searched the abstracts of congressional hearings held by committees and subcommittees with jurisdiction in each of the four domains during the 95th–97th congresses, noting the number of hearings at which organizations testified. Less publicly partisan and more specialized organizations are revealed by this procedure. In light of the enormous number of hearings covered in the Congressional Information Service (CIS) database, we restricted the search to the first sessions of the 95th, 96th, and 97th congresses and to select major committees active in each domain.

Third, during July 1982, we interviewed 20–23 government officials in various policy-making positions in each domain in the Congress and the executive agencies, noting the number of officials mentioning an organization as one that frequently contacted them or which was representative of organizations that contacted them episodically. This method is especially likely to identify organizations having direct dealings and concerns with particular executive agencies and their regulatory initiatives. Two criteria were used in selecting individuals to be interviewed: (1) the position of the individual in the unit and (2) his or her tenure in the unit. An attempt was made to avoid relying exclusively on politically appointed officials or on those with less than two years' tenure in office.

Finally, for each domain we compiled a list of organizations appearing under the industry headings raised to the domain in *Washington Representatives* (1981), an annual publication that canvasses various public sources and surveys organizations in an effort to list organizations represented before the federal government. Organizations that are self-professed lobbyists before Congress and the executive agencies are especially likely to be identified.

Each source method of nominating organizations for inclusion in the population of claimant organizations has distinctive features that sets it apart from the others (Salisbury 1984). If we had relied only on the listing produced by the *Washington Representatives*, we would have underestimated the population of interested organizations by more than half in each domain. (The percentage of organizations *not* contained in the *Washington Representatives* directory was 70.4% in agriculture, 52.8% in energy, 67.1% in health, and 80.3 in labor.) Domains differ substantially among themselves with respect to the amount of newspaper attention given them, the raw numbers of organizations identified as active, and the number of organizations engaged in repeated efforts to influence policy outcomes in their respective domains. The energy domain seems to have the largest number of organizations attracted to its concerns, with agriculture and health roughly tied in scale of participation with almost a third fewer organizational participants, and labor placing a rather distant fourth. While the CIS ratios of the number of mentions to the number of organizations mentioned are remarkably stable across the four domains, the NYTIS ratios vary considerably across domains.

There is a high ratio in energy, for example, suggesting the relative prevalence of "repeat players" in the domain.

For each domain we drew a random sample of 100 organizations, with each of the four sources contributing equally, but with each organization in the first three sources weighted by the number of mentions in that source. Because, for all but the listing from *Washington Representatives*, the probability of selection increased with the number of mentions, our sampling procedure reflected each organization's level of activity in the domain. We had strong reasons to adopt this weighting procedure. Knoke and Laumann (1983) had demonstrated that there was a high correlation (.75 and .72 for the energy and health domains, respectively) between the number of organizations active in a domain that named an organization as among the most influential actors in the domain and the number of mentions in newspaper stories, appearances in congressional hearings, and mentions by government officials. Hence, there was solid evidence for treating the number of mentions in the various sources as a measure of perceived organizational influence. The sampling procedure thus generated a list of organizations to be interviewed that disproportionately included the more influential and active organizations in the domain, while also allowing the selection of less influential and active organizations. Simple inspection of the samples reveals that we were quite successful in including many of the most prominent and influential organizations, with an admixture of less visible, more peripheral organizations. This mixture of organizations will permit us to investigate what, if any, systematic differences are to be observed in modes of participation in policy deliberations across different types of organizational actors.

Having sampled the client organizations, we then identified the representatives they employed or retained by conducting telephone interviews with client informants in a minimum of 75 organizations in each domain, 316 organizations in all.[2] These informants were identified by using published listings of organization officers, supplemented with direct inquiries of the organizations to determine who had operating responsibility for the organization's involvement in federal policy in the appropriate domain. The informant was asked to name up to four individuals inside the organization (employees, officers, member volunteers) and up to four individuals external to the organizations (employed in outside firms, trade associations, and so forth but not falling within the definition of an internal representative) who acted as key representatives for the organization in the policy area. It is this listing of nominated individuals that constituted the population of representatives.

The client interviews generated between 400 and 450 names of representatives in each domain, for a total of 1,716 individuals. (Representatives could appear on the lists as many times as they were mentioned; about 5% appeared in more than one domain.) Random selection from these lists produced samples of 257 to 261 representatives per domain, with a realized sample ranging from 192 to 216 across the four domains. The overall response rate of representatives was 77%. About 10% of the representatives contacted declined interviews; the rest could not be scheduled for various reasons. Slightly over two-thirds of the respondents were based in Washington and were personally interviewed there. Another 15%, based in other major cities, also were interviewed personally. The remainder of the sample was interviewed by telephone using an adapted format.

The final set of actors to be identified were the government officials most often the targets of representational activity in a given domain. These target government officials (including those holding elected, appointed, and career positions) were identified by asking the representatives we sampled to give the names and positions of "the five government officials or staff members you contact most often in the course of your work" in the appropriate policy domain. From these lists we sampled from 101 to 108 names in each domain, and successfully interviewed about 72%. About 8% of the government officials declined to be interviewed.

NOTES

The data analysis in this paper is the work of Paul Johnson now of the University of Kansas. His contribution has been both technical and substantive and altogether invaluable. We also acknowledge with gratitude the assistance of Tony Tam of the University of Chicago. Support for our research has been provided by the American Bar Foundation and the National Science Foundation. An earlier version of this article was presented at the 1986 annual meeting of the American Political Science Association, Washington.

1. For a presentation of the specific data see Nelson et al. 1987.

2. The response rate was 78% with 10% of the organizations refusing interviews. Another 12% of the organizations could not be located, were located overseas, or had ceased to exist. Refusals did not follow any discernible pattern and were not regarded as a significant source of bias.

REFERENCES

Bentley, Arthur F. 1908. *The Process of Government*. Chicago: University of Chicago Press.

Berry, Jeffrey. 1977. *Lobbying for the People*. Princeton: Princeton University Press.

Bonnen, James T. 1980. Observations on the Changing Nature of National Agricultural Policy Decision Process, 1946–76. In *Farmers, Bureaucrats, and Middlemen: Historical Perspectives on American Agriculture*, ed. Trudy Huskamp Peterson. Washington: Howard University Press.

Browne, William P. 1986. Lobbyists, Private Interests, and the 1985 Farm Bill. Central Michigan University.

Browne, William P., and Robert H. Salisbury. 1972. Organized Spokesmen for Cities: Urban Interest Groups. In *People and Politics in Urban Society*, ed. Harlan Hahn. Beverly Hills: Sage.

Chubb, John E. 1983. *Interest Groups and the Bureaucracy: The Politics of Energy*. Stanford: Stanford University Press.

Dahl, Robert. 1961. *Who Governs?* New Haven: Yale University Press.

Dahl, Robert. 1985. *A Preface to Economic Democracy*. Berkeley: University of California Press.

Guither, Harold D. 1980. *The Food Lobbyists*. Lexington: Lexington Books.

Hadwiger, Don F. 1982. *The Politics of Agricultural Research*. Lincoln: University of Nebraska Press.

Hanson, John Mark. 1985. Congressmen and Interest Groups: The Development of an Agricultural Policy Network in the 1920s. Paper presented at annual meeting of American Political Science Association, New Orleans.

Knoke, David, and Edward O. Laumann. 1983. The Social Organization of National Policy Domains: An Exploration of Some Structural Hypotheses. In *Social Structure and Network Analysis*, ed. Nan Lin and Peter V. Marsden. Beverly Hills: Sage.

Laumann, Edward O., John P. Heinz, Robert Nelson, and Robert Salisbury. 1986. Organizations in Political Action: Representing Interests in National Policy-Making. Paper presented at annual meeting of American Sociological Association, New York.

Laumann, Edward O., and David Knoke. 1987. *The Organizational State: Social Choices and National Policy Domains*. Madison: University of Wisconsin Press.

Lindblom, Charles E. 1977. *Politics and Markets*. New York: Basic Books.

Lindblom, Charles E. 1983. Comment on Manley. *American Political Science Review* 77:384–86.

Moe, Terry. 1980. *The Organization of Interests*. Chicago: University of Chicago Press.

Nelson, Robert L., John P. Heinz, Edward O. Laumann, and Robert H. Salisbury. 1987. Private Representation in Washington: Surveying the Structure of Influence. *American Bar Foundation Journal* 1987 (Winter):141–200.

Olson, Mancur. 1982. *The Rise and Decline of Nations: Economic Growth, Stagflation, and Social Rigidities.* New Haven; Yale University Press.

Olson, Mancur. 1965. *The Logic of Collective Action.* Cambridge: Harvard University Press.

Salisbury, Robert H. 1969. An Exchange Theory of Interest Groups. *Midwest Journal of Political Science* 13:1–32.

Salisbury, Robert H. 1979. Why No Corporatism in America? In *Trends toward Corporatist Intermediation,* ed. Philippe Schmitter and Gerhard Lehmbruch. Beverly Hills: Sage.

Salisbury, Robert H. 1984. Interest Representation: The Dominance of Institutions. *American Political Science Review* 78:64–76.

Schattschneider, E. E. 1960. *The Semi-Sovereign People.* New York: Holt, Rinehart & Winston.

Schmitter, Philippe, and Gerhard Lehmbruch, eds. 1979. *Trends Toward Corporatist Intermediation.* Beverly Hills: Sage.

Schlozman, Kay L., and John T. Tierney. 1985. *Organized Interests and American Democracy.* New York: Harper & Row.

Shapiro, Andrew. 1984. Sampling Memorandum Describing Procedures Employed in Washington Representatives Project. University of Chicago. Mimeo.

Starr, Paul. 1982. *The Transformation of American Medicine.* Cambridge: Harvard University Press.

Walker, Jack L. 1983. The Origins and Maintenance of Interest Groups in America. *American Political Science Review* 77:390–406.

Wilson, Graham. 1982. Why Is There No Corporatism in the United States? In *Patterns of Corporatist Policy-Making,* ed. Gerhard Lehmbruch and Philippe Schmitter. Beverly Hills: Sage.

Wilson, Graham. 1985. *Business and Politics: A Comparative Introduction.* Chatham, NJ: Chatham House.

9

U.S. Congressman as Enterprise

*E*ven the casual watcher of the congressional world cannot fail to observe the incredibly complex array of personnel and activities on and around the Hill. Some of the confusion results from the surfeit of tourists, bus-trippers, and other visitors to the nation's Capitol. Some is due to the publicity whirl mutually compounded by politicians and the media. Much of the scurrying, the crowding, and the frenetic pace, however, stems from the sheer volume of personnel employed by Congress. The number of members has remained constant, but in the years between 1967 and 1979 the number of congressional committee staff and personal staff employees grew from 7,014 to 13,276; the total number of employees (staffers and others) is now well over thirty thousand. This fact has been noted by several observers, and some of its implications have been explored (Fox and Hammond, 1977; Machowsky, 1978; Malbin, 1980). Nevertheless, the impact of staff growth on the members themselves has not, we think, been fully appreciated.

In this essay, we wish to argue that as a consequence of staff expansion each member of Congress has come to operate as the head of an enterprise—an organization consisting of anywhere from eight or ten to well over one hundred subordinates. These organizations, varying in complexity, structure, and function, constrain and shape the behavior of the members in ways that help make the Congress itself a "loosely coupled" collection of these enterprises, a very different institution than it was. Much of what we will say grows out of, or is at least compatible

Kenneth A. Shepsle coauthored this article. It is reprinted with permission from *Legislative Studies Quarterly* 6 (November 1981):559–76.

with, other recent analyses of congressional change (Ornstein, 1975; Dodd and Oppenheimer, 1977). We do not seek to elucidate fully its dimensions or to identify all of the factors involved. Institutional reforms, incumbency effects, party decomposition, and leadership debility have all been at work. Nevertheless, we think that an emphasis on the transforming effects of staff growth on member functioning warrants close attention.

Structural Components of Member-Centered Enterprises

The core of any congressional enterprise is the personal staff of the member. This is so in part because the personal staff is unequivocally and entirely dependent on the member for hiring and promotion. Its explicit responsibility is to serve the member's needs and interests, and its primary normative commitment is loyalty to the member. There is considerable variety in the ways that members organize their staffs. Some place a large fraction of the casework personnel in the state or district, for instance, retaining principally the legislative aides in the Washington office. Some sharply differentiate among staff functions so that the responsibilities of the press aide and of the administrative or legislative assistants seldom overlap. In other offices, on the other hand, "everybody does everything as needed—we hope." Some offices are organized along strict hierarchical lines with authority concentrated in the hands of a single senior aide, while other members prefer less clearly delineated lines of authority and responsibility (Fox and Hammond, 1977, Table 14; Loomis, 1979).

There is not much evidence to suggest that organizational form as such affects the substance of what members do. It may affect the efficiency with which things are done, especially in processing casework. In addition, the choice of organizational style may often reflect the member's own conception of his or her role and the functional priorities associated with it. Thus a member who puts most of the staff in the district is seen thereby to be stressing casework and constituency service and *ceteris paribus* may reasonably be regarded as placing a high value on reelection as against legislative achievement.

It is dangerous, however, to stress the pattern of personal staff arrangements, precisely because a large proportion of the members have additional staff components within their total enterprise. Most committee and subcommittee staff are appointed by, or think of themselves as primarily subordinate to, a particular member. Prior to the "democratization" movement of the early 1970s, the primary appointing member was generally the committee chairman. The recent wave of reforms, however, has vested de facto and generally de jure authority in subcommittee chairs, minority members, and, in some cases, every member of a particular committee. As a consequence, all members of the Senate and most members of the House have at least some voice in the selection of committee or subcommittee staff members. This means that a given member is able to draw not only upon the skills and talents of his or her personal staff but on certain committee or subcommittee personnel as well. A committee chairmanship thereby adds a sizable cadre of assistants to a member's enterprise. A subcommittee chairmanship likewise yields significant assistance. A Democratic senator in 1980 (but not 1981!) might reasonably expect to head one full committee and/or one or more subcommittees; the resultant staff increments available therefrom might range from a low of about twenty to a high of over one hundred. Individual House members do not profit so richly from the available staff resources; indeed, not every House member, even of the majority, is able to profit at all. Those House members who do gain committee or subcommittee staff assistance may thereby gain a relatively larger advantage vis-à-vis their lower-ranking colleagues. Still, in the House as in the Senate, committee staff are distributed among a large number of members. Decentralization of power is thereby enhanced. And for a large number of members, the problem is posed as to how to manage this organization, this collection of personnel differentiated by political function and legal status, but nevertheless subordinate to the specific member.

Other Personnel Resources

Before we pursue this question, let us look briefly at four other types of personnel resources that may contribute to the strength of particular members. One derives from the auxiliary agencies, such as the Congressional Research Service (CRS), the Office of Technology Assessment (OTA), the Congressional Budget Office (CBO), and the General Accounting Office (GAO), where some members may have particularly effective access. For example, it was widely alleged that Senator Kennedy (D.-Mass.) had used OTA as a source of quasi-patronage such that some of its staff would be especially attentive to the senator's needs (Greenberg, 1977; Cohen, 1979). Kennedy's influence over OTA staff was derived from his position as chairman of the committee overseeing the operation.

A second kind of extended staff dependency may result from proliferation of "alumni networks," composed of people who once worked for
a member and now work elsewhere on the Hill, but continue to carry
the more or less clearly acknowledged blessing of their erstwhile principal. Thus one hears of "so-and-so" who now is assistant general counsel of committee X but who was brought to Washington by Congressman
Q and remains in close and faithful contact with the congressman. Indeed, he may owe his present job to the member's recommendation.

A third variety of "once-removed" enterprise member is the former
staffer now comfortably ensconced in a trade association, labor union, or
law firm located in the downtown Washington "K Street Corridor."
Though no longer involved exclusively in legislative machinations, he
may nevertheless serve his former boss as a source of information and
occasional assistance.

Finally, there are the executive-branch alumni of the enterprises of
particular legislators. In 1977, for instance, five assistant secretaries for
congressional relations in executive departments had served previously
on the staff of a single Democratic senator. Clearly, that senator had the
makings of a network of interaction and collaboration that might carry
his influence well beyond what he as an individual could have imagined.
In a very real political sense, that senator had come to head an enterprise that reached deep into the administration as well as extending directly into three subcommittees and, via the personal staff, throughout
his home state.

Given the variegated character of the personnel system of a senator
or congressman, to regard him as an isolated individual or even as a personality buffered against and buffeted by contending outside forces is inappropriate. To do so is to err, in the same way that it is mistaken to treat
the actions of a corporate executive primarily in terms of his (or, rarely,
her) personality rather than as constrained by the context of forces well
beyond his or her individual uniqueness.

In this discussion, we will not discuss the relationships members develop with particular groups of other members, including special interest caucuses, ideological coalitions, state delegations, and so on. These
interactions, insofar as they are effective, certainly complicate the structure of congressional action, but as they contribute no additional staff
resources as such (indeed, they often require member contributions of
staff), they do not alter the enterprises themselves. Collusion among a
particular set of firms does not as such alter the character of the firms,
and so it is with congressmen.

The Consequences of an Enterprise Perspective

If we are to contend that a particular frame of reference is analytically superior to extant alternatives, we are obliged to indicate what difference it makes to adopt the recommended perspective. What questions are we led to that we might otherwise overlook or undervalue?

The principal advantage of this perspective is that it allows us to incorporate the phenomena of congressional staff systematically with the analysis of Congress rather than awkwardly appending it to a discussion of congressmen as discrete individuals. The effect of extensive staff has been to transform the individual member in much the same fashion that presidential staff has transformed the chief executive. One does not dwell for long on Richard Nixon, Jimmy Carter, or Ronald Reagan in isolation; rather one incorporates their staff assistants into the analysis, not obliterating the president as a unique individual but interpreting his actions in a different way than one might do with a Lincoln or a Jefferson whose agonies of office were largely suffered alone. The Henry Jackson (D.-Wash.) enterprise and the Jacob Javits (R.-N.Y.) enterprise were different and more complex phenomena than could be expressed by either senator's personal presence alone; each in 1980 comprised well over one hundred people, incorporating expertise and active involvement in multiple policy areas. Done in his name and almost always within the bounds of his desires, the activities of the senatorial enterprise are nevertheless both more than and different from those of the senator himself. The result of the actions and interactions of one hundred senatorial enterprises, moreover, generates a quite different institution than the one of a century ago, or even of a few decades ago, consisting of individual senators acting more or less alone.

The literature on the modern Congress recognizes fully that the institution has been transformed and generally points accurately to the reasons behind the transformation. We do not seek here to contribute so much to the explanation of this change as to articulate a useful way to characterize it. By considering congressmen as organizations, we are led to investigate some critical questions of organizational behavior that we might not think of if the members were regarded solely as individuals. Froman (1968) and, especially, Cooper (1975, 1977) have argued the utility of thinking of Congress itself as an organization and we are, in a sense, moving their case down to the level of the member.

Where is the Bottom Line?

Congressional enterprises "produce" a mix of outcomes that varies, in part, according to member motivation and opportunity and, in part, according to season and necessity. Fenno (1973) has developed a trichotomy of member motives that will serve us, initially at least, in developing the point. He suggests that members may in their committee work seek to emphasize their own reelection, the enactment of sound public policy, or career advancement within the congressional institution. We would broaden and modify this formulation to recognize that members pursue those basic purposes, with varying emphasis, in all aspects of their activity and that most members pursue all three kinds of goals simultaneously and continuously. Now if we were considering the members only as individuals, we could not accept that reformulation of Fenno's typology. When the individual member is engaged in floor debate, he cannot also be doing casework, negotiating with the "other body," and soliciting campaign funds. But the member's enterprise can indeed do all those things and more and, with shifting emphasis and variable efficiency, does.

Promotion Activities

Every member-enterprise engages in member-promotion activities on a continuous basis. Media-related efforts, casework, newsletter production, trips to the district, and the wide range of credit-taking ploys of which the modern member is a master generate attention and, hopefully, support that ultimately will be revealed in the next election. Not every member feels the same need for promotional efforts, of course. Some, on the other hand, seem interested in little else. Senators may accentuate promotional work in the period prior to a reelection campaign and slack off a bit at other times, but increasingly the style seems to be to routinize much of the promotional work and at a high volume. Even the member who has already announced the intention to retire generally continues the publicity mill at an undiminished pace.

Much of the member-promotion is done by the personal staff, of course, and as every member has such a staff regardless of seniority, committee assignment, or leadership responsibility, it may fairly be regarded as the core of the member-enterprise, the sine qua non of the other functions. But, as Fenno has shown, committee work often has its promotional aspects, too, and it is obviously a mistake to assume that policy-centered efforts, from bill sponsorship to floor management, have no implications or are not exploited for the advancement of the member's career. A subcommittee staff counsel is often as attentive to the constituency needs of the subcommittee chairperson as the latter's press aide or campaign manager.

The relationship of the member-enterprise to the reelection campaign itself is often tricky legally and ambiguous organizationally. No congressional funds may be used to pay people who are working on a campaign staff or to purchase campaign materials. Nevertheless, it is common for individual staffers to move from a personal or, less often, committee payroll to the campaign payroll for all or part of the campaign and then return to a Hill position, either the old one or another within the member's enterprise. This movement of individuals among formal organizational units need not affect very much what they actually do. A speech writer or a press aide may carry on in much the same manner whether employed by the member-representative or the member-candidate. The point is that in either capacity the staffer is part of the member's enterprise, the latter having been enlarged and somewhat modified in function for the duration of the campaign proper, and the niceties of legal restrictions on who may be paid by whom for what only marginally affect the behavioral realities of member-staff interactions.

Policy Formation

Every member-enterprise engages in public policy formation. At minimum, the member votes on the floor and in committee. We do not suggest that members vote against their preferences or the interests of their constituents. Despite occasional conspiracy theories to the contrary, it rarely occurs that the enterprise—that is, the staffers tied to the specific member—will decisively alter this direction of member voting. Nevertheless, the sheer scope and complexity of the legislative agenda make it impossible for even the most indefatigable member to master the substance of every issue sufficiently well to reach in isolation a judgment about how to vote. While the Administration, congressional party leaders, and other cue-givers provide important guidelines for member behavior (Kingdon, 1973; Matthews and Stimson, 1975), one consequence of the growth of member enterprises is that substantial guidance can come from within the enterprise, i.e., from the staff.

Beyond the "simple" acts of voting, member-enterprises are engaged in bill and amendment drafting and sponsorship, participation in floor debate, and involvement during committee and subcommittee sessions including hearings, investigations, markups, and report preparation. That the individual member may not always personally perform each and every function does not diminish the impact of the work, or the member's ultimate responsibility for what is done in his or her name. Sometimes, as in voting, the member cannot delegate, and generally the extent to which member-enterprises are dependent on the visible performance by the principal is far greater than in most small business enterprises where even the most charismatic of proprietors may occasionally leave subordinates in charge. Nevertheless, staffers do enormously expand the scope and range of each member's policy-relevant activity. Much of it may have promotional effects, of course—a bill designed for election purposes with no real intention of pushing it through to enactment, an amendment intended to benefit a district interest, or a floor speech to be distributed under the frank throughout the state.

It may often be that committee staffers give less explicit attention to the promotional implication of an action than would a member's personal staff. Some policy specialists within a given member's enterprise—foreign policy advisers, for example—may be instructed not to worry about the back-home implications of an issue. In general, however, we may expect the distinction between policy-oriented and promotional activity not to be sharply drawn. A very large proportion of what any member-enterprise does affects both promotional and policy goals and any attempt rigidly to compartmentalize the two would force the enterprise into a thoroughly artificial and generally misconceived situation.

Building Influence

Fenno's third motivation affecting congressmen in committees is achieving influence within the House. We may adapt this for our purposes by suggesting that many, though perhaps not all, member-enterprises seek to build influence, not only within the House or Senate but in some meaningful political arena(s). It might be a committee or even a subcommittee. It might be a "cozy triangle," a policy subsystem involving member-enterprises, executive agencies, and interest groups. It might be a state delegation, a party caucus, an ideological grouping, or some combination of all of these. The influence in question might

remain quite diffuse, taking the form of a general reputation as someone to be reckoned with. Or it might be very specific, having as its objective the protection of an agency's jurisdiction or even election as
Speaker. Since motivation is so intertwined with opportunity, the prudent member will seldom delimit the objects of ambition unnecessarily.
You never can tell what might develop.

The point is that in seeking power within the institution, the modern
member utilizes not only his or her personal skills and opportunities but
those afforded by the whole enterprise the member heads. It follows
that, by and large, the bigger and more well-placed that enterprise in its
various elements may be, the better the chances for additional power to
be secured. Hence a committee chair confers power, not simply anymore
by the sheer authority of the position but through the increment of staff
to the member-centered enterprise. Each subcommittee assignment carries staff resources for the member, sometimes small and sometimes
very substantial. Seniority of service is likely to be accomplished by a
growing corps of "alumni." The wider distribution of staff resources resulting from such developments as the Subcommittee Bill of Rights, S.
Res. 60, H. Res. 5, and so on, however, has decentralized power and rendered member-enterprises somewhat more equal.

Survival and Success

In a fundamental sense, the "bottom line" is measured by enterprise
survival in the relevant electoral arena and by success in the arenas
of policymaking and institutional power. Within a given member-
enterprise, however, these imperatives will often be too imprecise to
animate and guide the diverse individuals who comprise the "organization." It is, therefore, a consequence of this perspective that we must pay
attention to the structure of signals and incentives that operates within
member-enterprises to constrain and shape behavior.

Our perspective may seem to subordinate the elected senator or representative by placing him or her in an organizational context, but it
must be remembered that it is the member who hires and fires, fixes salaries and sets responsibilities, and generally establishes the framework
of expectations, substantive and procedural, that will define the enterprise and constrain its members. It is the member individually who must
be reelected and whose policy priorities must nearly always have first
claim on staff effort. Yet in many specific situations, these acknowledged
obligations constitute no more than a general guide to action. "The boss

wants to do something for consumers. Fine—but what?" The staff must develop a legislative proposal. More commonly, "The boss needs to look like he's been effective up here. He needs to be able to take credit for doing something." The staff must devise the "something."

Some members give close guidance to staff, monitoring the choices of substance and strategy and supervising every stage of the enterprise. Other members delegate some areas—casework, for example—while retaining certain substantive policy areas for personal input. Still others are content to front for the organization and let staffers do nearly all the day-to-day detail work. Different enterprises play it in different ways. It may be that senior Southern Democrats and a few other "old style" members tend to delegate less and control more directly and tightly the work of their enterprises than do the newer members who are more accustomed to extensive staff support. Apart from this very tentative observation, we have not been able to discern systematic differences in the closeness of articulation or, alternatively, organizational slack or flaccidity. Our main concern is to suggest that among the members heading these congressional enterprises, there are important variations in style that follow very different lines from those observed in the past by students of individual-level congressional behavior.

Above the Bottom Line: Staff Styles and Ambitions

Staffers, too, have diverse styles and ambitions, of course, and we must note how these affect the functioning of congressional enterprises. Price (1971) has distinguished between "professionals" and "policy entrepreneurs" in assessing staff motivations. A "professional" is a staff member whose primary commitment is to a particular role and its attendant norms, such as that of parliamentarian, appropriations clerk, or tax lawyer concerned with the technical niceties of the Internal Revenue Code. A "policy entrepreneur" is seeking to use his or her staff role to advance a particular policy objective. Both these types of staff may readily work in many different member-enterprises, though the policy entrepreneurs are presumably constrained by ideological limits and would comfortably fit only in "right-thinking" companies. One might wish to add to Price's pair a third type of staffer, the "politico," whose overarching concern is to serve neither role nor policy but rather the career of the member who heads the enterprise. Politicos may move among several distinct roles and pursue multiple policy objectives, but these are always subordinate to the needs of the member.

In general, it is our strong impression that during the past two decades both professional and entrepreneurial staff types have become fewer in number while member-serving loyalty at all levels of staff performance has become more and more pervasive. Insistent policy entrepreneurs often seek (or are encouraged) to move outside the realm of the congressional enterprise, to executive branch, think tank, or interest group settings where essentially similar policy objectives may be pursued apart from the constraints of the member-enterprise (though, of course, constrained by other forces). Certain types of professionals can also find opportunities outside the congressional milieu, though others have specialties for which Congress provides the only institutional market. Sometimes politicos can transfer from one enterprise to another; sometimes, the personal component of the enterprise—"We're a real family in this office"—is too salient to stand the move.

There are many combinations of motives and ambitions, rewards and alternatives, giving shape and direction to staff behavior. When these are linked with diverse types of leadership provided by members, the resulting patterns of member-enterprise operation, organizational efficiency, and substantive purpose are so numerous that generalization at this stage of our understanding is hazardous. We believe that systematic empirical work couched in terms of the member-as-enterprise conception of Congress will in due course yield illuminating results. Meanwhile, we offer some tentative hypotheses and/or restatements that grow out of our own use of the enterprise conception.

Hypotheses, Conjectures, and Hunches

The Product

First of all, consider the organizational "product." Much has been said of late concerning the enormous expansion of casework and the potential effects of casework in insulating members against adverse electoral tides. It is axiomatic that casework on a large scale requires staff; conversely, a large staff can generate casework (Johannes, 1980; Johannes and McAdams, 1981; Fiorina, 1981). In either case, a comparatively large congressional enterprise will devote much larger resources to "producing" casework than could even the small member operation of two or three decades ago.

Similarly, a large member-enterprise can "produce" bills and amendments in much greater profusion than could the members working alone. And so they do.[1] But member-enterprises cannot pass legislation any more easily. Indeed, as they grow in size, they may also grow unwieldy and awkward in negotiating the compromises essential to coalition building.[2] It is only the member individually who votes and, despite the often important role of staff in negotiating legislative substance, a great deal of the bargaining over policy details can finally be done only by the principals themselves. For example, expanded staff adds relatively little to their personal capacities to mark up legislation where, inasmuch as markups have been opened to public observation, members do not wish to be seen as uninformed, uninvolved, or too dependent on their staffs.

Hence, we would expect to find, as indeed we do, that there has been a rather massive increase in the number of bills introduced, the number of amendments put forward, the number of committee and subcommittee meetings held, and the number of hours spent in session, but a substantial decrease in the number of bills actually passed.[3] The congressman-as-enterprise, no doubt in company with numerous other factors, produces a very different product mix—dominated by casework and policy proposals—from the legislator acting substantially alone.

Member Interaction

A second line of reinterpretation growing out of our enterprise conceptualization deals with the bases of member interaction and collaboration. One historically important mode of cooperative action among members rested on the widely shared norms, described by Matthews (1960) and others, that characterized congressional life, especially during the 1950s. These norms were rooted in the need to cultivate substantive expertise among members in a legislative body whose members had little professional staff, and to assure that those who became experts would have a persuasive impact on their colleagues. Apprenticeship, specialization, and reciprocity were all geared to the elusive goal of building majorities on the basis of scarce but, when the norms were fully operative, sufficient substantive competence.

The expansion of member-enterprises, however, has undermined those norms. By giving staff resources to each member, the potential range of expertise of each member-enterprise is greatly expanded. By encouraging a shift in the product mix from policymaking to position-taking in the fashion noted earlier, the relevance of specialized member expertise and reciprocal deference is reduced. Further, new members need not wait until they can earn a reputation among their colleagues for mastery of a subject; with able staff they can begin immediately to fashion proposals, publicize positions, and serve constituents, which is what apparently returns the best yield to the individual member-enterprise anyway.

As the norms of member division-of-labor give way, the capacity of congressional leaders to aggregate interests into majority coalitions is also very much weakened. Sam Rayburn's advice, "To get along, go along," no longer needs to be taken as seriously, since each member will in any case have substantial resources under his or her control and hence may get along nicely without going along at all. Instead of committee chairmen disciplining maverick members, one observes chairmen appealing to yet-to-be-sworn-in members for their support in the party caucus. The decentralizing of committee power and the rise of the caucus as a relevant decisional arena exacerbate the effects of staff growth by enhancing the position of each individual member and reducing the incentives to cooperate with either partisan or seniority leaders. And if the 1980 election results are at all prophetic of the future, congressional leaders will be special targets of national ouster campaigns and consequently even less able to dominate the norm-shaping processes of the institution.[4]

If leadership is weakened and expertise-centered norms are undermined, on what bases does cooperation among members occur? Clearly, there are such bases, since we observe that Congress does pass legislation from time to time. Part of the answer lies in the traditional sources of shared values among legislators: partisan unity, ideological cohesion, and executive pressure. All of these factors still operate, and while the member-as-enterprise may be somewhat differently affected by them than were the more individualistic senators and representatives, it would be a grave mistake to assume that the enterprise somehow removes the member entirely from these political forces. The most important effect of member-enterprise growth, however, may have been to strengthen another very traditional source of American political action, log rolling to fill the pork barrel.

Distributive Politics

We need not review the salience of pork barrel politics in American history nor underscore the pervasiveness of distributive public policy. Our point is that the transformation of Congress from a body of individuals to a collection of enterprises, primarily through the growth of staff, has accentuated these disaggregative tendencies and rendered policy still more distributive than ever. Part of the reason is the weakening of other norms leading to collective action and the further depreciation of leadership we have described. In part, however, it is the growth of member-centered staff that has promoted disaggregation. With extensive staff resources, member-enterprises can actively seek out district-related aspects of policy proposals or of programs already in operation. They can tack on amendments with special district appeal. They can articulate whatever differential district advantages there may be in a particular program. By extensively monitoring what is happening elsewhere in Congress and in the executive branch, a member's staff can often discover possibilities that, in the absence of staff help, would go unnoticed.

In turn, of course, the member-enterprises take credit for the positive district benefits of programs in operation or proposed. Credit-claiming also requires staff assistance and is facilitated further by the expanded staff located in the district itself as well as by the increased frequency of trips home by the member. Congressmen have always taken credit whenever feasible, to be sure, and have always pursued their full share of pork. Moreover, it is no new development for members who do not keep their constituency fences mended to find themselves in political difficulty. What is new is the scale on which credit-taking and district-massaging can now occur, thanks partially, at least, to the expansion of staff resources. And, further, to the extent that this strategy is politically successful, i.e., wins reelection, members are more and more persuaded to pursue it.

One result is that policy issues are increasingly defined, not in the language of national interest, efficiency, growth enhancement, justice, or some other broad objective, but in terms of the tangible and symbolic benefits accruing to specific sets of constituents. Farm commodities, defense contracts, mass transit grants, and differential oil price effects on geographical regions are the basis on which policy coalitions are built. Log-rolling coalitions have always been difficult to fit within either party or ideological packaging and they still are. Despite rhetoric to the contrary, the pragmatic propensities of "politics as usual" are encouraged in a system of members-as-enterprises, perhaps for the same reasons of prudent necessity that persuade corporations so often to "rise above principle" and accommodate themselves to labor unions and a myriad of governmental controls.[5]

Vertical Integration

Finally in the list of consequences of the emergence of members-as-enterprises, we can observe a phenomenon we may call "vertical integration." By this we mean the tendency of each member-enterprise to pull inside its organizational orbit an array of functions that formerly were done in other organizational settings. Where once the local party organization might mobilize voters and campaign funds and provide important channels for constituency communication, now these are done largely by the member-enterprise itself, augmented for election campaigns but large and active all the time. Relations with mass media are usually handled "in house." Some member-enterprises, as Macartney (1975) notes, operate as the local organizational focus for assembling otherwise scattered groups and interests so as to resemble local party organizations.

The rapid expansion of political action committees has led to a considerable nationalizing of the financing of congressional campaigns as well as a sharp rise in the cost, but the actual spending decisions remain within the candidate enterprise, as do the strategic calculations and plans that guide specific member (or challenger) action. Again, our point is that the member of Congress is not most usefully viewed as an isolated individual, but as the visible director of an organizational structure. During elections especially, this structure grows quite complex in design and extensive in function.

Members of Congress and the Direction of Enterprises

It follows from our discussion that the elected members of Congress find themselves occupying roles that impose substantial responsibilities for internal management and administration. Personnel must be recruited, incentives for performance established, operating routines developed, rewards and discipline distributed, and, in general, the enterprise managed so that reelection is not jeopardized and policy decisions are not botched. A certain amount of institutional assistance has been provided in recent years to help members manage their offices and locate capable personnel, and both chambers have undertaken study and reform efforts aimed at further improving internal management. In addition, trial and error has generated a kind of experience and folk wisdom that is used to help resolve management dilemmas. Nevertheless, it remains true that few are elected to Congress with much background as executives, few recognize the complexities of their own administrative responsibilities until rude experience has forced their attention, and many simply are not very good at making tough managerial decisions. Said one senator's administrative assistant: "The boss will never fire anyone. He may hire somebody else and hope the first one gets the hint, or he may send the bad one over to the committee payroll, or if it's a real disaster, he'll tell me to get rid of the person but not to make any waves."

One consequence of the organizational revolution within Congress may be to give former mayors, governors, or business executives some advantage over, for example, "mere" lawyers in more quickly establishing effective enterprises and hence securing both reelection and influence within the institution. Another, already partly accomplished, will be to enlarge the service functions of House and Senate agencies designed to assist with management tasks. A third is the appearance of private consultants who advise members on how best to operate their enterprises.[6]

Efficiency is seldom a neutral criterion, of course, and there will be potential losers who fear that reduction in office or committee chaos will also damage access to their member. And this is the other side of the growing managerial responsibility of members; staffers complete for member time and attention, pursue ambitions and rivalries, involving both personal careers and policy commitments, and generally play out the processes of bureaucratic politics.

Conclusion

When we consider Congress as an organization, we tend to focus on the formal structural units of committees, leadership posts, and the like.[7] Individual members are characterized in terms of their respective memberships in these units, and their behavior is described in terms of moving back and forth from one structurally-determined set of activities to another; now working on subcommittee business, now serving constituents, now participating in the party caucus or helping develop leadership strategy. We do not recommend abandoning this formulation of reality. Rather, we would integrate it with another perspective which emphasizes that, in every one of these so-called roles, the member is working with and through associated staff personnel who share an identity and a set of goals not because of the payroll they are on, the office they work in, or the tasks they perform, but because of their loyalty and commitment to that particular member.

This "structure," which we have called the member-as-enterprise, cuts across the lines defining the formal organizational units, of course. But it is not as informal as an ad hoc work group or a caucus that has not yet been officially constituted. Most of the staff resources of any particular member-enterprise are specified in the formal rules indicating who may appoint whom and under what terms. The size and scope of an enterprise is not therefore simply a reflection of a given member's skills at making contacts and attracting personal loyalty. Its parameters can be determined in large measure by examining the official documents and formal specifications of authority. But the member-enterprises are not identical with the institutional structure of Congress. It is member-centered, and consequently it, and the whole array of behavioral patterns affected by it, are very importantly shaped by the characteristics of the individual members.

Our final observation derives from this point. Matthews, Huitt, Fenno, Polsby, and other perceptive students of Congress have sought in various ways to articulate key institutional developments, only to find that what they had thought were generic properties of the system were in fact highly dependent on the particular characteristics of key personnel and their respective political values and situations. Normative constraints on congressional behavior have always been defined by the members, and different members have defined them differently. The influence of a Sam Rayburn or a Lyndon Johnson in shaping the "system" does not last forever. Moreover, the growth of member-enterprises and the extension of each into so many different institutional nooks and crannies magnifies the effects of member turnover. A Senate without Warren Magnuson or Jacob Javits is a somewhat different institution. Republican control in 1981 affects Senate "folkways." New members combine with new staff to remake agendas and styles of work. This does not mean that Congress is the sort of phenomenon that permits us only to tell stories about interesting people and situations, however. There are generic features permitting theoretical arguments to be constructed which, if they are not quite timeless, will last beyond the useful life of journalists and anecdotes. We think these generic features are to be found, in important part, in the conjunction of personalities with institutional components that define each member-as-enterprise.

NOTES

The authors gratefully acknowledge the research support of the John M. Olin Foundation. They also thank Professor Barry Weingast and an anonymous referee.

1. According to data provided by Bibby, Mann, and Ornstein (1980), the average number of bills introduced per member grew dramatically in the House and smoothly, if undramatically, in the Senate. In the 80th Congress the mean for House (Senate) members was 17.5 bills (33.2 bills). By the 95th Congress the mean had grown to 36.4 bills (38.0 bills), though, in the interim, it had grown as large as 50.7 bills in the 90th Congress (48.7 bills in the 91st Congress).

2. The ratio of bills passed to bills introduced has declined monotonically and precipitously in both chambers. Between the 80th and 95th Congresses, this proportion has fallen from .228 to .065 in the House and from .524 to .282 in the Senate.

3. Time-in-session has grown from 1224 hours in the 80th Congress to 1898 hours in the 95th in the House; comparable numbers for the Senate are 1462 and 2510 hours, respectively. Committee and subcommittee meetings have grown in number from 3210 in the 84th Congress (numbers not available earlier) to 6771 in the 95th Congress in the House, and from 2607 to 6656 in the Senate. The number of bills passed in the House (Senate) has declined from 1739 (1670) in the 80th Congress to 1027 (1070) in the 95th.

4. An early sign of this came in March, 1981, when the National Conservative Political Action Committee announced it would invest heavily in attempts to unseat House Majority Leader Jim Wright, Ways and Means Committee Chairman Dan Rostenkowski, and Budget Committee Chairman James Jones.

5. The Reagan-Stockman budgetary initiatives of 1981 stand as a strong challenge to this proposition. Their success might seem to require a reformulation of the preceding argument. Nevertheless, aggressive congressional leaders have repeatedly encountered political difficulties of their own in recent years.

6. A few examples will suffice here. The Congressional Research Service produced occasional studies on how to organize Washington and district offices, e.g., Marc Yacker, "Congressional Office Operations: Aspects of Staff Organization in Washington and the Congressional District," CRS, 76–233G, November, 1976. So, too, do the Democratic Caucus and Republican Study Committee, and various adjuncts to the Offices of the Sergeant-at-Arms. In the private sector there are a number of private management and computer services firms which provide advice and counsel on administrative matters for a fee. Finally, in the not-for-profit private sector are such organizations as the Congressional Management Foundation, financed by public-spirited businessmen, whose mission is to bring administrative efficiency to Capital Hill.

7. A mid-1978 inventory (Salisbury and Shepsle, 1979) of all those organizational entities within Congress possessing some staff capability yielded a total of 990 separate units. They include the following:

100 Senate offices
435 House offices
 15 Senate standing committees
 22 House standing committees
112 Senate subcommittees
148 House subcommittees
  6 Senate select or special committees
 10 House select, special, or ad hoc committees
 32 House commissions, task forces, ad hoc subcommittees, advisory groups, or policy groups
  4 Joint Congressional committees with 5 subcommittees
 18 Senate party leadership offices
 10 House party leadership offices
  3 Senate administrative units
  6 House administrative units
  3 Senate campaign or research offices
 11 House campaign or research offices
  4 Senate informal caucuses or coalitions
 24 House informal caucuses or coalitions
 14 Joint informal caucuses or coalitions
  5 Congressional support offices
  3 Joint administrative offices

REFERENCES

Bibby, John F., Thomas E. Mann, and Norman J. Ornstein. 1980. *Vital Statistics on Congress, 1980.* Washington: American Enterprise Institute.

Cohen, Richard E. 1979. "The Watchdogs for Congress Often Bark the Same Tune," *National Journal* (September 8):1484–1488.

Cooper, Joseph. 1975. "Strengthening the Congress: An Organizational Analysis," *Harvard Journal on Legislation* 12:307–368.

———. 1977. "Congress in Organizational Perspective," in Lawrence C. Dodd and Bruce I. Oppenheimer, eds., *Congress Reconsidered,* New York: Praeger.

Dodd, Lawrence C. and Bruce I. Oppenheimer, eds. 1977. *Congress Reconsidered.* New York: Praeger.

Fenno, Richard F., Jr. 1973. *Congressmen in Committees.* Boston: Little, Brown.

Fiorina, Morris P. 1981. "Some Problems in Studying Resource Allocation in Congressional Elections." Social Science Working Paper 344, Pasadena: California Institute of Technology.

Fox, Harrison W., Jr. and Susan Webb Hammond. 1977. *Congressional Staffs: The Invisible Force in American Lawmaking.* New York: The Free Press.

Froman, Lewis A. 1968. "Organization Theory and the Explanation of Important Characteristics of Congress," *American Political Science Review* 62:518–527.

Greenberg, Daniel S. 1977. "The Saga of the OTA," *The Chronicle of Higher Education* (August 1):11.

Johannes, John R. 1980. "The Distribution of Casework in the U.S. Congress: An Uneven Burden," *Legislative Studies Quarterly* 5:517–545.

Johannes, John R., and John C. McAdams. 1981. "The Congressional Incumbency Effect: Is It Casework, Policy Compatibility, or Something Else?" *American Journal of Political Science* 25 (August): 512–42.

Kingdon, John W. 1973. *Congressmen's Voting Decisions.* New York: Harper and Row.

Loomis, Burdett A. 1979. "The Congressional Office as a Small (?) Business: New Members Set Up Shop," *Publius* 9:35–55.

Macartney, John D. 1975. "Political Staffing: A View from the District." Ph.D. Dissertation, University of California at Los Angeles.

Machowsky, Martin. 1978. "On the Growth of Committee Staff." Paper presented at the annual meeting of the Midwest Political Science Association.

Malbin, Michael J. 1976. "Congressional Staffs—Growing Fast, But in Different Directions," *National Journal* (July 10):958–965.

———. 1980. *Unelected Representatives: Congressional Staff and the Future of Representative Government.* New York: Basic Books.

Matthews, Donald R. 1960. *U.S. Senators and Their World.* New York: Vintage Books.

Matthews, Donald R. and James A. Stimson. 1975. *Yeas and Nays: Normal Decision-Making in the U.S. House of Representatives.* New York: Wiley.

Ornstein, Norman J., ed. 1975. *Congress in Change: Evolution and Reform.* New York: Praeger.

Price, David E. 1971. "Professionals and Entrepreneurs: Staff Orientations and Policy Making on Three Senate Committees," *Journal of Politics* 33:316–336.

Salisbury, Robert H., and Kenneth A. Shepsle. 1981. "Congressional Staff Turnover and the Ties That Bind." *American Political Science Review* 75 (June): 381–96.

Part III

◆

Interests and Citizenship:
Perspectives on Democratic
Theory

The two essays in this section raise questions that are often left implicit in interest group analysis but are there nevertheless and vitally so. Why do people join associations? What motivates participation in the political arena? Too often the answer is thought to be obvious; people participate to advance their interests. In fact, however, participation is more complicated in both motives and consequences, and these papers explore some of that complexity, partly at a theoretical level and partly with reference to some research findings.

10

Modes of Participation and Policy Impact in American Education

T*here is a pervasive*—in modern social science parlance, paradigmatic—point of view among Americans regarding how, fundamentally, public policy decisions come to be. At one level of sophisticated abstraction this perspective is expressed thus in the Eastonian depiction: environmental circumstances give rise to popular demands, which, in turn, are pressed upon the polity's decisional system to yield policy outputs.[1] In this characterization it may be concluded that there will be no public policy result unless demands (not to mention supports, diffuse and specific) are present to provide the efficient stimulus. Demands, in turn, may result from any or all of several varieties of activity: parties and elections, interest group lobbying, citizen contacting, and so on. But whatever the form, the concept of demands clearly rests on a prior assumption; namely, that individual citizens will, to some extent and in some fashion, become active, and that by means of their activity, they will create the demands that are a necessary (though not, except to the extremely naïve, a sufficient) condition of public policy outcomes.

Although David Easton intended his formulation to characterize a quite general process, it seems to me that it reflected a distinctively American approach to the concept of citizen participation. It is not so apparent to others, I think, that citizen "demands" are the motive force from which all policy springs. And this is because it is Americans who are especially and entirely suffused with the mythic, metaphorical heritage of John Locke.[2]

Reprinted with permission from the *International Journal of Political Education* 2 (1979):297–310.

In the Lockean world, as we all know, government derives its just powers from the consent of the governed. Beyond that, however, with the single exception of foreign policy,[3] the exercise of those powers is also to be shaped and constrained by the governed. Leaving aside the question of how, by what means, consent and constraint are effectively to be exercised, there is no doubt that popular judgments are, in the Lockean view, to dominate and give substance to public policy. And there can be little doubt, either, that such judgments must require popular activity or behavior, to make them explicit, and hence operational. Citizenship itself, as a status as well as a bundle of activities, is the primary condition, the starting place, from which all legitimate political action follows. The state, in short, is a derivative of participation.

Now it is clear that in much of the democratic world this does not accurately describe the case. Citizenship, in the view of many, is conferred by the state and dependent upon it, not the other way around.[4] And when this view prevails citizen participation is theoretically much less central and, indeed, may often be problematic in its policy significance.[5] The point is that in the United States the significance assigned to citizen participation is absolutely crucial. And this has meant that, (a) there are many institutional devices and mechanisms whereby citizens do, in fact, take a direct hand in shaping public decisions; (b) rhetorical appeals to the symbols of citizen participation will carry special persuasive power, especially in efforts at "reform"; but, (c) much of the participatory activity that, in fact, occurs will be of little policy relevance and perhaps even a kind of sham.

This general view has special application to public education in the United States. For the school, more than any other institutionalized program in American public policy, has depended upon the direct involvement of citizens for its direction and, indeed, its very existence. The fictions of legal phraseology do not fully reveal this dependence. When in 1642 the Massachusetts Bay Colony first mandated the provision of education at public expense, the doctrine of state responsibility was articulated, and it has been so ever since.[6] The state or its subdivisions, such as the city, county, or school district, will undertake to provide basic education, though at what minimum level has ever since been a matter of dispute.

In actual fact, however, the provision of schools was then left almost entirely to the local community and, in turn, to the concerned citizens. Whether there would be a school or not, in those early days, depended almost entirely on whether concerned individual citizens mobilized enough support, financial and otherwise, to provide one. Often this effort generated what was virtually a private academy. In the Southern states the impetus frequently worked through the Anglican/ Episcopalian parish. Indeed, there was little difference, in the early days of American education, between the level and type of citizen support involved in sustaining public schools, on the one hand, and private schools, on the other.[7]

Public education, to be sure, had its base in the legally compulsory tax rate, extracted from all citizens with or without school-age children. And as the scale and heterogeneity of American communities increased, this fact assumed increasing importance. Yet it should not be forgotten that throughout the nineteenth century in many rural and small-town communities there were few citizens who lacked school-age children. These were young communities with young families. And the latter took it as a major item of business to create the basic educational machinery their fledgling enterprises required. State legal control meant almost nothing until the last hundred years or so. Significant state financial support came even later. American schools had their fundamental basis in the voluntary efforts of the citizens of each particular community. That is a tradition not lightly surrendered.

In modern times this tradition has been expressed through several different modes of citizen participation. First is the formal dependence of schools in many states on voter approval of the tax rate providing local community financial support. Indeed, although there is much variation from one state to another in the frequency of direct referendum-type elections governing school policy matters, only two of the fifty states make no use of these at all.[8] Beyond this formal support there is a substantial degree of dependence, on the part of many schools, on informal support in the form of supplementary fund raising and direct auxiliary services. It is extremely difficult to estimate how much of this kind of participation there is or how much it contributes to educational programs, but it is not trivial.

As with most other local government bodies in the United States, schools are governed by citizens, whether elected or appointed, who participate without significant reimbursement. This reliance on citizen activism for policy governance is one of the most cherished prerogatives in the American political tradition, and it is linked to some deeply rooted values—the superior virtue of local control, for example, or the importance of maintaining *lay* rather than professional control over school affairs.

A further function of citizen participation is implicit in the principle of citizen governance. It is mainly through citizen activity that community norms and expectations regarding educational policy are articulated and pressed upon school officials. School professionals often have lamented such activity as pressure, and contended that it may result in distortions of sound educational practice. Conversely, it has been through citizen demands that many recent changes in educational priorities have been brought into operation, most dramatically in regard to racial integration in American core cities. However a particular set of demands may be interpreted, citizen involvement remains a basic mechanism, though not the only one, by which the substance of educational programs is determined. And, it should not be overlooked that participatory pressure goes in many directions. It has been private citizens who have sought to block sex education as well as seeking to bring about educational equality for racial minorities. Citizens both urge and block school busing for racial integration. There has seldom been a single policy direction resulting from citizen involvement, but there has seldom been much vitality in American education without the active participation of large numbers of ordinary citizens.

Some of the most important recent literature dealing with participation has been concerned to establish the categories or types within which participatory behavior falls. The work of Verba and Nie both exemplifies and dominates this endeavor, and it is useful to consider what they have done both in contrast to what had come before and in its relation to school-centered participation.[9] Until the Verba-Nie work the prevailing view was that political participation was unidimensional.[10] It ranged, for any set of actors, from much to little, with all the various acts thought to array themselves along this quantitative dimension. What Verba and Nie showed was that there were several distinct dimensions involved. Just because a person was active in electoral politics, for example, did not mean that he or she was active in community affairs and vice versa. Verba and Nie concluded that there were four distinct types of activity—voting, electoral campaigning, communal involvement, and personal contacting of officials; and these yielded six types of participants, those specializing in one of the four activity sets plus those who were altogether inactive and those who were active across the board.

To at least some extent both the unidimensional line of research and the Verba and Nie revision have displayed a generic tendency in social science to get the empirical results, and only those, foretold by the questions asked. Verba and Nie, for example, excluded protest demonstrations and other "irregular" modes of participation. Consequently they found no "protest type" in their data. Similarly, the older research had asked only about election-centered behavior[11] and so had found no evidence of communalist participation. Nevertheless, Verba and Nie have not been modest in asserting the generic quality of their typology. And as they have secured essentially similar responses to the same set of questions in the several other nations they have surveyed,[12] they have felt quite comfortable in this conviction.

A case can be made that the Verba-Nie line of analysis in fact has located its participation types within more or less distinct institutional boundaries, those delineating partisan elections, on the one hand, and community affairs, on the other. Insofar as this may be true, it might well turn out that an investigation of other institutional settings would turn up sets of people who were quite active in one or more of those settings but not in the ones Verba and Nie asked about. It is certainly as reasonable to expect to find active school "specialists" or church "specialists" as it is to find election campaign specialists. This is of particular importance if we wish to understand participation related to schools and attempt to draw inferences from the Verba-Nie findings.

A second consideration to be borne in mind regarding the Verba-Nie formulation is that it presupposes that participation is purposive. Participation, they contend, consists of those acts intended to influence government; that is, to affect policy decisions. Leaving aside whether this does not entail far too much rationalism for ordinary voters to bear, it plainly excludes from view much activity we might well want to examine in a study of participation. When an individual joins an organization such as the neighborhood school Parent-Teacher Association for example, it is seldom clear that he does so in order to affect school policy. Yet, having joined, he may find himself well situated to mobilize influence (if, someday, he comes to desire it). The joining of groups and the exertion of policy influence through those groups are conceptually and empirically distinct.[13] Often one type of behavior may be converted into the other should circumstances warrant, and the connections and relationships between purposive and non-purposive behavior are very much worth investigating. They must not be excluded by too narrow a definition.

In much of what follows I shall draw upon research recently completed involving rather lengthy interviews with some 507 school activists in six suburban school districts in the St. Louis, Missouri (U.S.A.), metropolitan area. Respondents were chosen from among those who displayed at least a minimum level of participatory activity, such as attending school organization meetings. No matched sample was constructed; we know nothing directly of how these people compared with non-activists in their respective communities. We do know a great deal about this set, however, and we can compare many subgroups within it to test a number of important arguments concerning patterns of school participation and the factors affecting them.

There are many distinct forms that citizen participation in school affairs may take. Surely the most common is membership in a school-related group. In 1974 an NORC survey reported that 17.5 percent of American adults belonged to some school organization. This is really an astonishingly large number. It represents something like twenty-two million people! But it only begins to characterize the number of Americans who take some kind of active part in school affairs. It is not wholly clear what is included in this set of activities, but we know that there has been a rather formidable number of people who march in the streets, contribute time or money to school election campaigns, participate in ad hoc or informal groups, or even go to court to seek redress. All of these people are purposive participants. They do indeed seek to affect educational policy through their activity. In that desire they may often be disappointed. They may or may not persist in their endeavors. But they do embody the traditions of citizen effort, and their whole socialization has led them, often with exaggerated expectations, to believe that the mere fact of their efforts will be sufficient to effect the desired result.

Purposive participation reflects some degree of unhappiness with the way things are. The citizen wants to change things, either for his or her own children or for the general welfare. This observation leads us to ask about the processes by which citizens are induced to play an active part. Virtually without exception school activists are brought into initial involvement in conjunction with the entrance of their eldest children into school. Regardless of what subsequently may occur, whether or not the involvement blossoms into a purposive crusade, it begins in support of the children's entry onto the school scene. Thereafter, some fraction of the parents become exercised and seek to *change,* or prevent change in, their children's educational setting. Another fraction, usually larger than the first, seeks only to provide *support* for the schools *as they are.*

Supportive participation may vary from much to little. In the former case there can be a quite frenetic pace, as mothers drive car pools on field trips, sew school play costumes, bake cookies, and otherwise display their parental devotion. In the same fashion, purposive participation may also range from less to more. Indeed, unless one probes the motivations it may be difficult to distinguish between the lethargic purposive activist and the modestly enthusiastic supporter of the schools. It is at the "high" end of activity that the difference is marked. The supportive enthusiast is uncritical, but spends much time in his or her activities. The purposive activist has policy goals that Parent-Teacher Association or committee or electoral work have to accomplish.

What factors account for different types and amounts of school-related participation? The St. Louis data provide a somewhat more complete set of answers than most other studies. First, there is almost no support for the argument that family background and/or socialization leads people toward greater or lesser amounts of school participation. No really significant relationships were found between respondents' participation level and interest or involvement in school affairs by their own parents. Secondly, there was a substantial class effect. Less affluent and/or less-well-educated people participated at a lower level of intensity, than those higher on the SES (socio-economic status) ladder. St. Louis area school participants generally were significantly higher in SES rank than the SES median for their communities and this matches the findings of nearly every national study of participation.

One thing that follows from this is that those communities displaying higher average social rank will also enjoy larger amounts of citizen activism. Conversely, communities of lower SES standing, including most core cities in the United States, have considerably less "natural" citizen involvement. We will return to this theme later.

School-centered participation has historically been the special province of women. In most areas of public life women participate less than men, a fact that has been taken to support the allegation that women occupy a prejudicially subordinate place in American society. The schools are an exception, or at least they appear to be, for two-thirds of the school activists, in St. Louis and elsewhere, are women. On closer inspection, however, it turns out that the participation of women is disproportionately supportive in intent and routine, almost reflexive in its motivating force. Women are brought into school-related activity by means of their parental role, but they are not provoked thereby to seek policy changes. Nor, for the most part, do they seek to rise through some hierarchy of participatory effort to positions of prominence and putative influence. At the "upper" reaches of school participation effort men occupy a much larger share of the relevant positions. So even in an arena that traditionally has been identified as "women's work"—the schools—men dominate the positions of real importance.[14]

This observation raises a question of fundamental importance. What significance is to be attributed to participation rates and forms? Are the lower levels of intensity to be interpreted as mere window dressing? Or, for that matter, do the upper levels, such as school board or citizens' committee membership, really carry effective power? It is certainly possible that although these positions are dominated by men, this domination reflects a societal mythology that puts men disproportionately in high office (or induces men to seek high office), rather than signifying that real power lies in their hands.

We have alluded already to the effect of community context in participation when we mentioned that different profiles of community social characteristics generate different patterns of citizen participation. Let us pursue this further. There are at least three quite distinct kinds of community impact on the patterns of school-related citizen participation. First, there is the SES effect already noted. It is quite clear that communities with high median social rank display more participation than those less affluent. Size may also be a factor that reinforces this tendency though neither the St. Louis data nor national surveys permit a close reading. It is reasonable, however, to suppose that the larger the community in the United States, the less participatory its citizens will be inclined to be, both because of the presumably greater atomization/ alienation of big-city life and because the authorities are more remote and insulated from effective pressure. It is not simply the SES distribution that counts, of course. Demographic trends (rising or falling enrollment, e.g.), social heterogeneity (many patterns of variations may still result in a common mean), and more subtle subcultural attitudes regarding education all have their effects.

A second contextual effect is structural. School districts are not always coincident in their boundaries with municipalities. In the St. Louis study one school district comprised twenty-three separate municipalities, while another embraced considerable farm country surrounding a central town. Such a structure depresses participation in at least two ways. Citizens do not know where to turn with complaints since, depending on the issue, the action route will be very different, structurally and even geographically. In addition, there are fewer opportunities for interaction withing the school district, since so much social business will take place within the smaller municipal fragments. Civic knowledge and social interaction both contribute to the ease and likelihood of further participation.

Complexity and confusion in the structure of public authority, the very hallmarks of American governmental design, inhibit citizen participation. And, it may be noted, legislative mandates to increase participation by adding ad hoc mechanisms for local participation, in schools, poverty programs, or community development, may in the long run exacerbate this tendency.

An additional structural factor involves the methods of school board selection and school tax approval. If these processes are closely tied to the broader political processes of the community—if, for example, the mayor appoints the school board—then school-related participation will also be part of a larger pattern of community involvement. If, however, as is far more common, school governance is structurally separated, school participation is much more likely to be the province of a group which is perceived as school specialists.

A third community effect is to be found in the issue context. Each community or school district has a history that is in some respects unique. Animosities and alliances may scar or heal in a manner reflective of who, in particular, said what to whom in times past. Some communities, for explicable but subtle historical reasons, place an especially strong emphasis on the quality of their schools. They attract residents (partly on that ground) who, in turn, take an active role in order to preserve the reputation (and attendant property values). In some communities the schools become the battle ground between the old and the new generation of settlers, or between differing social philosophies, or, most visibly and dramatically, between different racial or ethnic groups. Such conflicts not only have historical consequences—i.e. lasting through time—they may have profound social and economic effects. We can hardly escape the melodramas associated with racial change in American and British schools. We may overlook the more frequent but less visible experience of Americans whose real estate fortunes have been profoundly affected by property values associated with the putative quality of the community's schools.

We should not conclude that each school district is so distinctive that no general statements regarding "who governs and why" can be made. There will, however, be differences within any stratum of school districts regarding how much and what kind of participation there is. For example, in two of the St. Louis districts the active participants were quite similar in socioeconomic background and situation. One district, however, enjoyed a considerably larger tax base, while the other contained a significant minority of black students. The latter district faced the necessity of reorganizing to bring about racial balance. In the other district there really were no substantial problems, crises, or even dissatisfactions. Not surprisingly, the consequence was that in the problem-free district participation was substantial in amount (high SES level) and uncritically supportive. In the other case, where participants were drawn from very similar social strata, their involvement was highly purposive and intended to change school policy.

Surely, this is not a random result. The SES factor predicted the level of participation, the community context predicted its substantive focus. The variables are generic, even though the particular combinations are unique. There are two points to be remembered. First, we lack enough carefully drawn cases to be entirely sure of what truly are the central variables. Class composition and legacies of community conflict are certainly important determinants of school-related participation and many other things. But there may also be other relevant factors. Indeed, the St. Louis study identified some, such as structural integration of the community and rates of community growth and change. Second, in the United States it seems very likely that the level and character of citizen participation in the schools will be vitally shaped by circumstances in the *local* community rather than in the state, region, or nation. Contextual factors, operating through interpersonal networks, on the community level are of crucial importance, and in this respect the American case may be substantially different from European counterparts.

One mode of citizen participation in American school affairs involves membership on citizen committees, usually appointed by mayors, school boards, or school superintendents. These committees may be designed to provide an official examination of a school problem, or more general citizen counsel on school affairs; in some cases it is hoped that they will legitimate school policies. Unlike school boards, these committees do not set policy. And compared to the ordinary forms of participation they involve much heavier commitments of time and attention. Sometimes citizens' committee members have been co-opted, of course. The intended result of their participation is to induce them to give support, which otherwise might not have been forthcoming, to the educational status quo. Some fraction of this group, however, learns to be critical, developing in the course of their committee service a more exacting standard of what public education ought to be. The St. Louis data indicate that although citizens' committee members display considerable diversity they tend, in the aggregate, to be somewhat more critical of the schools and to be more affected by their participatory experience than those who follow the more routine participatory paths of parent organizations.

Still more substantial impact from school participation is reported by those who run for and serve on school boards. We are here talking about a very small fraction of the total population, or course, though there are nearly 16,000 local school boards and the total number of people who serve at one time or another, is in the vicinity of 90,000.[15] Board members, though unpaid, devote large amounts of time to the job. In very few cases does there seem to be any sort of further political ambition associated with school board service. Rather the motivations, at least those that are conscious and explicit, center around notions of citizen duty, service to children and the community, and a degree of intellectual interest in the affairs of the public schools. What is perhaps most instructive is that board members are more likely than other types of participants to report that their opinion of the schools has changed—for the better. Familiarity seems on the whole to breed approval rather than contempt, and this raises a general question of great importance. Do we expect that by and large more active participation will enhance attitudes that are supportive of the existing scheme of things, or will activism be an efficient mechanism for bringing about change? The St. Louis data suggest that for the most part participation is supportive, however critical participants may be of details, and that, therefore, the more activism there is, *ceteris paribus,* the stronger will be the existing institutions and practices.

The discussion thus far has perhaps implied that school-related participation takes place only at the local level and only within normal structural arrangements. This is probably true, though we lack appropriate measures of the matter, but it is not exclusively so. One arena of participation, for example, has been the so-called White House Conference on Education, held at national and state levels from time to time since the 1950s, and designed to mold and rally elite opinion in the direction of expanded support for public education.[16] Sometimes curriculum reform has also been included in the programs. A similar pattern of elite mobilization, usually by executive branch officials, is common also in such policy areas as foreign affairs.[17] There is little evidence that much "trickle down" of influence occurs, as mass opinion is usually not much affected. But within the elite itself there may well be a legacy of enthusiasm, even of zealotry, that carries over to motivate a small number of very active influentials, and this may be quite enough to alter some aspects of public policy.

If insistent individuals can sometimes affect school policy so also can protesting groups who express their concerns outside the normal channels, taking to the streets or the picket lines.[18] Few policy sectors have been more obviously or profoundly affected by citizen protest activity, especially that related to racial integration. At another, *very* different, level, U.S. school activists practically invented the strategy, later emulated by environmentalists and others, of utilizing the courts to secure their policy desires.[19] Still another mode of citizen involvement entails working through organized interest groups such as the National Education Association, the Council on Basic Education, or the Citizens for Educational Freedom. Such groups lobby, of course, often at the national level and are, indeed, the chief means by which citizen activism is brought to bear on state and national educational policy.[20]

This should remind us that citizen participation is, among other things, a strategy for pursuing policy objectives. Mobilizing such participation will be appealing when one's policy cause is likely to draw broad, or at least intensely felt, popular support. Those arenas will be utilized in which a group's participatory resources are most readily mobilized, even though broad participation may not always be the most effective technique to achieve a particular objective. Thus it may be appealing to take to the streets because you can mobilize a crowd even though the decision is to be made in court—or vice versa.[21] Although American civic mythology does not fully understand it, there can be no assumption that simply because citizens take some action—whether it be a protest march, a tax vote, a lobbying effort, a petition to the school board, a mass meeting, or an election campaign—they will certainly win. Active citizens can and do lose, just as do those who remain relatively inert.[22]

The primary research objective of the St. Louis study was to investigate the impact that participation had on the participant. We sought to determine whether such scholars as Aristotle and John Stuart Mill were really correct in asserting that active citizens would be changed by their activity. Impact could take several forms. It might involve the acquisition of new information or it might extend to the changing of one's attitudes and opinions. It might involve new patterns of social interaction or expanded participation in organizational settings other than the schools. Impact might also entail, as Mill expected, some transformation of the self, enhanced personal capacities, a growth in self-confidence, and the like. The problems of measuring impact are formidable. Whatever the notion means, it is both subtle and complex in its manifestations. Much of the impact we would expect to result from participation may show up only several years later, and without good longitudinal data our ability to identify impact effects and sort out causal connections will be limited. Nevertheless, we went ahead and asked respondents a variety of types of questions bearing on the matter of impact, and our findings may be of interest.

Participation, even at a relatively modest level, does result in opinion change. Different formulations of the question produced different proportions of affirmative responses concerning such change, but never less than one-third. More interesting than the fact of change was its direction. Those who reported changing their opinions as a result of their involvement were more critical of the schools than those who remained unaffected by their experience. Thus our earlier comment about the continued supportiveness of highly involved citizens requires some modification. Substantial proportions of school participants reported information effects and personal growth. The more active the respondents were, the more likely they were to stress the personal growth component, suggesting that indeed Mill was right.

There are long-term effects of school participation on other organizational involvement, but their assessment is a bit complicated. Our data show clearly that a sizable fraction of school activists expect to move into other civic activity once their children are out of school and that arena no longer particularly interests them. (The close connection between family age structure and *both* entry into and exit from school participation gives this realm of citizenship a distinctive character.) The more active in school affairs, the more likely to move subsequently into other community arenas. Thus the schools become something of a staging area, or springboard, for civic participation generally. Many of the people who follow this course, however, are individuals who by reason of their social class and particular histories and inclinations would in any case have been likely to become active in the community even if they had been childless and hence not concerned about schools. Only a small fraction can be said to have moved into broader civic participation only because of their experience in school affairs. Yet even this handful, cumulating over time, may have a significant renewing effect on a community's activist elite. In any event, we need to give more careful consideration to the overlapping patterns of participation among different arenas of public life and, in particular, how, individually and in the aggregate, these change through time.[23]

We may conclude this discussion of impact by noting another relationship, which may very well represent an effect of participation, but which at least indicates an important attitudinal dimension of school activists' views about the political world. In the St. Louis study we asked a series of questions, adapted from other surveys, that sought to tap what generally is referred to as "trust in government." We asked those questions separately for each of five levels of government, national, state, county, city, and school district. There are some complexities in the data, but the main result is strong. The schools are the most trusted level of government. Beyond this, however, the smaller and closer to home the government unit, the more trusted it was. In this immediate post-Watergate period it is not surprising that the national government ranked at the bottom. It is more significant that the schools, and after them local government, ranked at the top. Moreover, the estimate of trustworthiness for these levels was quite high. It seems clear that active participation is closely linked to approval of the participatory area involved.

In these days of precipitous decline in overall levels of trust it may be especially important to take this finding seriously. If participants are more trusting and confident, while cynics remain on the sidelines, the argument for expanded citizen involvement transcends the pursuit of self-interest or the enhancement of self-confidence and individual capability. Participation becomes a key mechanism by which to strengthen popular belief in, and support for, the essential governing processes in the society.

NOTES

1. Perhaps we would have come to some such formulation anyway, but it is David Easton's schema that has defined the world within which policy-oriented political science has worked for two decades. *A Systems Analysis of Political Life*, New York, Wiley, 1965.

2. Louis Hartz's explication of this argument remains persuasive. *The Liberal Tradition in America*. New York, Knopf, 1955 and "Democracy: Image and Reality," in Wm. N. Chambers and Robert H. Salisbury, *Democracy in the Mid-Twentieth Century*, St. Louis, Mo., Washington University Press, 1960.

3. See Locke's *Second Treatise of Civil Government*, Ch. XII.

4. See T. H. Marshall, *Class, Citizenship and Social Development*, Garden City, N.Y., Doubleday, 1965.

5. Recent discussions of the significance of participation in democratic politics seem to have missed this point. See, *inter alia*, Carole Pateman, *Participation and Democratic Theory*, London, Cambridge University Press, 1970; Dennis Thompson, *The Democratic Citizen*, New York, Cambridge University Press, 1970.

6. It is hoped that the reader will be able to recognize the distinction made in the use of the term "state." Here we are using it in the American context, meaning the major units of the federal system, rather than as a generic term for authoritative government.

7. On the history of American education, generally, see R. Freeman Butts and Lawrence A. Cremin, *A History of Education in the United States*, New York, Henny Holt, 1953.

8. See Howard Hamilton and Sylvan Cohen, *Policy-Making by Plebiscite: School Referenda*, Lexington, Mass., Lexington Books, 1975.

9. S. Verba and N. Nie, *Participation in America: Political Democracy and Social Equality*, New York, Harper and Row, 1972.

10. See, for example, Lester Milbrath, *Political Participation*, Chicago, Rand McNally, 1965. But cf. the revised edition, with Goel, 1977.

11. The most substantial data sets were generated by the Survey Research Center's biennial polls.

12. See S. Verba, N. Nie and J. O. Kim, *The Modes of Democratic Participation: A Cross-National Analysis*, Beverly Hills, Calif., Sage, 1971.

13. The classic statement of this argument is, of course, Mancur Olson, *The Logic of Collective Action*, Cambridge, Mass., Harvard University Press, 1965. See also my "An exchange theory of interest groups," *supra*.

14. We would not wish this conclusion to imply support for a sexist view. In fact, if education and experience are controlled, women appear to hold their own even at higher levels of school participation. But many more of the supportive participants are women.

15. See Harmon Zeigler and Kent Jennings, *Governing American Schools*, Scituate, Mass., Duxbury Press, 1974.

16. See George Grassmuck, "The White House Conferences On Education," presented at the 1977 meeting of the Midwest Political Science Association.

17. See James Rosenau, *National Leadership and Foreign Policy: A Case Study in the Mobilization of Public Support*, Princeton, Princeton University Press, 1963.

18. See Michael Lipsky, "Protest as a Political Resource," *American Political Science Review*, December, 1968.

19. See the magisterial work by Richard Kluger, *Simple Justice*, New York, Alfred Knopf, 1976.

20. See the relatively recent discussion of school lobbies in *Congressional Quarterly*. The Washington Lobby, 2nd ed., 1974.

21. It is instructive to observe the spring 1978 demonstrations articulating the desire of blacks and others to secure a favorable outcome in the historic Bakke case involving so-called reverse discrimination.

22. A profoundly important finding apropos of this point is John Mueller's report that American public opinion followed almost exactly the same curve of increasing disapproval during the Vietnam War as it had during the Korean War. In the latter case there were few protests or sit-ins but in both instances opinion changed as a logarithmic function of the casualty rate. See *War, Presidents and Public Opinion*, New York, Wiley, 1973.

23. See my paper "Overlapping Memberships, Organizational Interactions, and Interest Group Theory," presented to the American Political Science Association, 1976.

11

The Local Community:
An Arena for Citizenship in the
Federal System

A*ll democratic governments* are arenas of civic action. Individuals and groups contend in each arena for the prizes that can be won there, and the actions they take are the activities of citizenship. The prizes are the rewards, material and symbolic, that the authority of a given arena permits to be awarded. To continue the metaphor, in the United States there is an exceptionally large variety of arenas with significant differences in the scope and substance of prizes available. In a very important sense, this is the essence of federalism; multiple arenas of action—national, state, and local—with each having limited authority to allocate some values but not others among interested claimant citizens. In turn, this means that citizens must continually assess which arenas are the most appropriate settings for them to pursue whatever goals they have. That assessment must take into account not only which prizes can be won where, but what political resources can be mobilized in one arena as against another.

The specific nature of American federalism, much less a matter of constitutional law than of historical tradition and continuing political reality, has been characterized by the profusion of more or less autonomous local governments—arenas with limited but meaningful policy prizes to win. The creation and re-creation of these arenas has been an extremely important part of American civic experience with a meaning often neglected or misunderstood. But the local governmental arenas do not stand by themselves, like football stadiums or the Roman Colosseum,

Reprinted with permission from Stephen L. Schechter, ed., *Teaching About American Federal Democracy* (Philadelphia: Publius Books, 1989), pp. 49–56.

monuments to be admired and occasionally filled with cheering throngs. Civic institutions take their meaning from the activities people engage in to create them, sustain them, and use their authority to generate public policies of one kind or another.

In short, government derives its significance from the kinds of citizenship undertaken by those who live in and are affected by the public authority in question. A richly endowed arena of broad scope, like the federal government, will attract the active interest of many competing groups scrambling for the prizes. A small institutional setting with limited authority to act may attract few contenders.

Citizen action is never automatic, of course; just because the stakes are potentially very high does not assure that everyone will enter the contest. Nor will all of us understand correctly which arenas offer the best choice of securing the prizes we deem most valuable, and hence we may invest our civic energy inappropriately. In any event, the central idea employed here is one in which citizenship consists of people creating and making use of governmental arenas, including local arenas, to realize their diverse purposes. In so doing, they employ such resources as may be available to them—votes, money, rhetoric, protest, and so on—all of which can be subsumed under the heading of citizenship action.

In completing this introduction, let me outline two quite different conceptions of citizenship which have especially important applications to the consideration of local political communities.[1] One form we may call *instrumental* citizenship. We refer by this term to the familiar activities whereby individuals, groups, and organizations pursue their own interests, seeking to persuade governmental officials to decide in their favor and, if there is opposition, against the other side. Self-interested citizens need not invariably be selfish. Common Cause, environmental groups, and the prohibition movement have all sought public policies from which they would not personally derive specific benefit, but they did hope to see their values embodied in policy and they all have had opposition. Instrumental citizenship thus is rooted in political disagreement. The citizen acts in order to obtain some substantive policy result that others resist. Votes are mobilized, lobbying campaigns mounted, coalitions constructed, demonstrations organized, and so on. The forms of action are familiar to us, and we are quite accustomed to linking them with policy objectives.

There is a second conception to citizenship, however; and, especially with reference to local government, this conception has been widely admired and practiced throughout American political experience. We shall refer to this as *republican* citizenship. Republican citizenship involves active civic participation, but it is not primarily intended to achieve particular policy results. Rather its essential purpose is to create and maintain the institutions and processes of community governance. The republican citizen serves, doing his or her civic duty, because of the deeply held conviction that without a viable community no private interests can effectively be secured. That is, unless the "system" works, one's own self-interest cannot be achieved, and so one must pitch in to make it work. Public service, from this perspective, does not spring from a sense of *noblesse oblige,* nor from private ambition or the quest for group advantage. Republican citizens regard civic duty as the job of everyone, and see all citizens as having an essentially equal share of both the obligation to serve and the responsibility for keeping the political order in effective working condition.

The idea of republican citizenship has its roots in the theories of Aristotle and the practices of Athenian democracy, and it was integral to the thinking of Jefferson, Adams, Madison, and indeed most of the Founding Fathers. For many Americans that conception may now seem mainly of antiquarian interest, as modern politics appears to consist overwhelmingly of instrumental action in behalf of self-interest. In the course of the following discussion, I will argue that local political arenas not only have been created but are still very largely maintained and made to work by the devoted actions of republican citizens. This argument carries with it a very important pedagogical message as well; namely, that students must learn that while self-interested citizenship is very often the appropriate and relevant focus of effort, in other situations civic duty is also necessary. Civic education should exclude neither type of action. The rational and concerned democratic citizen must be able to tell the difference and to know how to practice both modes of citizenship without either cynicism or despair.

In this essay, I hope to show that much of the community experience in the American federal system is an expression of both types of citizenship, republican and instrumental, and the tensions between them. We begin with a discussion of the role of republican citizenship in the founding of communities. This discussion then leads to the thesis that social homogeneity has very often been a precondition of effective community-making and a principal objective of republican citizenship. We then consider the thesis of the American system as a pluralistic society of instrumental citizenship; however, this thesis is found to be inadequate. In the course of this discussion, I will argue that the quest for homogeneity and conformity has impelled not only the creation of communities but also their maintenance, precisely because of the influence of pluralism in the larger arenas of state and national politics.

The Constituting of Communities in America

From the founding of Jamestown and Plymouth down to the planned communities of today, Americans have been at work creating their local communities by official action, endowing them with legal indentity and authority, and, in the process, establishing arenas of citizenship in which people could contend for the things they value. This reliance on formal legal action to establish communities was not inevitable. In many societies it has been more common for local settlements to develop slowly through more or less unplanned processes of accretion. In the prototypical case, function tended to generate the urban formation rather than the other way around, as a transportation junction, a religious institution, or a defense outpost might give rise to a larger community. But America was a new country, lacking the centuries of social history and established institutions. Moreover, we lacked a feudal past, and the deep social divisions that grow out of that kind of history. This factor is often held to explain the broad acceptance of a Lockean liberal ideology. It also has meant that many of our communities were founded before their functional feasibility was even known, much less the dominant factor.

Community founding in America has followed several distinct patterns depending on when, where, by whom, and for what purposes the founding occurred.[2] For example, the Puritans of New England were anxious to assert the autonomy of local institutions against any more central authority, in part because they had so recently experienced in England the struggle in which Charles I attempted to centralize authority. Two centuries later, however, on the frontier of Michigan, Florida, Arkansas, and eventually much of the Trans-Mississippi West, it was the federal government that "remained the paramount force in solving the many problems associated with the frontier condition."[3] New England towns were created as covenanted moral communities while many in the South and West were designed from the start as commercial ventures.

During the Progressive era, municipal reforms witnessed the creation and re-creation of many units of local government in which the dominant design criterion was efficiency, and the dominant social group benefiting disproportionately from the structural changes was the middle class. Recent scholarship has emphasized (perhaps unduly) the deleterious effects of Progressive era changes in local government on citizen participation, noting that as the points of access to local authority were consolidated in the name of efficiency voting turnout shrank,[4] especially among the working class, and governmental responsiveness suffered.

Americans are still creating local communities, constituting them officially as authoritative governing units, in large numbers. Nowadays, this process seems directed more often toward merger and consolidation of local units than toward making new towns or districts. But as recently as the 1950s the incorporation of new suburban municipalities and special districts was a familiar experience, and in the preceding three and one-half centuries there was hardly ever a time when counties, towns, school districts, and other local governments were not being established somewhere. As a rough estimate, the total has probably been close to 150,000. And this is in marked contrast to the infrequency of nation-building or state-making. However dramatic the constitutional period of the 1780s was, it occurred only once, and we have made only five new states in the twentieth century.

There is a more important point here than simply the numbers and frequency of community foundings. Each governmental unit provides an arena in which people may act, seeking to utilize the authority of the unit for their purposes. At the same time each governmental unit in a democratic society requires its residents, or some of them at least, to serve, hold office, and exercise the authority of the body. Thus each is an arena for both forms of citizenship, republican and instrumental. That is, the very fact that we have made so many distinct and separate local units has enormously increased the opportunities for civic action,[5] and, while making it necessary for citizens to participate, we have also made democratic citizenship considerably more complicated than it otherwise might have been.

Why should Americans, more than any other people, have created such an extraordinary profusion of local governments? Part of the reason, no doubt, has been the necessity of governing a large and diverse society, located in a huge land mass with great variation in physical and social circumstances. Part has been the consequence of a federal structure of institutional authority which makes ample room for new communities and governmental structures to be established and to function without much centralized direction or control. In part, the explicit construction of legally defined local jurisdictions is made necessary by the absence of long-established norms and customary conceptions of who has the authority to do what and to whom. In the Progressive era, a frequent justification for establishing independent school districts and a variety of other reorganizations of local governmental arenas was the need to remove the function in question from "politics."[6] I want to suggest that in addition to these factors a more encompassing and powerful force has been at work, and provided much of the meaning these other partial explanations contain. My thesis is this: *the American community founding process has sought to create homogeneous cultural groups.*

The United States has been and is, in Robert Wiebe's terms, a segmented society,[7] and a very large portion of the segments are and have always been local. Each has sought to create an island of like-minded people, separated from one another spatially and sociologically, governing itself within boundaries by consent and often consensus but, when necessary, operating to suppress dissent and interest conflict as they might arise. New England towns were established by covenant, and newcomers were subsequently admitted only after signing on. It was not only the covenant that bound people together, however. As Thomas Bender points out, membership in the town "was fundamentally spiritual and experiential, often based upon previous and long-established friendship."[8] When a town grew more diverse it was not uncommon for the new elements to be "hived off" producing two "purer" communities where before there had been only one. In the Middle Atlantic colonies also, cultural group segregation was the norm. Later, as ethnic and religious diversity grew more marked in the nation as a whole, individual communities continued to display astonishingly little internal social diversity. It was far more common for a midwestern town of the nineteenth century to be overwhelmingly Methodist or Lutheran, Scandinavian or Yankee, than to display any significant amount of cultural pluralism. Even today, of course, ghettoization is not unfamiliar. Cultural homogeneity within particular suburbs or urban neighborhoods, often enforced by zoning and districting arrangements, is seldom either complete or lasting, but it obviously continues to be a powerful norm affecting the lives of millions of Americans of all classes, races, and cultural backgrounds.

This effort to establish homogeneous communities and to defend their homogeneity against the forces of diversity has had enormously important implications for many facets of American political life. It has inspired generations to clamor for states' rights and other rhetorical versions of local autonomy in order to keep control over "our" affairs in the hands of people "like us." It has led to suburban sprawl, as earlier it encouraged successive waves of outward movement inside city boundaries by the urban middle class. Today it fuels the defense of neighborhood schools, and while there is certainly a component of racism in that defense the drive toward homogeneity goes well beyond race to include ethnic, religious, social class, and other cultural elements as well.

From this perspective the establishment of functionally specific local districts, typically justified as efforts to insulate them from partisan or "special interest" politics, can be seen in another light. Autonomous school districts, in particular, provided an institutional framework in which educational interests did not have to cater to competing social groups but could design the "one best system" of programs for a presumptively unitary community according to a unitary standard of professional values.[9] Even though the school districts were not really homogeneous, therefore, they could be treated as though they were for purposes of elementary and secondary education. Similarly, sewer districts, park districts, and other such arrangements could pretend there was no group conflict within their jurisdictions because their governing arrangements effectively screened out most of the particularistic demands and conflicts. Efforts to establish metropolitan area structures for broader governmental purposes, on the other hand, have generally foundered in America, precisely because, in the proposed new and far larger and more diverse arena, political uncertainty as to outcomes would jeopardize so many of the spatially concentrated interests in the area, each of which controlled its own territorial jurisdiction, however restricted its capacity to act effectively.

The culturally homogeneous community provides a very particular and quite limiting kind of arena for the practice of citizenship. Given homogeneity, it is an arena in which broad consensus may be assumed and conflict regarded with suspicion. It is an arena in which it is difficult to challenge established patterns, in which those who do may be branded as troublemakers and, if they persist, encouraged to exit.[10] Further, it is an arena in which, lacking mechanisms for competition or protest and without the normative acceptance of social conflict, potential problems or incipient conflicts are often ignored or papered over. Robert Wood once characterized suburban politics as having these features.[11] I am suggesting that they have been characteristic of all local community development throughout the American experience.

The homogeneous community is also a setting in which community service is relatively easy to undertake. Since cultural and other barriers do not block or constrain ambition, one may move in and out of civic life, neither threatening nor enhancing one's private values but "doing one's duty" to keep the communal enterprise afloat. That is, this consensual community is the natural locus for republican citizenship. From Aristotle through Jefferson, the advocates of this form of civic virtue assumed that a necessary feature of a virtuous republic was a rough equality of status and condition among its citizens. Without that equality, the striving, conflict-oriented, competitive citizenship of instrumental action in pursuit of scarce values might be the only kind that makes sense. In a diverse, pluralistic community, instrumental citizenship will typically predominate, and the larger the unit the more likely will be, as Madison tells us in *Federalist* No. 10, a diversity of factions and interests. Republican citizenship can flourish only among relative equals, and only in culturally homogeneous groups is equality of status not an open issue. This, I suggest, is the underlying logic, from the perspective of civic theory, that has driven American community-building.

We must keep in mind that in a sense American social history has been dominated by a continuous process of social differentiation as new cultural groups came to our shores, new economic classes emerged in the context of capitalist expansion, new interests were differentiated and institutionalized in corporate and organized group form, and the scale of almost every collective enterprise grew larger and larger. Those forces of diversification have surely affected every part of the land so that even the most out-of-the-way places in Mississippi or Maine have been "modernized"; i.e., have encountered enough social diversity that at least some of the old consensus has broken down and a certain amount of pluralism is tolerated. Over the long run, however, these diversifying forces not only have been resisted in local communities (and indeed in states as a whole so long as they were substantially homogeneous), but they have also been resisted in significant degree *by means of* creating new communities.

Homogeneity and Pluralism in the Federal System

My emphasis on homogeneity may seem peculiar inasmuch as the predominant concept long associated with American social development has been pluralism. Madison, Tocqueville, Calhoun, and a great many others, past and present, have stressed the diversity of cultural streams that have produced the multicolored American social fabric. Moreover, a central principle governing the constitutional design was precisely the need to accommodate and control the effects of diverse factions and groups. Cultural pluralism, regional differences, religious diversity, association profusion—all are hallmarks of the nation, past and present. Nevertheless, it is in the nation as a whole that pluralism can be seen, not necessarily in a given community. The quest for homogeneity has energized the creation of distinct local governments precisely because in the larger arenas of state and, especially, nation, there was such pluralistic richness. Establishing and protecting local authority was the only way to preserve the autonomy of the locally dominant group, and, in one community after another, that group was so overwhelmingly strong that pluralism was a meaningless phrase. Massachusetts was not originally pluralistic. For decades Utah had little experience of religious pluralism, and neither did the overwhelmingly Catholic, Lutheran, Baptist, Methodist, or Congregational towns elsewhere. Even today the religious map shows that in large parts of the nation one denomination claims over 50 percent of the church adherents.[12]

The growth in aggregate American social diversity has generated two distinct tensions with this homogeneity orientation. One is the tension that underlies federalism, which arises even though in a legalistic sense local government has no constitutional autonomy vis-à-vis the nation. The tension here is between the diversity of groups and the differently weighted political mix of those groups operating in the state or national arena and the homogeneous community whose values are in some way out of step. The result is often that in the larger and more inclusive political arena groups prevail which could not win in the local arena and they then make demands for local actions which local elites do not like.

Local autonomy is pitted against national standards in many substantive areas of public affairs, and in each there is this tension between local homogeneity and national diversity.[13] Wiebe has argued that in modern times this tension has often been expressed as a conflict between the relatively tolerant liberal accepting values of national elites and the much more insular views of the "locals".[14] The national perspective stresses interdependence and an emphasis on abstract rules and impersonal forces. The local view holds on to personal relations, homogeneous values, and suspicion of outside "alien" forces. Localism need not always mean parochialism, however, nor do the forces of good inevitably control the national scene.

The second tension comes from the processes of fission and diversification that have affected the local community itself. Former social, ethnic, or religious monopolies have given way before mobility of population, growth, and change. The modal response to this tension, as we have noted already, is the "hiving off" process, incorporation of a new community, schismatic separation of a religious congregation, moving to a new neighborhood, or perhaps just closing down street access to an area "threatened" by social change.

The quest for homogeneity, however strong and enduring, has ultimately foundered in most parts of America, or at the least grown more difficult to achieve. Diversity of values and expanded zones of tolerance for that diversity have gradually displaced an insistence on the one true way. Or it may be that a middle class town now accepts racial and religious pluralism but not social class pluralism. Local minorities have made increasingly effective use of the tension of federalism, appealing their case, both legal and political, to the broader national arena and using the national levers of power to alter local policy. But the fact that even in the local community most forms of pluralism have increased does not alter the related fact that the tradition of community-building in America has been (and, where new subdivisions are built today, still is) rooted in the desire for cultural homogeneity. And further, some forms of citizen action make sense only in a context of substantial homogeneity of values and statuses.

Community Purpose, Community Attachment and Citizenship

The segmented society perspective of Wiebe and others is considerably broader than needed here, for it extends to all kinds of communities—those found in the professions, in large corporations, in academic departments, and any place else where shared norms bind some people together and exclude others. Wiebe argues, for example, that as the normative unity of local communities broke down in the late nineteenth and early twentieth centuries the rise of professional, corporate, and other large organizational milieus provided mechanisms to preserve autonomy and value cohesion, albeit with rather different justifications.[15] From the perspective of local governments, these functional communities, cutting across and severely weakening the lines of local attachment, posed a basic problem. How could loyalty to the home town be claimed against a "higher" loyalty to one's career? How could the commitment of active local citizenship be expected from one whose morally compelling community was no longer where he lived but with his professional peers? And, if most of the residents who were linked to trans-local communities pursued their main concerns in those arenas, who would be left to display the civic virtue necessary to govern the community?

One answer, of course, is to abandon the local community as an instrument of autonomous government and turn it into an administrative subunit directed by state or national elites. In this event, groups with effective access to those elites may gain their purposes quite nicely (and sometimes not so nicely), and utilize the standard methods of instrumental citizenship to do so; namely, voting, campaign contributions, pressures on congressmen, and so on. Those local residents lacking access or ineffectual in exploiting it and who dislike the policy results may move to a more congenial setting where their values prevail. National or state domination need not, in the American case, mean uniformity of policy. The same groups do not win out every time or in every place. Insofar as national programs have dominated the scene since the New Deal, as many argue they have, they still tend to be allocated in disaggregated constituency-specific ways, subject to differential political pressures from diverse groups. What nationalizing of political action has occurred does not mean the end of effective citizenship, but it does virtually limit the citizen to instrumental action. The republican virtues of creating the institutions, vitalizing the processes, and serving the needs of the society are hardly relevant for more than a handful at best if the locus of significant decision making is Washington, D.C.

Republican citizenship, for most Americans, is practical primarily in the local community. Let us be clear what this means. First, it means that largely voluntary service intended to help make authority function effectively will be an option available to most people only if there are quite large numbers of governmental units with sufficient autonomy to make participation more than a sham. Second, however, the substantive purposes that such a government can accomplish may, because of resource limits or the dominant values, be quite limited. There may not be enough money or enough effective control to do what is needed. Republican service does not guarantee satisfaction on instrumental grounds. Third, since rough equality of status is required for sustained republican virtue, the community must be quite homogeneous in its values. It cannot tolerate much conflict, partisan or otherwise.

These conditions were generally met in American communities prior to the modern era, as we have seen, and there is certainly a significant residue left. But consider some other characteristics of such segmented, insulated communities where republican citizenship could thrive. If conflict was suspect then wide ranging debate over alternative courses of action could hardly be expected. The town meeting model has too often been depicted as one where debate was encouraged and the vigorous joining of issues was a regular feature of life.[16] Not so, nor could it be. The rarity of meaningful political argument in America stems precisely from the fact that each American has grown to political maturity among people with whom most values were shared.[17] Disputes occur only at the margin of each community's consensus. There are multiple communities and each may have a somewhat different set of core values, but insofar as each segment remains separate from the other no "real" debate need occur, nor can it.

A corollary of this point is that dissent within the consensual community is commonly either repressed or treated as a harmless eccentricity. In either case it is not taken seriously. This is supremely ironic. It means that in a society that so values the liberty of each community against the interference of others, the individual within each community has little freedom to express opposing views. In the early days of convenanted communities, it was fairly easy for a nonconformist to confess error and be welcomed back, but without penitence there came expulsion. Running people with locally unpopular views out of town is an American practice with a long history, notwithstanding the First and Fourteenth Amendments.[18]

The paradox of community autonomy resting upon individual conformity reveals, on the one hand, the very real limits that may be accomplished in terms of substantive purposes by means of republican citizenship. If one cannot argue much or openly disregard the dominant norms, what good is the opportunity to serve as an active community-building citizen? Or, to put it differently, why should we not regard this so-called republican virtue as a cover, a mask that hides the status quo power distribution and suppresses any challenge to those who benefit from it? The answer is, first, that republican ideology is not, despite its association with the American Revolution, an ideology of social change. It is, as Cicero and Jefferson both hoped it would be, an ideology of social stability and decent order. Civic duty sustains the institutional framework of community life. It is supportive—indeed, patriotic—rather than being designed to criticize or attack the broad patterns of society.

Second, since Aristotle, active citizenship has often been held to be a basic necessity for individual development and self-actualization. The conditions that appear to characterize the republican milieu may set quite distinct limits to how far and in what directions individual growth can go. Participation may well enable the individual to become more fully human only as that is defined by the norms and values dominant in his particular community. Insofar as the human potential requires engagement in conflict or striking out in novel directions, republican citizenship cannot assist.[19] Nevertheless, within those limits there is much testimony in support of the view that an active civic life expands the individual value and satisfaction of that life. And it follows that in the United States the very profusion of local governments, resting as it has on the voluntary participation of the citizens, has been the main structural foundation of this Aristotelian self-realization.

Two further aspects of what we are calling republican citizenship underscore its importance for present-day communities in the American federal system. One is the fact—at least it is probably true though no systematic social science has really been utilized to test it—that despite great spatial mobility Americans tend to derive a significant part of their social identity from their "home town" or local neighborhood. Moreover, there appears to be a powerful tendency to value that place of origin very highly indeed; to regard it as "the best little" town/neighborhood/city/etc. in the country/world. The opportunities for armchair theorizing and pop social psychologizing about American identification with place are immense, and pending the availability of serious evidence, should probably be resisted. It may be noted, however, that insofar as one's local community is a central point of self-defining reference, it may not be foolish to work as an active citizen in order to make that community as attractive and highly regarded as possible.

The second point to make here is supported by contemporary social science data. In recent years, reversing earlier patterns, Americans have come to *trust* local governments more highly than state or national authority.[20] In a period when trust in authority generally has suffered severe decline, and when the power of local government to deal effectively with most of life's problems may reasonably be doubted, it is a bit startling to discover that the trust factor has held up so well. Perhaps what this means, however, is that, whatever the "objective" functional concerns of modern life may seem to be, many citizens continue to seek and value the attachment to accessible local institutions in which they may play a part, a part reflecting their continued commitment to the norms and obligations of republican citizenship.

Instrumental Citizenship in the Local Community

For two centuries or more, the dominant motivation underlying active citizenship in Western democracies has been presumed to be instrumental, that is, people take part or attempt to in order to secure some service, status, privilege, or right that without civic action would be denied them. The history of suffrage extension and especially the efforts by American blacks to obtain their full civil rights amply illustrate the point. With respect to citizenship in the local community, however, the instrumental case for action is not without complication. Two issues may be noted. First, there are today a great many goods, services, and needs that cannot be provided by local government unaided no matter how powerful politically a group may be. Blacks have been elected mayor in Newark, Gary, East St. Louis, and Mound Bayou as well as Chicago, Detroit, Atlanta, and Los Angeles, but the citizens of those places, who were impoverished before, find their condition little improved on average by access to local political power. They might well be entitled to ask what good it had done them to be good citizens. The decisive arena of action for a very large share of the economic goods and services provided by public authority is clearly national not local.

A second factor helping to weaken the instrumental impact of local citizen participation is the relative ease of exit from any particular jurisdiction. Why struggle in one city to gain power, especially group power, when it is so much easier to move to a community where your group already has power? Such is the logic of much of the schismatic town founding which, as we have noted, has been so prominent a feature of American civic history. They exit option has also been the obvious choice of large segments of the middle class who fled central cities for suburban refuges against one wave of immigrants after another. Historically, the flight was almost entirely white and during the past forty years or so the effect was mainly to segregate communities on the basis of race. Most recently, however, black middle class citizens have also exited in quite large numbers, leaving the city versus suburb differentiation more sharply defined by social class than by race as such.

The point, of course, is that to secure lower crime rates, better schools, nicer parks, and newer street lights it may well seem easier to move to where they exist by reason of the class composition of the community than to fight for them through political activity. As a consequence of, or at least in full compatibility with, this perception, voting turnout, the most direct measure we have of local level citizenship, is consistently and substantially lower for local elections than for state or national contests.

Nevertheless, many people do vote in even the most lackluster local elections and sometimes, as in the 1983 Chicago Democratic primary, participation reaches very high levels indeed. Some of the voting turn-out may well be motivated by the norms of civic duty (republican citizenship), but there are instrumental goals as well that local action can rationally be seen to affect. First, there are jobs. Local governments employ nearly nine million people (just over three million are teachers). Political participation is not always or everywhere a necessary condition for obtaining or keeping one of those jobs, but it has been known to be of some use. One category of local government job is that of elected official of which there are, according to 1977 figures, some 475,344 in the country. Active citizenship is certainly required to obtain these positions, and while most Americans seem not to harbor ambition for office the supply of aspiring candidates remains quite substantial.[21]

A second bundle of instrumental objectives toward which citizen action may be directed is the array of goods and services provided by local authority. Even though the figures seem dwarfed by the defense budget or federal welfare expenditures, the amounts of money and especially perhaps the salience of locally determined services remain significant. The recent literature examining how much effect political pressure has on service distribution has not provided conclusive answers and there is surely much variation over time and among communities.[22] Nevertheless, it is not mere democratic mythologizing to suggest that civic participation bears some instrumental relationship to local service levels and the satisfaction therewith that citizens enjoy—or complain of.

Finally, we should note a somewhat more indirect but nevertheless important instrumental effect of autonomous local community citizenship. Despite their economic and social vulnerability, local officials possess substantial legal authority to act in geographically defined jurisdictions in which that authority operates. In short, they have turf, literally and symbolically. They are concerned to protect that turf and to secure the resources necessary to serve its needs and demands. In effect, by constituting local communities and conferring upon them significant autonomy, we have at the same time created an array of vested interests with built-in lobbyists who will work at every level, public and private, to enhance those interests.

In recent years, the organizations of public officials have greatly expanded in number and perceived political impact. The U.S. Conference of Mayors, the National League of Cities, the National Association of Counties, the American Federation of State, County and Municipal Employees (AFSCME), the National Education Association, unions of firemen, police, and other workers—all of these and more have helped build a structure of public policies which, wherever the decisions are formally made, greatly enlarge the resources and protect the continued autonomy of action and authority of the local community. Thus, despite all the nationalizing and centralizing forces at work in the modern world, the American political process continues to reflect the instrumental impact of local political action.

Yet there are limits to what even the most vigorous and sophisticated political action can achieve. Ghost towns and abandoned villages reflect not only the forces of social change but often the failures of politics as well. The struggle to prevent school closings in the 1980s lest the neighborhood suffer decline had its analogue decades earlier when the little red school houses were consolidated out of existence. No matter how big a vote there is or how much protest, some policy changes grind on inexorably. Citizen action even then can play a part, of course, helping to guide and shape the direction that consolidation and centralization processes take, but it is not a sufficient guarantee of success. Not only are different citizens often on different sides of an issue, but citizenship alone does little to build houses, create jobs, or discover new energy resources. It is vital that citizen education convey both the possibilities of civic action and its very real limits.

Toward a Conclusion

In the contemporary world, the melodramas of national and international politics so dominate the civic theater that serious attention to the local community has come to be regarded by academics, journalists, and many thoughtful citizens as either eccentric or an exercise in nostalgia, a harking back to simpler days. In a technologically sophisticated, interdependent world, the local community seems at the mercy of forces beyond its control, powerless to resist the tides of fortune, good or ill. The ocean provides political society with its most apt metaphor; vast, mysterious, powerful, often cruel, immensely promising but never bothered by any particular fish or ship or social reformer. So, from a world-historical perspective, the local community and its citizens may appear to have little to say or contribute, either to the fate of mankind at large or even to one's own particular condition.

If this perspective were the most appropriate one from which to view the end of the twentieth century, there would be little point in urging young people to take part in the civic rituals of participation in their local community, or to build a more satisfying life by working with one's neighbors. If multinational corporations, the arms race, and Malthusian population pressures really shaped our future, to teach students that they have an obligation to revitalize their local communities through hardworking citizenship might be merely to invite their cynical disbelief in the dogmas of democratic faith.

Even if it were true that the functional requirements of modern life could no longer be met from the resources available within local jurisdictions, it might still be possible to draw the money and authority from the larger public and carry out important programs on a decentralized local basis. The war on poverty of the 1960s was based, in part, on this assumption, and its record suggests two basic problems. One is political and pragmatic; it is difficult to sustain a program that taxes at one level and spends at another, where different groups benefit and different political constraints operate at one level compared to another. And, second, if the *real* authority is national, with local units having little choice about what to do or for whom, there is not much room for meaningful citizenship in the subordinated local community. To encourage local citizenship then would be to invite frustration and more democratic rage than commitment, and this is often what occurred in local community action programs.

Many observers have argued for some time that in American urban communities the social cohesion and moral consensus necessary for effective republican citizenship have, in any case, long since broken down.[23] In this view, the modern city is a place of alienation and anomie, not of community; of inequality and Hobbesian conflict, not of shared concern to build and keep the institutions of civil society. If the local community is not a viable locus of citizenship, it makes sense to evaluate it in terms of the efficiency with which services are provided, environmental quality is maintained, and life chances improved for its residents. The uses of local government will be regarded more as matters of convenience than as institutional arenas necessary for the very existence of citizenship practice.

Yet American local communities continue to exist in rich profusion, resisting the tendencies to consolidate in the name of efficiency, a tendency so readily observable in the corporate business world. The local arena still provides the occasion for active civic participation for large numbers of people. I suspect this persistence is not simply the result of inertia, nor of the resistance of local office holders anxious to retain their petty principalities. The quest for homogeneity is still part of the dynamics of the United States, and the local community is still its chief institutional mechanism. Americans still value the instrumental values they can secure locally: the zoning change, the street repair, the nuisance abatement, the pupil assignment (sometimes), and even, still, the job. Active citizenship in the local community cannot accomplish everything we need or hope for, but, as the founding generation of America saw so clearly, it can still mean a great deal to the quality of our lives.

NOTES

1. A fuller discussion of these conceptions of citizenship may be found in two earlier papers of mine: *Key Concepts of Citizenship: Perspectives and Dilemmas* (Washington, D.C.: U.S. Office of Education, 1979); "Republican Virtue and Affirmative Citizenship," paper presented to the Conference Group on Political Theory, Washington, D.C., 1980.

2. In this discussion I have drawn on the work of many scholars. Among those I found particularly helpful were Page Smith, *As a City Upon a Hill* (New York: Alfred Knopf, 1966); Thomas Bender, *Community and Social Change in America* (New Brunswick, N.J.: Rutgers University Press, 1978); John Reps, *Town Planning in Frontier America* (Princeton, N.J.: Princeton University Press, 1965); and Malcolm Rohrbough, *The Trans-Appalachian Frontier* (New York: Oxford University Press, 1978).

3. Malcolm Rohrbough, *The Trans-Appalachian Frontier,* p. 220.

4. Actually, I do not find that Schattschneider, Burnham, and the other scholars who have described the decline in voting after 1896 make much of this point, but it is surely a logical component of their argument concerning "the system of 1896." See E. E. Schattschneider, *The Semi-Sovereign People* (New York: Holt, Rinehart and Winston, 1960) and Walter Dean Burnham, *Critical Elections and the Mainspring of American Politics* (New York: W. W. Norton, 1970).

5. In his celebrated analysis of American civil society Alexis de Tocqueville placed much emphasis on the importance of local institutions as schools of responsible citizenship essential to meaningful liberty. *Democracy in America,* Phillip Bradley, ed. (New York: Alfred Knopf, 1945), especially in Volume 1, Chapter 5.

6. See the analysis of Samuel P. Hays, "The Politics of Reform in Municipal Government in the Progressive Era," *Pacific Northwest Quarterly* 55 (October 1964): 157–169.

7. I cannot express too vigorously my admiration for Wiebe's *The Segmented Society* (New York: Oxford University Press, 1975). More than his other admirable works, *The Search for Order* (1967) and *Businessmen and Reform* (1962), *The Segmented Society* offers a most persuasive and remarkably holistic interpretation of the essential American experience and it is a provocative delight to read and to ruminate upon.

8. Thomas Bender, *Community and Social Change in America*, p. 64.

9. See David Tyack, *The One Best System, A History of Urban Education* (Cambridge, Mass.: Harvard University Press, 1974).

10. See Albert O. Hirschman, *Exit, Voice and Loyalty* (Cambridge, Mass.: Harvard University Press, 1970).

11. Robert Wood, *Suburbia, Its People and Their Politics* (Boston Houghton, Mifflin, 1958).

12. See Douglas W. Johnson, Paul R. Picard, and Bernard Quinn, *Churches and Church Membership in the United States* (Washington, D.C.: Glenmary Research Center, 1974).

13. I am paraphrasing the language sometimes employed by the Supreme Court in its struggle to find acceptable verbal formulas to resolve obscenity disputes, among others. For the most part, the Court in recent times has insisted on a simple interview standard, for example, in cases involving race, defendants' rights or, usually, religion. In obscenity issues, however, the *Miller* case restored the legitimacy of "community standards" as one criterion. I take this to indicate that despite setbacks on the issue of neighborhood schools, the local homogeneity cause is not wholly abandoned. See *Miller* v. *California*, 413 U.S. 15 (1973).

14. Wiebe, *The Segmented Society*, p. 107, *passim*.

15. See also Burton J. Bledstein, *The Culture of Professionalism* (New York: W. W. Norton, 1976); Paul Starr, *The Social Transformation of American Medicine* (New York: Basic Books, 1982); Peter D. Hall, *The Organization of American Culture, 1700-1900* (New York: New York University Press, 1982); Alexandra Oleson and John Voss, eds., *The Organization of Knowledge in Modern America, 1860-1920* (Baltimore: The Johns Hopkins University Press, 1979). One is tempted also to regard the home rule movement for local government as part of this same process of developing insulation against the forces of diversity and conflict. Home rule for cities and professionalization did occur together in time and surely shared many basic value orientations.

16. For an encomium to this model of disputatious town meeting democracy, see Paul Y. Ylvisaker, "Some Criteria for a 'Proper' Areal Division of Governmental Powers," in Arthur Maass, ed., *Area and Power* (Glencoe, Ill.: The Free Press, 1959), pp. 27–52.

17. Although many have remarked the decline of political oratory in America this interpretation has not commonly been offered. I do so here with some trepidation, therefore. For a recent survey of the American oratorical tradition, see Barnet Baskerville, *The People's Voice, the Orator in American Society* (Lexington, Ky.: University of Kentucky Press, 1979).

18. The Supreme Court has almost never provided unpopular speakers even doctrinal protection against a hostile audience. And from Roger Williams to the antebellum abolitionists (see Russell B. Nye, *Fettered Freedom*, rev. ed. [East Lansing: Michigan State University Press, 1964]) on to the Viet Nam protesters this "tradition" has remained operative. It is true, of course, that a much larger share

of the population today affirms the values of tolerance for dissent, but this is a distinctly modern development, not an outgrowth of the dominant tradition of American life.

19. For a persuasive statement regarding the importance of conflict in stimulating the growth of effective civic consciousness, see W. Lance Bennett, *The Political Mind and the Political Environment* (Lexington, Mass.: Lexington Books, 1975). At the same time, however, it may be that the citizen in office who struggles to figure out a solution to a community problem may grow as much as one who argues fiercely with his neighbors over what to do. In other words, the conflict Bennett and Ylvisaker praise may be found in the battle against uncertainty as much as in dialectical debate.

20. Between 1968 and 1976 the proportion of Americans expressing greater confidence in national rather than in state or local government dropped sharply—from 43 percent to 29 percent for whites and from 59 percent to 29 percent for blacks. See David B. Hill and Norman Luttbeg, *Trends in American Electoral Behavior*, 2nd ed. (Itasca, Ill.: F. E. Peacock, 1983), p. 125.

21. The best study of recruitment of candidates for local (or any other political) office remains Kenneth Prewitt's *The Recruitment of Political Leaders: A Study of Citizen Politicians* (Indianapolis: Bobbs-Merrill, 1970).

22. See, *inter alia*, Kenneth R. Mladenka, "The Urban Bureaucracy and the Chicago Political Machine: Who Gets What and the Limits to Political Control," *American Political Science Review* 74 (December 1980): 991–998 and Bryan D. Jones, "Party and Bureaucracy: The Influence of Intermediary Groups in Urban Public Service Delivery," *American Political Science Review* 75 (September 1981): 688–700.

23. This was the classic view of the "Chicago school" of sociology, exemplified by Louis Wirth and others. See the collection of Wirth's essays, *On Cities and Social Life* (Chicago: University of Chicago Press, 1964).

Part IV

◆

*Interests and Institutions in
the Local Community*

Much of my early field work dealt with urban politics, and I continue to regard the city not only as the setting for many of life's most civilized pleasures but as an appropriate context for exploring generic political questions in a relatively manageable milieu. In the heyday of urban politics research much of the best work was done by scholars who were not urban specialists but who found the city a useful site for empirical investigation of fundamental questions. I think this remains true, and I offer these examples from my own work in the hope that young scholars may be encouraged to spend part of their research careers exploring the ground around them.

12

The Politics of Geography in America

*P*erhaps it is true, as so many have said, that the United States was the First New Nation. The United States was the first, and is still the foremost, nation to have been wholly fashioned by the conscious decisions of political men. We have no mythological past, no Arthur and his Round Table, no Romulus and Remus, no Abraham or Moses. We have only history; our dramas are all documented and our useful fantasies are debunked. Romance must contend with reality, an ever more fully revealed reality, while heroes and their sacred causes are reduced to television parodies.

One very important feature of this manmade nation is that all of its geographical parts, its social spaces, have boundaries that have not been set by fiat, but established explicitly by public officials. From the granting of the first royal charters to the most recent legislative redistricting, the places of America have been created. None is "natural." Even Yosemite and Grand Canyon exist as national parks, not as natural wonders. And when we identify with some place of origin or present habitation, a state or a town, the attachment has little meaning except in the context of the political processes that once established and now maintain those places. Our geography is an artifact of our politics.

Four quite different kinds of social meaning have been investigated in our places. At different times and situations one or another may loom especially large but all are present and, among other things, provide the basis for deciding whether a particular place is good or bad, a delight or

Reprinted from Milica Banjanin, ed., *The Idea of Place* (St. Louis: Washington University, 1983), pp. 1–10.

a disaster. I will consider each category of meaning: the political, the commercial, the moral, and the personal. Despite the fact that the categories, like the places themselves, are manmade I will probably be unable to keep from violating their boundaries. Not to worry.

Political Spaces

Americans have invented or appropriated a bewildering array of terms to denote the geographical units in, by, and through which they are governed. Cities and villages, townships and towns, districts and authorities, wards and regions coexist in a jumble, at once fearful and wonderful. Some 90,000 local government units (actually down 40 percent since World War II) exercise some kind of authoritative jurisdiction over us. Without trying very hard I can think of at least seventeen separate and distinct geographically defined governmental units that contain the house in which I live. John Stuart Mill believed that the opportunity to participate in local government would be a wonderful training ground for the English working class, but the American scene offers such an embarrassing richness of these opportunities that, as we know, many, perhaps most, of us remain ignorant of and uninvolved in most of the public business, especially that of local government.

Nevertheless, the fundamental structures of American politics are, by design and in operation, geographical. Every member of Congress is elected by the voters in one and only one state or district. He or she is first and foremost dependent on the continued approbation of those who live, or at least vote, in that place. Applause in Washington does not necessarily translate into votes back home (though it may come to be valued more highly, so that the member quits Congress in order to hang around the capital). Voters and members alike are local. Only in the specific community can one vote, never in the nation as a whole. No one votes for Congress, only for individual members. This is familiar enough. And its main corollary is also familiar; namely, that public policy tends overwhelmingly to be formulated in disaggregated district- or group-specific terms. It is less often a matter of environmental protection in general than a struggle of economic development interests in Colorado or Wyoming against the hikers and backpackers from eastern cities; less the national interest in a strong defense than contracts for tanks, shipyards, and air bases; less the national need for scientific research and more the advantages that redound to the areas around Boston, Palo Alto, Berkeley, Ann Arbor, Madison, St. Louis, and other locales where the research universities are located. Prudent congressmen articulate their district interests, and the resulting packages of public policy reflect the aggregate effects.

When government is expanding, it is relatively easy to negotiate coalitions big enough to enact programs and fund them. Indeed, the votes may approach unanimity as each district stands to benefit. When there are cutbacks, on the other hand, or some form of policy conflict with clearly defined winners and losers, the struggle will generally display a strongly geographical definition. Snow Belt versus Sun Belt is only a recent version of an historic pattern. The Civil War and later on the Civil Rights struggles, the tariff, free silver, Jacksonian Democracy, the Constitution itself: all were fought out by politicians whose primary imperatives were the particularistic interests of local communities. And this was so because unless or until one is president of the United States there is no other institutional framework in which political support can be found.

It must be noted that to define political life in terms of geographical space is *not* to condemn that life to the eternal repetitions of old formulas and commitments. A spatial configuration may, in principle, contain any number of combinations of politically relevant interests and values. Alabama, for instance, is no longer a political space occupied by whites in fear of the prospect of black citizenship. George Wallace courts black voters, with some success, and so does Strom Thurmond in nearby South Carolina. Nevertheless, the distinctiveness of a politics constructed out of spatially defined units depends upon the existence of separate and perhaps conflicting interests differentially distributed across the spaces. If, for instance, every state had an identical proportion of its work force belonging to labor unions, then labor-management struggles over policy might be very much the same all over the nation and geography wouldn't matter much. But Detroit is not the same as Phoenix or Dallas. North Carolina's union work force is less than one-fifth that of New York or West Virginia. So their respective political complexions also differ, and it makes a great difference not only who wins but where. A politics of geography is thus highly particularistic, somewhat dynamic in the long run, and also, in a heterogeneous society, filled with the bases of conflict and disagreement.

It is hardly surprising that where the match-up between socioeconomic interests and geographical districts has such massive significance for the shape and substance of public policy there would be recurrent struggles over how to define those geographical units. The Missouri Compromise, the Kansas-Nebraska bill, and other great names from the past exemplified the centrality of sectional politics and the necessity of compromise among geographically defined interests if the Union was to endure. *Baker* v. *Carr* and the associated cases and developments involving one man-one vote provide a modern illustration of how critical is the question of election district design and of who will decide.

Electoral districts are not the only spaces determined by means of political decisions, however. The functional layout of American communities also has been shaped, not wholly but in critically important ways, by the decisions of governmental authorities. Indeed, it can be argued that the only kind of government planning that has ever been widely accepted in the United States is town planning. From the beginning, New England towns were "laid out." They did not just grow by accretion; they were planned. So also in the South. And in Virginia, when the natural processes of growth failed to sustain the projected communities, county courthouses were built anyway and lawyers had to come to them. L'Enfant's Washington plan was distinctive in its geometry, and it postulated multiple monuments and public buildings to fill the projected spaces. But on a lesser scale most other American towns were also designed by official action, and I want to note two particular aspects of this fact.

One is the centrality of public buildings and public functions. The courthouse square is a national phenomenon, sometimes obscured today in large cities that have grown in ways that lose track of where the center used to be, but still clearly identified in most of the 3,000-odd county seats of the country. An extension of the same idea, of course, is the central location of state capitals, not everywhere, but in all but four or five states. And, of course, Washington itself was chosen for its then central position, geographical and political.

Obviously, to locate public buildings in the middle of town is to stress symbolically the importance of public affairs, just as the medieval cathedrals reflected the relative preeminence then of spiritual concerns. More than that, however, the concept of a courthouse square was quickly enriched by the growth of commercial activity around its edges. Whether the civic institutions dominated the commercial or vice versa, the symbiosis was surely inescapable, symbolically and in everyday life.

The other aspect of conscious town planning is the grid street pattern. Again, it is not quite universal; Boston comes to mind, as does L'Enfant's Washington, and a few others. But it is remarkable how consistently the grid has been employed in America, even when, as in San

Francisco, to insist on it must require builders to ignore every principle of physics. Commercial ease and simplicity no doubt recommend a grid pattern most of the time, though in some instances it is only recently that its conveniences have been fully appreciated—providing rapid access for fire engines, for example, and escape routes for bank robbers. My point is that this fundamental fact of American community structure, the grid pattern of streets, was imposed by governmental authorities, from the seventeenth century on.

Geography as Commerce

A second aspect of American space making involves the commercial impulse. At the beginning it was in the South where town making was unabashedly also a money-making enterprise, in Jamestown, not Plymouth. The New England town was a moral device, the "city on the hill," an idea we will come back to in a moment. The "southern idea" involved the planning of a community that would induce investors, small or large, to locate there, enhancing property values and making the founders rich. There is no way to underestimate the importance of real estate speculation as a dynamic force in shaping the United States, nor of the role of government in fueling that dynamic. A road, a courthouse, a canal, a railroad, a college, all these were public or quasi-public inducements to location and commercial growth used in the same way as tax abatement and other financial gambits are employed today. In recent times, of course, we have witnessed the effects of zoning, municipal boundaries, VA and FHA mortgage policy, highway construction, and above all the selective effects of real estate tax shelters and mortgage interest deductions. Suburban sprawl and central city decay are ubiquitous, in big cities and small, but let no one suppose that they are "natural." Shopping malls are no more the inevitable creations of impersonal social and economic forces than was the courthouse square or the New England common. We have *made* all our places, and if they seem tawdry, even unlivable, it may well reflect the moral quality of the motives that shaped our designs.

The Moral Community

The Puritans intended to create a morally superior community, made virtuous in part by the Calvinist character of its inhabitants but in part also by its design. For the next two centuries the issue went back and forth as to whether the virtuous character of Americans was sufficient to guarantee their liberty or whether, as Madison put it, auxiliary precautions were required. With the death of classical politics in 1787, the Founding Fathers accepted the need for structural precautions. Nevertheless, the concept that a nation had been founded that was and would forever be morally superior to all others was firmly embedded in our schoolbooks, our public rhetoric, and our international relations. We had made a virtuous place as well as a prosperous one and indeed each aspect was pretty much proof and guarantor of the other.

The imputation of moral superiority to a geographical place is especially American. Other countries have their nationalisms, but generally they are more linguistic or religious than geographical. Here the nation, the region, the state, the county, the city, all are objects of intense affection and home town loyalty. We fight, cheer, and otherwise struggle for the honor of these fractions against competitors. Nostalgia sanctifies the shabby results of the real estate speculator and mayor who conjured up Sunnyvale Village out of seventeen acres of swamp and bracken, or their counterparts who went in the night to steal the county records so as to make their town the county seat. We identify with places, whatever their origins, and that attachment shapes our behavior.

Personal Geography

Actually I speak too glibly when I say we identify with places and that it matters. Social scientists have asked a great many questions during thirty-some years of sophisticated polling, but I am not aware of any efforts to ask people how they value particular spatial configurations or what it might mean to them to do so. I speak, however, if not with confidence, at least unembarrassed by systematic evidence to the contrary. And my unsupported hypothesis is that Americans, far more than other folks, define themselves geographically. They are New Yorkers, Virginians, or Iowans; from Chicago, or Boston, or Dallas; Macoupin County, the East Side, Kerry Patch, or Parkview. Moreover, paradox extraordinary, these attachments sit snugly amidst the enormous geographical mobility that has ever characterized American life. Most people in this country have not, in fact, lived out their lives within a single geographical unit, be it village, city, or even state. Even when gross population figures have been static, there has been enormous turnover of individuals. It may be, of course, that it is this very mobility that has bred such strength of psychological attachment, the anchor of home town giving some modicum of stable location to an otherwise directionless life.

At another level a passionate commitment to local places, like nationalism on a larger scale, can serve to express the yearnings that go largely unfulfilled in a humdrum world but are animated every Friday night at the local high school basketball game against Naperville or Glen Ellyn. How very significantly our lives are shaped by our attachments and loyalties to places, and all those places have been created by political action. They have been made, not found and so, therefore, have we.

We Are Not All Locals

By now many of you will be quite restless, muttering to yourselves and one another that not everyone is so parochial, even in this country, and that it is my particular midwestern myopia that prevents me seeing the significance of larger, nongeographical forces such as social class and multinational corporations. Further, you may mutter, localism may well have dominated our historic self-images, but it has surely lost both relevance and power in the face of great metropolises, vast bureaucracies, and all the other comforts of the modern world.

Who can deny these considerations? The world has changed and technology has without question rendered geography far less meaningful than it used to be. Spatial location does not much constrain our interactions nowadays as it always did before. Technology invites us as easily to cheer for Atlanta as for St. Louis, more's the pity. Suburban towns have no clear physical definition and in any case commonly bear no relation to school districts, shopping neighborhoods, and the other spatial configurations we use. It should follow either that specific geographical loyalties are weakening or, at the least, that they are relevant only for larger and more inclusive units, mainly the nation. And it might also follow that identity would be derived increasingly from functional attachments; church, party, union, corporation, profession. This tendency would be further accentuated to the extent that geographical spaces become more and more heterogeneous socially. It is by no means clear that neighborhoods today are more integrated along lines of social class or race than they used to be, but it is true that in terms of religion and national origin the erstwhile ghetto barriers have broken down.

For purposes of this discussion let me concede most of these points and then go on to argue that nevertheless geographical configurations are of great continuing significance in the United States, especially in our political life. Before I do that, however, I want to point out that the tension between localism and universal criteria of worth and merit is hardly new in America.

One sees it in the artistic world, for example. In the early days of the Republic, Americanism was characteristically expressed in classical form. The simplicity and virtue of the Roman Republic supplied much of the inspiration for writers and artists who appropriated those qualities to impose orderly and often heroic definition on American materials. Horatio Greenough's statue of Washington, clad in a toga, was perhaps the culmination of this aesthetic tendency but, of course, in architecture Roman and Greek models continued to provide the major symbolic form of dignity and civic gravity suitable for public buildings.

In the postclassical age, however, which in the arts came a bit later than in politics, localism came to be the hallmark of Americanism in art. The Hudson River School, Mount, Bingham, and many others chose themes and developed styles that were unlike their European counterparts. So did some of the popular writers of ante-bellum days. It may well have been the scarcity of wealthy patrons that pushed American artists to use local scenes and modes of life rather than the classical allegories and other universal themes of the previous generation. In any case, the depiction of ordinary people in identifiably American settings encourages Americans to think of themselves in essentially geographical terms—in relation to specific states and regions, rivers and mountains—to define themselves in terms of place.

One way of characterizing the progress of the arts in America since the early nineteenth century is in terms of a kind of dialectical alternation between localism and universalism, between Inness or Eakins and Ryder, between Ives and MacDowell or Horatio Parker, between Wood or Curry or Benton and Pollock, between Gershwin and Roger Sessions. Incidentally, in this context a frequent synonym for universal is academic, and sometimes a synonym for academic is uninspired.

To most modern American intellectuals, attachments to local places have long been suspect. Local is juxtaposed to cosmopolitan as narrow is to broad, simple to sophisticated, stodgy to exciting. Serious people read the *New York Times* wherever they live and cheerfully ignore the neighborhood news contained in the shopper throwaway. Exercised over the large events of the world, they are taken by surprise, uncomprehending and briefly furious, when their neighbors vote to ban a book or exclude an adolescent halfway house. But, after all, they are "them," the locals, Mencken's Booboisie, Gopher Prairie—not us. *We* don't live *there*. Modern intellectuals don't live anywhere in particular. And, consequently, in the United States—though not so much elsewhere in the world—their political impact is negligible.

Conclusion

Returning now to the political side, my penultimate contention is that, despite all the massive societal forces conspiring to destroy viability of local communities and local identities, the American political order continues to be based upon the assumption that they are real, and to a certain extent politics continues to make them real. Efforts by practical reformers and utopian schemers alike to transcend the institutions of local government in favor of larger units more apposite to the structures of economic life have not caught on. For example, the creation of the Tennessee Valley Authority in 1933 was heralded as the harbinger of a new, more "national" approach to river basin development, but after that one "slip-up" state and local officials, abetted by the Army Corps of Engineers, managed to stave off further uses of the regional model. The organization of banking and of the courts has given public authority a regional structure, and the federal government administers many of its programs through regional offices. Few of us identify much with the Kansas City regional office of HUD or the Fifth Army headquarters, however, and those geographical constructions remain mere administrative conveniences, lacking political meaning of their own. A regional office gets its *political* substance from the concerns of state and local officials within the region.

So we are back where we began, with a politics of place, of cities and counties and states and districts as the units of effective political action, loyalty, and scorekeeping. In an age of super organization and global interaction, how can this localism survive? And, more important, what will it mean for *our* survival? The first of those questions is easier to answer. Political localism survives in America because that is the framework within which public officials are elected and in that process develop the patterns of responsiveness that shape their actions. *If* there were a strong disciplined party system, or *if* Exxon or Jesse Helms or the AFL-CIO could fully dominate the national political agenda, then things would be truly different. In fact, however, the centrifugal forces generally overpower the centralizers, at least in the political arena. School prayer, at most, becomes a state or local option. Defense against the Russians dissolves into district-specific contracts. It is the budgets of each city and county, each school district and university that come to reflect Reaganomics and the war on inflation, and it is the hosts of officials from these units that mobilize to keep things as they have been.

I would not argue that political localism is the only centrifugal force tending to fragment American public policy and in the process to expand the size of the public budget. Congressional committees and subcommittees have a similar effect. Uncoordinated administrative units—interservice competition in the Pentagon, for instance—further the result. Interest groups, so vigorously and multitudinously represented in Washington, are largely oriented toward the maintenance and enhancement of specific policy advantages to their particular constituencies and alertly redefine any proposal for policy change into terms that specify its effects on each group's interests. Interest group liberalism and the policy immobilism that accompanies it draw important sustenance from the *geographical* localism of which the American political order has been constructed.

Now—and at last—can America survive? Can local interest policy solutions solve global problems? Can micropolitics produce effective macrostrategies of action? These are hardly new questions, of course, and I shall not propose new answers. Let me observe, first, that there are several lines of argument suggesting that localism, even in an advanced modern age, is a preferred political option. Various strands of participatory radicalism, for example, have urged the further devolution of power to neighborhoods and other small forms of community as a more or less conscious riposte to the large-scale bureaucratization of modern life and the accompanying dehumanization of the spirit. Efficiency may be sacrificed but so be it; human values will flourish. A second argument stresses the traditional virtues of federalism; limited commitment, experimentation, diverse approaches, and so on. In today's world the contention might give more emphasis to human ignorance—we need openness and diversity to find workable solutions to problems we don't seem to understand very well—rather than states' rights or generalized suspicion of governmental power. But much of the rhetoric advocating decentralization of political action has a long-familiar ring to it.

A third justification for encouraging the continued vitality of localist politics is what might be called the decollectivization of public policy. The ideological and symbolic trappings of this argument can vary a good deal, but at bottom what is asserted is this: Do you say that the problems of housing, agriculture, education, poverty, and so on are collective concerns involving the interests of all of us which can be solved only by comprehensive national action? And do you say further that a fragmented system of political action such as ours cannot act effectively in the general interest? Nonsense! No such action would in fact *work* to "solve" those "problems." They are not in fact, national problems. They do not really affect all of us, at least not equally. In any case, we don't know how to "solve" them through comprehensive action. We will make better aggregate programs in small steps, in small spaces, than through national declarations.

This argument might, in principle, be thought equally as applicable to abortion, school prayer, and tobacco price supports as it is to student loans, food stamps, and housing. The actual politics of things today, however, puts Senator Helms on one side of the table for some issues, and quite as genially on the other side if that logic is more useful. Localism, like most elements of American constitutional and political design, cuts several ways.

There is a Panglossian quality about our world. Public opinion polls report that we generally distrust all large organizations, public and private. We are far more suspicious than we once were of public officials and our fellow citizens alike. We express deep concern about the future of the world. And we gravely doubt our collective capacity to do much about it. At the same time, however, we say that we are remarkably happy personally. Our finances, despite Reaganomics, are not bad. Our sex lives are fine. We allege to the pollsters that we pray a great deal and are pleased with the response thereto. And even with crime in our streets and homes, the undependability of our appliances, cars, and other durable goods, grim employment prospects in the core industries and the principal human services professions, and so forth, even so, we claim to be happy now and optimistic about our personal futures. Economists like to talk about the fiscal illusion, whereby people embrace a program's benefits without seeming to realize how big a tax bill accompanies them. Perhaps the supreme illusion of American life is our high level of civic satisfaction in the quality of our lives regardless of the reality. If so, I would agree political localism is a large part of the answer. For it is that localism that persuades us, no matter how contemptuous we are of Congress, to love our congressman nonetheless. And if, with Hamilton, we think "the people" a great beast, we might still conclude that the folks next door are not so bad.

How profoundly that sentiment—Hamilton's, Archie Bunker's, and ours—was and is the bedrock of a kind of social conservatism, how closely entwined it is with political localism. That localism has contrived to maintain a fundamentally conservative structure of political values throughout our history. But it is only a certain kind of conservatism, one that makes common cause with neighborhood groups and participatory democrats and elevates human processes of a sort above tangible accomplishment, citizenship before efficiency. Perhaps that cause is doomed, but was it only in the Old South that Americans could be political romantics and resist history?

13

Urban Politics:
The New Convergence of Power

*E*conomically, culturally, and in many ways even politically, the United States has become a thoroughly urban nation.[1] One aspect of this urbanization is that scholars have increasingly paid attention to phenomena occurring in cities. Sociologists, political scientists, economists, geographers, and historians have all developed urban subfields of specialization; and in recent years the subfields have been infused with the great enthusiasm of virtual armies of researchers. When these efforts are combined with those of architects, planners, social workers, administrative managers, and all the other urbanists asking questions about life in the city, the resulting stack of data, reports, proposals, admonitions, and manifestos is truly staggering. Inevitably, perhaps, concern for the substance of city life gets mixed with concern for the methods of inquiry. Both, of course, are legitimate and important areas of concern. Each helps illuminate and is illuminated by the other. Specifically, the study of power structure—a basic issue for all political inquiry—has come to focus very largely on the city. In the process, both the substantive and methodological issues surrounding this generic political question—the question, as Dahl puts it, of Who Governs?—have been involved in virtually every discussion of urban affairs in recent years.[2]

Yet despite, or perhaps because of, this special ferment some important gaps on this question—who governs the city?—have remained. Many of these relate to the basic criticism to be made of almost all urban studies, the absence of comparative dimensions. Serious, theoretically sophisticated social and political analysis of urban data is relatively new

Reprinted with permission from *The Journal of Politics* 26 (1964): 775–97.

on the scholarly scene, however. It is perhaps not so surprising therefore that so little genuine comparative work has been undertaken. One may be encouraged by the emergence of a number of comparative studies.[3] Most of these, however, deal with relatively small communities. One who is interested in general patterns of big city politics must deal with a series of case studies, each study dealing with a single community. Each study then serves its author as the empirical foundation for a series of generalizations about politics (or society—the sociologists have been firmly in the tradition since the days of the Lynds). Some of these are brilliant. At best, however, they are sophisticated insights and theoretical conjectures built upon descriptions of a single case which, one hopes intuitively, may fit a larger number of cases.

The limitations of the data are compounded by variations in conceptual apparatus and/or data-gathering technique. One wishes that there were a clear basis for determining that Atlanta was or was not a pyramid-shaped monolith; that Springdale was "really" controlled by a caucus, and that New Haven actually conforms to Dahl's analysis.[4] None of these three was studied in a manner which permits accurate comparisons with the other two (or twenty more which might be named), and hence no generalizations about either of two central points is possible. First, what is (are) the structure(s) of power in American cities? Second, what are the principal independent variables affecting the shape, scope, and operation of these putative structures? It may turn out that each city is unique and no useful generalizations can be made using the city as the unit of analysis. Or the city may really be the most useful microcosm of the political system in which all essential processes, structures, and relationships can be found. The professional conclusion probably lies somewhere between. We will not know without systematic comparative study.

One major effort at synthesis of exciting materials about city, principally big city, politics is that of Edward C. Banfield and James Q. Wilson.[5] To a large extent they draw upon the same materials as this essay, and there are many areas of agreement. There are important differences, too, however, both in conclusions and approach. Thus Banfield and Wilson give only passing attention to the historical dimension of urban politics. I propose to examine the question of the structure of power and do so over time. By viewing the city historically a number of critical elements, particularly those which have changed, can be seen more clearly than if a more strictly contemporaneous study were made. My discussion focuses upon the big cities in the United States that experienced major growth prior to World War I. The pattern I shall describe may apply to other communities as well, but my model city in what follows is heterogeneous in ethnic and racial terms, contains considerable industry and a suburban ring, is experiencing core city decay, and is, in short, what those who write about urban problems generally have in mind when they refer to "the city."

Anyone who talks about urban structures of power must take a stand on two related questions: what is meant by power and how does one go about trying to establish its empirical dimensions. By "structure of power" I mean the set of relationships among community roles, durable over time, through which relationships scarce resources are allocated in a community. I am primarily concerned with those allocations which involve decisions by governmental agencies. We should recognize, however, the shifting importance over time of public allocations to the total of allocations made in the community, and remember, too, that public and private actions are always mixed together, nowhere more than in the city. I shall not give attention to the allocation of all those resources that might be deemed scarce, but only those that are of substantial volume or scope. I recognize the difficulty of drawing clear distinctions between "important" and "unimportant" decisions, but there *is* a difference, and it is recognized by decision-makers in a city. Thus the structure of power affecting a primary fight over the nomination for recorder of deeds may bear no relationship to the structure within which the city's urban renewal program is determined. In such a case it is only the latter that is of much interest; the decisions involve much more substantial resource allocations and the structure of power involved is therefore a more important one.

In short, we shall examine the most crucial structures of policy-relevant power in the large American city and attempt partly to identify and partly to postulate a pattern of development that seems warranted by the histories and present circumstances of several such cities. In doing so we must necessarily make comparisons among fragments of data drawn from sources that are widely diverse in concept and method. The result must obviously fall short of definitive status, but hopefully it may at least provide some stimulus to systematic comparative research in urban data.

II

Two systematic historical studies of urban power structure are those of New Haven by Dahl and Cibola by Schulze.[6] Both identify patterns of change that, despite considerable differences between the communities, are roughly similar. Much of the other published material on American urban history can be read as confirming this general pattern.[7]

Dahl finds that political office in New Haven was dominated first by the "patricians," then by the "entrepreneurs," and finally by the "ex-plebes." Patrician dominance rested upon oligarchic control of all of the major resources from which influence could be fashioned. "[S]ocial status, education, wealth, and political influence were united in the same hands."[8] The entrepreneur's prominence emerged as wealth and social standing were separated, and the new men of business displaced the patricians in controlling economic resources. The entrepreneurs, moreover, were popular as the crabbed patricians were not. But the increasing immigrant labor force led to changing standards of popularity, and by about 1900 "[P]opularity had been split off from both wealth and social standing. Popularity meant votes; votes meant office; office meant influence."[9] The resulting pattern Dahl refers to as one of "dispersed inequalities." Many actors possess politically relevant resources but none possesses enough to dominate a broad range of actions. Particular actors exercise influence over particular policy decisions depending on the resources relevant to that decision, and several types of coalitions may aggregate the influentials concerned with specific problems, but no continuous structure of influence is operative for the broad range of public decision.

Robert Schulze describes a similar historical pattern in Cibola except that Cibola, a much younger community, had no patrician era. Instead it experienced two stages, local capitalism and non-local or absentee capitalism. In the former stage, until 1900, the economic dominants were also the political dominants. They held public office as well as controlling local economic resources and their preeminent social standing reinforced their hegemony. After 1900 Cibola increasingly became an economic satellite and local economic resources came increasingly under the control of national firms. Local officials of these firms did not involve themselves in the active influence structure of the community, much less hold office. Rather, there developed a separate category of influentials, the public leaders, whose influence rested primarily upon such factors as popularity and commitment to the locality. Schulze describes this as a bifurcation of power, but it may not be amiss to suggest that Schulze's data permit the inference that Cibola is more polylithic— influence is widely dispersed and discontinuous—than the bifurcation image implies.

Both Dahl and Schulze give support to the general view that roughly from the end of the Civil War until 1900 American cities were dominated by the merchantry. Where the community had long existed as a substantial population center, notably in the East, the entrepreneurs were likely, as Dahl describes, to have displaced the patricians. Where there hardly had been a city in the ante-bellum years, there were no patricians to displace, and the commercial elite, relatively open to talents and money, but an elite nonetheless, dominated all the major institutions of the community. Political offices were typically held for short terms with each important merchant expected to contribute some time to the marginal activity of public office-holding.

Although the economic elite of the mercantile city dominated political institutions as well, it is unlikely that much additional influence accrued to them as a result. Public authority did relatively little in this stage of urban development. Only gradually were such elemental functions as water supply and sewage disposal, street construction and maintenance, police and fire protection undertaken.[10] In many cases, too, the initial phases of service were provided by a mixture of public and private position held by influentials. Public improvements were undertaken not only to make life possible in the increasingly crowded and extended city, but also as "booster activities." "Let's put good old ——— on the map!" was an oft-repeated watch-word of civic promotion. As McKelvey notes, chambers of commerce were formed to promote economic development in a number of post-Civil War cities,[11] and the promotion of canals, railroads, exhibition halls, and—the classic booster gimmick—the World's Fair, all were part of the merchantry's effort to sell their particular community to the nation. Boosterism, even for the one-shot, short-run promotion, almost invariably involved a complex intermixture of public and private efforts and rested, therefore, on an elite which dominated both public and private office.

The gradual expansion of public services, however, had a significance for the structure of influence that booster gimmicks did not. Water and sewer systems, schools, streets, parks, police, and fire were functions that required continuous operation by larger and larger corps of public employees. With the industrial growth of the city, the object for which boosterism strove, more and more people, requiring near-geometric increases in services, came to the city. Further, the new immigrants came to work in the new industries. Whereas the mercantile city had been as nearly classless as the frontier itself, the industrial city was the site of a differentiated class structure; differentiated by income and life chances, by ethnic origins, by religion, and by political potential.

At the same time, the industrial economic giant viewed the city very differently from the merchant. He was far less dependent on local sales or real estate values and thus less concerned with growth itself. His was a contingent investment in the community—gradually in the several communities housing his several branches—and his civil liability was therefore limited just as the corporate form limited his legal liability. His participation in the allocation of community resources, while potentially great, was infrequent and discontinuous. He was concerned only to protect his relatively narrowly defined corporate interests, not a generalized pattern of influence.

The merchantry had been deeply committed to the city in an economic and emotional way that was missing from the industrial manager. In the industrial city the modes by which civic obligations were discharged became more diverse and more specialized. Service on special boards or committees for libraries or schools, or parks, or slum dwellers was increasingly the way that the local notables—and their wives!—made their community contributions. These were likely to be structurally separated from the main body of governmental institutions and something of a preserve for "the best people," insulated from "politics." In addition, the slowly growing concern for planning the City Beautiful and reforming inefficient or corrupt government provided larger and larger amounts of "program material" for the luncheon clubs and merchants' association.[12] That occasionally reform campaigns would actually elect a mayor or effect a change in governmental operation did not cancel the fact that economic and social influence had been separated from political influence, and that each now (ca. 1900) rested on a different social base.

An autonomous political elite was, of course, a function of expanded governmental activity and a growing working class population that altered the numerical balance of the city. As Dahl points out, not only were the political entrepreneurs now more popular than the economic entrepreneurs but the criteria of political popularity changed. Effective representation of the booster spirit and promotion of industrial growth gave way to effective representation of the needs of the poor for elemental services and the promotion of the political organization itself. The boss and his machine we now recognize to have been functional for the newly industrial city; a growing army of public job-holders was recruited, a vast immigration was socialized and provided means of advancement in the urban society, welfare needs were at least minimally provided for, further extensions of public improvement programs were constructed, albeit expensively, and specific services were rendered to the economic elites as well. Railroad spurs, street car franchises, assessment adjustments, police protection of imported labor, and a variety of other benefits could be conferred upon business by governmental agencies, even though the latter were no longer controlled by the businessmen themselves. Although businessmen were often appalled and sometimes intimidated by the "new men" of city politics, they rarely intervened or even protested against the system in any continuous way.

Surely a portion of the reason that the boss remained in power was that although government was far more formidable in this period than formerly, the major decisions allocating resources in the city were still made by private interests. Governmental functions were no doubt of crucial importance to the machine itself and to its followers, but, for the most part, they were of marginal importance to the private sector of the economy. It therefore made relatively little difference whether they were done well or not. This is the obverse of the point that economic notables tended to withdraw from civic involvement after about 1900. Not only did the changing city pretty well force them out of office; it was quite rational for them to tend their private gardens and only enter the political arena on behalf of specific policy questions with an immediate payoff to their specialized economic concerns.

What Schulze describes as the bifurcation of power between economic and political elites was thus a function of a changing industrial and social order in the city supported by the enlarged opportunities for political entrepreneurs in the growth of governmental activity. At the same time, the economic and social notables were fragmented by the split between absentee and local capital, the diffusion of energies in a myriad of specialized civic but largely non-political enterprises, and finally by the exodus from the city's corporate limits of the middle class. The efforts of the Progressive WASPs to reform local government, to cleanse the stables of municipal corruption, were in the main doomed by the inexorable movements of people. The middle class moved to suburbia and put political popularity—the ability to get elected—permanently on a working class basis.

The final seal on the bifurcation was effected by the shift of the voting habits of the urban working class to overwhelming Democracy. From the beginning of the New Deal more and more of the large cities became safely Democratic. The metropolitan middle class maintained its

Republican loyalties with respect to the national scene, but in local matters a modus vivendi on a business-like basis with the Democratic leadership—a matter of necessity for those with local interests at stake—was often achieved.

Yet the Democratic partisan hegemony provided a kind of cover by which middle class values could reappear in the public decisions of a working class city. By the end of the 1940's the machines were fading. The disciplined delivery of votes was rarely possible, at least on a city-wide basis, and the professionalization of the city bureaucracy was well along. Political office still went to those who mustered majorities from a predominantly working class city electorate but the circular pattern that characterized the era of "Politics for Profit"—votes gave power, power provided favors, favors provided votes—was increasingly broken. It is significant that a move toward "Good Government"—meaning rational policy making—came from within the political stratum itself in these years in Chicago, St. Louis, Pittsburgh, and New Orleans. This move coincided with a change in the agenda of urban resource allocation, and this change in turn has led to a change in the structure of influence.

III

I propose to designate the contemporary structure of urban power as the "new convergence." It is similar in many ways to what Dahl calls the executive-centered coalition. It is headed, and sometimes led, by the elected chief executive of the city, the mayor. Included in the coalition are two principal active groupings, locally-oriented economic interests and the professional workers in technical city-related programs. Both these groupings are sources of initiative for programs that involve major allocations of resources, both public and private. Associated with the coalition, also, are whatever groups constitute the popular vote-base of the mayor's electoral success. Their association is more distant and permissive, however. Their power to direct specific policy choices is severely limited. In the following pages I shall examine each element in the coalition as well as some of the groups in the city that largely lack power. In all cases I am concerned with power that is relevant to key resource allocation decisions.

In the period roughly centered on the turn of the century business leadership was transformed from local to absentee capital, from merchantry to corporate managers. Accompanying this shift in economic organization was a shift in community political commitment and orientations, and this shift, in the direction of reduced interest, coincided with and reinforced the burgeoning autonomous political organization. Now, however, I am saying that business plays an important role in the structure of city affairs. The apparent contradiction points to some complexities in the notion of "business."

First, some kinds of business never experienced the nationalizing effects of industrial reorganization. These often remained intimately associated with politics throughout the era of the bosses. Real estate dealers, building supply firms, insurance agents, and corner confectioneries were always likely to have an iron or two in the political fire. They still do, but these interests are not part of the coalition we are examining. Their interests are small with respect to resource allocations, and they deal in channels that are peripheral to the main body of decisions. Their politics is a kind of eternal process which goes on in many different kinds of worlds without affecting them. Petty business and petty politics are thus handmaidens but irrelevant to the larger issues of power.

The large international corporation continues to regard the local scene with the same investment calculus described earlier. In general, the branch plant will do only as much about the community as is required to develop and maintain an image of good corporate citizenship, and this is far less than is necessary for power or even concern about community resource allocation.[13] Occasionally, the needs of the firm may require it to intrude into the community political system, but such intrusions would be very much on an *ad hoc* basis. The same is likely to be true of large, nationally-oriented unions.[14] The exception occurs when the union or the firm has a large home office or plant in the city or has grown large from a base in a particular community. Then "good citizenship" may require more than charitable work and involve the company or union leadership in larger urban policy issues.

The most active business firms in the new convergence, however, are those with major investments in the community, which are dependent on the growth of a particular community, and which have come to recognize that all the major issues and decisions of the city affect their interests.[15] Furthermore, they all share a growing concern with that congeries of problems labeled "core city decay." They include the major banks, utilities, railroads, department stores, large real estate firms, and metropolitan newspapers. Functionally, the list is remarkably similar from city to city. Also similar is the fact that active concern with community affairs is relatively recent, largely post-World War II, and coincides with the perception of threat to tangible "downtown" economic values. Finally, the reentry of these groups into the active quest for power coincides with the weakening of the party-political dominance of the governmental arena. This permitted the numerically inferior business groups to assert their claims on a more continuous basis than formerly had been the case. In Chicago, where the machine did not weaken so much, the loop businessmen continued to operate on a largely *ad hoc* basis.[16] Elsewhere, however, the downtown business interests articulated their concerns more forcefully and organized their community-centered energies more efficiently than ever before. Instead of boosterism, business-centered groups helped to trigger a variety of problem-solving programs such as redevelopment and traffic revision and provided continuing support for efforts at solving other problems such as delinquency and crime. Much of the lay leadership of public campaigns for bonds, for example; much of the stimulus to action itself; and much of the private portion of new investment necessary to redevelopment came from this newly organized group. It is important to recognize, however, that, although the support and stimulus of downtown business was and is an essential element in the coalition that dominates decisions in the city, downtown business does not constitute a power elite. It does not run the city, or call the shots for its puppets.

The second element in the coalition—one would be tempted to call it the Civic Establishment except that the term may connote more tradition-based power than this coalition possesses—is composed of the technician, the professional, the expert. As Barry Karl has pointed out, the innovative function of the Progressive reform groups has largely been taken over by the professional.[17] The social worker has replaced Jane Addams. The social scientist in a Charles Merriam has replaced the amateur politician/reformer. Police administration, comprehensive budgeting and capital programming, systematic traffic control, land use planning, and renewal and rehabilitation have all become, in one degree or another, the domains of the expert. Technical criteria play a far greater role than before in determining choices, and the specification of alternatives is likewise largely a function of the technician who, often alone, knows what is possible.[18]

Perhaps the policy area most obviously dominated by the expert is that of public education. Teachers and school administrators not only set the agenda for action. They provide most of the arguments and evidence relevant to the choices that can be made and constitute the most active and powerful interests participating in the decision-making process. If nonprofessionals protest against certain policies—Negroes denouncing *de facto* segregation, for example—the professional educators cite technical educational criteria as a sufficient justification for their decisions and frequently carry the day.

The existence of professional skills relevant to city problems is, of course, a relatively new feature on the urban scene. Even now we are a long way from a technocracy, for the skills fall far short of the problems. Nevertheless, the growth of what broadly may be called applied social science has added a significant number of new people in new roles to the urban system, and these people help articulate and specify the problems and alternative courses of action for the other interests in the coalition. In this way the technician exercises power over resource allocation that is every bit as real as that of the economic interests or authority-wielders.

Let us turn to the peak of the loose coalition of interests that dominate today's urban scene, the mayor. He presides over the "new convergence," and, if the coalition is to succeed, he must lead it. More than anyone else he determines the direction of urban development; yet his sanctions are few, his base of support insecure. The mayor is both the most visible person in the community and, on questions of public policy, probably the most influential. Yet his is a classic example of the separation of influence and power.[19] Few big-city mayors have significant patronage resources. Even fewer use their appointments to give themselves direct leverage over policy. Although the mayor in a partisan city is necessarily elected through processes that involve the ward organizations, no big-city mayor can be regarded as the creature of the machine. Rather the mayor is an individual who has 1) sufficient mass appeal and/or organizational support to win election, 2) enough awareness of the complexity of urban problems to rely heavily on a professional staff for advice and counsel, and 3) the ability to negotiate successfully with the economic notables in the city to mobilize both public and private resources in efforts to solve core city economic and social problems.

Successful electioneering in the city requires that the candidate be palatable to a lower income constituency, especially to African Americans. Where there remain vestiges of party organization with vote-delivering capabilities the successful candidate must have some appeal for them, too. An ethnic background or family association that evokes support from the delivery wards is often helpful. At the same time, however, the successful mayoral candidate is likely to appeal to that portion of the urban electorate which historically has been reformist or mugwumpish in orientation.[20] He personifies good government by his espousal of professionalism in local administration. Frequently his personal style, despite his name or political forbears, is thoroughly white-collar and middle class. He is relatively articulate on local television, and his campaigns are likely to stress his competence at communal problem-solving rather than the particular group benefits that may accrue following his election. Nor is this mere campaign talk. His administration concentrates on solving or alleviating particular problems rather than building memorials or dramatizing the city's commercial prospects. Again, this posture requires collaboration with those processing the relevant resources, the experts and the businessmen.

Obviously, there are variations in the way the mayoral role is played. From city to city and mayor to mayor many differences may appear. The main lines of demarcation may be twofold, however. Some mayors, possessing the gifts of self-dramatization, may more fully personify the programs of the city than others. This has little effect on the content of the decisions but may have consequences in terms of support. Mayors may also differ in the degree to which they actively seek out problems and solutions. Banfield describes Daley waiting for things to come to a head; other mayors more actively seek either to forestall the problem entirely or to structure the whole process through which the issue develops. The latter distinction may be related to the structure of the city; the larger and more diverse the city, the less effectively can the mayor actively shape the problem-solving process.

Of what is mayoral influence composed? Much of it is contained in the office itself. Of all the roles in the community none is so well situated with respect to the flow of information concerning the city's problems. This alone gives the occupant of the office a great advantage over other influentials. He knows more about more things than anyone else. Although his patronage power may be relatively slight, his budgetary authority is typically substantial. Insofar as he, by himself or in a board or commission, presents the budget to the council, he is determining much of the agenda for the discussion of public affairs, and no one else in the city can compete with him. Third, his ability to co-opt persons into *ad hoc* committees is unmatched in the city. As the only official with formal authority to speak for the entire city, he can confer legitimacy on co-opted leaders as no one else can. Thus, if he chooses to, a shrewd mayor may have a good deal to say about who shall be regarded as leaders and who shall not. Negotiations on civil rights issues in a number of cities illustrate the point well. Finally, as noted earlier, the mayor is, or soon becomes, far better known in the community than anyone else, and is far better able to command and structure public attention.[21]

A considerable factor in the mayor's ability to structure public debate is his superior access to and influence over the press. City hall reporters not only cover his office closely but their view of city problems is very largely gained through their daily contacts with the official city fathers. The latter, in turn, are cordial and by being helpful can be reasonably assured that most of the news stories out of city hall will reflect mayoral interpretation. The newspapers as major businesses with their economic future tied to the local community and its elites are likely to favor editorially a mayor whose style embraces their interests. Thus even though the editors may differ with some specific recommendation of the mayor, they give him general support, while through them the mayor communicates his conceptions of city problems and program. One result, of course, is to make it difficult for others to challenge successfully the incumbent mayor for re-election.[22] Thus despite the unstable character of the coalition's base—predominantly low income voters and downtown businessmen—the mayor, once elected, may serve a good many terms. No outsider can find a sufficiently sharp wedge of controversy to drive between the disparate elements, or sufficient visibility to exploit whatever gaps develop.

Nevertheless, the mayor is influential only relative to other groups in the city. He is not powerful relative to the problems he tries to solve. The mayor cannot determine by fiat or, apparently, any other way that the economic resources of the city shall increase, that crime and poverty shall decline, that traffic shall move efficiently. He only has rather more directly to say about how the problems shall be approached than anyone else.

This discussion omits those cities which have adopted the council-manager form of government. In Kansas City or Cincinnati, for example, the aggregative and legitimating functions are less likely to be performed by the mayor who is seldom more than the ceremonial head of the city. The manager can rarely perform these functions either, since they are largely incompatible with his professional role. The result may be that the functions are not performed at all. On the other hand, the manager does possess some of the elements of leadership, especially information. As Banfield and Wilson note, the manager "sits at the center of things, where all communication lines converge. In the nature of the case, then, the councilmen must depend on him for their information. Whether he likes it or not, this gives him a large measure of control over them."[23]

IV

The "new convergence" we have described actively seeks out solutions to certain problems it regards as critical to the city's growth. This activist posture may be viewed as somewhat at variance with the approaches to decision-making described by Dahl and by Banfield. Dahl suggests that in New Haven the coalition led by Mayor Lee actively sought to resolve certain major issues with Lee serving as the principal negotiator among the contending forces. But, says Dahl, Lee selected issues with a view towards their effect upon his chances for re-election. Permanently conditioning the mayor's strategy was the fact that "the mayor and his political opponents were constantly engaged in a battle for votes at the next election, which was always just around the corner."[24] So far as most large cities are concerned, this may greatly overstate the impact of the necessity for re-election on the specific choices made by the mayor and his allies. We shall try to suggest both the role of the electorate and some of the more immediate restraints upon mayoral choice-making in a moment.

Banfield's analysis of Chicago in the late 1950s leads to the conclusion that issues are raised primarily by large formal organizations, some of which are governmental and some of which are not.[25] As the maintenance or enhancement needs of the organization required governmental decisions they entered the political arena and usually sought the support of Mayor Daley. Daley himself, however, operated in primarily a reflexive fashion. Although he desired to "do big things," he had to move slowly and cautiously, fearful of generating further controversies, and aware that the ponderous and intricate structure of power he headed could be disrupted and his influence capital used up if he moved too soon or too often. But Banfield selected issues that illustrate this argument. His cases fall far short of representing the range of major resource allocation decisions for Chicago. It may still be true, therefore, that Daley initiated or actively participated in the process involved in making other decisions. Certainly it seems that other big-city mayors do.[26]

I focused originally on the processes of allocating scarce resources. These processes may sometimes involve bitter conflict among rival interests. They may sometimes be resolved, however, in a highly consensual way. Particularly is this likely to be the case when the technical experts play a large role in shaping the decision. Much of the time such major areas of public policy as expressway planning, zoning, and budget-making are determined in ways that evoke little complaint or dispute. The fact that no one in the city effectively objects to the decision makes the decision no less important in terms of resource allocation.

A closely related aspect of urban decision-making is that a great many decisions are made in a fashion that may best be described as habitual. The pressures on the time and attention of decision-makers are such that many decisions must continue to be made (or avoided) as they have been in the past. No continuing calculation can be made of the costs and benefits for each area of possible choice. Much is done routinely. Much is left undone in the same way. Control of the routine is largely in the hands of the technicians with the mayor in the best position to alter it at the margins.

Some issues are forced "from the outside," of course. Things which city leaders would prefer not to have to deal with may be pressed in the fashion Banfield describes. Race relations issues generally come under this category. Almost every large city mayor has been compelled to take action, not because he or his coalition particularly wanted to, but because they were forced to by external pressure.

The recent demands of militant Negro groups have often been concentrated on city hall, however, even when the substance of the demands dealt with jobs in private employment. Black leaders have correctly identified the mayor as the appropriate figure to convene local elites in order to negotiate agreements that will open job opportunities to African Americans. Militant blacks have often greatly overestimated the power of the mayor to effect a satisfactory solution, however. For while he is in a stronger position than any other person or group or functioning organization, his resources and those of his allies may fall short of the requirements.

Pressure from the constituency would not be the usual way for policy to be initiated, however. The bulk of the city's working agenda is made up of proposals drawn up by the city's own technicians to meet problems identified by them or by their allies in the problem-oriented sectors of the community. The need for new revenue sources, for example, is perceived by the mayor and his staff long before public pressure is exerted, and it is the mayoral coalition which seeks a viable solution to the problem.

Not all mayors, not all corps of technicians, and not all downtown business groups are equal in ability to perceive problems, devise solutions, or negotiate settlements. One of the significant variables that distinguishes one city's political system from another is the energy and imagination of its newly convergent elites. In some cities solutions may be found that escape the leaders of another. It is probably true, however, that these differences have been narrowed somewhat by the collaboration among urban elites throughout the nation. The American Municipal Association and the U.S. Conference of Mayors provide organized communication networks that link the political executives. So does HHFA in its field. So do the various associations of urban technicians in their respective specialties. The metropolitan press facilitates a certain amount of interchange with respect to both problems and solutions in urban areas. Thus there has developed some degree of consensus as to what should be done and some uniformity in the structure of power by which action may be accomplished.

Cities vary with respect not only to energy and skill of leadership but in tangible resources, public and private and may be mobilized for reallocation. In Pittsburgh, for example, there was probably no available substitute for the Mellon cash. In St. Louis the scarcity or stodginess or both of local private capital has made the redevelopment task more difficult. These are variables involved in the power structure of a community. That there are also variations in the range and severity of the problems cities face is obvious and complicates further the task of comparative analysis.

V

I have suggested that a large portion of the content of urban public policy is provided directly by one or more of the three main elements of the governing coalition; the mayor, the technical experts, and the downtown business community. They identify the problems, they articulate the alternative actions that might be taken, and they themselves take most of the relevant actions. This structure of decision-making provides no immediate role for the community-at-large, the voters; and, although Dahl may overstate the significance of their role in limiting New Haven's executive-centered coalition, they do play a role in resource allocations, and so do the organized groups that represent segments of the electorate that are outside the dominant coalition.

Dahl's attribution of "weight" to the electorate seems to be based on the relatively intense partisan competition in New Haven, and it may be reinforced by the need to run every two years. But in many cities the direct competition for office is neither so sharp nor so frequent. The tenure in office of prominent mayors such as Tucker, Daley, or Wagner suggests that survival in office may not always require the close attention to voter desires that Dahl suggests. Particularly is this likely in a city where elections are partisan, for the safety of the Demcratic ticket is not often in question in many of these cities. The primary may occasionally present peril to the incumbent, and in both partisan and non-partisan cities incumbents sometimes lose. But there is little evidence to show that mayors, or other elected executives for that matter, have any reliable way of perceiving voter needs very accurately or consciously building support for himself among them. The new mayor may say, with Richard Daley, that "good government is good politics," in part because he doesn't have the option to engage in any other kind.

Nevertheless, generalized constituency sentiment remains a factor that affects policy-making, albeit in a secondary, boundary-setting way. It works primarily in three ways. First, the technician as social scientist often takes into account the interests and needs of the public he hopes to serve when making his plans and recommendations. If he proposes an enlarged staff of case workers for the Welfare Department, he does so partly because in some sense he expects the public to benefit. It is rarely, however, because any public demand for the larger staff is expressed. Rather, the technician believed the proposal would be "good" for the constituents. Secondly, the electorate must make certain broad choices directly. Bond issues and tax rates must often be voted upon; other types of referenda must be approved; key policy-making officials must be elected. Very often this involves "selling the public" on the desirability of the proposal. They have not demanded it. They often have no strong predispositions one way or another except perhaps for a class-related bias on public expenditures in general. But this approval is required, and in anticipation of the limits of tolerance the key decision-makers must tailor their proposals. This is influence, of course, but of a general and largely negative kind. Thirdly, there is the active demand stemming directly from the constituents to which policy-makers respond, but which response would not have been made in the absence of the public demand. Some of these demands go counter to the policies espoused by the coalition; spot zoning, for example, or construction unions' demands on the building code. In some instances the coalition may have the power to block the demands; in other cases, not. Some demands, however, are more difficult to deal with because, if they arise, they cannot be blocked by the exercise of power, but at the same time they are so controversial that almost any solution is likely to damage the overall position of the leaders. As we have noted, many of the issues of race relations are in this category. The city fathers have not agitated these issues, but once raised they must be met.

As we assign "the public" to a largely secondary role, we must also relegate those officials most closely associated with immediate constituency relationships to a similarly secondary position. Councilmen or aldermen, ward leaders, and other local party leaders are likely to play only supportive or obstructive roles in the community's decision-making process. The demands for action do not come from or through them, they are not privy to the councils either of the notables or the experts. They may well play out their traditional roles of precinct or ward politician, but, unlike the machine leader of yore, these roles are separated quite completely from those of policy-making. Even in Chicago, where the mayor's position in part depends on his vote-getting strength through the party organization, very little participation in policy-making filters down to the ward leaders. Similarly, William Green's rise to power in the party organization in Philadelphia had little effect on the content of public policy. It is essential to see that the difference between the policymaking leadership and the "politicians" is more than rhetorical. It carries a substantial impact on the content of policy.[27]

Even though neither the party professionals nor the electorate generally are active participants in the process of resource allocation, is not the top political leadership, specifically the mayor, constrained by his desire for re-election? In part, of course, the answer is yes. In partisan cities the mayor must be nominated and elected on the party ticket, and, particularly in the primary, this may involve getting party organization support. In a non-partisan community too, the mayor must get enough votes to win. It does not follow, however, that there is much connection between what is needed to gain votes and the specific decisions made once in office. Dahl emphasizes the vote-getting popularity of Richard Lee's program in New Haven, especially of urban renewal. Yet that popularity was not really evident in advance of the decisions and was largely dissipated within a very few years. Doubtless Mayor Collins increased his popularity in Boston by rationalizing and reducing the fiscal burden, but, if Levin is at all correct, his election was not a mandate for *any* particular decisions he has made.[28] The same, I think, could be argued for Dilworth, Tucker, and others of the "new mayors." Certainly the limits of public understanding and acceptance constitute restraints upon the decision-making system, but these are broad restraints, rarely specific in directing choices, and operating largely as almost subconscious limits to the kinds of choices that may be made.[29]

VI

It may not be amiss to conclude this discussion by juxtaposing three quite different strands of thought concerning the urban scene. On the one hand, Dahl and his associates have generally denied the existence of a single structure of power in the city. We have argued, not contradicting Dahl but changing the emphasis, that on a substantial set of key issues such a structure may be discerned. Hunter *et al.* have stressed an essentially monolithic structure heavily weighted in behalf of the economic elites. We have stressed the central role of elected political leadership. Finally, such writers as Lewis Mumford and Jane Jacobs, less interested in the problems of power, have doubted the capacity of the urban community to serve man's essential needs at all. In a sense, we are suggesting that each may be partly correct, partly wrong. The coalition of interests headed by the mayor may indeed lack the resources, public and private, separately or combined, to solve the communal problems now dominating the civic agenda. This is the irony that lies behind the convergence of power elements in the modern city. Where once there seemed to be ample resources to keep what were regarded as the major problems of urban life within quite tolerable limits, now, with far more self-conscious collaboration of governmental and private economic power than ever before, and with those structures of power themselves larger and more extensive than ever, the capacity to cope with the recognized problems of the environment seems almost pathetically inadequate. Partly, this may be because the problems have changed in magnitude, and, partly, that we perceive their magnitude in more sophisticated fashion. In any case, it makes the notion of an elite with ample power to deal with the urban community if ever it chooses to, seem a romance, a utopian dream. Like other municipal utopias—Progressive-era reform or today's metropolitan reorganization—it may be yearned for but largely unrealized.

NOTES

An earlier version of this paper was presented to the 59th Annual Meeting of the American Political Science Association, New York, September 5, 1963.

1. For a most comprehensive and thoughtful history of urban growth in America see Blake McKelvey, *The Urbanization of America* (New Brunswick, N.J.: Rutgers University Press, 1963).

2. Robert A. Dahl's study of New Haven was a classic of political science almost before it was published. See *Who Governs?* (New Haven: Yale University Press, 1961). Dahl chose not to integrate his findings with those available concerning other communities, and in a number of respects one may argue that his conclusions are limited to the New Haven context. One cannot deny, however, that the larger question of how to approach the study of power has been given theoretically sophisticated stimulus from the work of Dahl and his associates. See Nelson W. Polsby, *Community Power and Political Theory* (New Haven: Yale University Press, 1963). For a convenient summary of many of the items in the large monographic literature on community power structure, see Charles Press, *Main Street Politics* (East Lansing: Michigan State University Institute for Community Development, 1962).

3. Attempts to engage in genuinely comparative analysis include Oliver P. Williams and Charles Adrian, *Four Cities* (Philadelphia: University of Pennsylvania Press, 1963); Amos H. Hawley, "Community Power and Urban Renewal Success," *American Journal of Sociology* 8 (1963): 422–31; Leo F. Schnore and Robert R. Alford, "Forms of Government and Socioeconomic Characteristics of Suburbs," *Administrative Science Quarterly* 8 (1963): 1–17.

4. See the categorization suggested by Peter Rossi, "Power and Community Structure," *Midwest Journal of Political Science* 4 (1960): 398.

5. *City Politics* (Cambridge: Harvard University Press, 1963).

6. Robert Schulze, "The Bifurcation of Power in a Satellite City," in M. Janowitz, ed., *Community Political Systems* (New York: The Free Press of Glencoe, 1961), pp. 19–81.

7. The volume of historical work dealing with American Cities is immense in weight but often disappointing when it comes to the questions of greatest interest to political scientists. McKelvey's work is masterful both as a summary and as an introduction to the literature. *Op. cit., passim.*

8. Dahl, *op. cit.*, p. 24.

9. *Ibid.*, p. 51.

10. See McKelvey, *op. cit.*, pp. 12–13.

11. *Ibid.*, p. 43.

12. The suggestion that civic reform issues provide "program material" and sometimes little else is developed in Edward Banfield, *Political Influence* (New York: The Free Press of Glencoe, 1961), pp. 298, ff.

13. See the provocative essay by Norton Long, "The Corporation and the Local Community," in Charles Press, ed., *The Polity* (Chicago: Rand McNally & Co., 1962), pp. 122–36.

14. See Banfield and Wilson, *op. cit.*, pp. 277–80.

15. See *Ibid.*, Ch. 18.

16. See Banfield, *Political Influence*, pp. 291, ff. Banfield himself emphasizes the tangible conflicts of interest which divide Chicago business interests. Even so, however, one may suspect that without the Daley machine Loop business interests would have developed more commonality of interests.

17. See *Executive Reorganization and Reform in the New Deal* (Cambridge: Harvard University Press, 1963), ch. 1.

18. Banfield and Wilson note that the city manager often acquires power by virtue of "his virtual monopoly of technical and other detailed information," *op. cit.*, p. 175. They pay little attention to the possibility that other technicians in the city bureaucracy may acquire power over limited segments of policy in the same manner. Banfield and Wilson do note that in many cities it is the bureaucracy which can initiate and implement change but do not concede increasing significance to this group. See pp. 218–23.

19. Banfield and Wilson suggest that as the mayor's machine-based power has declined his formal authority has increased, by virtue of reformers' efforts to achieve greater centralization. They recognize, of course, that the increased authority does not compensate for the loss of power. Moreover, in the contemporary city the scope of the perceived problems and needs is often so broad that the strongest political machine could have done little about it from its own resources. Providing investment capital to rebuild downtown or opening employment opportunities for blacks must be negotiated in the broader community. The mayor is likely to be the chief negotiator and neither formal authority nor political clout is as effective as bargaining skills. *Ibid.*, p. 336, ff.

20. Lorin Peterson greatly overstates the case for connecting contemporary urban influentials with the mugwump tradition, but there is something in his argument. See *The Day of the Mugwump* (New York: Random House, 1961).

21. Scott Greer found that Mayor Tucker was the only person in the St. Louis community, city or suburbs, with any substantial visibility with respect to community-wide issues. *Metropolitics* (New York: John Wiley & Sons, 1963), pp. 106–07.

22. Banfield and Wilson note that the city hall reporter "is likely to be in a symbiotic relationship with the politicians and bureaucrats whose activities he reports," *op. cit.*, p. 316. They do not conclude, however, that this relationship strengthens the elected leadership. Indeed, they imply the opposite. See, e.g., p. 325. This difference in judgment calls for more systematic empirical analysis than is presently available.

23. *Ibid.*, p. 175. Banfield and Wilson, however, do not make this point concerning the position of the mayor in nonmanager cities.

24. *Who Governs?* p. 214.

25. *Political Influence,* p. 263, ff.

26. In addition to Dahl's discussion of Mayor Lee's active role, one may cite as particularly pertinent the discussions of Philadelphia, Detroit, Nashville, and Seattle reported in the appropriate volumes of Edward Banfield, ed., *City Politics Reports* (Cambridge: Joint Center for Urban Studies, mimeo). My own research in St. Louis, the initial foundation for much of the argument in this essay, certainly leads to this conclusion.

27. For an illustration, see the essay "St. Louis: Relationships Among Interests, Parties and Governmental Structure," below.

28. See *The Alienated Voter* (New York: Holt, Rinehart and Winston, 1960).

29. Banfield and Wilson also discuss a shift in the contemporary city, at least in political style, from working class to middle class. They conclude that the new style politician, reflecting middle class values in a working class city, will be compelled to offer broad inducements to the electorate in the form of major civic accomplishments if he wishes reelection. *Op. cit.,* p. 329 ff. This argument, like Dahl's, seems to me to assume that the urban electorate "shops" more actively than I think it does. It also assumes that political leaders in the urban community are more acutely conscious of their reelection problems than I think they are.

14

Organized Spokesmen for Cities:
Urban Interest Groups

A *familiar leitmotif* of American political analysis develops the key words "pressure group," "lobbyist," "access," and "special interest" into a fabric of explanation of the policy-making process. One may choose the benign views of a Herring (1940) or a Truman (1951), or prefer the critical posture of a Schattschneider (1960) or a McConnell (1966), but one can hardly escape giving central attention to the organized groups at work to influence public policy outcomes. Although disputes about concepts and methodology have not infrequently substituted for the empirical treatment of group activities, there exists a sizable body of literature treating various aspects of interest group activity concerning major sectors of policy. However, despite the recent emergence of concentrated academic attention on matters involving intergovernmental relations between cities and states as well as cities and the federal government, surprisingly little attention has been given to the associations of municipal officials that often serve as intermediaries in the negotiations and discussions that precede the programs that develop. It is the aim of this essay to add to the existing literature on interest groups by discussing some of these major organizations of municipal officials, and at the same time to consider further some generic questions of interest group theory.

Interest groups have generally been regarded as a topic of pertinent concern to political scientists because of their efforts to affect policy outcomes; in short, as lobbyists. Moreover, the traditional theoretical

William P. Browne coauthored this article. It is reprinted with permission from Harlan Hahn, ed., *People and Politics in Urban Society,* Urban Affairs Annual Review 6 (Beverly Hills, Calif.: Sage Publications, 1972), pp. 255–78.

283

formulation of the origins and growth of interest groups stresses their importance as mechanisms for the expression of discontent. Groups are seen mainly as instruments for affecting policy, making claims upon other groups through the medium of favorable governmental decisions. This analytic emphasis has generally been accompanied by the assumption that although organized groups might be subject to the operation of Michels' Iron Law of Oligarchy, this made no great difference to the group's lobbying efforts since in basic values the members of the group could be assumed to be pretty much in agreement.

Recently, this orientation toward interest groups has been called into question (Olson, 1965; Salisbury, 1969). It has been shown that organized groups are often not, in fact, cohesive on value and policy questions. It has been shown further that lobbying is often not the main incentive for joining such groups nor the central activity that sustains them. Organized associations are undoubtedly units of importance in American political life, but the nature of that importance needs further amplification if we are adequately to understand how groups operate.

In the urban field the group universe is large and diverse, and considering the conventional wisdom about the importance of groups, it makes it all the more bewildering that there is not more literature examining municipal interest groups. Standard works on American interest groups do not mention the National League of Cities or the National Municipal League, and urban politics texts make, at most, only passing reference to these organizations.

The discovery by professional political scientists of the organizations composed of municipal officials is quite recent and their treatment is largely restricted to the policy lobbying focus referred to earlier. Suzanne Farkas' analysis of the U.S. Conference of Mayors (1971) gives little attention to the internal life of that organization, nor did Connery and Leach (1960) in their brief discussion of the former American Municipal Association and USCM. Clement Vose (1966) has described some of the specialized "lobbying" of such groups as the National Institute of Municipal Law Officers, and there have been several accounts of the rather differently motivated National Municipal League (for example, Willoughby, 1969).

None of these studies adequately recognizes two quite central facts about the contemporary processes of urban political life. First, there has developed an elaborate and variegated network of formal associations of city officials which far exceeds in scope and importance anything Louis Brownlow (1955) may once have envisioned for his "1313" group of organizations. These early organizations of government officials were originally drawn together to provide a variety of technical services. But today a large share of the nation's cities are included in these organizations and officials of these cities depend upon them both for lobbying representation in Washington on behalf of urban interests and for a variety of services and benefits of direct utility to their respective communities. At the top, this network has been integrated organizationally by means of close cooperation. The largest, best staffed and most lobby-oriented of these groups, the National League of Cities and the U.S. Conference of Mayors, have largely combined their staffs and recently formed a third organization, NLC-USCM, Inc. Other organizations such as the National Association of Housing and Redevelopment Officials and the International City Management Association also work closely with the merged staffs so that despite the existence of many separate organizations of city officials there is an extraordinary degree of coordination of lobbying policy and a closeness of communication linkages among them. NLC-USCM has gone so far as to establish a State, County, City Service Center to coordinate not only the municipal associations but other interest groups as well, including the National Association of Counties, National Governors Conference, and Council of State Governments.

The second fact of importance about these organizations concerns their impact, not on public policy, but on those who belong. Perhaps the most important effect of the growth of urban interest groups is the cultivation and encouragement by the group leadership of professionalism in their jobs on the part of members, whether they be mayors or other kinds of public officials. The delineation of official role expectations has been fostered as the organizations work with members and bring them into contact with one another. Mayors, city planners, municipal law officers, and other groups of officials have achieved self-conscious identities through participation in their respective organizations. Moreover, through training programs and information services, the organizations have enhanced a level of performance in the roles which could reach closer to the expectations.

Part of our discussion of urban group development will be put in historical terms so that the emergence of different types of groups and different activities and relationships can be related to the historical context in which they first appeared. One implication of this approach should be acknowledged here. It is this. The groups we will consider have not been notable for changing their activities or adapting their programs and goals as circumstances altered. Rather, as organizations they have tended to maintain traditional roles and identities. When new conditions or needs arose, new organizations have been formed, often by individuals who belonged to and remained in the old ones. Functional differentiation is thus fostered among organizations rather than adaptation by one organization to new tasks.

Our examination will focus mainly on the "peak" associations of urban officials, the National League of Cities and the U.S. Conference of Mayors. These are the largest and most prominent of the many urban interest groups and they have the greatest and most far-reaching impact on the formation of national urban policies. Table 1 conveys some sense of the scope and variety of these organizations. Much of our discussion is based on extensive interviews with officials and members of these or-

TABLE 1
Some Urban Interest Groups

Associations of Units of Government: American Association of Port Authorities, Council of State Governments, National Association of Counties, National Governors Conference, National League of Cities, National School Boards Association, National Service to Regional Councils, U.S. Conference of Mayors.

Professional Based Associations: Airport Operators Council International, American Association of School Administrators, American Association of State Highway Officials, American Institute of Planners, American Public Power Association, American Public Welfare Association, American Public Works Association, American Society of Planning Officials, American Society for Public Administration, American Transit Association, American Water Works Association, Inc., Building Officials and Code Administrators International, Inc., Institute of Traffic Engineers, International Association of Auditorium Managers, Inc., International Association of Assessing Officials, International Association of Chiefs of Police, Inc., International Association of Fire Chiefs, International Bridge, Tunnel, and Turnpike Association, Inc., International City Management Association, International Institute of Municipal Clerks, Municipal Finance Officers Association, National Association for Community Development, National Association of Housing and Redevelopment Officials, National Association of State Mental Health Program Directors, National Association of Tax Administrators, National Institute of Governmental Purchasing, Inc., National Institute of Municipal Law Officers, National Recreation and Park Association, Public Personnel Association, Water Pollution Control Federation.

Independent Associations: National Municipal League, Public Administration Service, Urban America, Urban Coalition, Urban Institute.

ganizations and on intensive observation of a state municipal league and a local county league of municipalities. Quotations not otherwise attributed are drawn from personal interviews.

Social Movement Versus Role Cultivation

We will not attempt a treatment of the organized municipal reform movement, but we should take notice of the important distinction between the expressive values of reform which led to the formation of the National Municipal League and the professional improvement objectives of the contemporaneous League of American Municipalities and most of the successor groups of city officials. At the beginning, in the late 1890s, the latter were anxious to avoid the political stigma of reformism. Reform appealed variously to the business community or the anti-vice crusaders or some other section of "the better elements" of the community, but it was not an appeal that moved the hearts of most urban officials themselves. They were more often the targets of reformers, not the protagonists. If anything, they wanted technical advice and assistance from a national organization along with a forum for mutual discussion. The LAM sought to provide precisely this kind of instrumental benefit and so did the state leagues of municipalities which began to be formed after 1898.

The LAM and the NML were never hostile to one another. Their programs had a good deal in common, and both organizations were surely manifestations of the "Progressive Ethos" that dominated urban middle-class conceptions of America during the period (Hofstadter, 1955). Their memberships were based on different principles, however, and this distinction is crucial. The NML sought the support of anyone interested in the cause of municipal reform. The LAM was designed to serve the interests of municipal officials, and it was they, or rather the municipality as such, which constituted the unit of membership. As an early state municipal league director who supported LAM put it, "We are not reform groups! We are like a service organization for municipal officials." Essentially it is this concept of membership which has been utilized in the formation of the major organizations active today. Either the municipality itself as a legal entity or the holder of official municipal office qua office is the member. Sympathizers, former office holders, or other supporters of the policy goals of the organizations have no place as dues-paying members.

Eventually the League of American Municipalities failed as an organization because its staff and leadership were unable to provide enough services that officials found truly useful. The reforming NML concentrated its efforts on "model" governmental *structures* and sought to convert "the people" to their ideal formulations. The LAM went beyond such generalized objectives and developed a series of model *programs* in such areas as finance or licensing which LAM officials would attempt to adapt to the special circumstances of a given community in an effort to increase the efficiency of its governmental performance. In addition, LAM collected data and served as a clearinghouse of information concerning municipal practices, and to further these objectives. LAM encouraged the formation of state leagues of municipalities and specialized associations of officials. However, as the latter began to provide organizational meeting grounds and proved more responsive to the felt needs of the members, LAM had little to offer except statistics and model reform programs. As John Stutz of the League of Kansas Municipalities observed, LAM was an organization "looking for something to do" (National League of Cities, 1964). On the other hand the state leagues were successful because they "offered municipal officials something, something that they felt they had a need for and could apply [to their own duties]." The organization went out of business in 1912, its staff and its functions taken over by organizations it had helped to create, but the example of a national organization of cities remained.

The Process of Professionalization

In a sense, what both the NML and the LAM sought to do was to improve cities. The state leagues of municipalities, which achieved a more enduring organizational identity in the early years of the twentieth century, concentrated on raising the competence of public *officials*. The goal was professionalism. Its criteria of accomplishment were largely those of job efficiency and in this spirit the league efforts joined the forces of Taylorism that were making comparable inroads in facilitating the role differentiation of school superintendents among others (Callahan, 1962). The idea of a professionalism produced by efficient performance had important implications for the role of the leagues also. By assisting officials—holding conferences, establishing short courses, disseminating information, and giving on-the-spot advice—a league could professionalize the man whose only actual training was on the job. Experience and example were taken as the sources of wisdom and professional officials were those who were wisely efficient.

The leagues thus appealed to those who were in fact the potential members, city officials without formal training for their jobs. The approach fitted exactly the organizational imperatives of associations seeking the dues-paying support of municipalities, which meant in practice the office holder. At the same time, the leagues generally eschewed programmatic promotion. Such controversial proposals as city manager government were left to such groups as the NML. The leagues assisted managers but avoided advocacy, for advocacy might alienate, and the leagues needed, first of all, the support of as many cities as possible. Controversy might mean the loss of membership and organizational bankruptcy. Failure was no abstract threat; about one-third of the state leagues have gone out of business at one time or another.

The leagues were not without their own research orientation. But their research was of the most practical nature directed at providing information of direct assistance to the members. Information of a comparative nature about municipal costs and wages and various regulatory codes was most often the content of their research projects. Projects were reflective of a particular need of the time, including such items as "Municipal Licensing Practices, 1928," "Regulation of Hogs within Municipal Boundaries," and "The Communication of Glanders [an infectious mouth disease among horses] in Municipal Watering Tanks." Research conducted by groups within the Chicago "1313" complex was often somewhat broader in scope than that of state leagues, but on the whole it was comparable both in its intent and its orientation. The Chicago groups, in fact, regularly collected league reports and frequently attempted to draw them together for their own purposes. After Brownlow was able to attract the organization of state leagues, the American Municipal Association, into the complex, communication and the exchange of information were greatly increased.

Professionalism through self-improvement appealed initially to the heartland of progressivism. California, Iowa, Kansas, Wisconsin, Minnesota, and Michigan were leaders in early successful league creation, and within those states it was mainly the smaller cities which responded to league appeals. In the large urban centers the immediately relevant professionalism was that of party politics, and the leagues had little election advice to offer the politicians. The industrial states from Ohio east were, with four exceptions, the last to develop state leagues of municipalities. In many other states, too, however, the effort was not without its perils.

Some eighteen state leagues failed in the years before the Depression and in many states only a handful of cities found the concept of professionalization sufficiently attractive to pay their dues. An ironic competition developed between the leagues and the state universities. Initially many leagues sought assistance from the universities for their executive staff, and they generally encouraged the universities to cultivate bureaus of government service to provide research and advice to local officials. To a very substantial extent, however, these service bureaus offered the same services as the leagues and they were supported by taxes instead of dues. This necessitated that the leagues offer new services in order to preserve their distinctive appeal.

In time the leagues developed a more diverse service potential. During the Depression, for example, state leagues often provided legal assistance to individual cities which enabled the community to save the money it would normally have spent on attorney fees, especially in the preparation of new municipal ordinances. Comparable help was offered on problems of municipal finance and accounting as well as applying for and utilizing federal programs such as those sponsored by the Public Works Administration. This trade-off of league dues for direct services was so attractive that between 1934 and 1937 nine new state leagues were able to successfully organize.

The Emergence of Lobbying

State leagues of municipalities gradually developed a fairly extensive array of advisory and technical services for city officials which supplemented their educational functions and added to the benefits of information exchange afforded by newsletters and periodic meetings. These services did not, however, include lobbying. It was relatively rare for a state league official to be seen testifying before legislature committees in the pre-Depression years, and only the New Jersey director went so far as to define himself, in 1931, as a "lobbyist, politician, counsellor." What efforts the leagues did make to influence public policy dealt mainly with the legal authority of municipalities and were couched in legalistic terms rather than as issues of who in the community ought to get what. When, in the early 1930s, American cities turned to the federal government for financial help, they found, rather to their dismay, that the American Municipal Association, which since 1924 had been the national federation of state leagues of municipalities, was not disposed to represent city claims for money in Washington. There was some rather complicated maneuvering among various leaders of the AMA and some of the leading American mayors, but the result was the formation, in February 1933, of the U.S. Conference of Mayors. The new organization was designed from the beginning to be a national lobbying organization, concentrating on getting money from Congress and from administrative agencies, which money would go as directly as possible to the nation's cities. USCM membership was originally limited to cities over 50,000 population, and for many years its effective constituency were the big cities, while AMA generally represented the sentiments of smaller cities and towns which provided the bulk of its members.

USCM was created with the support of AMA and its first executive director, Paul Betters, doubled as AMA executive director. AMA opened a Washington research office and for a time the USCM relied on the older group for its research. By late 1935, however, serious tension had divided the two organizations. There were policy differences, especially over how federal aid programs should be allocated among different-sized cities, and there were administrative troubles over how organizational funds should be allocated. Finally, Betters resigned from his AMA post, and the two groups went their separate ways. The AMA returned to Chicago and "1313" to continue its nonpartisan, efficiency-oriented research and service work. Betters and USCM settled down in Washington to look for money.

The future was in Washington. In 1948 the AMA began to issue formal pronouncements on proposed national policies affecting cities. In 1954 their headquarters was moved to Washington and in 1963 the Chicago research office was closed. In 1964 AMA became the National League of Cities and through the 1960s a series of steps led to the present close reintegration of the two organizations into what amounts to a single coordinated lobbying and service enterprise. The organizations share the same set of offices. Issue positions are compromised in advance of public statements and since 1969 there has been a single person serving as Director of Congressional Relations who supervises the combined staffs of the two organizations.

Sophisticated Services

The main basis of organizational strength and stability for the leagues of municipalities at every level of their operation has been the services they provided their members. As we have seen, these services have evolved from the initial program assistance of the old LAM, through a period of self-help professionalization, and then an emphasis on the collection and dissemination of municipal data. At every one of these stages, a primary concern of the organization was whether or not member officials would continue to pay their dues. As the organizations grew they had more resources to devote to expanding and improving their offerings. The increasing number of involved officials also began to demand more tangible returns for their investment in the group. To a large extent this meant money, and as the scope of city budgets grew and the range of state and federal programs carrying financial aid for cities also increased, the most salient service to city officials was helping them get more federal and state money. As we have noted, this was the original purpose of USCM and AMA/NLC eventually came to share it.

This raises the question of whether their lobbying efforts warrant the continued membership support of both the major organizations; NLC and USCM, by the same set of municipalities. This is an important theoretical issue as well as one of practical concern to city officials. Mancur Olson (1965) has argued that no rational person would join an organization in order simply to lobby for policy support which, if the lobbying were successful, would bring him its benefits regardless of whether he had belonged to the lobbying group. Funds for urban renewal or poverty programs are not restricted to group members. We have contended elsewhere, however, that under many conditions the group strength required to lobby successfully is a matter of great uncertainty (Salisbury, 1969). Hence, within quite broad limits rational men may join a group to give it, as their collective spokesman, the political weight necessary to be persuasive. This would appear to cover the case of the early days of USCM. In addition, however, it is not always true that public policy benefits for cities go to them equally or according to some impersonal formula. Some get more than others. It is not impossible that cities whose leaders were most active in USCM received a somewhat disproportionate share of the federal funds available. And this very possibility might well persuade otherwise reluctant officials to participate in the organization.

But Olson is surely right in stressing the importance of selective benefits, available only to members, in keeping an organization going. And urban groups have all sought ways to provide useful services to their members. In recent years such older forms of service as self-improvement have lost much of their appeal. A much larger proportion of today's urban officials have received formal training for their roles. Professionalization through self-help has largely given way to more academic processes, and as noted earlier the universities also provide many of the advisory technical services pioneered by the leagues. On the other hand, the expansion of urban government services has, in a sense, left the old-style leagues with too big a task. Although a professional league staff can contribute at the margins of contemporary efforts to cope with urban crises, to many cities, despairing over both their problems and their budgets, traditional conceptions of league-type, research-based assistance may well seem trivial indeed. "I can't afford the time for any organization," said the mayor of one of Missouri's largest cities, "that keeps telling me things I already know and does nothing but feed me beer and sandwiches. What I need is someone to help me get to the money I need, not just tell me where it potentially is at."

And they may appear just as trivial to the leaders of these organizations themselves! A well-respected and veteran state league director offered the following comment. "I'm faced with a problem of demonstrating to my constituents [member officials] that something is being done with the money they give me. They expect to see something for everything I do but that takes a great deal of time. I don't like the term 'urban crisis' but that is what we are faced with and that is what we had better work on." The most dramatic organizational result has been the creation of the National League of Cities-U.S. Conference of Mayors, Incorporated. NLC-USCM, Inc., is an independent corporation formed primarily to contract with federal agencies in order to assist in the development and implementation of government programs. The corporation contracted with such agencies as the Departments of Labor; Health, Education and Welfare; and Housing and Urban Development. Projects involved the organization in operational manpower programs, "State Plan Programs" for HEW, and an evaluation of the Model Cities program.

The new organization also provided all the traditional services of advice and technical assistance to member cities. The organization's inquiry service handled approximately 1,000 requests for information on various facets of municipal government in 1970. Staff members make field visits upon request for direct consultation with municipal officials. In addition, a wide variety of technical, advisory, and general information reports are issued from NLC-USCM headquarters. In fact, the staff attempts to release pertinent information on as many of their projects as possible. These activities are on the whole very reminiscent of those undertaken by the state municipal leagues.

The contracting role was expected to be of substantial benefit to other member-service activities. As a senior staff member said, "Every person that is employed by this organization is contributing to the dissemination of information to our members. If we employ someone because of a federal grant or Ford money, it still means that the individual is doing work for us." These contracts provide budgetary support for the organizations; in 1970 only about one-fourth of the NLC and USCM total budget (which was nearly $4 million) came from membership dues. Contract work has underwritten very important staff expansion with spillover benefits for member cities. Finally, the organizations have gained further legitimacy in the eyes of their members and of official Washington as well from enlarging the scope of their activities and adding the expertise derived from the administration of urban program contracts. In the size of the organizational budget and in conception of the benefits to be provided through the association, NLC-USCM, Inc., is a far cry from the days of "1313."

What Do the Members Pay—What Do They Get?

Membership in the U.S. Conference of Mayors, the National League of Cities, and in state and regional leagues of municipalities has a somewhat unusual character compared to most voluntary organizations. In USCM it is the mayoral office of a city which really belongs, not the man who holds the office. In the leagues it is the city itself. Individuals participate by virtue of their official positions with their respective cities. Moreover, membership dues and at least most, if not all, of the expense of attending meetings comes from the municipal budget. The only costs of membership falling directly on the individual members are those of time and energy. Individuals make the decision to join or not, of course, and despite the fact that membership costs them nothing, many officials in the past felt the organizations were not worth even a tiny fraction of their municipal budgets. USCM was heavily subsidized beyond the regular dues structure by a few of the "more involved" cities during its formative years. It was felt that a population-based dues structure which was high enough to maintain the group's endeavors would prohibit many cities from lending their support to the organization at a time when their lobbying strength was important. Similarly, AMA was able to raise a budget of only $165 from ten state municipal leagues for its initial operation in 1924.

As we noted earlier, the rather direct, tangible benefits generated by many state leagues and by USCM during the 1930s overcame much of this resistance. It is probably fair to say that today, even in fiscal crisis, few American mayors would be likely to conclude that the dues for these organizations constitute good items to cut to save the city money. In a survey of St. Louis County municipal officials, we found support to be widespread and firm. They felt that the various municipal associations had been instrumental in obtaining increased revenue from the states and federal government. Not only that, they were able to secure information and assistance from the organizations which enabled them to cut corners in their own governmental operations. Ordinances were obtained and copied without a legal fee for the city attorney, and a variety of cheaper and more efficient procedures were picked up and instituted on topics from clerical filing systems to street repair.

An important aspect of financing is that these organizations are essentially low-cost groups. Given the great size of municipal budgets, the total dues paid by a city are most often inconsequential. New York, which has the highest dues of all cities, pays NLC $7,000 per year and USCM $5,000. Combined with their dues to all other municipal associations to which New York and its officials belong, the total disbursement is less than is spent on their individual lobbying expenses in Washington, D.C., alone. Or to put it in different terms, these dues are roughly equivalent to the cost of employing three beginning maintenance employees. This implies that, given the organization's potential for increasing city revenues, there is really very little risk of any financial sort involved in the decision of whether a municipal government affiliates with these groups.

Among the other dimensions of membership costs are those derived from the positions taken by the organization on policy questions. Mayors are, after all, elected officials. If they maintain membership in an organization which takes a stand that offends large numbers of their own constituents, they may encounter political troubles. In general, all of the organizations we have examined try to avoid taking a position on issues they expect will divide their members. NLC, for example, avoided making pronouncements on the Vietnam War on this ground, and in 1970 the leadership used this argument to persuade sponsors to withdraw a motion condemning the SST. Even revenue-sharing, a prime legislative goal of USCM, threatens the perceived interests of enough cities which comprise the membership of NLC and its affiliate state leagues to lead that organization to soft-pedal the issue.

None of these organizations is primarily concerned with expressive goals, however (Salisbury, 1969: 16). They seek more tangible benefits for their members, and the members, for their part, seek mainly material services in return for their membership dues. USCM and NLC make many public pronouncements on policy issues, of course, but the main task of broad agitation for urban goals is left to such groups as Urban America and the Urban Coalition. In terms of their primary organizational concerns, therefore, USCM and NLC can afford to remain quiet on potentially divisive issues.

Active participation by members in these organizations presents a number of interesting aspects. As in nearly every organizational setting activism falls short of involving everyone. Some mayors are indifferent; some are inexperienced; some are both and likely to avoid organizational settings they do not understand or care about. No mayor depends for reelection on his activity in these groups, and few have much time on their hands for peripheral functions. Some mayors have short political lives and hardly learn the names of the organizations before leaving office. In a sense, it is surprising that attendance at meetings is as heavy and service on committees as broadly distributed as it is. Part of this activism results spontaneously from the benefits which activity confers on those who participate, and part of it is the result of conscious efforts by the leadership to gain broader involvement.

Perhaps the most important single incentive to attract the active involvement of city officials in organizations like USCM or NLC is the prestige gained from recognition by one's peers. Mayors, like other people, are gratified by the recognition of their colleagues. They are flattered by the attention. And as they become acquainted with one another at annual convocations their interest in the affairs of the organization is quickened and the value they place on success within it is raised. As a staff member said: "Officials certainly don't join our organization to come to our conventions, but at the same time these meetings are helpful hunting grounds for us to recruit active participants. We know those people that come around regularly are the ones that are interested; they come to be quite enthused about the worth of the group through these informal contacts."

Most mayors, even those of large metropolitan centers, do not have much prospect of moving on to higher political office though sometimes a state municipal league may be a useful forum in which to campaign for statewide office. Consequently, a prime source of what national recognition is available to holders of mayoral office is high position within one of the major national organizations of cities. Not only recognition from peers is involved. Attention from the national press is considerable. Network television appearances and official statements to congressional committees grow out of USCM or NLC office. On a lesser scale there is comparable prestige and attention along with peer recognition in state and metropolitan area leagues to encourage at least some officials to be active. Unlike some organizations, neither the rules nor the norms are restrictive regarding activism. Participation is welcome and open to all who will take the trouble. A former officer in county, state, and national associations of both municipalities and city attorneys said, "This is really a personal thing and people get involved largely for their own egos as well as some prestige that they see associated here. If you stand up and try at all you can be anything you want in organizations like these."

If there is oligarchy, it is mainly because so many members do not want a share of the active roles. The executive staff, which plays a crucial part, tries assiduously to attract new members into committee and officer roles. But they depend nevertheless on the active leadership of a group of veterans. Many mayors and other city officials do not serve more than a term or two. In order for USCM and NLC to retain a core of members with some degree of knowledge about the workings and the affairs of the organization, they must rely on what is in many cases an unrepresentative group of officials in leadership roles, but a group which is self-selected according to the criterion of interest and willingness to work. "A Lindsay or a Yorty may be actively sought after soon upon his election," said a ranking staff man, "but for the most part we want officials who have demonstrated over time that they understand the goals of the organization."

Both NLC and especially USCM need active contributions from the mayors of the largest ten or fifteen cities in the country in order to give legitimacy to the organization's claims to speak for the nation's cities. If, for example, the mayors of Chicago, Detroit, and Pittsburgh failed to take any part in the affairs of USCM, it would seriously undermine the organization's standing. A staff member once told a group of over twenty California city executives that faced with a choice between them and Los Angeles, USCM would have to choose Los Angeles. Generally big-city mayors themselves have more experience and better staff work to bring to national organization affairs, and their statements carry more news value and command more political attention than would the same statements coming from the mayor of one of the Springfields. The executive staff tries to involve some of the smaller-city people too, of course, in order to give them a sense of identification with the organization. But the main stress is on getting the big-city people and keeping them sufficiently interested to give their time.

This strategy, however, must be kept in careful balance when it comes to the pursuit of policy goals. Although the organizations are most dependent on the larger cities, the legislators with whom they must work, especially those on appropriations subcommittees, often have little common grounds for understanding with big-city officials. Moreover, NLC-USCM has recently been subjected to a good deal of criticism because the feelings of the small-city officials are not in evidence as frequently as many federal officials would like to see. In response, the organizations have been making concentrated efforts to bring such officials in to testify before Congress. Accordingly, this means that these officials too must be convinced that they should devote the time to become involved in these organizations.

One incentive of special relevance for this purpose is the professional recognition of peers already noted. In the same manner that value is placed on being a senator's senator in conforming to the folkways and gaining peer recognition (Matthews, 1960), there is a premium attached to gaining the respect of other mayors through appropriate participation. This is evidenced by the comments of a small-city mayor: "To be frank, I felt that by testifying in Washington, D.C., that people would understand and see that you don't have to be from a metropolis to be a good mayor. It only takes hard work." For the large-city mayor who constantly interacts with other mayors, this is an even more important feeling. For a mayor, however popular or powerful in his own city, to be acknowledged by his colleagues as a good man is to gain a real reward in these days when mayors have all too few successes and too many crises.

More tangibly, the usefulness of the NLC-USCM lobby in securing federal programs of aid to cities, assisting in winning the money to fund those programs, recruiting and advising the personnel administering them, and generally bringing help to beleaguered municipal officials has been great and acknowledged to be so by most of the big-city mayors. Indeed, their efforts through these organizations may do more for their city budgets than most other things they might spend their time on.

One other incentive to activism may be mentioned. The meetings of the national associations, like those of many other such groups, are occasions of social pleasure as well as instrumental benefit. The St. Louis County League of Municipalities gets its biggest attendance at its annual barbecue. The USCM host city gives its guests the most generous hospitality, and the convention can be a most pleasant semi-vacation to which many members bring their spouses. For newly elected officials and those from smaller cities the chance to meet their peers, share their problems, and gain a national perspective are often highly valued. Many members indeed, especially if they are less involved in the national lobbying work, would regard these "solidary" benefits as the principal personal value derived from membership and rank these values alongside the more tangible services to their administration and their community. In the words of a mayor from a St. Louis County municipality, "My wife and I have gone to NLC's Congress of Cities for years. We wouldn't know where else to go on our vacation. What do I like best? Obviously the variety of people I've met there." Membership in USCM and NLC involves both the individual official and his city and both receive benefits from belonging.

Urban Group Leadership

Governing organizations like NLC and USCM present several special problems. We have already referred to the importance of the big cities in giving the organizations necessary political weight. At the same time, however, in most of the state and national organizations the voting rule is: one city—one vote. Smaller cities might, therefore, exercise decisive power within the organizations. But they do not. The big cities, in fact, play the predominant role, especially in the national organizations. It is they who control the bulk of both the formal offices and the informal influences. Big-city hegemony is partly derived from the way decisions are made. The rules make it easy for city officials not to bother very much with affairs of the organization unless they are really interested.

In both groups decisions are made by those who choose to get involved in the organization. And, since the decision-making involvement of members is limited to matters of general policy and the selection of officers, it behooves larger-city representatives to take an active part in order to affect the more specific elements of the organization programs. They are, after all, the primary recipients of federal programs, and their work in NLC and USCM has proportionately greater payoffs. On the other hand, small-cities officials are less likely to get involved as long as they believe that they are being effectively represented and that their colleagues from cities of similar size are included in the operational structure. The major difference between the two organizations in this respect is that state municipal league directors take an active role in leadership positions of NLC since they are still affiliates of that group.

Official policy for both groups is formally adopted on the floor at the annual conventions. However, there is but a limited amount of discussion and only a few minor changes have ever been made in the course of floor debate. This activity is mostly a ratification of decisions that have been made earlier in the various standing committees and their subcommittees. These specialized committees have much autonomy to develop policy and strategy in their respective areas of concern. USCM has only four such committees and they are rather small. NLC has eight and they are large (150 members each) with very active subcommittees that do most of the actual work.

The formal device of most importance in centralizing organizational control is the executive committee composed of the officers of each organization. The committees are each headed by the organization's annually elected president and vice-president. The other twenty-one members of NLC's executive body are elected for two-year staggered terms. This contrasts with that committee of USCM which includes the past presidents of the group and eight elected trustees all of whom serve for the remainder of their time in office. Their authority to control lobbying tactics and strategy and to develop the details of policy positions is very broad since all major policy decisions are considered by these committees. Both organizations also have advisory boards which serve partly as mechanisms for screening prospective executive committee members and partly as loci for cooptation and socialization of the more vocal dissidents among the membership. The selection of these committee and board members, like those of the substantive committees, is formally left to the current organization president. But here, as in so much else, it is actually the executive staff which exercises most of the real initiatives.

The Role of the Staff

We need not review all the advantages and sources of power available to full-time staff personnel of large organizations (Truman, 1951). In the case of NLC and USCM the key factors are these:

(1) the executive directors are vastly more experienced in the affairs of organizations of city officials than any members;

(2) the executive directors have more staff, more contacts, and more information regarding what is going on in Washington and in the other cities of the nation than has any member;

(3) the executive directors are in a position to suggest promising nominees for association office, and to provide program and policy guidance which, with very rare exceptions, the members are happy to adopt;

(4) the executive directors have over the years provided services and done favors for many of the member officials which cumulatively strengthen the directors' positions.

With regard to experience, John Gunther was executive director of the USMC for more than thirty years, and Patrick Healy, director of the North Carolina state league as early as 1934, led the NLC from 1953 into the 1970s. Both organizations have drawn their principal staff people heavily from state leagues and from complementary functional organizations such as the National Association of Housing and Redevelopment Officials (NAHRO). Indeed, there is considerable movement of staff personnel among the many urban organizations, both along a local-state-national axis and among the different national organizations, and this has greatly facilitated the interorganization coordination of lobbying in recent years.

At the top the directors of these organizations receive rewards commensurate with their organizational success. There are a few salaries above $40,000 per year. NLC-USCM, Inc., employed 130 staff members at the beginning of 1971 and ten state leagues had ten or more employees. In the larger organizations, moreover, nearly half the personnel are professionals of one kind or another with appropriate formal academic training. In the small-state leagues, by contrast, the staff director generally suffers a syndrome of lower salaries, little or no assistance, and the reputation among their peers in other states of being "unprofessional."

The contemporary picture of the executive staff of the urban lobby organizations contrasts sharply with the situation of a generation ago. For the first decade of its existence, from 1924 to 1930, the National League of Cities (neé American Municipal Association) had its headquarters in the office of the Kansas state league. Then the executive secretary, founding father, and general entrepreneur of the AMA was John Stutz, who continued also as director of the Kansas league, In 1932 Paul Betters was hired to succeed Stutz as AMA director, and, as we have noted, Betters also became the main moving force behind the formation of the USCM. When Betters came under fire in his dual role, it was Stutz who was particularly critical of Betters' emphasis on Washington lobbying. Stutz's position in AMA was still formidable and Betters resigned to go full-time with USCM, where he remained until his death in 1956.

Stutz never accepted the more expressly political role which USCM undertook nor was he oriented toward Washington. Neither was his entire generation of state league organizers and catalysts. Several came from state universities and returned to academic life once their respective leagues were well under way. AMA gave money to help organizing efforts, and Stutz sought to identify promising organizers and place them in state leagues which were in organizational trouble. Through this process and the complementary energies of Louis Brownlow and his "1313" array of research and improvement organizations in Chicago, a generation of urban group leaders (and of political scientists interested in city affairs!) was given shape. Until the post–World War II era a large share of the state groups depended heavily for their success on the skill of their particular director. For example, the highly successful Georgia league collapsed when its director, John Eagan, died in 1934, and in New Jersey the death of Sedly Phinney had a substantial negative impact on that vigorous state organization. The postwar years, however, have seen a steady growth in staff and budget of nearly every urban group, and among the state leagues and two principal national organizations, survival would no longer seem to depend quite so much on the personal qualities of the executive directors. Their guidance in the substantive business of the association, however, is probably more significant than ever. The old-style leagues with few members and small budgets had little choice but to stress research and self-improvement. Today the urban lobby groups are large, vigorous, and comparatively well-financed, and this gives their leaders many more options and the opportunity for far more extensive autonomous initiative than their predecessors could enjoy.

Urban Groups and Group Theory

Let us conclude this discussion by noting some of the implications for interest group theory which seem contained in the phenomena of organizations of city officials. One already mentioned is the fact that contrary to Olson's argument, organizations of rational men can under some circumstances be formed in order to lobby for collective policy goods. It seems clear that USCM was so formed and that the 101 mayors who joined in 1933 had reason to believe that their joint effort would be de-

cisive in obtaining federal aid. Secondly, however, and in partial contradiction to the above, membership in USCM and in the other groups of
interest to us here is not personally costly. It is the city which pays, and
therefore the rational choice component of membership is placed in a
different context. If membership is essentially free to a mayor, then once
the group is going and he is part of it, inertia will operate to keep him
in rather than force him to reexamine his position. Today, the groups
are firmly established and inertia, even apathy, may work to their advantage rather than constituting an obstacle as it does with groups
whose members must weigh the benefits against their direct costs in the
form of annual dues.[1]

The urban lobby groups provide their members first of all with material benefits. The tangible assistance of information, advice, and guidance, especially regarding the programs and processes of the federal
government, is joined with impressive lobbying on behalf of additional
financial and service aid for cities. In part, given the nature of NLC-
USCM membership, this lobbying itself is a form of direct service. As
important political executives in their own right, mayors would generally seek, and be expected to have something to say about, programs affecting cities. The organizations and their staff help to organize and
coordinate these statements, facilitating the performance of a task most
big-city mayors at least would have to do anyway but with greater difficulty and less effect. Material benefits are supplemented for some members by the solidary benefits of interaction with peers and the resultant
recognition and camaraderie. Expressive benefits, on the other hand,
are seldom of much importance. More often members find themselves
frustrated because the organizations will not speak on some question for
fear of alienating a segment of the group. Seldom are NLC, USCM, or
the state leagues found taking a public position which is subject to much
disagreement among the members. The members are a very select
group, of course, and where, as is often the case, there is widespread
agreement among urban officials concerning what policy ought to be
adopted, the organizations speak vigorously. But public expression is not
the most important way by which these groups seek policy results. In order to optimize their political effectiveness and, at the same time, avoid
offending members who might not share the leadership policy preferences, key staff and activist members do much of their work quietly. One
staff veteran put it this way: "If many people understood all that we
were trying to do, we'd be in trouble trying to promote the legislation we
feel is essential."

The other side of this coin, as we have noted, is the tendency to form new organizations to express new value concerns rather than adapt or enlarge old organizations in ways that might too severely alter the established ways of either the executive staff or the members. In the urban field this has resulted in a large and complex network of organizations which are, for much the greatest part, complementary to one another in political impact rather than competitive. And through the interchange and interaction of staff, but not very much through their very considerable overlapping membership, these organizations have achieved a well-coordinated lobbying effort in Washington. They have also greatly enlarged the communication among urban officials themselves. At one time a central contribution of urban groups was the upgrading of competence and professionalization of city officials. This still goes on, but the more important contribution perhaps comes from the greatly intensified interaction among city officials. All big-city mayors, for example, come very quickly to be familiar with the conditions, problems, and efforts at solution of every other city. They all operate as part of a communications network which under NLC-USCM, Inc., auspices has been sufficiently active to make the urban crisis of America truly a national crisis and not simply a collection of diverse local concerns.

NOTE

1. We are talking only about holding the organization together, not mobilizing its political strength for lobbying purposes. In the latter situation membership inertia is the bane of the executive staff.

REFERENCES

Brownlow, L. (1955) *A Passion for Politics.* Chicago: Univ. of Chicago Press.

Callahan, R. (1962) *Education and the Cult of Efficiency.* Chicago: Univ. of Chicago Press.

Connery, R. H. and R. H. Leach (1960) *The Federal Government and Metropolitan Areas.* Cambridge: Harvard Univ. Press.

Farkas, S. (1971) *Urban Lobbying: Mayors in the Federal Arena.* New York: New York Univ. Press.

Herring, E. P. (1940) *The Politics of Democracy.* New York: W. W. Norton.

Hofstadter, R. (1955) *The Age of Reform: From Bryan to F. D. R.* New York: Alfred A. Knopf.

McConnell, G. (1966) *Private Power and American Democracy.* New York: Alfred A. Knopf.

Matthews, D. R. (1960) *U.S. Senators and Their World.* Chapel Hill: Univ. of North Carolina Press.

Olson, M. (1965) *The Logic of Collective Action: Public Goods and the Theory of Groups.* Cambridge: Harvard Univ. Press.

Salisbury, R. H. (1969) "An Exchange Theory of Interest Groups." *Midwest J. of Pol. Sci.* 13 (February): 1–32.

Schattschneider, E. E. (1960) *The Semi-Semi Sovereign People.* New York: Holt, Rinehart and Winston.

Truman, D. B. (1951) *The Governmental Process.* New York: Alfred A. Knopf.

Vose, C. E. (1966) "Interest Groups, Judicial Review, and Local Government." *Western Pol. Q.* 19 (March): 85–100.

Willoughby, A. (1969) "The Involved Citizen: A Short History of the National Municipal League." *National Civic Rev.* 63 (December).

15

Schools and Politics in the Big City

A*fter decades of silence,* both social scientists and educators are at last explicitly examining and re-examining all the options regarding the relationship between the political system and the schools. Descriptive analysis has greatly enriched our understanding of how alternative structures operate. A full menu of recipes for changing the structures has been developed and here and there implemented. And while we are far from realizing closure on our uncertainties, the art of social engineering with respect to school-community relations is finally getting an underpinning of evidence and systematic analysis.[1]

Broadly, there seem to be three themes running through this new wave of literature. One is primarily descriptive: How are educational decisions made, and what variables are relevant for explaining alternative outcomes? A second theme merges this descriptive task with a special concern: What accounts for variations in the money available to the schools, and implicitly, how might more money be made available? The third theme is a bit different. It raises a more complex question, and answers depend not only upon careful descriptive analysis but also upon performance criteria that are very difficult to work out: How may the school system do a more effective job in the total context of community life?

It is apparent that the "context of community life" is a concept fraught with snares and difficulties. I propose to look at it mainly with reference to the problems of the core city; there, it encompasses major

Reprinted from the *Harvard Educational Review* 37 (1967):408–24. Coyright © 1967 by the President and Fellows of Harvard College. All rights reserved.

facets of the problems of race, of poverty, of physical decay and renewal, of perennial fiscal trauma, indeed most of those troubles we label "urban problems" in contemporary American society. The issue I wish to ruminate about here is whether one type of political-system–school-system-relationship might be more effective than another in attacking these dilemmas of urban life. Specifically, I propose to consider the thesis that direct political-system control of the schools (historically anathema to educators) might have significant virtues in making the schools more effective instruments of social change and development.[2]

We know that many big-city school systems operate with substantial formal autonomy. They are not run by the political or administrative leaders of the city, but are insulated from those leaders and the interests they represent. In part this autonomy is a consequence of various formal features of local government which give to the schools the authority to run their affairs with little or no reference to the demands of other city officials. Perhaps in larger part, however, the insulation of the schools may be a function of the ideology, propagated by schoolmen but widely shared by the larger public, that schools should be free from "politics," i.e., the influence of nonschool officials. Insofar as this view is shared, it has made formal independence a less relevant variable, and most of what evidence we have suggests that the formal structure of school-city relations does not matter very much: the schools are largely autonomous anyway.

It has been argued that autonomy for the schools means that professional educators would be free to carry out educational policies which they, as professionals, deem most effective without the intrusion of conflicting and educationally deleterious demands from nonprofessionals. But autonomy and insulation may also result in other things. Autonomous schools may be unresponsive to important groups in the community whose interests are not effectively served by the dominant values of professional schoolmen. Autonomy may mean a fragmenting of efforts aimed at solving community problems because of inadequate coordination and planning. And autonomy may also bring vulnerability as well as insulation. If the schools are separated from the rest of the community's political system, they may be more easily exposed to the protests or demands of groups which are disaffected from that system, unable to work their will within its often labyrinthine structures, but able to organize direct popular support. And if they attempt direct protest action, they can make life most difficult for schoolmen who are unable to retreat into positions of mutual support among city officials with many programs and agencies and client groups. Unable to trade off one group against another, the schools may be and often are the targets of protest which may well have its roots in other facets of the city's life, but is directed against the schools precisely because they are autonomous and vulnerable.

The argument that the costs of "political control" far exceed the costs of autonomy needs re-examination. I have been struck by the frequent reference in that argument to the allegedly baleful effects of Big Bill Thompson's 1927 campaign for election as mayor of Chicago in which he concentrated much of his flamboyant oratory on the issue of control of the public schools. Big Bill promised to sack the superintendent who was, said Thompson, a lackey of King George and the British. Educators have ever since been agreed that a mayoral campaign subjecting the schools to this kind of educationally irrelevant attack was ample evidence of the need for protection from big city politics. Thompson's rhetoric was, of course, so blatantly demogogic that he makes an easy object lesson, but behind the rhetoric the issue has other features which make its moral much less clear.

In a most interesting book, called *School and Society in Chicago*,[3] George S. Counts examined the 1927 election soon after it happened. Counts's assessment is one of considerable ambivalence. On the one hand, he has no sympathy for Thompson's tactics of catering to his anti-British constituents by threatening to "punch King George in the snoot." Yet Thompson, in denouncing Superintendent McAndrew, was exploiting a very real conflict within the schools which had already engaged major socio-economic sectors in the community.

William McAndrew had come to Chicago in 1924 in the wake of a series of political scandals and convictions affecting members of the school board. McAndrew was looked to as a reformer who would use his office more vigorously than had his predecessors. Particularly, he was expected, apparently by all the most interested parties, to establish the superintendency as the center from which the schools would thereafter be run. Professional educational criteria were to prevail. No more politics!

McAndrew interpreted this mandate to mean that *he* would select the criteria; the classroom teachers would not. He believed that *professional* educators should embrace teachers and administrators in the same organizational units, so he effectively discouraged the previously vigorous teachers councils in the Chicago schools. Chicago had a strong and long-standing set of teacher organizations including units of the American Federation of Teachers, and McAndrew's unsympathetic view of their status led to abiding tension. Counts reports that the teachers' groups provided effective support for Thompson's election.

In addition, McAndrew had alienated organized labor in general. Not only had he rejected the propriety of the teachers' unions. He had introduced the junior high school. Chicago labor spokesmen construed this to be a step toward separate vocational training for working-class children. They viewed the junior high as an early breakaway from an equalitarian curriculum and this, they feared, was aimed at producing a docile, cheap labor force. Finally, McAndrew was a champion of the platoon system, or, as it was generally referred to, the Gary Plan. He favored the alleged efficiencies of the Plan and justified them quite frankly in a business-oriented way. Moreover, he actively and often consulted with representatives of the Chicago Associaton of Commerce; never with spokesmen of labor.

The result was a fairly considerable class conflict over McAndrew and his policies, both inside the school system and in the community. William Hale Thompson exploited these tensions and, in a way, helped resolve them. At least, after Thompson won, McAndrew was fired.

The important morals of this story seem to me to be the following: First, McAndrew provoked a severe conflict among the schoolmen themselves. The alleged intrusion of "politics" into the schools was really more the widening of a breach that already existed. Breaches among the schoolmen have been rather exceptional, from McAndrew's time until very nearly the present. Educators have proclaimed their fundamental unity of purpose and interest; and to a remarkable degree, they have lived up to it. But as teachers' unions grow strong and make demands and, occasionally, strike, and as community-wide controversies develop over the location, programs, and financing of the schools, the myths and practices which lead educators to maintain a united front in facing the outside, nonprofessional, world cannot survive. And, if there are conflicts, they will be exploited. The only question is, "By whom?"

The second lesson of the Chicago case of 1927 relates to the ultimate problem-solving machinery. McAndrew and the schools became a central issue in a partisan political race. Was this an appropriate mechanism for resolving a virtual class conflict involving the largest category of public expenditure? If it was not, then what is the regular political process for? Why are educational issues not properly determined in this arena? Why not indeed, except, perhaps, that Big Bill made the final determination. This dramatic fact has been enough to cinch the argument whenever some hardy soul could be found to play devil's advocate.

Later in this paper I shall explore further the two features I have drawn from the Chicago case; the political significance of unity among the schoolmen, and the possible consequences of determining school questions within the regular political processes of the community. Before I do, however, I would like to consider further what seems to me an important element of the context of school politics, in Chicago and every other city, then and now. This is what I shall call *the myth of the unitary community.*

George Counts concludes his analysis of the McAndrew affair by calling for "the frank recognition of the pluralistic quality of the modern city. Such recognition would involve the extension of a direct voice in the control of education to the more powerful interests and the more significant points of view."[4] The recommendation troubled Counts. He believed that it would really only "regularize practices already in existence," since these groups were already actively engaged in the struggle for influence over the schools. Still Counts recognized that he was making a "radical" proposal. It went directly counter to an historic perspective which has long pervaded the thinking of educators: namely, that the city is a unity for purposes of the school program. That is, regardless of ethnic, racial, religious, economic, or political differences and group conflicts in other arenas of urban life, educational need not, and should not if it could, recognize or legitimize those differences. Education is a process that must not be differentiated according to section or class. Learning is the same phenomenon, or should be, in every neighborhood. Physical facilities and personnel should be allocated without regard to whatever group conflicts might exist in the community.

Schools have not always been run this way in reality. In the nineteenth century, some concessions were made to such prominent ethnic groups as the Germans by providing special classes in the German language; but in St. Louis, these were discontinued in 1888, or just about the time that ethnic heterogeneity really blossomed in the city. In recent years, a good many departures from the norm can be observed. In many cities, ethnic representation on the school board has been accepted as a hostage to the times, though the tendency is generally to deplore the necessity of special group recognition. Representatives of labor, of Negroes, and of Catholics hold big-city board memberships today and their constituents would complain if they did not. But the prevailing doctrines have not altered as much as the practice, I suspect, and the perspective which denies the legitimacy of group conflicts over school policy is certainly still widely held.

Surely an important element of this view of the city was the egalitarian democracy espoused by a large portion of professional education's intellectuals. The common school, later the high school, and now the community college have been urged and supported as mechanisms for equalizing the life chances of everyone in the community. To introduce programs for one group that were not available to another, or to build different kinds of school buildings for different neighborhoods, would cultivate group and class differences in the twig-bending stage which would lead to deeper socio-economic cleavages in the adult community. Most people, it seemed, never considered the possibility that the have-not groups might receive *more* and *better* education than the middle class.

It looked like the poor could only get short-changed in a system of differentiated education and a caste system would result. This was the position not only of educators but probably of most actively concerned lay citizens too. It was an operative theory to guide education policy, and it was linked to a view of the community beyond the school system. For a consensual, integrated, organic community was and is an abiding standard for many American intellectuals. A proper city should manifest no deep-seated social or economic cleavages. Groups and classes with opposing interests are considered dangerous to the continued tranquillity of the polity. When they exist, as they increasingly did in the industrial city of turn-of-the-century America, it becomes necessary to adopt programs, such as universal education, and institutions, such as nonpartisan local government or at-large elections, that overcome the threatening heterogeneity.

But burgeoning immigration, the rise of the urban political machine, the emergence of corporate economic interests, and the enormous increases in scale of the urban community were parallel and closely connected phenomena of the 1880–1910 era. The metropolis which emerged threatened to erupt in group conflicts that would engulf the schools unless defenses could be found. The unitary-community perspective, more or less accurate as description a generation before and still serviceable for many smaller communities outside the metropolis, from that time on has been primarily a myth for the big city.

Still, it is a useful myth, and its uses were and are many. First, it served as a sharp contrast to the "political" world. Urban politics in the muckraker era was plainly a politics of group conflict and accommodation. The boss was a broker of social and economic tensions, and part of his brokerage fee to the community was the heightening of group consciousness. Ethnic identity for many Europeans was first achieved through the processes of American ward politics. Irish, Italian, or Czech nationalisms, for example, were much promoted in the cities of this era, as candidates and parties sought ways to secure the loyalties of the urban electorate.

With the political arena patently corrupt and marked by the conflicts of a myriad of "special" interests, the unitary-community perspective of education could justify the institutional separation of the schools from the rest of the political community. Independence from "politics" would keep out the selfish aims and corrupt tactics of the politicians.

Independent schools systems were not new of course. Institutional separation had always been a prevailing pattern. But in the larger cities, until the end of the nineteenth century, the structure of the independent school systems had been highly political.[5] Many school boards were chosen by wards. Some were selected by the city council, some by direct and frequent election. Ward representation was not originally viewed as a way of representing diverse group interests in the city as much as it was a means of keeping the board in close touch with the electorate. It resulted, however, in highly "politicized" school boards, sensitive to neighborhood pressures, particularly in the area of school-building. The ward system promoted log-rolling among sections of the city over many components of the school program. Neighborhoods sometimes traded off advantages, thereby probably facilitating rapid construction in many cities. Wards might also block one another, however, and thus retard the whole system.

The development of the professional educator to fill the newly created position of superintendent of schools inaugurated a different approach to education in which lay control would operate in increasing tension with the professional expert. With ward representation, this tension might well have been unbearable, at least to the professional educator. But parallel to the rise of the superintendency came the elimination of the ward system, and at-large election systems were rapidly adopted for the selection of school-board members.

The unitary myth was and is of great use in justifying an at-large school board. If the community is an organic whole with a single public interest in education, the board member should be protected against local, "selfish," interests by giving him a city-wide constituency. Moreover, since there are no legitimate "special" group interests in education, any responsible citizen can serve on the board, and there is no reason to give particular groups in the community a seat. To give a seat to labor, for example, would be wrong because it would constitute recognition of a special-group perspective on educational policy. Indeed, in a unitary community, there is really no such thing as representation on the school board, since there are no interests to represent. If, as George Counts and others found, urban school-board members were drawn predominantly from middle class, WASP, business-oriented strata of the community, it was a fact without significance in a unitary community.[6] In a recent study of school desegregation in eight northern cities, Robert Crain found that business and professional persons who serve on the school board, do so as individuals, not as class or elite spokesmen, and that such "nonrepresentative" individuals have been more acquiescent to integration than board members elected by party or ethnic constituencies.[7]

The myth has thus been important in underwriting equalitarian educational programs, in separating the school systems from the main political process of the city, and in validating middle-class control of the schools. In addition, it was a useful adjunct to the emergence of professional expertise in education and school administration. Expertise rested on the assumption that valid ways and means to run the schools existed and were independent of the particular interests and values of particular groups. A good school system is good for everyone, not just a portion of the community. Experts, those people with professional training in the field, are qualified by their specialized training to tell good from bad, and laymen, if they are sensible, should defer to this expertise. If the unitary assumption is undermined, however, then no one, however well trained, can identify or administer a "good" school system. One may then ask only, "Good for whom? For which groups?"

Apart from a social scientist's perverse interest in exploring the myths we live by, is there any point to this discussion of the unitary-community myth? I believe the answer is "Emphatically, yes!" When educators treat the community as a unitary phenomenon, they are less able to offer programs and facilities which are differentiated to serve the diverse needs and values of particular subgroups in the city. It is an indictment of educational political theory that head-start projects for the urban poor only began on a large scale in 1965. Not that schoolmen did not often recognize the differential needs of slum children and sometimes tailor programs to fit those special needs. Rather, they had to do it in an inarticulate, often *sub rosa*, fashion since such programs went counter to the mainstream of schoolmen's thinking. And so the programs were generally ineffective in meeting a problem of such magnitude.

The unitary-community idea was not simply for the guidance of educators. As we have seen, it helped protect the independence of the schools from the community's political processes. Or did it? Raymond E. Callahan has argued that the independent urban schoolmen were, in the period from about 1910 to 1930, extremely vulnerable; not, perhaps, to partisan political pressure, but to the dominant socio-economic interests of the community.[8] In this period, business was pretty generally dominant, and Callahan attributes the rise of the "cult of efficiency" in educational administration to the desire of vulnerable schoolmen to please the influential businessmen. In a way. Counts's story of Chicago confirms this point; during the relatively "nonpolitical" period when McAndrew was exercising full authority, the Association of Commerce occupied a very influential place while labor was excluded from school affairs. The "intrusion of politics" under Thompson meant the return of the teachers and other nonbusiness interests to active and influential positions.

Independent schools, operating according to the myth of the unitary community, were and are rather feeble instruments for seeking public support, and this weakness is one key to the business domination Callahan has described. School-tax rates and bond issues and, in some states, the annual school budget, may require specific voter approval in a referendum. How are the schoolmen to persuade the electorate to say yes? They have relatively little of what in urban politics is sometimes called "clout." They have no network of support from groups and interests for whom the educators have done favors in the past and who now can be asked to reciprocate. They may sometimes get the teachers and the parents and the children to ring doorbells, but such efforts are often ineffectual compared to the canvassing a strong party organization might do. Since approval of a school referendum invariably costs the taxpayers money immediately—there is no intervening lapse of time as there is between the election of a candidate to a city office and the possible future increase in taxes—a sizable negative vote may normally be assumed. Where is the positive vote coming from? Educators have gone on the assumption, quite probably correct, that the benevolent patronage of the business leadership was necessary if they were to have a chance of referendum success.

Today, in the big city, the structure of the situation has not changed. Only the interests which effectively make demands upon the schools have changed. Blacks, the poor, middle-class intellectuals, and teachers have partially, perhaps largely, displaced the businessmen. The unitary-community myth is still used as a defense of the schools. In order to persuade predominantly Catholic, lower-middle-class voters of Irish or

Polish descent to support higher taxes for public schools, it is very important to emphasize the undivided benefits which all residents receive from an undifferentiated educational program. The difficulty is that today the pitch is no longer believed. It is evident, for example, that African Americans do not buy the myth that the community is unitary. They know better. Moreover, even though a school board with a unitary-community perspective may permit integration, blacks demand a differentiated school program with compensatory facilities to help them fight prejudice and poverty, to help them reach a high enough level so that equal educational programs will no longer leave them behind. Meanwhile, those ethnic groups whom Wilson and Banfield have shown to be comparatively unwilling to vote for public expenditures for *any* purpose are especially unenthusiastic about putting high-cost programs into slum schools that serve racial minorities.[9] Unions are anxious about job competition from the products of improved vocational programs. And although property taxes for schools may be only a minor problem for large corporate business, they are often severe in their effect on smaller business and on small householders. The latter groups, especially, are potential city dropouts; that is, they may move to suburbia if taxes go up, and the result may be to depreciate further the city's tax base while its educational needs increase. The unitary-community myth no longer serves to quiet the demonstrations or to pass the tax increase. It has largely outlived its usefulness. Yet it is still frequently articulated by schoolmen and lay supporters of the schools, perhaps because, as the inveterate gambler said in explaining his continued patronage of the crooked card game, "It's the only one in town."

There is another dimension in which unity has been emphasized with respect to schools. Educators have tried very hard to achieve and maintain consensus among all those engaged in the educational enterprise. Unity is a prerequisite to a reputation for expertise, and it thus adds to the bargaining power of schoolmen as they seek public support. Unity inside the school helps justify independence from "politics." In the Chicago case of 1927 and again today, in Chicago and elsewhere, the vulnerability of the schools to group pressures from the community depends heavily on the extent to which the board, the superintendent and his administrative associates, and the teaching staff remain as professional allies rather than splitting into conflicting camps.

The consensus among school interests is equally sought after at the state level, and as my colleagues and I have suggested in our study of state politics and the schools,[10] a number of devices have been developed to help achieve and preserve unity, even at some cost in terms of goal achievements—dollar volume of state aid, or teacher tenure law protection, for example. The point I wish to make here, however, is that unity among schoolmen is frequently a considerable handicap for big-city school interests, particularly in their efforts to get increased state aid.

Let me illustrate my point with a discussion that leans heavily on experience in Missouri. There, a moderately malapportioned legislature for many years exhibited great fiscal prudence. They spend more than they used to, but the state still ranks much lower in comparison to other states in expenditures than in income. Education is no exception, but, thanks largely to the skillful efforts of the Missouri State Teachers Association, both district consolidation and equalization grants under a foundation program have steadily improved the financial condition of most *rural* schools. But these programs are of much less benefit to schools in the large cities.

St. Louis and Kansas City schools receive state aid, to be sure, but on a somewhat different basis from other districts. State aid is legally less assured in the large cities, and it gets a smaller portion of the job done. The city of today has high-cost educational needs as compared to noncity areas. The core-city wealth, which is effectively taxable by local action, is comparatively less great than it used to be. State-aid programs which aim at providing minimum per-pupil expenditure do not solve big-city needs, and the states have not been receptive to extra demands of urban educators any more than they have responded to other urban interests.

When the city-school interests go to the state capital to press their special claims, they carry with them the norms of their professional colleagues everywhere, the norms of unity. All educators are united in favor of education, one and indivisible, to be provided equally for all. Yet this same delegation comes to ask special treatment from the state, either in the form of additional state money or additional authority to act for themselves. Moreover, the statewide education interests normally take no stand on the requests of the city-school interests. The statewide groups are interested in equalization, not special programs for the cities. They might even oppose urban-oriented school legislation since it would either compete for monies desired for equalization or, at the least, serve the needs of "the city," a symbol which noncity school leaders look on with suspicion. And these school leaders occupy the state department of education and dominate the state teachers association. From the point of view of the city schools, the best thing, and the usual thing, is to have the state groups stay out.

The urban school forces, assuming they have at least the neutrality of the state educational groups, confront another unity norm when they arrive at the state capital. This is the unwritten rule of the state legislature for dealing with all "local" issues, and the school needs of a city like St. Louis are treated within the same system of legislative practice as a proposed salary increase for the sheriff. They are all local issues. The rule provides that the legislators will approve a request from a local community provided that the state representatives from that community are substantially united in their support of the request.

One might suppose that, since the school groups all strive for internal unity, the legislators' prerequisite would be easy to fulfill. Such is not the case, and much of the reason lies in the separation of the schools from the political system of the city. The problem lies in the relationship, or rather the lack thereof, between the spokesmen for the schools and the city delegation in the legislature. City legislators are not interested in the schools. They avoid service on education committees, take little part in debate on school issues, and generally are thought by other legislators who are concerned about state school policy to contribute very little. Urban legislators are likely indeed to be profoundly uninterested in the concerns of *any* groups which successfully keep themselves apart from the political system of the city. They, after all, are products of that system and their points of reference are mainly contained within it. The school representatives cannot eschew politics and still make meaningful contact with the legislature.

Although most state legislators would be merely indifferent to the schools' plea for state help, some may actively, though covertly, oppose the requests. In the St. Louis case, a number of influential city legislators identify themselves with the "state" as a fiscal entity apart from the "city," and resist increased state expenditures of any kind for the city. Others may reflect a Catholic constituency and say, for instance, that unless money is provided for transportation to parochial schools they will oppose extra funds for public education in the city. Still others have been known to be engaged in various kinds of alliances, for instance with school-building and maintenance crews, and hope to gain benefits for their allies by helping to block the school board's requests in the legislature. Most of the city-based legislative opposition will be behind the scenes. In a roll call vote it would seldom show up. Nevertheless it may effectively block passage of the program.

The key to the problem is in the fact that the schoolmen have no way to reach the pivotal legislators where it counts. There is no network of mutual obligation and support connecting the two groupings. The school board can cash no influence checks in payment for past or future favors done for legislators. There are a few favors the school can do for a highly political legislator, but every element in professional education training and ideology contributes to the refusal to think in these terms. Parenthetically, it might be noted here that lay board members seem to get more righteously indignant than professional superintendents at the suggestion that they do a little trading if they want their program passed. Political naiveté, especially at the level of articulated ideology, helps reinforce the incapacity of urban school interests (though not necessarily in rural areas where schoolmen are often highly skilled in the arts of "forks of the creek" politics) to get what they want from the state. Not only the congenital opposition of educators to these elemental political tactics, but the widespread misconception of the source of their opposition further confounds them. Newspapers and other "spectator elites" such as academics have assumed that it was the rural interests that were doing in the urban claims. The inability to understand that urban legislators were often unresponsive, not only regarding school problems but on many other desires of some city-based interests, has led to invalid inferences about what to do next. One of these has been simply to reassert the evils of politics and the importance of insulating the schools against their bitter breath. The second is to await with confidence the coming of reapportionment. "Give us an urban majority and our urban programs will pass," is the assumption underlying this optimism. But an urban state legislative majority may still not care much about the schools; and, without more political savvy than they have displayed in the past, the spokesmen for city school interests will continue to get unsatisfactory treatment.

There is, obviously, the now genuinely optimistic prospect of federal funding, especially rich for urban schools serving slum populations. I shall not explore this dimension in detail, but I want to note an important point: urban interests have for years done much better at the federal level than in the state capitol. The reasons are complex and not very well understood, but among them is the strong, warm, and skillfully administered relationship between city political leaders and federal officials. Federal officials in all the relevant branches and agencies have come to be responsive to political leaders and politically skillful administrators in the cities. Mayors, urban-renewal directors, and local poverty-program administrators are especially skilled, individually and through their national associations, at bringing their points of view to the sympathetic attention of Washington.

Earlier I raised the question of the significance of deciding the McAndrew affair within a partisan electoral process. Let us return to that dimension of our general problem. I have suggested that autonomy and isolation have serious disadvantages for urban schools. What is to be said on the other side? What would it be like if the schools were a more integral part of the urban political system; if, for example, they were made a regular line department of the city government with a director appointed by the mayor to serve at his pleasure? How would such a process work? What would be the substantive effects on educational policy and on the city generally?

To examine this issue directly, we need to be clear about how city political systems actually function. No single formulation will do justice to the complexities of the question but at least three points seem especially pertinent. First, political scientists generally have found that in large cities, and some of the smaller ones too, influence is rather widely dispersed, specialized, and exercised in a discontinuous fashion. That is, one person or group will be active and influential on one set of issues while quite a different array dominates the next set. This tendency is perhaps accentuated when a specialized set of issues, such as education, is determined within a specialized institutional framework. But the institutional framework is primarily reinforcing, not by itself determining. A second, related, finding of political scientists' examinations of the urban community is that great pressure is generally exercised in questions of substantive policy program (though not so much on elections or top level personnel appointments or tax rates) by the program's professional and administrative experts. In urban renewal or public health and hospitals, to take two examples from regular city government, the professional personnel run the programs about as completely as schoolmen run the schools; perhaps, more so.

A third finding is rather different from the first two, however. In many cities, though by no means in all of them, a critical and continuing role of substantial import is played by the mayor. He is the chief organizer of the dominant coalition of interests and the chief broker among them. He is the chief negotiator in balancing not only the disparate and often conflicting groups in the city but also in representing city needs to state and especially to federal agencies. More than that the mayor is the single most important problem-solver. He is committed, out of sheer re-election necessity if for no other reason, to rebuilding the slums, attracting new business, renovating downtown, implementing equal rights and opportunity and, as federal money is at last making it possible, improv-

ing the life chances of the urban poor. Not all mayors face the same circumstances, of course. Some are weak in formal authority to control
even their governmental environment; many are lacking in the fiscal
and human resources to get the necessary leverage on the social and
economic environment. Nevertheless, there is a substantial similiarity in
the orientation and role of big-city mayors, and this convergence has
been especially pronounced during the past decade. In style or substance, mayors of today have little in common with Big Bill Thompson.
Actually, mayors might not relish taking more direct responsibility for
the schools. Why should they take on another large problem area when
they too can fall back on the argument that the schools should be non-
political? If they were to accept a more active role, it might be because
they really want to resolve the complicated difficulties of urban life, and
solutions *must* include effective use of the schools.

These three generalizations are all relevant to my question but in
somewhat different ways. They suggest that if the schools were integrated with the urban governmental system, the educators would continue to make most of the technical and administrative decisions but the
mayor and his coalition of community support would play a major role
in giving over-all program and fiscal direction. The schools would compete more directly than now with other city programs for available
money. Their programs might be more differentiated among different
segments of the community, as the mayor tried at once to solve problems
and ease tensions and to please the major elements of the coalition that
elected him. Their top administrative personnel might be more vulnerable to the vicissitudes of electoral fortune, though mayors might be
only slightly more effective in breaking through the defenses of the educators' bureaucracy to choose (or fire) their own men than are independent school boards now. Educators might find themselves and their
programs more often subordinated to other agencies and programs
than is presently the case, but this subordination might be more a difference in perception than reality; an independent school system already must compete for money and support, but in an indirect and
segmented manner. It is not clear that mayor-directed schools would be
more generously financed from the local community but neither is it inevitable that they would be poorer.

In my judgement, the principal difference between the existing arrangements for the government of urban public education and this hy-
pothetical control by the mayor would be in the schools' relationship
with the increasingly pluralistic and tension-filled community. An inde-

pendent school system asks for community support directly, unprotected by any of the confusions of mandate that attend the election of political officials. The schools are naked against community pressures except as their unitary-community ideology and whatever rational citizen demand there may be for their services may shield them. I have argued, and so do the protest demonstrations and the negative votes in referenda, that these are not sufficient protection if the urban schools are to perform the extraordinarily difficult, high-cost tasks of educating the urban poor. It is not coincidence, I think, that recently the schools have been so often the target of the alienated and disaffected elements of society. Whether protesting against *de facto* segregation, double taxation of Catholics, or alleged Communist infiltration, the pickets know that the schools are vulnerable to direct assault. No other programs or interests get in the way. No other issues or loyalties intrude.

But the processes involved in electing a mayor and a council, especially on a partisan ticket, but also in a large, heterogeneous city with nonpartisan government, do mute these kind of pressures. Mandates *are* vague; constraints on the specific policy choices which the officials will subsequently make are loose. And the protection afforded to the professionals is considerable. They may administer their programs while someone else takes the heat, and diffuses it.

There is evidence that in the controversies over fluoridation those communities in which the voters decided the question in a referendum were often in the process racked by deep social conflict. In those cities where a mayor played a strong role, on the other hand, fluoridating the city water supply by administrative order, there was little untoward excitement.[11] The schools have far more substantive impact on urban life than fluoridation, of course; the latter seems to be mainly symbolic. But educational issues are laden with affect, and they may come more and more to resemble fluoridation as a focus for the manifold discontents of the city. The broader political process might help to protect the schools against becoming the urban community's battlefield.

In all that I have said thus far, my principal points appear to be as follows: (1) more direct and effective political (mayoral) control of the schools will be difficult to engineer because of the resistance of schoolmen, regardless of formal governmental structure, to "nonprofessional" direction; and (2) big-city school interests might get a more receptive hearing in state and national capitals and be partially screened from local direct action protests if they merge their interests more fully with the over-all city administration. But would this type of result lead to more effective education? This, in my judgement, is precisely the *wrong* question. In the urban center, there is no education which is separate from the issues of race, poverty, housing, crime, and the other human problems of the metropolis. The issue we need to face is whether greater mayoral control would lead to changes in school policy (e.g., better coordination and cooperation with urban renewal, recreation, and poverty programs) which would make the educational program more effective in solving the larger complex of community problems. In a simpler era, one could argue that Big Bill Thompson may well have done just this in Chicago. And, forty years later, one might well feel that, in the same city, Mayor Daley might have achieved more effective integration than Superintendent Willis seemed disposed to provide had the mayor chosen to violate the educators' code of independence and exert more direct control of the situation.

At the same time, there should be no mistake about the fact that greater administrative integration of schools with city would, in many cases, mean subordination of the schools to the city government. Moreover, such subordination might often mean that the schools were being used as instruments to achieve policy goals which extended well beyond more narrowly defined educational objectives. To some extent, of course, this is happening anyway, and indeed it has always been so. But the issue of political control forces us to be explicit about the question of how the many goals we wish to achieve in the city can best be approached. If it turned out that education was not at the head of the list, educators would be compelled to acknowledge that fact in a situation where they had to bargain for their share of the local resources against the direct competition of other programs as well as against the fiscal prudence of the electorate.

Direct competition for local money; subordination of educators to other public officials with other interests and programs; the self-conscious use of the schools as instruments to fight poverty, improve housing conditions, or fight city-suburb separation: these have been virtually unthinkable heresies to devoted schoolmen. Yet, are they much more than an explicit statement of steps and tendencies already being taken or implicit in present practices? I think not; we are already moving this way, to some extent we always have been doing so, and the real question to be faced is: How might we do these things better? A greater measure of local political leadership in education and coordination of the schools with other portions of the community might well contribute to this end.

NOTES

The original version of this paper was delivered as the Alfred Dexter Simpson Memorial Lecture at Harvard University, November 12, 1965. I am grateful to the Harvard Graduate School of Education and the New England School Development Council, under whose auspices the lecture was presented, for extending to me the opportunity to formulate the arguments presented in the paper.

1. I have chosen not to try to provide a full array of bibliographical citation to the relevant literature. Partly, this decision is based on my desire to present an argument which raises questions for public examination and debate rather than to assert that some things are so and others not. Partly, however, this particular body of literature is growing so rapidly that reference footnotes would be incomplete virtually as soon as they were written.

2. I have explored some facets of this question in briefer compass in my essay, "Urban Politics and Education," in Sam Bass Warner, Jr., ed., *Planning for a Nation of Cities* (Cambridge, Mass.: MIT Press, 1966), pp. 268–84.

3. New York: Harcourt, Brace and Co., 1928.

4. *Ibid.*, p. 357.

5. See the discussion in Thomas McDowell Gilland, *The Origin and Development of the Power and Duties of the City School Superintendent* (Chicago: University of Chicago Press, 1935), esp. ch. vi.

6. George S. Counts, "The Social Composition of Boards of Education: A Study in the Social Control of Public Education," *Supplementary Educational Monographs* 30 (July 1927): 83. See also the findings of Roy Coughran, "The School Board Member Today," *The American School Board Journal* 6 (December, 1956): 25–26, reprinted in August Kerber and Wilfred R. Smith, eds., *Educational Issues in a Changing Society*, rev. ed. (Detroit: Wayne State University Press, 1964), pp. 284–87. W.W. Charters argues cogently that whatever the political significance of middle-class membership on school boards may have been, there is little empirical basis for concluding that membership really has meant policy control anyway. See his "Social Class Analysis and the Control of Public Education," *Harvard Educational Review* 23 (Fall 1953): 266–83.

7. Reported in "Educational Decision-Making and the Distribution of Influence in Cities," paper presented to the American Political Science Association, September 7, 1966.

8. *Education and the Cult of Efficiency* (Chicago: University of Chicago Press, 1962).

9. James Q. Wilson and Edward C. Banfield, "Public-Regardingness as a Value Premise in Voting Behavior," *American Political Science Review* 58 (December 1964): 876–88.

10. Nicholas A. Masters, Robert H. Salisbury, and Thomas H. Eliot, *State Politics and the Public Schools* (New York: Alfred Knopf, 1964).

11. See Elihu Katz, Robert Crain, Donald Rosenthal, and Aaron J. Spector, "The Fluoridation Decision: Community Struture and Innovation," manuscript, March 1965. The processes by which an affect-laden issue like education may ignite previously latent community tensions has been inadequately explored. James S. Coleman's highly suggestive synthesis of the then existing materials, *Community Conflict* (Glencoe, Ill.: The Free Press, 1957), has not been followed by much further empirical work.

16

St. Louis Politics:
Relationships Among Interests,
Parties, and Governmental Structure

*P*olitical scientists have been troubled in recent years by just what it is they mean when they talk about a political party. Whether the discussion concentrates on the American scene or includes comparative data from other countries, the ambiguity of party as an analytical tool remains. Particularly difficult and very largely untouched by specific empirical analysis are the relationships which connect core party organizations, the social and economic interest group configuration, and the formal governmental structure of a community. Whereas some political scientists have assumed the crucial importance of the formal structure in shaping the political life of the community, others have tended to regard structure as largely irrelevant and to argue instead that the only significant variables were embraced in interest group activity. This paper will offer a synopsis of the situation in one city, St. Louis, Missouri, in an effort to suggest the ways in which the three factors mentioned are interrelated.

The burden of the argument here is that a somewhat peculiar bifurcated structure of local government plays a crucial role in shaping the nature and scope of political conflict in the city. Two broad interest groupings in St. Louis, each composed of rather loosely allied groups and each pursuing different sets of goals in the political arena, are enabled to live under the same party label by the fact that each grouping can control one segment of the governmental structure and from that control secure the portion of its goals most vital to it. Neither group gains complete satisfaction thereby, but the consequence is that the two

Reprinted from *The Western Political Quarterly* 13 (June 1960):498–507 by permission of the University of Utah, copyright holder.

groups are not forced into the full range of sharp competition that a more centralized and monolithic structure might require.

The Interests

The constellation of social and economic interests which make up the body politic of St. Louis is like in some ways and in some ways unlike that of other major American cities. In common with other metropolitan centers, the St. Louis area has experienced rapid growth in the post–World War II period, but unlike most other cities, this growth has taken place almost entirely outside the city limits, which were fixed by constitutional provision in 1876. The growth of the St. Louis area, further, has not kept pace with many other parts of the country, particularly because the hinterland of the city has not grown much. Consequently, St. Louis business leaders have been concerned to bring new industry to the city, and this effort has spurred the desire, shared by other metropolises, to solve traffic and transit problems, to renovate and rehabilitate slum areas, and to revive the downtown business district.

In common with many cities, St. Louis has experienced a great influx of Negroes and "mountain whites" in recent years with a resulting increased demand for various types of municipal services. As elsewhere, these "new immigrants" play the same role in relation to ward organizations of the party that nationality groups did in past decades. The tight and inflexible boundaries of the city have, at the same time, meant that St. Louis has lost upper income population to the suburbs. The combination of an increasingly lower income population and the desire to attract new industry and therefore to keep tax rates at reasonable levels has left the city in almost perpetual financial embarrassment in the postwar period, an embarrassment alleviated only by the imposition of an earnings tax of 1 per cent on all income.

If one looks at the major economic interests in the city, one can begin with familiar categories, labor and business, and discover some degree of conflict between these two groups. Yet no analysis can explain St. Louis politics satisfactorily by relying solely upon labor-management conflict. Labor, for example, is not monolithic. The largest unions are the Teamsters, the Building Trades, the Machinists, and the Auto Workers, while a number of smaller unions also play some role. These unions differ considerably in their local political significance. The Teamsters are the most active locally and the most controversial. They have a fairly fully articulated set of goals for St. Louis which includes general expansion of services for low income groups and which emphasizes heavily the betterment of race relations and equality for minorities. The militance of the Teamsters, with its ideological flavor, is in contrast to the unphilosophical bread-and-butter concerns of the Building Trades which seek jobs and contracts and find that extensive political alliances are of great assistance in securing these goals. They are not really interested in most of the program of the Teamsters, and the Teamster leaders sometimes express contempt for the unconcern with policy exhibited by the "pork chop" unions. Nevertheless, each group finds that under present conditions their channels of action often bring them into working agreements with each other on political questions. The UAW and the Steelworkers differ from each of the two types of labor groups mentioned above, since they are largely unconcerned with local politics. Their union interests are not much affected by decisions in the local arena, and though their leaders sometimes go through political motions, neither these unions nor the management of the plants where they work are normally active on the St. Louis political scene.

The business community is likewise divided along a number of lines. Dominating the public view are the industrial, banking, and commercial leaders of locally controlled large businesses, the "downtown" business community. These are the men who need more industrial development in the city, these are the men who have significant stakes in the rehabilitation of the slums and the consequent revival of the core city, and these are the men who also form the social elite of the city. The interests of this configuration are articulated by the metropolitan daily press, and they are identified with "Progress" and "Good Government," while they are against the "Politicians." The bulk of the middle and upper-middle income residents of the city and the professional, religious, and educational leadership tend strongly to identify their interests with those of this business elite.

The small business community, on the other hand, does not. Composed of small downtown enterprises like parking lot operators and of neighborhood commercial establishments, this group is concerned with specific, individual treatment at the hands of governmental authority. Specific tax measures, provision of stop signs, regulation of on- and off-street parking, zoning, and the like are their primary goals, and they very often line up with organized labor groups in political alliance against the "downtown" interests.

The social composition of the city is noteworthy in two main respects, the impact of the minority influx and the ethnic make-up of the city. More than one-fourth of the city's population today is black and they are achieving increasing political power. Six wards of the city's twenty-eight are represented by African Americans, and significant influence is exerted in at least three others. Desegregation of swimming pools, schools, and, to some extent, of places of public accommodation has followed the rise of blacks to influence. Until the New Deal and again during most of the 1940's the Negro community was predominantly Republican, but since 1949 Negro wards have produced overwhelming margins for any candidate bearing the Democratic label.

Nationality groups have not played as important a role in St. Louis politics as in many cities. St. Louis experienced a large German immigration and a significant Irish immigration during the mid-nineteenth century. For decades these two groups formed the backbone of the Republican and Democratic parties respectively. But the "late immigrants" from Eastern and Southern Europe largely by-passed St. Louis in favor of the heavy industrial centers. Thus the European "ethnics" in the city have had nearly a century to become assimilated, and today, except for one Italian ward, it is difficult to find many traces of genuine nationality identification. The heavily Catholic religious heritage of St. Louis remains, but national origin seems to have little meaning in St. Louis politics.

St. Louis thus displays two broad configurations of interests. On one side are the locally oriented labor unions, blacks, neighborhood businessmen, and lower income people generally. This grouping focuses its attention primarily on the specific bread-and-butter issues of jobs, stop sign, spot zoning, and the like, and exhibits a sharp antipathy toward any suggestion of increased tax rates. Downtown business interests and the middle and upper-middle income residents, on the other hand, are primarily interested in broader policy questions—economic growth, urban renewal—and their approach to problems of fiscal solvency is more sympathetic to the needs for more tax revenue.

The Structure of Government

The structure of St. Louis government is *sui generis* in many respects. The city is governed under a charter adopted by the voters in 1914. Some important aspects of the city's business, however, are not under home rule control. The police department, for example, is controlled by a Board of Police Commissioners appointed by the governor, and a Board of Election Commissioners is similarly appointed. Originally, the device was adopted to enable a pro-Southern state administration to have police control in a Unionist city. Later it allowed a Democratic state administration to have patronage to dispense in a normally Republican city. The contemporary significance of this arrangement is quite different as will be noted later. In the city a moderately strong mayor administers nearly ten thousand employees of whom he can appoint some seventeen without regard to civil service requirements. An elected comptroller acts jointly with the mayor and the president of the Board of Aldermen, elected at large, to form the Board of Estimate and Apportionment which prepares the city budget, a budget which the Board of Aldermen may cut but not increase. The budget includes in its provisions many of the most vital policy decisions affecting the city and the mayor is certainly the key figure in its preparation. The Board of Aldermen is composed of the president and twenty-eight representatives elected one each from the twenty-eight wards. The mayor and the members of the Board of Aldermen each serve four-year terms. The aldermen, of course, must pass all ordinances for the city, but even though a majority of the Board often opposes the mayor on policy issues, the latter clearly dominates the policy-making process.

Almost entirely separate from this portion of the city government are the so-called "county offices." St. Louis, like Baltimore, is not a part of any county. Nevertheless, under state law, the functions ordinarily performed by county officials must be performed in St. Louis by officials like sheriff, collector of revenue, license collector, recorder of deeds, magistrates, and others who are elected by the voters and are completely outside the control of the city administration or the city charter. These officials make few policy decisions of any importance, but taken together they provide nearly one thousand non-civil service jobs, and, as one of the few remaining sources of patronage in the city, they are prizes of great importance to those who are interested in patronage.

The Board of Education should also be mentioned here. It, too, is outside the budgetary control of the city. The Board is elected separately and its tax rate is determined through separate referendum elections. It, too, controls a substantial pool of patronage jobs in its building and maintenance departments, and patronage rather than educational policy is the major issue in Board of Education elections.

Thus the structure of St. Louis government contains two largely separate sets of offices. One is centered in the mayor's office and is the natural focus of attention for those interested in broad problems of municipal policy. The other is based upon the county offices, Board of

Education, and Board of Aldermen and consists essentially of a patronage pool and a means for securing individual favor with very little responsibility for policy.

The Party Situation

St. Louis has undergone two rather remarkable political metamorphoses during the past three decades. The first it shared with many other metropolitan centers, the change from consistent Republicanism to overwhelming Democracy as the New Deal coalition produced sizable pluralities on the local level. The shift to the Democrats embraced practically all elements of the community, but perhaps the most notable changes took place among the blacks, and among many of the German areas of the city. Silk stocking and delivery wards alike went Democratic during the thirties. But although the state and national Democratic tickets continued to carry the city comfortably, during the next decade, from 1941 to 1949, the Republicans returned to power on the local scene. We need not examine the reasons for this switch except to note that it took in much of the city, especially the blacks, and it was backed by much of downtown business and the metropolitan press. This Republican swing carried the party into the mayor's office (by a two-to-one majority in 1945), swept the Board of Aldermen nearly clean of Democrats, and helped elect Republicans to Congress, although the Democrats hung on to some local offices and Roosevelt won handily.

The period of Republican control ended in 1949, however, and since that time the Democratic sweep of all offices at all levels, save only a maximum of four aldermanic seats, has been complete. This time the black wards shifted overwhelmingly to the Democrats and have shown no sign of defecting despite that tendency in some other cities. The upper income areas—smaller now than formerly—have shown remarkable Democratic strength, largely undisturbed by the Eisenhower era. The lower income sections of the city, which include the Negro areas, are staunchly Democratic, to the extent that the Republicans are badly demoralized and have difficulty in finding either candidates or money to make a serious race for any political office in the community.

Yet this cyclical variation in the fortunes of the two parties does not conform to the configuration of interests in the community. As outlined above, the city is broadly divided along some sort of quasi-class basis into two groupings; labor, low income, small, neighborhood business, and at least recently African Americans, against large downtown business, the forces of "Progress," with the daily papers as spokesmen and the so-called "newspaper wards" as sources of voting strength. This general division of the community interests has not changed greatly during the past decade except perhaps as the proportion of racial minorities has increased while the old German Republicans have lost their ethnic identity. But these changes surely do not account for (a) the massive shifts in the strength of each party over a relatively short period of time, or (b) the absence of fairly sharp and relatively even competition between the two parties for local office. For this latter fact is perhaps most prominent; namely, that when one party has been dominant, the other party is moribund. This is especially true of the Republicans since 1949. With a constellation of interests that normally might be expected to support Republican candidates, the latter lose by margins exceeding three-to-one.

Interest, Party, and Structure in St. Louis

We cannot here go into all the reasons for the variation in party fortunes and the recent lack of Republican success. But we do want to examine the forms of institutionalization of this division of interests in the community. If it has not taken the form of inter-party conflict, how has it been expressed? The answer is that two fairly distinct groupings have appeared *within* whichever party was dominant in a particular period, one representing the larger business groups, the newspaper ward areas, and the forces of "Progress" generally, while the other is characterized by the "Politicians" who are spokesmen for a medley of lower income, labor, small business, and minority groups. Such a division was notable within the Republican ranks during the late 1940's. Such a division is quite obvious within the Democratic ranks today. *This division is not only one of conflict over economic and social interests in the community, it is also manifested in the formal structure of government.*

In both the Republican and the Democratic parties the intra-party division has followed essentially the same lines. On the one side, the downtown business groups and the other interests associated with them have found their representation in the office of mayor primarily, usually with co-operation from the comptroller and the president of the Board of Aldermen. All these officials are elected on a city-wide basis with substantial newspaper attention to their campaigns, which tend to cost considerable sums of money for publicity. These three, forming the Board of Estimate and Apportionment, make the key fiscal decisions of the city, and, however hard they try, the Board of Aldermen can alter these decisions only at the margins. Moreover, the mayor, as mentioned before, is by all odds the most significant policy-making official in the city. It is policy, of course, with which the large business constellation is concerned—broad civic policy affecting the location of industry, general tax rates, availability of full city services, the social climate of the community necessary to attract technical personnel for their businesses, and the social climate of the community necessary to preserve the status of an old-line, social elite whose autonomy of local operation is being eroded by the nationalization of business and labor alike. It is this group which wants civic reform and civil service, which sponsors the many Citizens Committees to study local problems, and so on. The group is not reactionary or even particularly conservative in the usual meanings of those terms. Some of its leaders are liberal Democrats on the national scene, and many are outspoken defenders of equality for minorities on all levels. Its co-operation with organized labor is never more than lukewarm, but again, on the national scene, the Teamsters and the Building Trades, the dominant labor groups locally, are not noted for their liberalism.

The other side is likewise focused on a set of public officials, the holders of the "county offices," supplemented by the dominant group on the Board of Aldermen. The county offices are filled in city-wide elections too, thus giving them the same formal constituency as the mayor and his associates. But these elections are not attended by wide publicity, they are held in conjunction with November general elections instead of the municipal elections in the spring, and the chief requisite of victory is a dependable vote delivered by an effective ward organization. The newspapers take little part in these elections and correspondingly have little influence on them. Instead they are dominated by the so-called "delivery wards" of the city, generally, the lower income and Negro wards. Again this was true when the Republicans controlled these offices as well as now when the Democrats are supreme.

The complex of interests which supports these political leaders also finds it important to have influence with the aldermen. In the wards inhabited by lower income residents aldermen are selected in the same way as the county office-holders; nomination dependent largely upon the support of the ward committeemen and election dependent upon an effective ward organization. Many county office-holders are also ward committeemen and the alliance between these elements of the party organization is firm. By and large, this element of the party is not particularly concerned with broad social or economic policy as such. It is concerned rather with the immediate needs of effective ward organization, and these needs are not notably different today than they traditionally have been. Patronage remains the lifeblood of the organization and, of course, the county offices are sources of significant patronage in the city. Consequently, control of these offices is vital to the organization. For the same reason, control of the Board of Education is important. More than that, however, the county office element of the party is concerned with the needs of its electoral supporters as the latter interpret these needs. This means broadly *individual favor.* Jobs are crucial, but so also are specific contracts for building contractors, stops signs and parking regulations, assistance in getting into a public housing project, route location for a throughway, and so on. Assistance for individuals in need, the classic basis of urban political organization, remains the basis for this wing of the party, and such assistance is necessarily funneled through the particular set of offices which this wing seeks to control; jobs through the county offices and Board of Education, and individual attention from the Board of Aldermen achieved through a log-rolling system know locally as aldermanic courtesy. These are the concerns of blacks, low income groups, the politically active elements of the local labor movement, and of many kinds of small businesses. Thus there is not much question of which element in the party these groups will support in a situation of conflict between the two party groups.

One interesting thing about this division, both of interests in the city and of offices, is that conflict between the two groupings is minimized. The group focused on the mayor is not interested in patronage, although from time to time its conception of good government requires that it advocate the further extension of civil service. By the same token, the county office group and many of its electoral supporters are profoundly indifferent to most matters of public policy. Aldermanic courtesy does create conflict, since the granting of individual favors—e.g., a stop sign in front of a confectionery—often runs counter to broader policy concerns—e.g., a master traffic plan. Nevertheless, there are many areas of policy and patronage where each element of the party is content to let the other element control. Each group needs the other. The county office people need the financial support for their precinct workers which the mayor-led group contributes to the party. The mayoral group needs the support of the delivery wards to get many of its policy goals put into effect. This mutual need is sufficient at least to permit the two groups to share the same party label, and perhaps to require it.

But there is always latent and sometimes manifest conflict between the two groups. Issues like the distribution of the tax load, recognition of labor organizations among municipal employees, and particularly charter reform, which might threaten the existence of the patronage offices, all activate not only the office-holders within the party but, more importantly, bring into operation most of the interest groups in the community which ally with one or the other faction. On such questions the mayoral group is sharply opposed by the majority of the aldermen as well as by the dominant elements in the city committee of the party, the ward committeemen—county office forces. The tendency toward conflict is reinforced by the fact that each group tends to view the other as an unholy conspiracy aimed at destroying its opponents. As it happens in St. Louis this conflict often takes the geographical form of what is nearly a north-south split with the south side and west end supporting the mayoral faction while the north side is the heart of the county office group strength.

A word should be said about the rather special effect that the structure of the police department, headed by a Board appointed by the governor, has on the political scene. Two consequences are apparent. In the first place, influence with the police department follows from influence with the governor, and consequently, successful gubernatorial candidates are much sought after figures in St. Louis politics. Secondly, although the police department is run on the merit system, there is a substantial amount of patronage available in the form of assignments and promotions. This patronage is, of course, of more interest to the county office group than to the mayoral group and the former seeks it more assiduously. In this quest the county office group joins forces with the representatives from St. Louis to the state legislature in an alliance that is facilitated by the dependence of the state legislators upon ward committeeman endorsement in order to win office. The close liaison between the state delegation and the county office forces means that the county offices themselves, established by state statute, are safe, and that the desires of the city administration for new state legislation will often get a cool reception from a state delegation allied with the opposing faction of the party. When the St. Louis delegation to the legislature is not united in behalf of the city's demands, they have little chance of passage, and policy requests from the St. Louis administration are blocked most often not by rural opposition, as so often is alleged, but by the county office faction of the St. Louis party.

Perhaps there is no way to prove categorically that the formal structure of government is the crucial variable in determining the particular form which the interest conflict in St. Louis politics has taken. Certainly the total political process in the city is complex. Yet it can scarcely be doubted that if the county offices did not exist and their meager functions were performed by regular administrative agencies of the city, the contending interest groupings in the city would have to find other channels for the satisfaction of their needs. Without the county offices there would be no patronage and hence ward organizations would be weakened. In that event, those interest groups, notably labor, which now work through the ward organizations, would be forced to play an even more direct role in the political process than they do now. Without the county offices there would be only one really important office through which to exert political power, for whatever purposes, and that would be the office of mayor. The aldermen, without effective ward organizations, would need to turn more directly to the interest groups of their wards, and again the conflict between the two broad interest configurations of the city would become more open. If the office of mayor became the chief and virtually the only prize for the contending groups, then it would seem that at least two consequences would follow, given the interest group line-up as it now exists in St. Louis. First, the two groupings which now form factions within the party would divide into two separate parties. This process might be slow. It might be effected through the use of "Blue Ribbon" slates running against "politician" slates, or it might in time result in the revival of the Republican party. In any case, the conflict would be more open than it is now. Secondly, it would be more continuous and involve a broader range of issues. Whereas now there is a substantial area of autonomous operation left to each faction, if the mayor's office were the only prize, then victory and the battle to achieve victory would cover all the issues in which the two sets of interests are even potentially in conflict. Either one side would win or it would lose, and there would be none of the present partial victories for both sides, which, however frustrating they are sometimes, at least give some satisfactions and some basis for compromise and mediation to each group.

If the present alignment of interests were altered in any significant way, a development which the militant and volatile character of the Teamsters and the increasing numbers and self-consciousness of blacks make possible, the significance either of the present structure or of any alternative arrangements would be altered too. Under the present conditions, however, this analysis seems to be valid and, indeed, is confirmed by each major political event in the city. Any discussion of the effects of a really different structure, of course, must be speculative, since the proposal to change the structure so as to abolish the county offices will be met with sharp resistance by those groups which utilize the offices to advantage.

If the data reviewed here permit one to offer a tentative statement about the relationships between interests, party, and structure, it would appear that the interest group system is, as the Bentleyans argue it must be, basic. At the same time, however, the governmental structure affects in crucial ways the manner in which these interests will be articulated into political parties, and in so doing it plays an important role in determining the scope and intensity of political conflict in the community. It seems doubtful whether one could say that a particular structural form would in every case bring about a particular party system or give a particular shape to the conflict, since the structure and the interest configuration interact in each case. If the interest groups of St. Louis were more amorphous and diffuse and not joined in any bimodal pattern, even the most centralized structure of strong mayor control could not be expected to produce sharply competing parties. On the other hand, the present, somewhat diffuse structure would not appreciably moderate the conflict if St. Louis were divided into rigid class groupings of a quasi-feudal nature. Perhaps the study of the relationships of interests, parties, and structure in other cities will permit comparative analysis of a manageable range of data, and in turn lead us to more confident generalizations about the problem.

Part V

—— ◆ ——

*Continuing to
Reinterpret*

Despite the undoubted continuities, many things in politics do not stay the same for long. We must identify the dynamic elements and track the changes, resisting the temptation to keep using our old notes, and accepting the inevitable fact that many of our most brilliant insights will become mere historical footnotes as "the system" moves on to another phase. This last essay will be superseded in due course, but its argument, intentionally drawn to contest the conventional wisdom, may be provocative nevertheless.

17

The Paradox of
Interest Groups in Washington:
More Groups, Less Clout

*O*_{ne of the} most startling events in the history of public policy in the United States was the Tax Reform Act of 1986.[1] It was startling not so much because of its content or its possible impact as, first, because it happened at all, contrary to the forecasts of all knowledgeable observers and, second, because it was fashioned and passed while virtual armies of lobbyists looked on in distress and frustration, unable to intervene to affect the outcome. The "Battle of Gucci Gulch" was fought by members of Congress, mindful, to be sure, of the needs and concerns of organized interests but operating in a context shaped mainly by broader policy, partisan, and institutional considerations. It seemed a heavy irony indeed that, just when the number and variety of organized interests represented in Washington were at an all-time high—with unprecedented numbers of lobbyists using high personal skill supplemented by elaborate modern technologies of analysis, communication, and mobilization—and in a policy area, taxation, that had acquired many of its bizarre existing contours from the pressures and demands of narrowly based interest groups, the ultimate decision process should largely screen out those interests.

This paradox of more interest groups and lobbyists wielding less influence over policy results does not manifest itself all the time, to be sure. The paradox, however, is substantially valid, if not in quite this stark form, then at least in more nuanced forms. In this chapter I argue

Reprinted from Anthony King, ed., *The New American Political System*, 2d version (Washington, D.C.: American Enterprise Institute Press, 1990), pp. 203–30, with the permission of the American Enterprise Institue for Public Policy Research, Washington, D.C.

the case that the growth in the number, variety, and sophistication of interest groups represented in Washington has been associated with, and in some measure has helped to bring about, a transformation in the way much public policy is made and, further, that this transformed process is not dominated so often by a relatively small number of powerful interest groups as it may once have been. I certainly do not want to be understood as saying that interest groups as a whole have weakened in the way, say, that party organizations have lost control over the nomination of candidates. Nor would I deny that in particular instances the old ways are still intact—the "veterans' system" comes to mind—with triangular symbioses linking groups, congressional committees, and executive agencies in nearly impregnable policy success. Moreover, policies such as social security may be quite rigid and largely beyond amendment, not so much because of organized group pressure as such as from the fear among policy makers that such pressure is potentially mobilizable and would soon follow any adverse policy revision. Still, I contend that a great many interest group representatives seek information more than influence, that in many ways they have become dependent on and are sometimes exploited by government officials rather than the other way around, and that much of what contemporary lobbyists do is to be understood as a search for order and a measure of predictability in a policy-making world that has been fundamentally destabilized by developments of the past twenty years.

Changes since 1960

The Explosion in Numbers

The number of organizations directly engaged in pursuing their interests in Washington, D.C., has grown dramatically since about 1960. We have no reliable base line of observation, but the following items suggest the magnitude of expansion in the interest group universe.

- The number of registered lobbyists increased from 3,400 in 1975 to 7,200 in 1985.
- The annual publication *Washington Representatives* managed to find and list more than 5,000 people in 1979; by 1988 it listed nearly 11,000.[2]
- The proportion of U.S. trade and professional associations headquartered in and around Washington grew from 19 percent in 1971 to 30 percent in 1982.[3]

- The number of lawyers belonging to the District of Columbia Bar Association (a requirement for practice in Washington) increased from 10,925 in 1973 to 34,087 in 1981.
- The number of business corporations operating offices in Washington increased from 50 in 1961 to 545 in 1982.[4]
- Some 76 percent of the citizens' groups and 79 percent of the welfare groups in Washington in 1981 had come into existence since 1960.[5]

The Shifting Composition

From Tocqueville to Truman and beyond, interest group scholarship focused almost exclusively on voluntary associations, organizations of members who joined together to advance some common purpose. Mancur Olson showed that the simple fact that people share some political values is not a sufficient basis for collective action.[6] But Olson and other scholars have identified a variety of factors, including the presence of political entrepreneurs, selective benefits, social pressure, philanthropic motives, coercion, and sheer uncertainty, that can account reasonably well for the substantial numbers of voluntary associations that exist and are active in the political arena. This large set exhibits considerable variety, however. Thus trade associations composed of corporations operate quite differently from citizens' groups, especially expressive groups where the problem of free riders is more difficult to control. Important changes have occurred among voluntary associations in both composition and relative importance. In addition, however, three other, rather different kinds of interest organizations inhabit the Washington community, each of which has attained a larger and more consequential place in recent years.

First are institutions. Individual corporations, universities, state and local governments, and religious denominations are active on their own behalf as well as often belonging to voluntary associations of similarly situated entities.[7] Some of these institutions are profit seekers while others are in the nonprofit sector, but they share the condition of being affected by public policy and hoping by their presence in Washington to turn policy to their advantage. Although some have long been influential—large oil companies, for example—it seems likely that in the past two decades individual institutions have been of greater importance in affecting national policy and certainly have devoted greater effort to keeping track of the policy process than they did before the 1960s.

A second category of interested participant, once not nearly so important, is the think tank. The American Enterprise Institute, the

Brookings Institution, the Heritage Foundation, the Urban Institute, the Institute for Policy Analysis, the Cato Institute, and a good many others have come to play a significant role in national policy making. Some of these organizations have been havens for out-of-office politicians who remain in Washington in the hope that the next election will return them to office. The principal mode of think tank operation, however, is to publish and publicize policy analyses and recommendations.[8] Think tanks do not usually insist that policy makers adopt their recommended positions to placate some organized constituency they represent. Rather, they depend on the logical power of their arguments or the persuasiveness of their evidence and analysis. They often seek more to shape the broad agenda of policy action than to push for specific decision outcomes. These are only tendencies, to be sure, and there is considerable variation among these organizations; but it is important to include them in any comprehensive picture of the nongovernmental participants attempting to influence the policy-making process. Moreover, it is important to recognize not only that they are more numerous than, say, in 1960 but that they have become considerably more visible. Their ultimate effect may be difficult to determine precisely, but policy institutes and other such think tanks are in no sense merely academic enterprises.

Third, Washington lobbying is carried on not only by organizations on their own behalf but by agents of various kinds retained to advance their interests. Thus many of the lawyers in Washington do not pursue much conventional law practice but concentrate on representing client organizations before federal regulatory agencies, assisting in the presentation of testimony before congressional committees, arranging for a discussion between a client and a high-ranking White House staff person, or approaching potential sources of campaign contributions to help a senator's reelection campaign. This last example highlights an important feature of the lobbyist-agent. Such figures often operate as go-betweens, building symbiotic connections between client organizations and public officials so that each can advance its own interests by helping the other. Some of the living legends of contemporary Washington lobbying—Thomas Boggs, Clark Clifford, Charls Walker—have served a wide range of clients in this manner, and as a consequence a considerable mythology has developed around the notion that Washington lawyers are formidable power brokers whose impact on the policy process is vast, largely undesirable, and sometimes scandalous. To the roster of Washington lawyers in private practice must be added the very considerable number of consultants, of whom Michael Deaver, Lyn Nofziger, and a good many other peddlers of influence are notorious though perhaps unrepresentative examples, and public relations firms, a few of which, such as Hill and Knowlton, have become large enterprises offering clients a broad array of services, including lobbying but extending to many other forms of contact with the public.

Inasmuch as these agents are free-standing rather than organizational employees, they must often hustle for clients, persuading them that policy expertise or connections with officials will yield payoffs more than matching the fees charged. It is understandable that, as the ranks of such agents expand, the competition for business may sometimes tempt people into actions that exceed the bounds of legitimacy. Of all the people engaged in interest representation in Washington, however, only a minority—20 percent according to the one major study, by Robert L. Nelson and others—are free-standing agents, "guns for hire," so to speak.[9] The remainder are employed by the organizations whose interests they represent; and although they must often keep their members happy, they do not have to be so anxious about obtaining clients, arguably a major source of legal or moral corruption in the process of interest representation.

The Fragmentation of Interest Sectors

In the "old days"—the 1950s, say—it was characteristic of many policy sectors for a few organizations, sometimes only one, to have hegemony. The American Medical Association (AMA) dominated health policy, the American Farm Bureau Federation (AFBF) was far and away the most influential group on agricultural matters, the American Petroleum Institute led the list of energy interests, and so on. In the late 1980s these are still substantial organizations, actively involved in making policy pronouncements and using the tactics of influence, but in most policy domains such quasimonopoly power has been undermined by a process of interest fragmentation that has greatly changed the distribution of influence.

This fragmentation process has two distinct components. First, the self-interested groups have increased in number, variety, and specificity of policy concerns. In agriculture the National Farmers Union gained a position as liberal Democratic rival to the conservative Republican AFBF, only to be challenged on specific issues by the National Wheat Growers Association, the Soy Bean Association, the Corn Growers Association, and dozens of commodity-based trade associations. Some, like the National Milk Producers Federation, had been around for decades but as relatively peripheral players. Others, like the corn growers, were newly organized, drawing on more self-conscious and, because of changes in farming technology, more differentiated groups of producers. But not just producers. Many of the groups now active in agricultural issues include corporations engaged in other stages of the chain linking the farmer to the consumer. The Grocery Manufacturers Association is one example, but there are scores of others in which farmers play little or no role. Commodity organizations and trade associations have been joined by numerous individual corporations, including giant agribusiness firms like Cargill or Archer-Daniels-Midland and firms like Coca-Cola or Pizza Hut, concerned about the prices they must pay for commodities they use.

In the mid-1980s William P. Browne identified well over 200 interests involved in shaping farm legislation.[10] With this massive expansion of private interest group participants, it has been necessary since at least the late 1950s to construct quite elaborate coalitions of these groups to get the support necessary to enact major farm legislation. In agriculture the farm bills still take broad multipurpose form and are enacted for terms of three to five years, after which there is another round of negotiation. The complexity of these negotiations defies quick summary, but it is clear that the peak associations no longer guide the process.

A similar story can be told of the health policy domain.[11] There no single legislative enactment brings into focus the full extent of interest fragmentation, although efforts to achieve national health insurance and sometimes medical cost containment issues have come close. Issues concerning hospital construction, medical research, veterans' health care, and drug regulation, however, have long been treated separately. Whatever the question, the AMA, once so imperiously powerful, is no longer the dominant voice even of organized medicine. The hospital associations now speak with quite independent voices. So do many organizations of medical specialists. Medical insurance interests, medical schools, corporations engaged in medical technology research and manufacturing, and of course the drug companies all get involved. Again, complex coalitions among diverse interests are necessary to enact legislation and secure its continued funding.

An alternative approach to the building of broad interest coalitions so that groups can secure stable and supportive policy attention is to carve out a small but vital slice of the total policy pie and try to insulate it from invasion by competing interest. Medical schools succeeded for a time in keeping medical student subsidies from rival claimants. Veterans' interests have successfully protected their hospitals. Tobacco growers have maintained their benefits separate from broader farm policy questions. Quite large numbers of examples of such cozy programs could be cited where at least for a time a program and its interest group constituency have bee effectively isolated from broader entanglements. But the fragmentation process has a second component in addition to the proliferation of self-interested groups just described, which puts even these narrowly bounded islands of policy stability at risk. This component may be called the "invasion of the externality groups."[12]

A major category of growth among interest groups has been citizens' groups. This label is attached to a broad array of motivating concerns and points of view, but it applies to all those groups for whom self-interest, narrowly defined, is not the primary organizing appeal. Members of taxpayer groups and animal rights enthusiasts may thereby express some private desire to save money to protect their pets, but even for them the collective purposes of the group bear only an indirect connection to their personal situations. In any case, the rapid growth of citizens' groups has affected the policy process in important ways.

Many of these groups are primarily expressive, or what Byron Shafer has called "issue organizations," formed around specific causes or categories of policy and mobilizing support on the basis of appeals to the deeply felt value commitments of some segment of the public.[13] It may not be accurate to call the right-to-life activists or the National Gay Rights Organization ideological if that term implies a comprehensive structure of articulated principles from which particular policy positions are deduced, but the emotional intensity and resistance to compromise and broker politics of these expressive groups are in sharp contrast to the pragmatism associated with more self-interested organizations. Moreover, some of these citizens' organizations employ quite encompassing language to articulate their guiding principles. Common Cause distributes its efforts across a wide range of issues under a broad banner of "reform in the public interest," and some of the think tanks, especially politically conservative operations like the Heritage Foundation (whose recommendations to the incoming Bush administration ran to more than 900 pages), speak out on practically every item on the public agenda.

The central importance of the newly prominent externality groups is that they further destabilize the policy-making process. The proliferation or fractionation of interests in particular policy domains has undermined the hegemony of peak associations in those domains, pushing some groups into small policy niches and forcing others into much more complicated coalitional efforts to secure their policy desires. To this has been added this further assortment, differing from one policy domain to another in their specific concerns but similar in their tendency to appeal to high moral principle as the only proper criterion for deciding who gets what, when, and how. Many of these groups have dubious political muscle in the usual sense, as measured by membership size, money, or even social status, although some are impressive in one or more of these respects. Regardless, however, of their ability to affect electoral prospects directly, these groups are assertive in their use of mass media and thereby make themselves felt regarding which items get on the agenda, forcing the recognition of values and concerns that might, if left to the traditional cozy triangles, receive little attention. Further, the externality groups often call into question the legitimacy of otherwise stable cozy relationships among self-interested groups and officials. The attacks on the so-called cozy or iron triangles have been mounted by reformers of both left and right, by think tanks and citizens' groups of diverse motives and persuasions; as these groups have grown more numerous, the arrangements they have challenged have become less cozy, less stable. Not only are policy processes more uncertain, they are more often contentious. Externality groups attract considerable hostility from the more self-interested institutions and associations, which doubt the seriousness of purpose or understanding of real world effects on the part of citizens' groups and assorted do-gooders.[14]

A major exception to the tendency for established patterns to be overrun by newly emergent specialized interests and externality interests occurs in the field of labor policy. There too we find conflict, but in the form of bipolar struggles between two self-interested coalitions, the American Federation of Labor–Congress of Industrial Organizations (AFL-CIO), supported by assorted individual unions, and the U.S. Chamber of Commerce, the Business Roundtable, and the National Association of Manufacturers, backed by a miscellany of corporate firms and trade associations. Externality groups seldom intrude, and policy concerns that might cut across the dominant dimension—affirmative action in hiring, for example—tend instead to be drawn into the basic oppositional structure. That structure has strong partisan overtones too, of course, which make it all the more difficult to transform labor policy issues into less contentious language. One result, as Terry Moe has shown, is considerable stalemate with neither side able to prevail over the other.[15] This does not mean that labor and business never cooperate on issues, of course. Rapport was good between trucking firms and the Teamsters Union in opposition to truck deregulation, for example, and between automobile manufacturers and the United Auto Workers on trade policy. It is on labor policy itself that the basic conflict exists, and this pattern, while hardly a conventional interest triangle, has not been destabilized by the developments at work in other policy domains.

Uncertain Structures of Power

The destabilization argument I have been developing affects the pattern of policy outcomes at two levels. In the formulation of legislation and the implementing of regulations it means that it is no longer accurate to account for outcomes by reference to the familiar metaphor of iron or cozy triangles wherein interest groups, congressional committees or sub-committees, and executive agencies operate in symbiotic interdependence. For some time, indeed, attentive observers have doubted the validity of the triangle interpretation. Charles O. Jones suggested that "sloppy hexagon" might come closer to expressing the shape of the policy subsystem.[16] Hugh Heclo abandoned geometric tropes entirely in favor of the notion of "issue network."[17] The quest for a suitably evocative phrase will no doubt continue, but it will be difficult indeed to capture in simple terms the shifting, almost kaleidoscopic configurations of groups involved in trying to shape policy.

At a more highly aggregated level, destabilization challenges the value of what for two decades has been the dominant conception of most U.S. policy, interest group liberalism. Theodore Lowi's view, embraced in at least substantial part by most observers, was that in the United States, since the 1930s at least, the major thrusts of policy decision reflected the demands of particularistic groups, opposed weakly if at all by competitors and enacted without much reference to standards of judgment drawn from outside the interest-dominated arenas of politics.[18] In a destabilized world of fragmented interests and multidimensional challenges from externality groups it becomes impossible for policy makers to identify which interests, if any, they can succumb to without grave political risk. They find themselves with choice and discretion, able to select policy alternatives and take positions knowing that almost any position will have some group support and none can prevent opposition from arising. We can easily carry this interpretation too far, denying all policy effect to organized groups, and this would be quite unwarranted. Nevertheless, as was illustrated by the Gucci Gulch example I began with, the presumption has been significantly altered: where interest groups were seen as the prime motive force pressing politicians to make policy decisions in their favor, now the officials very often exploit the groups.

This partial reversal in the flow of influence is not simply a product of the expansion in size and fragmentation in purpose of interest sectors. It is also closely linked with changes in the institutional configurations of Congress and the executive branch. I need not detail these developments here but merely identify those that have especially affected the position and practice of interest group politics.

First has been the diffusion of power in Congress. The weakening of seniority, the empowering of subcommittees, and the expansion of congressional staffs have all contributed to the result that many members are in a position to participate actively and meaningfully on a much larger number of issues than once was possible. Specialization is not so much required to gain substantive expertise—and not so much deferred to by others in any case. On any particular set of policy concerns there are multiple points of potentially relevant access as groups seek support in the Congress, but the depressing corollary for the groups is that none of them is likely to carry decisive weight in shaping policy. Indeed, the position-taking and credit-claiming competition among these many focal points may well mean that ultimately no action is possible in any direction.

Diffusion of power within Congress has been accompanied by the widely remarked increase in the electoral success of incumbents. Incumbents' electoral safety further undermines dependence on interest groups. As John Mark Hansen has shown with reference to the growth of interest triangles in agriculture, the influence of farm groups developed in the late 1920s as members of Congress gradually learned that farm issues were a perennial part of the legislative agenda and farm organizations were therefore continually active and more reliable sources of electoral support than the political parties.[19] Farm belt Republicans therefore defected from their party and forged independent, mutually supportive links with the farm groups. But what was learned can be unlearned. As members of Congress today find themselves increasingly secure beneficiaries of pork, casework, and name recognition, they learn that they can afford to stand aloof from many interest groups. There are important exceptions, but my argument is that in the Congress of the late 1980s interest groups are virtually awash in access but often subordinate in influence.

In the executive branch the most significant development affecting established interest triangles has been the centralization of policy initiatives within the Executive Office of the President and particularly the White House staff. Interest group access in the past has been greatest and most productive with line agencies and independent commissions. The White House is a much more difficult target for lobbyists to reach, and even though White House decisions will necessarily favor some interests over others, it will rarely be, in any direct sense, because of the groups' skill or power. The groups report regular contact with the White House only about one-third as often as with the leaders of their most significant cabinet departments; this reflects a difference in accessibility, not power.[20] The groups go where they can; but ever since Franklin D. Roosevelt executive authority has been brought more and more fully within the White House orbit, and most organized interests have been disadvantaged accordingly.

Interest Group Adaptation

Strategies and Tactics

Despite repeated efforts to reform them, the legal rules constraining the behavior of organized interests in Washington have remained essentially stable for several decades. Only in the area of campaign finance has the law undergone major revision since 1946. Yet the world in which interest groups must operate has changed profoundly. Growth and the changing composition of their ranks are part of this transformation; diffusion of power in Congress and concentration of initiative in the executive are another part; the increase in incumbents' security against electoral defeat has likewise been a factor. The result is that from the perspective of the private interests old patterns of access and influence cannot be depended on to suffice for policy representation needs. Relationships are often friendly but generally unstable, with new groups and new coalitions appearing and reforming while the officials become stronger, wealthier in campaign funds, and as autonomous as they choose to be vis-à-vis the multitude of supplicant interests. Given these changes in their environments, how have organized interests responded and adapted? I consider two levels of adaptive action, tactical and strategic. The tactical question is this: how do lobbyists allocate their time and energy so as to be effective in this uncertain setting? At a more strategic level, what organizational techniques and means of action do interests employ to maximize their impact?

For interest groups as for candidates for presidential nomination or party leader in Congress, fundamental choices of strategy must be made. One option is to go "outside," seeking to shape political agendas and policy outcomes by arousing public opinion, using mass media and indirect marketing techniques to attract attention and broad support for their causes. A significant part of their effort may be directed toward the electoral process, for if they can alter the composition of Congress or significantly affect the result of a presidential election, their influence thereafter may be very considerable. As Kenneth Godwin has shown, however, the appeals needed to arouse sufficient mass support must be vivid, even sensational and they tend therefore to be both extreme and negative.[21] Such appeals may work well in the short run, but they often fade nearly as rapidly as they flowered. What we call political movements tend especially to display these characteristics: rapid growth in numbers, fueled by extensive publicity, with a penchant for extravagant language and various forms of direct action, followed by an equally rapid decay.[22] The movements of the 1960s—civil rights, antiwar, student empowerment, and even environmentalism to some extent—displayed this pattern, and it seems that many of the causes generally referred to as the New Right, having flourished in the late 1970s and early 1980s, have fallen on hard times in the past few years.

Outside strategies, like inside straights in draw poker, can sometimes work, but the odds are generally against them. Godwin suggests that this was especially characteristic of the many citizens' groups, of diverse persuasions, that came into existence after 1960 to mobilize broad public support. Given the tendency for their appeals to decay swiftly, any particular configuration of citizens' groups might therefore be expected to have only a short-term effect on policy. To revert to the terms employed before, this means that externality groups, by reason of the basis on which their organization rests (mass appeals couched in vivid but ephemeral political imagery), will destabilize relationships between officials and interests. In other words, it is not simply their numbers but their organizational dynamics that make citizens' groups so troublesome to the long-term players in the Washington community.

I am painting this picture with a broad brush, of course. Some citizens' and externality groups have managed to solve their membership mobilization problems well enough to achieve a stable and significant presence in Washington.[23] Nevertheless, those groups whose interests are predominantly material rather than expressive have a strong tendency to be the more numerous and consequential participants in policy subsystems (however unstable some of those have become) and to work primarily in a framework of "inside" strategy and tactics.

The inside strategic options for interest groups have crystallized in recent years as the principal means of action have become more clearly differentiated and better documented. I will look in some detail at several of these options as they have been used by business corporations.[24] Since some of the data reported are nearly ten years old and corporate organization has been extremely volatile in many respects, changes have surely taken place in the use of these strategies. Nevertheless, these data allow us to examine systematically not only the frequency with which business firms employ one method or another but the factors that help explain their strategic selections.

A time-honored method of securing representation in Washington is to hire an agent. Washington has no shortage of people with formal credentials as lawyers, public relations advisers, or consultants with substantive policy expertise to whom groups can turn for assistance. Indeed, the supply of independent lobbying agents has increased massively in recent years. Nearly every really large manufacturing firm engages at least one such agent (98 percent of the leading 100 firms in sales volume do so), and organizations that can afford to often employ ten or a dozen for various purposes. Nevertheless, only about one-fifth of the interest representatives examined by Nelson and his colleagues were independent agents, and many of these are used for specialized tasks—litigation, for example—that are on the periphery of the interest group's policy agenda.

Despite the very sizable hourly rates charged by many Washington representatives, it is generally cheaper for a group to employ them ad hoc than to staff a Washington office all year round. The rapid growth of corporate offices in Washington therefore signifies a major increase in the investment that firms have found it useful to make in the tasks of policy representation. To be sure, some companies, often under pressure from Wall Street, have decided that a permanent D.C. establishment is too expensive and have closed down, but especially among the larger firms the proportions with Washington offices remains very substantial.[25]

Coalitions

As the relatively secure relationships of the 1950s were destabilized by the developments of subsequent years, a wide range of efforts ensued, in Burdett H. Loomis's phrase, to "build bridges in a Balkanized state" with more or less explicitly designated coalitions.[26] Coalitions of interests are generic components of the political process, of course, and not a recent invention. Moreover, there have long been relationships among interests, cutting across the lines of party, region, and economic sector, that mobilized in cooperative political effort the resources of disparate groups, sometimes on an ad hoc basis, sometimes in more enduring fashion. What is striking about the most recent period, however, is how numerous are the coalitions designated as such and also how many counterpart coalitions, generally called caucuses, have been formed in Congress. In each case the fragmentation of interests and the breakdown of older patterns of connection have made it attractive to construct so many new combinations.

A major form of interest coalition, which has been with us for more than a century, is the trade or professional association. There have been several spurts of growth in the number and variety of these organizations over the course of American development, and their number continues to increase as new specializations and new combinations of functions emerge. Nearly 2,000 such organizations are represented in Washington, and their effect on the commercial real estate and restaurant facilities of the nation's capital has been profound.

The most striking change, however, in cooperative interest representation strategy reflects the inherent limitation of nearly every trade or professional association. More and better coalitions are required by the complexity of effects of federal policy on the institutions of society.[27] Not all widgetmaking corporations or banks or universities will be affected in the same way by what the government does. Peer-reviewed research grants from the National Science Foundation are greatly admired by large research universities but are not much help to the colleges; the leading dozen or so private universities have somewhat different concerns from the public institutions, and so on. Some of these differences are reflected in different voluntary associations, of course; the Association of American Universities (AAU) is distinct from both the National Association of State Universities and Land Grant Colleges and the National Association of Independent Colleges and Universities. In addition, however, several smaller working groups of university lobbyists exchange information and try to orchestrate their actions for maximum, highly targeted effect.

Other universities may not possess the resources or be sufficiently affected by federal policy to invest in deploying their own lobbyists but may still see possibilities in being represented in Washington outside the framework of the formal associations. For such interests a lobbyist broker can be a useful intermediary, bundling a collection of organizations together when it is useful but serving each one's specific interests without being troubled by having always to represent all its "members" in the way that leaders of voluntary associations like the AAU or the American Council of Education (ACE) must try to do. Thus, in the quarterly report filed under the Regulation of Lobbying Act and published in the *Congressional Record* for November 10, 1988, Cassidy and Associates, a public relations and lobbying firm that specializes in such matters, listed forty-four college and university clients.

The growing numbers of coalitions and alliances cutting across the boundaries of formal associations are made possible because so many more individual business corporations, universities, and other institutions have established Washington outposts. While they continue to pay their association dues (often to several associations), they operate independently as well when necessary. Some of the independent action is aimed at affecting public policy. For example, eighteen large firms in the financial sector organized a group to push for banking reform legislation opposed by the American Bankers Association and the American Council of Life Insurance.[28] Quite often, however, a major purpose of the new coalitions is informational. At weekly breakfast meetings and the like, similarly situated interest representatives can share information and interpretation that would come more slowly, if at all, through the more bureaucratic channels of a trade association serving a larger and more diverse membership. One other feature of many of these new coalitions is that the groups and organizations that participate must spend considerable time lobbying one another, trying to persuade colleagues concerning the policy stance that the collectivity should adopt.

Groups vary a great deal in the forms of action they employ in Washington, and while it would be rash indeed to claim to know precisely how much variation exists or what factors affect it, we can examine the behavior of manufacturing firms in some detail. Table 1 presents the proportions of the largest 1,000 companies that employ independent agents (1982), have created political action committees (PACs) (1983), or have established Washington offices (1982).[29] It is obvious that firm size and the resources that go with size are of decisive importance. Big business is far more fully represented in Washington than smaller firms. But that is by no means the end of the story.

Are big firms more actively represented simply because they can afford it, or are other factors involved? A number of possibilities come to mind. Craig Humphries finds that the extent of government regulation

TABLE 1
Corporate Uses of Strategic Forms of Action
1982 and 1983
(percent)

Sales Rank	With PAC (1983)	Using Agent (1982)	With D.C. Office (1982)
1–100	89	98	85
101–250	73	77	63
251–500	44	32	17
501–1,000	15	16	3
Total	39	38	24

Source: Craig Humphries, *The Political Behavior of American Corporations*, Washington University, 1989.

of a firm's industry strongly affects whether the firm establishes itself in Washington.[30] Among regulated industries, those that are more concentrated (that is, with a smaller number of firms) are more actively represented. So also are firms with more diversified product lines. The threat of imports has some effect, but the degree of unionization is not very important, at least not for the entire array of 1,000 firms. Having government contracts is associated with establishing a Washington office but not with the hiring of an independent agent or the creation of a PAC.

A significant relationship exists among those three strategic forms. That is, if a firm has a Washington office or uses independent agents, it is likely also to create a PAC. Using agents is strongly related to establishing a D.C. office. The forms of action go together, reinforcing one another and to some extent creating the necessity for one another. A company needs a Washington office in part to supervise its agents and direct its PAC's selection of the candidates it will favor. But the office can seldom cover all the politically relevant bases it can identify; hence the agents. And without a PAC to finance attendance at fund raisers, a corporate presence in Washington may be dismissed by officials as worthless. This interdependence among strategic forms of action leads to the recognition that interest group representation is a dynamic phenomenon, driven not only by the "objective" needs of rational actors affected by what the government does to them or for them but also by the internal logic of the association or the institution. It also points up the importance of examining such highly publicized matters as PACs in the context of other forms of interest group action.

The Tactical Repertoire

I turn now to the more specific activities in which business corporations and other groups engage, in which the organizational means discussed above are employed. As I have done throughout the chapter, I emphasize those aspects that appear to have changed in recent years. The emphasis on change is tricky to implement because, as with so much else about interest groups, we lack good historical base lines. Nevertheless, whereas Kay Schlozman and John Tierney concluded that contemporary group practice mainly involved "more of the same," some quite important changes have occurred in the things groups do.[31]

Groups must first make choices regarding the political arenas in which they will invest money and effort. A plausible expectation would be that, as relative power to determine policy outcomes shifts within a governmental institution or from one institution to another, the lobbyists will follow. Thus it was said that as policy-making dominance in Britain moved from Parliament to Whitehall, the lobby shifted its efforts accordingly. There is a competing hypothesis, however, to the effect that lobbyists go anywhere they can, using the authority of any institutional arena that they are able to penetrate in the hope that, because in the United States authority to shape policy is shared by so many separate institutions, some influence on their objectives can be exerted. On the whole the latter argument is more persuasive. Accessibility of an institution is a key element in shaping the decision of a group to seek access.

Interests differ considerably in the ease or difficulty with which they can penetrate a particular institution, and these factors also vary over time. Obviously, what groups try to do depends not only on the relevance to their concerns of an institution's authority and its accessibility to their efforts but on the groups's resources as well. Not all tactical options to gain access and influence are available to every group. Choices must be made, and we need to examine some of them.

Byron Shafer has recently described a major shift in the process of nominating presidential candidates beginning in the 1960s, whereby interest groups of various kinds came to play an increasing part in sponsoring delegates, lobbying on the platforms, bargaining over the nominations, and mobilizing support in the election campaign.[32] The strong support of the National Education Association for Jimmy Carter and of groups from the religious right for Ronald Reagan in 1980 illustrate a development of long-term importance. Shafer contends that in this process mainly the ideologically motivated groups are active, not the more pragmatic interests that are willing to bargain and compromise; as a result, the presidential campaigns are more radicalized than in "the old days" when party organizations were stronger and could play a more effective brokering role.

In the electoral process generally, the PAC phenomenon, so often denounced in the media and by reformers everywhere, has seemed to move from one tack to another with little assurance of where, if anywhere, a stable equilibrium may be found.[33] Labor had long employed PACs, of course. Ever since the creation of the CIO-PAC in 1943 unions had used this device to assemble campaign funds and had increasingly dispensed them almost entirely to Democrats. After the 1971–1974 changes in the law unambiguously legitimated PACs for all interests, the rapid expansion of corporate, trade association, and unaffiliated (mostly politically conservative) committees seemed likely for a time to overwhelm labor's efforts, giving most of their money to Republicans. Especially in 1978 and 1980 Republican candidates, including challengers as well as incumbents, benefited enormously from PAC assistance. Great dangers to balanced electoral competition were prophesied, and proposals for public funding of congressional elections, usually advanced by Democrats, were accordingly dismissed out of hand by Republicans. Since then, however, the balance has shifted. Unaffiliated PACs continue to back conservative candidates, but their funding has not kept pace, and their influence has therefore provoked fewer anxieties. Business PACs meanwhile have redirected their contributions quite sharply in favor of incumbents. Inasmuch as a solid majority of the House and, since 1986, of the Senate are Democrats, they have been the beneficiaries. The pragmatism that has guided PAC contributions by business interests to congressional candidates is in sharp contrast to the ideological fervor displayed by interests active in presidential campaigns. PAC pragmatism is an important indicator of the power of incumbent congressmen—interest groups that depend on them for help on narrow but vital issues give them campaign support, regardless of the broader policy orientation that the incumbent members display.

Away from the electoral process, a broad array of activities may be undertaken by Washington-based lobbyists. The usual characterization of lobbying has emphasized the tasks of making formal and informal contacts with officials and presenting them with information and argument. Schlozman and Tierney found that virtually every group did these things and did them more now than before. Other research shows, however, that this direct lobbying is not the most timeconsuming or often the most important concern. Thirty years ago Lester Milbrath found that lobbyists spent a large part of their working time in their own offices, not on Capitol Hill or elsewhere, making contact with officials.[34] This remains true today. The tasks that are both the most time consuming and the most important are concerned not so much with persuading government officials to act one way or another as with keeping track of what is happening in the policy process, alerting the client organizations to developments relevant to their interests, and developing appropriate strategies of response or adaptation. Advocacy of one's cause continues to require attention, of course, and the ways and means of gaining influence over outcomes are in no sense ignored. Schlozman and Tierney are quite right in saying that groups do more of everything than they did two or three decades ago. Even litigation, one of the less highly valued modes of action, is reported to have been undertaken by nearly two-thirds of the interest organizations surveyed by Heinz and others. Nevertheless, there appears to have been a significant shift in the balance among the lobbyists' tasks, and that shift is closely related to the broad movement of groups toward a full-time presence in Washington.

Recall a "classic" model of lobbying. A group sends a representative to Washington to press its case for or against some policy option, or it hires one of the many would-be agents already located in the nation's capital, waiting like defense lawyers in the courthouse corridors for a paying client to come into view. The presumption in this model is that the group knows what its policy interest is. If the group is big enough to have great voting strength, it may expect to gain its ends through the electoral process. If it is small and its needs are limited, it may need only to add lobbying expertise to secure the desired result. Many of these group concerns, richly illustrated in the case study literature, have been ad hoc and discontinuous, adequately served by a single lobbying campaign. Others require continuing attention but may still be very stable with respect to the policy interests sought. Thus for many years the big oil companies maintained a firm lobbying commitment to the depletion allowance, home builders have never wavered in their defense of deducting interest on home mortgages, and veterans' groups have kept up the pressure to maintain Veterans Administration hospitals.

The great expansion in the scope of federal programs since World War II, however, has meant that many more elements of the society are far more extensively affected by what the government does and must, in their own interests, become more involved in trying to optimize those effects. This sea change has been accompanied by two other changes of great importance. One is essentially intellectual: we acknowledge far more fully than we once did that there are profound interdependencies and interaction effects such that any policy decision is likely to be seen as having a major effect not just on its primary target population but on diverse other areas of life. The second is that these external concerns have been the basis of substantial group formation and political action. In consequence, a widespread destabilization of many of the old influence relationships has occurred. But there has been another level of destabilization. In today's world of complex, interdependent interests and policies, it is often quite unclear what the "true interests" of a group or an institution may be. The policy that will be maximally advantageous to an association often cannot even be framed without prolonged and searching analysis involving extensive discussion among those who are knowledgeable about both the technical substance of the issue and the feasibilities of the relevant political situation.

Uncertainty concerning the substance of group interests, as well as about how best to achieve them, forces those we call lobbyists to shift much of their energy away from lobbying, that is, away from advocating policies and influencing government officials. Before they can advocate a policy, they must determine what position they wish to embrace. Before they do this, they must find out not only what technical policy analysis can tell them but what relevant others, inside government and outside, are thinking and planning. Often, indeed, a group may not even know that it has a policy interest requiring attention until it discovers the plans of an agency to propose new regulations or of a congressional subcommittee to hold hearings on a subject. Information, timely and accurate, is absolutely vital to the lobbyist.

This point is nicely captured in the opening paragraph of Edward Laumann and David Knoke's analysis of the organizational networks involved in energy and health policies:

> The executive director of a major petroleum-industry trade association was leafing through the Federal Register, his daily ritual of scanning the Washington scene. Buried in the fine print was an apparently innocuous announcement by the Federal Aviation Administration of its intent to promulgate new regulations that would require detailed flight plans to be filed by pilots of noncommercial aircraft. Recently, several planes had gone down, and search and rescue efforts had been hampered by lack of informa-

tion on the pilots' intended routes. The trade association director muttered, "We've got a problem," and spent a frantic morning on the phone alerting his group's membership to apply pressure on the FAA to set aside the regulation. The executive realized that once detailed flight plans were on record with the FAA, the open-disclosure provisions of the Freedom of Information Act would allow anyone to learn where his member companies' planes were flying on their aerial explorations for oil, gas, and minerals. The alert director's quick mobilization of collective response saved the corporations potentially millions of dollars worth of secret data that might have fallen into the laps of their competitors.[35]

Laumann and Knoke treat information as a resource of central importance in the policy process and, as I do, see policy interests as "continuously constructed" social phenomena.[36] Their emphasis is on the conversion of information resources into influence over policy outcomes, however, and while it would be extremely foolish to ignore this element, it is important also to recognize that information may often be necessary to adjust one's own behavior sensibly. A corporation that knows the intentions of the Federal Aviation Administration may decide to change its own policies rather than try to persuade the agency to change.

The point of my argument is that the descent on Washington of so many hundreds of associations, institutions, and their agents does not mean that these private interests have acquired greater sway or even a more articulate voice in the shaping of national policy. In many ways the opposite is true. Washington is, after all, the main source of information about what government officials are doing or planning to do. To get that information in a timely way, a continuous and alert presence in the capital is vital. Moreover, in this quest for information the interest representatives are very often in a position of profound dependence. They need access to officials not so much to apply pressure or even to advocate policy as to be told when something important to them is about to happen.

Specialized newsletters are often helpful in this situation, and these expensive aids have multiplied in recent years. Coalitions and trade associations are, among other things, means of enhancing the exchange of information, although trade associations must be careful not to circulate more data about members' intentions than the antitrust laws permit. Withal, the centrality of the need for information and its use by interest groups to help define interests and policy preferences, structure the workday, and adapt organizational behavior to emerging political

conditions are clearly reflected in the findings of Heinz and others regarding how lobbyists spend their time. Table 2 reports the relative
frequency with which 776 interest representatives in the policy domains
of agriculture, energy, health, and labor engage in the diverse tasks involved in their jobs. Formal interaction with government ranks well below more informal contacts. Information exchanges claim a higher
priority than position taking, and intraorganizational efforts along with
monitoring of the political environment are of central importance.

One further consequence of the lobbyists' overriding need to know is
that in their contacts with government officials they display considerably
less specialization than might have been expected. Rather than focusing
on a particular committee or administrative agency, interest representatives report making regular contacts with an average of four or five
government units. More often than not these contacts are in both the
executive and the legislative branches and include both Republicans and
Democrats. Their dependence on information requires the interest rep-

TABLE 2
Frequency of Lobbyists' Task Performance
(1 = never; 5 = regularly)

Alerting client about issues	4.3
Developing policy or strategy	4.3
Maintaining relations with government	3.8
Making informal contacts with officials	3.7
Monitoring proposed changes in rules and laws	3.7
Providing information to officials	3.5
Preparing testimony or official comments	3.4
Commentary for press, public speaking	3.2
Mobilizing grass-roots support	3.0
Monitoring interest groups	2.8
Testifying	2.7
Drafting proposed legislation or regulations	2.7
Making contacts with opposition	2.6
Making contacts with allies	2.5
Resolving internal organizational disputes	2.5
Litigation	2.1
Arranging for political contributions	2.0
Working for amicus briefs	1.6

Source: Salisbury et al., *Iron Triangles: Similarities and Differences Among
the Legs,* American Political Science Association Conference, September 1988.

resentatives to go wherever they can learn something useful. This may well mean that watchful attendance at hearings and markup sessions is more the modal lobbying task than position taking or policy advocacy in any form.

Conclusion

I come back to the apparent paradox with which I began, to the Tax Reform Act of 1986 in which the members of Congress made the choices, excluding the scores of interest group representatives from the process and forcing them to wait outside until it was over. The interpretation I have offered suggests that, rather than being a paradox, this situation simply registered important changes that have been taking place. Many of the old symbioses have given way, destabilized as a result of expanded group participation, of greater electoral security, increased staff, and lessened need or inclination to specialize on the part of Congress, and of more centralized control of the executive branch, which leaves the specialized agencies less able to create their own triangular policy deals.

The uncertainty generated by this political destabilization is compounded by the problematic nature of policy interests. Organizations are often unsure which among the live policy options might be most to their advantage; indeed, they are often in doubt about what the options are. They are engaged in a never-ending process of learning, assessment, and calculation; and timely information, much of it available only from government, is the sine qua non of this process. It would be too much to claim that interest group lobbyists have been wholly subordinated to public officials, but we would surely misread the American political process if we ignored the extent to which these groups have come to Washington out of need and dependence rather than because they have influence.

NOTES

1. Jeffrey H. Birnbaum and Alan S. Murray, *Showdown at Gucci Gulch* (New York: Random House, 1987).

2. Arthur Close et al., eds., *Washington Representatives, 1988* (Washington, D.C.: Columbia Books, 1988).

3. Craig Colgate, ed., *National Trade and Professional Associations of the United States, 1982* (Washington, D.C.: Columbia Books, 1982).

4. David Yoffie, "Interest Groups v. Individual Action: An Analysis of Corporate Political Strategies," Working paper, Harvard Business School, 1985.

5. Kay Lehman Schlozman and John T. Tierney, *Organized Interests and American Democracy* (New York: Harper and Row, 1986), p. 76; see also Jack L. Walker, "The Origins and Maintenance of Interest Groups in America," *American Political Science Review*, vol. 77 (1983), pp. 390–406.

6. Mancur Olson, *The Logic of Collective Action* (Cambridge, Mass.: Harvard University Press, 1965).

7. Robert H. Salisbury, "Interest Representation: The Dominance of Institutions," *American Political Science Review*, vol. 78, pp. 64–76.

8. See Lawrence Mone, "Thinkers and Their Tanks Move on Washington," *Wall Street Journal*, March 15, 1988. Think tank lobbying is described in David Shribman, "Lobbying of Bush Transition Office Is Turning to Matters of Policy from Personnel Choices," *Wall Street Journal*, January 3, 1989. See also Martha Derthick and Paul Quirk, *The Politics of Deregulation* (Washington, D.C.: Brookings Institution, 1985).

9. See Robert L. Nelson, John P. Heinz, Edward O. Laumann, and Robert H. Salisbury, "Private Representation in Washington: Surveying the Structure of Influence," *American Bar Foundation Research Journal* (1987), pp. 141–200.

10. William P. Browne, *Private Interests, Public Policy, and American Agriculture* (Lawrence: University of Kansas Press, 1988).

11. See Edward O. Laumann and David Knoke, *The Organizational State: Social Choice in National Policy Domains* (Madison: University of Wisconsin Press, 1987).

12. See my essay, "Washington Lobbyists: A Collective Portrait," in Allan J. Cigler and Burdett A. Loomis, eds., *Interest Group Politics*, 2d ed. (Washington, D.C.: Congressional Quarterly Press, 1986), pp. 146–61.

13. Byron Shafer, *Bifurcated Politics* (Cambridge, Mass.: Harvard University Press, 1988), chap. 4.

14. See Robert H. Salisbury, John P. Heinz, Edward O. Laumann and Robert L. Nelson, "Who Works with Whom? Interest Group Alliances and Opposition," *American Political Science Review*, vol. 81, pp. 1217–34. The excellent essay by Jeffrey M. Berry, "Subgovernments, Issue Networks, and Political Conflict," stresses the importance of increased conflict as a destabilizing force. Berry's essay came to my attention after I had completed my own, but it is clear that our thinking has moved along closely related lines. His work appears in Richard Harris and Sidney Milkis, eds., *Remaking American Politics* (Boulder, Colo.: Westview Press, 1989), pp. 239–60.

15. Terry Moe, "Interests, Institutions, and Positive Theory: The Politics of the NLRB," *Studies in American Political Development*, vol. 2 (1987), pp. 236–99.

16. Charles O. Jones, "American Politics and the Organization of Energy Decision Making," *Annual Review of Energy*, vol. 4 (1979), pp. 99–121.

17. Hugh Heclo, "Issue Networks and the Executive Establishment," in Anthony King, ed., *The New American Political System* (Washington, D.C.: American Enterprise Institute, 1978), pp. 87–124.

18. Theodore Lowi, *The End of Liberalism* (New York: W.W. Norton, 1969).

19. John Mark Hansen, "Choosing Sides: The Creation of an Agricultural Policy Network in Congress, 1919–1932," *Studies in American Political Development*, vol. 2 (1987), pp. 183–229.

20. Robert H. Salisbury, John P. Heinz, Edward O. Laumann, and Robert L. Nelson, "Iron Triangles: Similarities and Differences among the Legs" (Paper presented to the annual meeting of the American Political Science Association, Washington, D.C., September 1988).

21. R. Kenneth Godwin, *One Billion Dollars of Influence: The Direct Marketing of Politics* (Chatham, N.J.: Chatham House, 1988).

22. See my essay "Political Movements in American Politics: An Essay on Concept and Analysis," *National Journal of Political Science,* vol. 1 (1989), pp. 15–30.

23. See, for example, Andrew McFarland, *Common Cause: Lobbying in the Public Interest* (Chatham, N.J.: Chatham House, 1984); and Jeffrey M. Berry, *Lobbying for the People* (Princeton, N.J.: Princeton University Press, 1977).

24. Much of this section is based on the research of Craig Humphries, whose doctoral dissertation, *The Political Behavior of American Corporations,* analyzes corporate strategies of political action in careful detail. I am grateful to Dr. Humphries for permission to use some of his data and for his helpful comments on this paper.

25. See Kirk Victor, "Being Here," *National Journal,* August 6, 1988, pp. 2021–25.

26. Burdett A. Loomis, "Coalitions of Interests: Building Bridges in a Balkanized State," in Cigler and Loomis, eds., *Interest Group Politics,* pp. 258–74.

27. For a discussion of this development among manufacturing trade associations concerned about trade issues, see Leonard H. Lynn and Timothy J. McKeown, *Organizing Business: Trade Associations in America and Japan* (Washington, D.C.: American Enterprise Institute, 1988), pp. 110–12. See also Jeffrey M. Berry, *The Interest Group Society* (Boston: Little, Brown, 1984), pp. 202–05.

28. George Melloan, "What to Do When Your Own Lobby is against You," *Wall Street Journal,* February 16, 1988.

29. Actually, the N is 990; ten firms on the *Fortune Magazine* list were either subsidiaries of other firms or agricultural cooperatives. *Fortune Magazine,* May 3, 1982.

30. See n. 24.

31. Schlozman and Tierney, *Organized Interests and American Democracy,* chap. 7.

32. Shafer, *Bifurcated Politics.*

33. For a careful, measured analysis of PACs in American politics placed in their larger historical and political context, see Frank J. Sorauf, *Money in Amer-*

ican Elections (Glenview, Ill.: Scott, Foresman, 1988). A richly detailed analysis of corporate PACs is Theodore J. Eismeier and Philip H. Pollock III, *Business, Money, and the Rise of Corporate PACs in American Elections* (New York: Quorum Books, 1988).

34. Lester Milbrath, *The Washington Lobbyists* (Chicago: Rand McNally, 1963).
35. Laumann and Knoke, *The Organizational State*, p. 3.
36. Ibid., p. 15.

PITT SERIES IN POLICY AND INSTITUTIONAL STUDIES

Bert A. Rockman, Editor